D1569166

Bonds of Empire

Bonds of Empire presents an account of slave law that is entirely new: one in which English law imbued plantation slavery with its staying power even as it insulated slave owners from contemplating the moral implications of owning human beings. Emphasizing practice rather than proscription, the book follows South Carolina colonists as they used English law to maximize the value of the people they treated as property. Doing so reveals that most daily legal practices surrounding slave ownership were derived from English law: Colonists categorized enslaved people as property using English legal terms, they bought and sold them with printed English legal forms, and they followed English legal procedures as they litigated over enslaved people in court. *Bonds of Empire* ultimately shows that plantation slavery and the laws that governed it were not beyond the pale of English imperial legal history; they were yet another invidious manifestation of English law's protean potential.

Lee B. Wilson is Assistant Professor of History at Clemson University. A historian of colonial British America and the early modern Atlantic world, her research interests include the legal history of early American slave societies, colonial property law, and legal discourse.

Cambridge Historical Studies in American Law and Society

Recognizing legal history's growing importance and influence, the goal of this series is to chart legal history's continuing development by publishing innovative scholarship across the discipline's broadening range of perspectives and subjects. It encourages empirically creative works that take legal history into unexplored subject areas, or that fundamentally revise our thinking about familiar topics; it also encourages methodologically innovative works that bring new disciplinary perspectives and techniques to the historical analysis of legal subjects.

Series Editor
Christopher Tomlins, *University of California, Berkeley*

Previously published in the series

Robert Deal, *The Law of the Whale Hunt: Dispute Resolution, Property Law, and American Whalers, 1780–1880*

Sandra F. Vanburkleo, *Gender Remade: Citizenship, Suffrage, and Public Power in the New Northwest, 1879–1912*

Reuel Schiller, *Forging Rivals: Race, Class, Law, and the Collapse of Postwar Liberalism*

Ely Aaronson, *From Slave Abuse to Hate Crime: The Criminalization of Racial Violence in American History*

Stuart Chinn, *Recalibrating Reform: The Limits of Political Change*

Ajay K. Mehrotra, *Making the Modern American Fiscal State*

Yvonne Pitts, *Family, Law, and Inheritance in America: A Social and Legal History of Nineteenth-Century Kentucky*

David M. Rabban, *Law's History*

Kunal M. Parker, *Common Law, History, and Democracy in America, 1790–1900*

Steven Wilf, *Law's Imagined Republic*

James D. Schmidt, *Industrial Violence and the Legal Origins of Child Labor*

Rebecca M. McLennan, *The Crisis of Imprisonment: Protest, Politics, and the Making of the American Penal State, 1776–1941*

Tony A. Freyer, *Antitrust and Global Capitalism, 1930–2004*

Davison Douglas, *Jim Crow Moves North*

Andrew Wender Cohen, *The Racketeer's Progress*

Michael Willrich, *City of Courts, Socializing Justice in Progressive Era Chicago*

Barbara Young Welke, *Recasting American Liberty: Gender, Law and the Railroad Revolution, 1865–1920*

Michael Vorenberg, *Final Freedom: The Civil War, the Abolition of Slavery, and the Thirteenth Amendment*

Robert J. Steinfeld, *Coercion, Contract, and Free Labor in Nineteenth Century America*

David M. Rabban, *Free Speech in Its Forgotten Years*

Jenny Wahl, *The Bondsman's Burden: An Economic Analysis of the Common Law of Southern Slavery*

Michael Grossberg, *A Judgment for Solomon: The d'Hauteville Case and Legal Experience in the Antebellum South*

Bonds of Empire

The English Origins of Slave Law in South Carolina and British Plantation America, 1660–1783

LEE B. WILSON

Clemson University

CAMBRIDGE
UNIVERSITY PRESS

University Printing House, Cambridge CB2 8BS, United Kingdom

One Liberty Plaza, 20th Floor, New York, NY 10006, USA

477 Williamstown Road, Port Melbourne, VIC 3207, Australia

314–321, 3rd Floor, Plot 3, Splendor Forum, Jasola District Centre, New Delhi – 110025, India

103 Penang Road, #05–06/07, Visioncrest Commercial, Singapore 238467

Cambridge University Press is part of the University of Cambridge.

It furthers the University's mission by disseminating knowledge in the pursuit of education, learning, and research at the highest international levels of excellence.

www.cambridge.org
Information on this title: www.cambridge.org/9781108495257
DOI: 10.1017/9781108861762

© Lee B. Wilson 2021

First published 2021

A catalogue record for this publication is available from the British Library.

ISBN 978-1-108-49525-7 Hardback

Contents

Tables

Acknowledgments

When I began this project as a PhD student at the University of Virginia, I had little idea where it would take me. I started my scholarly career hoping to study constitution-making in early South Carolina, and I imagined that I would write an intellectual history that traced the roots of the colony's early legal development. In the years that followed, my sterile original plan morphed into something infinitely more complicated – and hopefully more interesting. As I hopped from archive to archive, dusting off obscure transactional documents and legal ephemera, I came to understand that it is not possible to understand early American legal history without first seeking to understand early American slavery. Try as I might to write a tidy constitutional history, the documents got in the way. Instead, they pointed to a messier story, one that defied my instinct to sort legally inflected activities into their proper silos. For all its messiness, this story yielded a broader truth: in colonial America, all law was slave law.

I would not have noticed this but for the support of friends and colleagues over the years. As a History major at Loyola College (now University) in Maryland, Joseph Walsh, Tom Pegram, Matthew Mulcahy, and the rest of the talented faculty nurtured my budding interest in the field. At the University of Virginia, I was fortunate to study with S. Max Edelson, who has been an unflagging source of support, criticism, and mentorship. Without him, this project would not have been possible. Paul D. Halliday guided me through the intricacies of English property law and transformed a staid subject into a riveting one by mere motion, as only he can. Chuck McCurdy and Risa Goluboff likewise helped me to place my work in dialogue with legal historians across time and space. I am immeasurably grateful for that grounding.

As I transformed my dissertation into a monograph, my colleagues at Clemson University have continued to offer support and guidance in countless ways. I am especially grateful to Steven Marks for his encouragement and my colleagues, Stephanie Barczewski, Caroline Dunn, Rachel Moore, and Criss Smith, for their mentorship and collegiality. Beyond Clemson, I benefitted from the thoughtful criticism of scholars from around the world as I presented chapters at various organizational meetings, including the University of Virginia's Early American Seminar, the American Society for Legal History, the Southern Historical Association, and the British Legal History Conference.

This project required extensive manuscript research, and I am indebted to all of the librarians and archivists who aided in locating documents and answering difficult questions. I am especially grateful to Faye Jensen and Mary Jo Fairchild at the South Carolina Historical Society in Charleston, South Carolina. Alex Moore and Nic Butler also were generous with their time and suggestions for new research possibilities. I have benefitted from the University of Virginia's financial support for my research, as well as support from the Harvard University and Cambridge University Joint Centre for History and Economics (Institute for New Economic Thinking), the Buckner W. Clay Endowment for the Humanities, and the Thomas Jefferson Memorial Foundation. Clemson University has also provided generous financial support in the form of travel grants, Humanities Hub research fellowships, and two Lightsey Fellowships. The American Historical Association and the American Society for Legal History likewise have supported my work. Taken together, their financial generosity made it possible for me to pursue research across continents and to carve out space for writing and revising.

I would be remiss if I failed to thank the kind souls who provided childcare for me as I completed this manuscript, and especially Ruth Ghowanlu and Anna Haen. I owe them a debt that I cannot repay. Likewise, my friends, colleagues, and family have made travel, research, and writing over the past several years more enjoyable. Nuala Zahedieh offered advice and hospitality in Edinburgh, while Perry and Alice Trouche were warm and welcoming in Charleston. My father, John David Wilson, taught me to love history in all its messiness. Barbara Wilson, Susan Reilly, and David Wilson have been behind me all the way, while my husband, Sasha, and our children, Ethan and Mia, remain a constant source of inspiration. Finally, my father-in-law, Kambis Ghowanlu, was an enthusiastic supporter of my work until his death this year from COVID-19. Quick with a question or a joke, Kami brought boundless joy to our lives, and his love of learning was infectious. This is for him.

A Note on Text

Throughout this monograph, I refer to modern-day Charleston, South Carolina, as Charlestown, the common spelling of the port city until it was incorporated as Charleston in 1783. All monetary values are in pounds sterling. Between 1725 and 1775, £100 sterling was approximately £700 in South Carolina currency. Where applicable, I have adjusted dates to reflect the beginning of the calendar year on January 1 rather than March 25.

Abbreviations

APC	*Acts of the Privy Council of England, Colonial Series,* W. L. Grant and James Munro, eds., 6 vols. (London, 1908–1912)
BL	The British Library, London, UK
BOD	The Bodleian Library, Oxford University, Oxford, UK
BPRO	Records in the British Public Record Office Relating to South Carolina, 1663–1782, ed. W. Noel Sainsbury, 36 vols., Emory University, Woodruff Library, Atlanta, GA
CSP	Calendar of State Papers, Colonial Series
ECCO	Eighteenth-Century Collections Online, Gale Group, gale net.galegroup.com
EEBO	Early English Books Online, Chadwyck-Healey, eebo .chadwyck.com
HLP	*The Papers of Henry Laurens*, eds. Philip M. Hamer et al., 16 vols. (Columbia: University of South Carolina Press, 1968–2003)
JNA	Jamaica Archives and Records Department, Spanish Town, Jamaica
LMA	London Metropolitan Archives, London, UK
LOC	Library of Congress, Manuscripts Division, Washington, DC
NARA	National Archives and Records Administration, Atlanta, GA
RG	*Royal Gazette*
RSCG	*Royal South Carolina Gazette*

SAL	*The Statutes at Large of South Carolina*, eds. Thomas Cooper and David J. McCord, 10 vols. (Columbia: A. S. Johnston, 1836–1841)
SCDAH	South Carolina Department of Archives and History, Columbia, SC
SCG	*South Carolina Gazette*
SCHM	*South Carolina Historical Magazine*
SCHS	South Carolina Historical Society, Charleston, SC
SHC	Southern Historical Collection, University of North Carolina, Wilson Library, Chapel Hill, NC
SNA	Scottish National Archives, Edinburgh, Scotland, UK
SP	*The Shaftesbury Papers*, ed. L. Cheves (Charleston: Home Press, 2010)
TNA	The National Archives, Kew, UK
WMQ	*The William and Mary Quarterly*, 3rd ser.

Introduction

In the summer of 1750, South Carolina colonist Peter Manigault traveled to England to acquire a legal education.[1] At first Peter, the son of wealthy merchant Gabriel Manigault, saw "nothing" in England that he preferred to his "Native Country." However, he quickly changed his mind, throwing himself into the hustle and bustle of eighteenth-century metropolitan life and peppering his father with requests for funds, including money to purchase a gold watch, "a very Necessary Article" in his "present Situation."[2] When he was not sampling the delights of London's social season, he dedicated himself to his legal studies, moving from Bow Street, which was "situated in the very Center of all the bad Houses in Covent Garden," to the Inner Temple. From this convenient location, he frequented the Temple Library and snagged "Bargains" on used law books at sales "about Temple Bar."[3] He also rode the Oxford circuit, an

---

[1] "Six Letters of Peter Manigault," *The South Carolina Historical and Genealogical Magazine* 15 (1914): 113–123. Peter Manigault was one of many South Carolinians who traveled to England to acquire a legal education in the second half of the eighteenth century. In fact South Carolina colonists sent more sons to be educated in England than any mainland colony in the late colonial period. Some of these students were less dedicated to their studies than Manigault, including Jack Garden, who concluded that "a person can not be a good Lawyer & an honest Man at the same time" and instead became a "Hackney Writer," or Billy Drayton, the son of a famous planting family, who became embroiled in a scandal over dueling. Peter Manigault to Ann Manigault, December 8, 1753, Manigault Papers, 11/275/11, South Carolina Historical Society, Charleston, South Carolina (SCHS).
[2] Peter Manigault to Gabriel Manigault, August 1, 1750, Manigault Papers, SCHS.
[3] Peter Manigault to Ann Manigault, July 20, 1752, Manigault Papers, 11/275/8, SCHS; Peter Manigault to Ann Manigault, September 25, 1752, Manigault Papers, 11/275/8, SCHS; Peter Manigault to Gabriel Manigault, October 18, 1752, Manigault Papers, 11/275/8, SCHS.

"expensive" enterprise that involved not only hazardous travel conditions, but also the tedium of "attending the Courts all day & writing out any Notes in the Evening."[4] Indeed, after making "Notes of all Causes of Consequence that ha[d] been argued" since he arrived in England, after filling his "Law Books" with countless "Remarks and References," and after listening to "very tedious affidavits" at Westminster, Manigault came to the conclusion that "Mirth and Law are incompatible." Thus resigned to the dullness of his chosen profession, he was called to the Bar in 1754 and returned to South Carolina, where he became part of that "Respectable Body of Men, who (provided they are well paid for it) make it their sole Business in this Life, to take care of the Lives & Estates of their Fellow Creatures."[5]

Manigault never lost his distaste for law. Although he did practice in South Carolina for a decade, he ultimately abandoned the profession, selling his books "at 10 per Cent lower than they were bought" because his "Inclination" to quit was "so strong."[6] Nonetheless, Manigault's English legal education continued to provide him with the wherewithal to make a living. Applying his legal expertise to the running of his own plantations and those of absentee South Carolina planters whose affairs he managed, he leveraged his knowledge of English law to ensure his clients the greatest return on their investments in land and, most importantly, slaves. Indeed, as Manigault and other South Carolina colonists were well aware, knowledge of English law was the sine qua non of mastery over slaves. Because slaves were colonists' most significant form of productive property, the ownership of enslaved people made it necessary to acquire at least a rudimentary English legal education. Local statutes provided a legal superstructure that allowed colonists to own, police, and punish slaves, but most daily legal practices surrounding slave ownership were rooted in English precedents and procedures. Colonists categorized slaves as property using English legal terms; they bought and sold slaves with printed English legal forms; and they followed English legal procedures as they litigated over enslaved people in court. They did

---

[4] Peter Manigault to Gabriel Manigault, October 18, 1752, Manigault Papers, 11/275/8, SCHS; Peter Manigault to Ann Manigault, November 30, 1752, Manigault Papers, 11/275/8, SCHS.

[5] Peter Manigault to Gabriel Manigault, September 27, 1753, Manigault Papers, 11/275/11, SCHS; Peter Manigault to Ann Manigault, September 27, 1753, Manigault Papers, 11/275/11, SCHS; Peter Manigault to Gabriel Manigault, August 18, 1753, Manigault Papers, 11/275/11, SCHS; Peter Manigault to Ann Manigault, February 19, 1753, 11/275/9, SCHS.

[6] Peter Manigault to unknown, [October] 1768, Manigault Papers, 11/278/7, 80, Peter Manigault Letterbook, SCHS.

so not merely out of a desire to emulate metropolitan culture.[7] Rather, English law provided colonists with a discourse and with plural modes of proceeding that aligned with the commercial imperative to treat people as property in a variety of transactions. Slave law was an organic part of, not separate from, English law in colonial South Carolina and throughout plantation America.

***

It is tempting to think of slave law in colonial British America as a legal aberration. Although English people owned slaves and traded them at English ports, England had no statutory law of slavery.[8] Parliament never explicitly authorized the ownership of human beings, nor did the English Crown issue a definitive statement outlining how enslaved people should be treated at law – there was no English equivalent to the Spanish *Siete Partidas* and *Recopilaciós*, or the French *Le Code Noir*.[9] This lack of statutory authorization was legally significant. As Lord Mansfield resoundingly claimed in the landmark case of *Somerset v. Stewart* (1772), slavery was "so odious" that it must be grounded in "positive law." Because it was not – because Parliament had never sanctioned chattel slavery, Mansfield concluded, a slave in England could not be detained against his will.[10] Scholars have shown that Mansfield's holding in *Somerset* was narrow in its application.[11] Nonetheless, his assertion has

---

[7] Robert Olwell, *Masters, Slaves, and Subjects: The Culture of Power in the South Carolina Low Country, 1740–1790* (Ithaca: Cornell University Press, 1998), 60–61; Christopher Tomlins, *Freedom Bound: Law, Labor, and Civic Identity in Colonizing English America, 1580–1865* (Cambridge: Cambridge University Press, 2010), 450–451.

[8] The custom of English merchants was to regard slaves as chattel property until they were sold. Moreover, English courts occasionally grappled with issues relating to slavery, including whether trover would lie for slaves as if they were chattels (courts initially held that it would), and whether assumpsit might be brought on the sale of a slave in England (no, but it would for the sale of a slave in Virginia). Additionally, "[s]laves were regularly sold on the Liverpool and London markets, and actions on contracts concerning slaves were common in the eighteenth century." J. H. Baker, *An Introduction to English Legal History*, 4th ed. (London: Butterworths Lexis Nexis, 2002), 475–477.

[9] Jonathan A. Bush, "Free to Enslave: The Foundations of Colonial American Slave Law," *Yale Journal of Law & the Humanities* 5 (2003): 422; Sally E. Hadden, "The Fragmented Laws of Slavery in the Colonial and Revolutionary Eras," in *The Cambridge History of Law in America*, edited by Michael Grossberg and Christopher Tomlins, 3 vols. (Cambridge: Cambridge University Press, 2008), 1: 259–260.

[10] *Somerset v. Stewart* (1772) 98 Eng. Rep. 499, 510.

[11] J. H. Baker cautions that *Somerset* – frequently misread by historians – did not specifically outlaw slavery in England, primarily because Lord Mansfield confined "himself to the narrow point that a slave could not be made to leave England against his will." Baker, *An*

left us with a lingering impression that "there was no slave law in England" and therefore that slave law developed apart from early modern English law.[12] From this presumption springs a portrait of legal deviance, of plantation colonists who warped English law to police their slaves, and of self-conscious slaveholders who became increasingly conflicted about the extent of their society's legal divergence from metropolitan norms over the course of the eighteenth century. By the early nineteenth century, according to historians, their strident defense of slavery masked an acute anxiety over treating people as things and hid a fractured system that was increasingly vulnerable to outside critiques and enslaved people's resistance.[13]

In *Bonds of Empire*, I follow South Carolina colonists of all sorts, from wealthy merchant-planters to illiterate sailors, as they used English law to maximize the value of the people they treated as property. I also place their activities in a larger Atlantic context, attending in particular

---

Introduction to English Legal History, 475–477. Elsa V. Goveia's reading of *Somerset* is, like Baker's, narrow. Indeed, according to Goveia, it was not because English law failed to recognize slavery that Somerset was freed, but due to "the lack of the superstructure raised on this basis." Prior to and after *Somerset*, "slaves were taken to and from England, as the case of the slave Grace shows; and so long as they did not refuse to serve, as Somersett did, it may be said that they remained property and did not become subjects in fact, though in theory this change was supposed to take place on their arrival in England." Elsa V. Goveia, "The West Indian Slave Laws of the Eighteenth Century," in *Caribbean Slavery in the Atlantic World: A Student Reader*, edited by Verene A. Shepherd and Hilary McD. Beckles (Kingston, Jamaica: Ian Randle, 2000), 584. See also George Van Cleve, "Somerset's Case and Its Antecedents in Imperial Perspective," *Law and History Review* 24 (2006): 602–603.

[12] Alan Watson, *Slave Law in the Americas* (Athens: University of Georgia Press, 1989), 62. An older historiography assumed *arguendo* that there was no English law of slavery, largely because England lacked a statutory framework that either authorized slavery or provided for the policing of slaves. Alan Watson, for example, begins his study with the premise that "[t]here was no slavery in England, hence there was no slave law in England." Indeed, "a law of slavery had to be made from scratch." *Ibid.*, 62. More recently, historians have begun to challenge this characterization. For example, Elsa V. Goveia argues that under both West Indian and English laws, "trading in slaves was a recognized and legal activity. Under both, there were provisions for regulating the mortgage of slaves and obliging their sale as chattels in cases of debt. This point is worth stressing. The idea of slaves as property was as firmly accepted in the law of England as it was in that of the colonies." Goveia, "The West Indian Slave Laws of the Eighteenth Century," 584.

[13] An older literature that suggested slavery became less economically viable over the course of the colonial period has been thoroughly debunked. See Kenneth Morgan, *Slavery, Atlantic Trade, and the British Economy, 1660–1800* (Cambridge: Cambridge University Press, 2001); Trevor Burnard, "'Prodigious Riches': The Wealth of Jamaica before the American Revolution," *The Economic History Review*, new ser. 54 (2001): 506–524.

to Jamaica and other Caribbean colonies. Emphasizing legal practice rather than proscription, I offer a different narrative, one in which English law imbued plantation slavery with its staying power even as it insulated slave owners from contemplating the moral implications of owning human beings. Rather than describing a system destined to collapse under the weight of moralist critiques in an Age of Revolutions, I depict a legal culture of astonishing flexibility that emerged unscathed at the dawn of the new republic.[14] In fact, following plantation colonists as they cobbled together legal systems from the bottom up reveals that they engaged in the same practices of creative legal adaptation that scholars have observed in English colonial settlements around the world, from Bombay to Botany Bay. American slave owners were participants in a wider English legal culture, one in which settlers harnessed English law's astonishing flexibility to establish their societies at the expense of enslaved people and indigenous populations. Despite our tendency to conflate English legal and political institutions with liberty, the extension of English law into imperial spaces was not an unequivocal good; from India to Ireland to Australia, English law was a ready vehicle for dispossession and exploitation. Plantation slavery and the laws that governed it were not beyond the pale of English imperial legal history. They were yet another invidious manifestation of English law's protean potential.[15]

[14] This perspective supports and extends scholarship that depicts colonial Lowcountry planters as "calculative participants" in a transatlantic economy, as intelligent market actors who zealously pursued profit maximization. S. Max Edelson, *Plantation Enterprise in Colonial South Carolina* (Cambridge: Harvard University Press, 2006), 5; David W. Galenson, *Traders, Planters, and Slaves: Market Behavior in Early English America* (Cambridge: Cambridge University Press, 1986), 1. Also, it links with recent early republic and antebellum scholarship that characterizes planters as capitalist modernizers who were not immune to larger economic and cultural trends. Joyce E. Chaplin, *An Anxious Pursuit: Agricultural Innovation & Modernity in the Lower South, 1730–1815* (Chapel Hill: University of North Carolina Press, 1993); Michael Tadman, *Speculators and Slaves: Masters, Traders, and Slaves in the Old South* (Madison: University of Wisconsin Press, 1989); Walter Johnson, "The Pedestal and the Veil: Rethinking the Capitalism/Slavery Question," *Journal of the Early Republic* 42 (2004): 299–308; Steven Deyle, *Carry Me Back: The Domestic Slave Trade in American Life* (Oxford: Oxford University, 2005); Calvin Schermerhorn, *Money over Mastery, Family over Freedom: Slavery in the Antebellum Upper South* (Baltimore: Johns Hopkins University Press, 2011).
[15] For recent work on the impact of English legal plurality in colonial environments, see Tomlins, *Freedom Bound*; Lauren A. Benton, *A Search for Sovereignty: Law and Geography in European Empires, 1400–1900* (Cambridge: Cambridge University Press, 2009); Ken MacMillan, *Sovereignty and Possession in the English New World: The Legal Foundations of Empire, 1576–1640* (Cambridge: Cambridge University Press, 2006); and

THE PROBLEM WITH MANSFIELD

When Lord Mansfield opined on the primacy of positive law in *Somerset v. Stewart*, he did so at a historical moment in which legislation was in the ascendant. Throughout the early modern period, as Parliament morphed from an event into an institution, statutes became an increasingly significant source of English law and ultimately eclipsed other sources of binding legal authority. This trend began with the English Reformation, as King Henry VIII sought to ground his ecclesiastical authority in statute and continued through the eighteenth century, when most Britons conceded Parliamentary sovereignty.[16] This pattern also held in the American colonies and in the independent United States, where positive law has retained its importance into the twenty-first century. After all, when a modern-day American asks what "the law" is, they likely expect to receive a substantive answer, one based upon information gleaned from local or federal statutes. This conflation of "law" with legislation is understandable, but it was not always the case. In fact, in the early modern period (as well as today), law was much more complex and multifaceted than this emphasis on statutory law suggests. Legal historians have done much to promote this perspective, dispelling older assumptions about what law was and how people engaged with it throughout history. Rather than viewing law as something separate from society, scholars now see it as deeply imbricated within the very fabric of past societies. This broader definition of legal culture has had profound consequences for the study of legal history, freeing scholars to understand "the legal"

Lisa Ford, *Settler Sovereignty: Jurisdiction and Indigenous People in America and Australia, 1788–1836* (Cambridge: Harvard University Press, 2010).

[16] As Mark Knights notes, Parliamentary elections were held frequently after 1679. There were "sixteen general elections" between that date and 1716, and these elections were increasingly contested. "After 1689, there were sessions every year without fail," which in turn resulted in an increase in legislation. Between 1660 and 1688, "parliament passed on average about 26 statutes per session; between 1689 and 1714 this rose to 64 per session." Mark Knights, *Representation and Misrepresentation in Later Stuart Britain: Partisanship and Political Culture* (Oxford: Oxford University Press, 2005), 11–12. Justices of the Peace increasingly found their duties enumerated in statutes, and judges were "manifestly being discouraged from the creative exegesis they had bestowed on medieval statutes" as statutes became longer, and preambles became more specific. To complicate matters further, this sixteenth-century growth of legislation also can be attributed to a more amorphous but important shift in *mentalité*, as "humanist legislators confident in their ability to improve things by the right use of power" sought to shape society through statutes. And emphasis on the importance of positive texts was both driven by and contributed to significant changes in printing technology. Baker, *An Introduction to English Legal History*, 207.

much more broadly and therefore to tap underutilized sources to great effect. Whereas legal historians once focused solely upon narrow doctrinal disputes, statutes, or judicial opinions, we now peer past the sovereign-as-lawgiver and attend to how law shaped the lives of everyday people and how they, in turn, shaped law.[17]

Applying these insights to early modern England, scholars have already begun to uncover a legal culture that was much messier but infinitely more interesting than a fixation with statute implies. Law in early modern England "was a layered and hybrid affair, resting on multiple constitutional foundations and constantly negotiated."[18] It was astonishingly varied from a procedural as well as an institutional perspective. Parliamentary statutes, of course, were an important source of legal authority, but so too were proclamations, charters, and letters patent. English men and women also engaged in a variety of legal transactions that historians can never quantify: they made contracts and executed bonds; they bought and sold merchandise; they made wills and gave inter vivos gifts to sons and daughters. In fact, these quotidian activities are difficult to trace and recreate precisely because they were so commonplace.

Although much of law's daily business never saw the inside of a courthouse, a hodgepodge of courts also dotted early modern England's crowded jurisdictional landscape. These legal institutions proceeded in distinct ways and grounded their authority in different sources.[19] From the central courts at Westminster, to Vice Admiralty Courts, to ecclesiastical courts, to manor courts, each of these jurisdictions had its own rules, vocabularies, and practices, which in turn shaped the behavior of litigants who came to them for remedies. Adding layers of jurisdictional complexity, other institutions exercised judicial power in addition to executive and legislative functions. Parliament, the Privy Council, and the Council of the Marches and Wales, for example, also acted as judicial bodies on specific occasions. Moreover, corporate entities

---

[17] Hendrik Hartog, "Pigs and Positivism," *Wisconsin Law Review* 4 (1985): 934.

[18] Phillip J. Stern, *The Company State: Corporate Sovereignty and the Early Modern Foundations of the British Empire in India* (Oxford: Oxford University Press, 2012), 10.

[19] As J. H. Baker has noted, "we have made an error if we have treated the history of the common law solely as a history of decided cases. There is a whole world of law which never sees a courtroom." J. H. Baker, "Why the History of English Law Has Not Been Finished," *Cambridge Law Journal* 59 (2000): 78. Amy Louise Erickson, *Women and Property in Early Modern England* (London: Routledge, 1993), 5; Tomlins, *Freedom Bound*, 188.

like the East India Company ran Company courts as part of a broader exercise of their corporate "statehood."[20] Jurisdiction – the power to "speak law" – resided in many places and spoke in many competing voices in the early modern English world.

In this pluralistic jurisdictional landscape, legal procedure was often more significant than substantive law. This, in turn, owed much to the early development of English common law, which coalesced around a set of formal procedures and rules administered by the king's central courts in Westminster. Among the most important of these was the writ system, which gave litigants access to remedies in the Court of Common Pleas and the Court of King's Bench. Plaintiffs who sought relief in these new royal courts were first required to purchase a writ, which "worked like a pass admitting suitors to the kind of justice for which they had paid." Although there were a number of different writs that were used in various circumstances, what is important for our purposes is that the formulae of the writs were "frozen" in place in the thirteenth century and remained so until Parliament ushered in a series of sweeping legal reforms in the nineteenth century. A plaintiff who sought a remedy at common law therefore could not "concoct" a new writ to suit the facts of a case but was required to fit his complaint within a preexisting writ form.[21] As a practical matter, this was important because it meant that "remedies were only available, to the extent that appropriate procedures existed to give them form." Legal procedure acted as a barrier to entry and shaped the trajectory of litigation from start to finish, and this ultimately "gave rise to a formalistic legal culture which affected legal thought at every turn." As a result of this reification of form, early modern litigants, judges, and lawyers did not think of "law" as a creature of substance, as we do. Rather, they encountered "law" first and foremost as a creature of procedure.[22] For John Rastell, writing in the sixteenth century, this meant that law was as much a verb as it was a noun. "Law," he explained, was "when an action of debt is brought against one."[23] Contrast this definition with William Blackstone's perspective nearly two centuries later. When the first Vinerian Professor of English law penned his *Commentaries on the Laws of England*, he defined law as "a science,

---

[20] Stern, *The Company State*, passim.
[21] Baker, *An Introduction to English Legal History*, 55–56.   [22] *Ibid.*, 53.
[23] John Rastell, *Les Termes de la Ley: Or, Certain Difficult and Obscure Words and Terms of the Common and Statute Laws of England, Now in Use, Expounded and Explained* (Boston: Watson and Bangs, 1812), 277.

which distinguishes criterions between right and wrong." Blackstone's definition conforms more closely to the vernacular understanding of law today, but it was itself the product of centuries of evolving legal thought rather than an inevitability.[24] Before Blackstone, early modern participants in English legal culture understood it first and foremost as performative and procedural.

In a world in which "law" was an action rather than an object, early modern litigants transformed legal procedure into a site of innovation. Although the common law writ system was rigid in form, clever litigants, advocates, and judges learned to work within its confines in order to accomplish their particular legal goals. They found ingenious ways to jump the writ system's barrier to entry by making new facts fit old forms. Legal fictions were a particularly useful tool in this regard. For example, early modern attorneys fine-tuned the fictitious "Bill of Middlesex," which allowed them to sue in debt in the Court of King's Bench without a writ.[25] The point of this complicated dodge was to allow a plaintiff to seek a remedy at common law, but without the constraints of the traditional forms of action. Instead, the plaintiff could initiate suit with a bill, which was a petition to the court setting out the facts of the case and demanding relief. More "convenient" for litigants, bill procedure allowed plaintiffs to bring multiple claims before the court simultaneously. Bills also were open-ended, unlike highly formulaic writs, and this gave litigants ample room to expand upon their many grievances.[26] The availability of the Bill of Middlesex in King's Bench, then, attracted business to the court, where the number of lawsuits "rose as much as tenfold" between 1560 and 1640.[27] Indeed, early modern litigants were savvy forum shoppers, preferring to sue in jurisdictions that offered the most advantageous procedures at the lowest cost. Judges, in turn, encouraged this by actively supporting procedural innovations that would "win back the patronage of litigants" from other jurisdictions and therefore increase their fees.[28] For example, in the sixteenth century, the central courts at Westminster all engaged in "an internecine struggle for business" by streamlining their procedures.[29] Two centuries later, Lord Mansfield himself attempted to drum up business for King's Bench when he allowed "actions on the case to enforce informal promises and negotiable

---

[24] Sir William Blackstone, *Commentaries on the Laws of England*, 4 vols. (Chicago: University of Chicago Press, 1979), 1: 27.
[25] Baker, *An Introduction to English Legal History*, 42.   [26] *Ibid.*, 41.   [27] *Ibid.*, 43.
[28] *Ibid.*, 40.   [29] *Ibid.*, 41.

instruments of credit," which other jurisdictions would not do.[30] By tweaking procedures that no longer seemed relevant in an increasingly commercial society, Mansfield responded to the needs of litigants who wanted courts to recognize handshake deals and newer systems of monetary exchange. Like countless legal actors before him, he worked within the confines of extant procedures, creatively adapting them to meet the needs of legal consumers.

AN ENGLISH LAW OF SLAVERY

As colonists sought to impose order upon New World societies, they drew on an English legal culture characterized by diversity, not uniformity, one in which legal change occurred at the level of procedure. *Bonds of Empire* shows that this was as true in plantation societies organized around slave labor as it was in Massachusetts, Nova Scotia, or Delhi. Slave law was a natural extension of England's hybrid, improvisational legal system rather than an outlier. This idea that the legal practices of slavery were normative only becomes apparent, however, when we loosen the grip of positive law on our legal imaginary. Scholars – taking a cue from Mansfield – have conflated the law of slavery with the slave codes promulgated by colonial assemblies.[31] Cobbled together on an ad hoc basis, these statutes are among our only prescriptive sources for understanding the development of plantation legal regimes. Primarily comprised of criminal and policing provisions, they reveal how colonists erected an apparatus of legal terror to support white supremacy and promote their economic interests. They were bloody and punitive, prescribing tortuous punishments for alleged legal infractions while at the same time stripping enslaved people of the rights that English men and women had come to expect as their birthright. Occasionally, such laws attempted to set standards for the ways in which masters were to treat those they enslaved in the hopes of forestalling violent reactions. Recently, scholars have used slave codes to document the manifold ways in which slaves resisted their captivity and to highlight moments in which whites reckoned with their

---

[30] David Lemmings, *Professors of the Law: Barristers and English Legal Culture in the Eighteenth Century* (New York: Oxford University Press, 2000).

[31] David Barry Gaspar, "'Rigid and Inclement': Origins of the Jamaica Slave Laws of the Seventeenth Century," in *The Many Legalities of Early America*, edited by Christopher L. Tomlins and Bruce H. Mann (Chapel Hill: University of North Carolina Press, 2000), 78–96; William M. Wiecek, "The Statutory Law of Slavery and Race in the Thirteen Mainland Colonies of British America," *WMQ* 34 (1977): 266.

humanity. Because slave codes punished rebellion, marronage, and running away, they stand as an enduring testament to the personality of individual enslaved people in the face of a legal system that treated them as property. As alleged criminals, enslaved people put the lie to the legal fiction inherent in chattel slavery, and their stories remind us that transforming people into property was always aspirational rather than fully descriptive of reality.[32]

Although slave codes are an invaluable resource for historians, a myopic focus on prescriptive law has left historians with an incomplete view of slave law in plantation America, one that emphasizes criminal law at the expense of so-called private law and proscription over daily practice. In *Bonds of Empire*, I seek to correct this. Probing a wide array of neglected sources – including litigation records, personal papers, and transactional documents – I emphasize more quotidian manifestations of slave law. Without discounting the significance of criminal law, I focus upon the routine "private" practices and civil litigation that made slavery work on a daily basis. Doing so gives us a more complete view of what slave law was and how it functioned. Indeed, when we broaden our source base, we begin to see that throughout British plantation America, all law was slave law. Rather than finding a narrow system devoted to policing enslaved people and preventing insurrection, we encounter a pervasive set of rules and practices designed to manage slaves as capital, labor, and property. Slavery and the legal practices that undergirded it not only set master against slave in a coercive relationship, it organized every aspect of white and Black colonists' lives. Slave mortgages bound white colonists to one another, while the availability of slaves as collateral shaped their economic choices when insolvency loomed. Shipwrecks triggered litigation over the ownership of Black mariners, pitting white sailors against their captains and the Crown against colonists as litigants claimed property rights in people. And a father's death set in motion acrimonious bickering over the ownership of hired-out slaves, fracturing customary working arrangements on plantations. State-sanctioned violence and the threat of physical brutality were key components of a legal culture that was built from the bottom up to control enslaved people, but this legal culture also worked quietly and invidiously to commodify enslaved people on a daily basis. In quotidian acts of economic exchange and in

---

[32] Philip J. Schwarz, *Slave Laws in Virginia* (Athens: University of Georgia Press, 1996), 1; Jeannine Marie DeLombard, *In the Shadow of the Gallows: Race, Crime, and American Civic Identity* (Philadelphia: University of Pennsylvania Press, 2012), 4.

litigation that proceeded from the assumption that people were things, white colonists adhered to the "chattel principle," the notion that monetary value inhered in the bodies of people of African descent.[33] The perception that enslaved people were property ultimately worked a violence of its own sort, not only by transforming slaves into valuable commodities, but also by teaching white colonists to view Black people as less than human.

Perhaps more important, moving beyond prescription to describe legal practice lays bare the English legal origins of slave law. Colonists may have mined a variety of other legal systems for precedents when constructing the more coercive elements of slave regimes in the New World, but English law supplied the forms, procedures, and vocabulary that made slavery possible and profitable on a daily basis.[34] "Chattel" is, after all, an

---

[33] Walter Johnson, *Soul by Soul: Life inside the Antebellum Slave Market* (Cambridge: Harvard University Press, 1999), 2; D. R. Berry, "'We'm Fus' Rate Bargain': Value, Labor and Price in a Georgia Slave Community," in *The Chattel Principle: Internal Slave Trades in the Americas*, edited by Walter Johnson (New Haven: Yale University Press, 2004), 55–71; Phillip Troutman, "Grapevine in the Slave Market: African American Geopolitical Literacy and the 1841 *Creole* Revolt," in *The Chattel Principle: Internal Slave Trades in the Americas*, edited by Walter Johnson (New Haven: Yale University Press, 2004), 203–233.

[34] Alan Watson, for example, has insisted that the law of slavery in the Americas "came into being bit by bit," often influenced by custom, but more importantly as judges in the late colonial period borrowed from Roman law. Watson, *Slave Law in the Americas*, 64. Elsa V. Goveia points to Spanish influence in the developing slavery regimes of the West Indies, although she also emphasizes the role that slave-owning planters played in adapting the Spanish system of slavery to meet their local needs. Goveia, "The West Indian Slave Laws of the Eighteenth Century," 580. In 1965, Arnold A. Sio offered a similar comparative analysis of Roman and American slavery. Arnold A. Sio, "Interpretations of Slavery: The Slave Status in the Americas," *Comparative Studies in Society and History* 7 (1965): 289–308. And Christopher Tomlins, while allowing that English common law adaptations were important in a developing law of slavery, suggests that the rationale for slavery as well as some of its most important legal doctrines emerged from the *ius naturale* and *gentium* (the law of nature and the law of nations), which legitimized the enslavement of captives and "brutes." Tomlins, *Freedom Bound*, 418. While a majority of scholars argue for the Continental jurisprudential origins of slave law, several historians aver that colonists looked to their English legal heritage when they cobbled together slave codes. These historians, however, primarily link slave law with English policing statutes or criminal law. Bradley Nicholson, for example, suggests that England's "often brutal police law," developed in the sixteenth century as a response to the problem of "masterless men," provided a template for laws meant to control and police a lower stratum of people. Bradley J. Nicholson, "Legal Borrowing and the Origins of Slave Law in the British Colonies," *The American Journal of Legal History* 38 (1994): 41. Olwell likewise finds that "while inimitable in fact, the example of English criminal justice was nonetheless a very real presence in the mental worlds of South Carolina jurists" as they crafted and interpreted slave legislation. Olwell, *Masters, Slaves, and Subjects*, 61. Thomas D. Morris

English legal term, and colonists did not settle upon this classification scheme by happenstance. As we shall see, English merchants and settlers began treating slaves as chattel property – first by custom and later by statute – in order to fit their human property into an extant English legal system, one that had evolved over the early modern period to maximize the power of owners to alienate chattel property without restraint. Properly categorized as chattel, slaves could be slotted into preprinted bills of sale, mortgages, trusts, and conditional bonds. They also could be substituted for other moveable property in common law causes of action or in Vice Admiralty litigation, where they could be treated as cargo.

By allowing white colonists to analogize slaves to ships, cows, or horses, the language of chattel slavery unlocked a host of ways of proceeding that suited plantation colonists' need to manage their slaves as a species of property.[35] The legal category of chattel itself became a site of innovation, as colonists perpetuated the most consequential legal fiction in the history of English law. Indeed, the sleight of hand by which human beings were transformed into property was purposeful; colonists carefully weighed their legal choices before committing to concepts, instruments, and conventions. At the same time, they inhabited a broader legal culture in which their decisions were to a certain extent dictated by a set of extant categories and formulas. The language of English law limited colonists' practical options and guided them toward workable solutions. Acknowledging this not an act of exoneration; rather, it is a reminder that law's language operates autonomously, shaping our perceptions of the possible and therefore channeling behaviors on the ground.

SLAVE LAW IN THE LOWCOUNTRY

In *Bonds of Empire*, I reconstruct an English law of slavery using records from South Carolina, and I supplement this with evidence from the West Indian colony of Jamaica. These two colonies dominated a Greater Caribbean region that was vitally important in both strategic and economic terms to the broader British imperial project. American slavery may have originated in Virginia, but historians have increasingly recognized

---

has proven the boldest advocate of the English origins of the "Southern" law of slavery, rooting slave law in English property law. Morris, however, focuses almost entirely upon nineteenth-century slave law. Thomas D. Morris, *Southern Slavery and the Law, 1619–1860* (Chapel Hill: University of North Carolina Press, 1996), 42.

[35] Watson, *Slave Law in the Americas*, 64.

that the first colony was an outlier rather than a bellwether. Instead, the developmental trajectory of the Greater Caribbean region – which was characterized by the exploitation of African labor and the production of agricultural commodities for Atlantic markets – was more typical.[36] South Carolina was a vital node in this dynamic region. Although there is still a tendency to associate the colony with its neighboring mainland southern colonies, South Carolina's history, climate, and economic trajectory made it more like Britain's West Indian colonies and less like North Carolina or Virginia.[37] Settled by Barbadians with experience using enslaved labor to cultivate sugar, South Carolina colonists adapted this plantation model to the Lowcountry's unique environment, ultimately finding in rice and, later, indigo, the cash crops that would make their fortunes.[38] Rice transformed South Carolina from a marginal frontier province into the wealthiest colony on the mainland. Indeed, South Carolina was second only to Jamaica in per capita wealth by the middle of the eighteenth century, and its residents – including Peter Manigault – ranked among the richest in the British Empire.[39] Jamaica followed an even more dramatic trajectory. There, the refinement of a Barbadian plantation complex devoted to the production of sugar transformed the former pirate haven into Great Britain's most valuable colony on the eve of the American Revolution.[40]

Settlers in both South Carolina and Jamaica built their economic success on the backs of enslaved Africans. The agricultural labor that made colonists rich depended upon a steady supply of slaves, which were transshipped across the Atlantic and sold in the port cities that became vital nodes in the transatlantic slave trade (Charlestown in South Carolina and Kingston in Jamaica).[41] In both places, the voracious

---

[36] Virginia plays an outsized role in older studies of slavery, including Edmund S. Morgan, *American Slavery, American Freedom* (New York: Norton, 1975).

[37] For a discussion of the historiography of the Greater Caribbean region, see Matthew Mulcahy, *Hubs of Empire: The Southeastern Lowcountry and British Caribbean* (Baltimore: Johns Hopkins University Press, 2014).

[38] By 1710, Charlestown merchants exported 1.5 million pounds of rice, a number that increased to 6 million pounds by the 1720 shipping season. Trevor Burnard, *Planters, Merchants, and Slaves: Plantation Societies in British America, 1650–1820* (Chicago: University of Chicago Press, 2015), 13.

[39] Russel Menard, "Financing the Lowcountry Export Boom: Capital and Growth in Early South Carolina," *WMQ* 51 (1994): 659.

[40] Burnard, "Prodigious Riches," 508.

[41] Jamaica accounted for fully one-third of all British slave imports in the eighteenth century, and Kingston, Jamaica, was the "major market" for slaves that were sold to Jamaican planters and also slaves that were resold into Spanish America. Trevor Burnard and

demand for slaves roughly tracked cycles of agricultural development. At the turn of the eighteenth century, when South Carolina planters began staking their fortunes on rice production, they also accelerated their commitment to African slavery. Colonists purchased African slaves in increasingly large numbers after 1700 – an earlier trade in Native American slaves effectively ended after 1715 – and Blacks outnumbered whites in the colony by 1710.[42] Slave imports nearly doubled each decade until the 1740s, only to accelerate again in the 1750s.[43] By "1760 all but three Lowcountry rural parishes were more than 70 per cent black."[44] The prevalence of Black people in the Lowcountry led Swiss settler Samuel Dyssli to observe in 1737 that "Carolina" seemed "more like a negro country than a country settled by white people."[45] South Carolina's demography, in fact, made it less like Virginia and more like Jamaica by the eighteenth century. There, the sugar boom of the 1740s combined with appalling life expectancy to fuel the "largest demand for slaves of any British colony in the Americas."[46] In fact, Jamaica received between 40 and 50 percent of African slaves that crossed the Atlantic in British vessels, and enslaved people comprised nearly 90 percent of Jamaica's population by the middle of the eighteenth century.[47]

The slaves toiling in Jamaican sugarcane fields and Lowcountry rice swamps were valued primarily for their productive labor. However, enslaved people also comprised a "large component of white wealth" in both colonies.[48] Colonists in South Carolina and Jamaica perceived enslaved people to be a form of human capital, and they learned to exploit the value inherent in Black bodies. Although slave prices fluctuated in tandem with a variety of economic factors, they rose in secular terms over time, making slaves a profitable form of investment for colonists as the eighteenth century progressed. Mortgaging the value of the slaves they owned in order to purchase more slaves, colonists used enslaved people to

Kenneth Morgan, "The Dynamics of the Slave Market and Slave Purchasing Patterns in Jamaica, 1755–1788," *WMQ* 58 (2001): 205–206.

[42] Edelson, *Plantation Enterprise*, 64.

[43] Philip D. Morgan, *Slave Counterpoint: Black Culture in the Eighteenth-Century Chesapeake and Lowcountry* (Chapel Hill: University of North Carolina Press, 1998), 59–60.

[44] *Ibid.*, 95.

[45] R. W. Kelsey, ed., "Swiss Settlers in South Carolina," *SCHM* 23 (1922): 90.

[46] Burnard and Morgan, "Dynamics of the Slave Market," 205.

[47] Burnard, *Planters, Merchants, and Slaves*, 169.

[48] Burnard, "Prodigious Riches," 508.

build a perfect "white man's country," a place where the acquisition of slaves and land enabled upward mobility for white colonists from a variety of backgrounds.[49]

English law facilitated this process of commodification. Using categories, procedures, and forms that had congealed long before New World colonization, plantation colonists elaborated legal systems that made it possible in theoretical as well as practical terms to treat human beings as property. This was particularly true in South Carolina, where from the colony's founding in 1670, stakeholders in plantation society began to graft African slavery onto an extant English legal framework. In fact, we can see the beginning of this process in South Carolina's first governing document, the *Fundamental Constitutions of Carolina* (1669). Drafted by proprietor Anthony Ashley Cooper and his secretary, John Locke, the *Constitutions* made it clear that African slavery was compatible with a legal system that otherwise hearkened back to a feudal English past. Alongside passages that established a hereditary aristocracy and allowed subinfeudation, the document endowed settlers in Carolina with "absolute power and authority over [their] negro slaves."[50] This blend of old and new was meant to assure aspiring colonists (many of whom were living in the Black-majority island of Barbados) that their property rights in people would remain secure in the fledgling colony. Simultaneously

---

[49] Menard, "Financing the Lowcountry Export Boom," 667. See also Bonnie Martin, "Slavery's Invisible Engine: Mortgaging Human Property," *The Journal of Southern History* 76 (2010): 820.

[50] *The Fundamental Constitutions of Carolina*, March 1, 1669 (hereinafter, "FC"), ¶110, available at Yale Law School, Avalon Project, http://avalon.law.yale.edu/17th_century/nc05.asp. Louis H Roper, *Conceiving Carolina: Proprietors, Planters, and Plots, 1662–1729* (New York: Palgrave, 2004), 29. Contemporary accounts discuss the *Constitutions* in both the singular (as a document) and plural (as a series of constitutional provisions).

Although most scholars agree that Ashley and Locke collaborated in drafting the *Constitutions*, it is difficult to quantify how much each figure contributed to this intellectual endeavor. David Armitage has recently suggested that John Locke played a greater role in drafting the text and in guiding the colony than previously has been thought. David Armitage, "John Locke, Carolina, and the Two Treatises of Government," *Political Theory* 32 (2004): 602–627. Vicki Hseuh, countering Armitage, has characterized Locke's role as that of an "administrative functionary." Vicki Hseuh, *Hybrid Constitutions* (Durham: Duke University Press, 2010), 70. Ashley's biographer has suggested a more collaborative relationship. K. H. D. Haley, *The First Earl of Shaftesbury* (Oxford: Clarendon Press, 1968), 242. For a recent discussion of John Locke and slavery, see Holly Brewer, "Slavery, Sovereignty, and 'Inheritable Blood': Reconsidering John Locke and the Origins of American Slavery," *American Historical Review* 122 (2017): 1038–1078.

a practical acknowledgement of colonial realities and an advertisement for Carolina, the *Constitutions* assumed *arguendo* that "negro" slavery was compatible with English law.

When Ashley and Locke grafted slavery onto their utopian New World scheme, they previewed the type of legal adaptation that would become typical of the colony's subsequent legal development. South Carolina colonists ultimately rejected the *Constitutions* and its elaborate system of governance, but the document remained a "compasse" that they "steere[d] by" in one key respect: its presumption that people could be property under English law.[51] Unlike Virginia, where legislators elaborated the legal status of slaves over time, South Carolina colonists treated people of African descent as slaves from the beginning, and they assumed that English law's categories and procedures could accommodate human property. Treating slaves as chattel property in practice and later, via statute, they fit slaves into a legal system that maximized the power of property owners to control human beings as a type of property, with few restraints.

As a practical matter, classifying enslaved people as chattel property also allowed them to slot slaves into extant legal procedures and forms as they litigated in the colony's multiple jurisdictions. In contrast to Virginia, where county courts blended features of common law and equity courts, South Carolina possessed institutionally distinct jurisdictions for common law (Court of Common Pleas and Court of General Sessions of the Peace), equity (Court of Chancery), ecclesiastical (Court of Ordinary), and Vice Admiralty (Vice Admiralty Court) from an early date.[52] This legal landscape changed little over time, despite sporadic attempts to introduce county courts in the colony.[53] Centered in Charlestown, the availability of different jurisdictions multiplied colonists' options when it came to litigating over slaves. Such jurisdictional plurality also made South Carolina's jurisdictional landscape seem more English. In fact, legal practice in South Carolina defies the traditional "Anglicization" narrative,

---

[51] Ashley to Maurice Matthews, 6/20/72, *SP*, 399.

[52] John Edker Douglass, "The Creation of South Carolina's Legal System, 1670–1731" (PhD diss., University of Missouri-Columbia, 1984), v. By 1731, the colony had four courts of record, located in Charlestown, as well as magistrate and slave courts that functioned at the parish level. The Court of Common Pleas was a civil jurisdiction that sat four times a year. The Court of General Sessions of the Peace heard criminal cases twice per year. Both common law courts were presided over by the Chief Justice. Douglass, "The Creation of South Carolina's Legal System," 153, 285.

[53] *Ibid.*, 84.

which posits that colonists increasingly conformed their laws and institutions to those of England over the course of the eighteenth century.[54] Certainly, the education of attorneys in South Carolina improved over time – more students from South Carolina studied at the Inns of Court in England in the late colonial period than from any other mainland colony – and pleading, particularly in the common law Court of Common Pleas, became more elaborate.[55] But throughout the colonial period, South Carolina colonists conformed their institutions and practice as closely to that of England as possible, and this early emulation meant that those who sought a judicial resolution to disputes over slaves could take advantage of multiple jurisdictions and a variety of ways of proceeding at law.

Like Britons elsewhere, South Carolina colonists were consumers of law, and they displayed a surprising degree of legal literacy. Indeed, the economic importance of slaves meant that South Carolinians of all sorts became adept at buying, selling, and litigating over slaves in order to access credit and expand their plantation and mercantile enterprises. The legal proficiency of merchant, planter, and official Henry Laurens suggests that some colonists achieved an astonishing degree of expertise in this regard. Although historians most commonly have viewed Laurens as a merchant or political figure, an examination of Laurens's voluminous correspondence reveals that he was also legally literate, attaining significant "knowledge of the laws and legal process" of the colony.[56] Laurens deftly managed his business affairs in the colony's common law, Vice Admiralty, and equity jurisdictions. Similarly, he acted in a legal capacity for his business associates in England and the West Indies, arbitrating disputes over debts and offering legal advice as to the timing and utility of initiating lawsuits. And he, like many other merchants, served as an appraiser in South Carolina's Vice Admiralty Court, applying his expertise in slave trading to the valuation of prizes or lost slave cargoes.

Laurens was among the colony's wealthiest men, but those of more modest means also understood that mastery of English law was essential to

---

[54] John M. Murrin, "Anglicizing an American Colony: The Transformation of Provincial Massachusetts" (PhD diss., Yale University, 1966), *passim*.

[55] Robert M. Weir, *Colonial South Carolina: A History* (Columbia: University of South Carolina Press, 1997), 251; William E. Nelson, *The Common Law in Colonial America, Volume II: The Middle Colonies and the Carolinas, 1660–1730* (New York: Oxford University Press, 2013), 70.

[56] Mary Sarah Bilder has provided this useful definition of "legal literacy" in the Atlantic world. Mary Sarah Bilder, "The Lost Lawyers: Early American Legal Literates and Transatlantic Legal Culture," *Yale Journal of Law and the Humanities* 11 (1999): 60.

maintain mastery over slaves. Take Arthur Matthews, who in March 1743 complained that a marshal had attempted to seize "some Negros" that had been mortgaged to him. Matthews prevented the officer from removing the slaves, insisting that he had "[a]cted in all Cases as the Law Directs in Relations to Negros under Mortgage." Satisfied – according to his own assessment of what the law was – that his actions had been entirely proper, Matthews ended his missive on a defiant note: the "Gentlemen that has Directed you to Sease right or wrong may Com on Me for the Slaves," he dared, but "I Shall Defend them Till I am Sattisfied."[57] Cloaking the human tragedy of slavery in a distinctively English idiom of property law and inheritance, colonists like Matthews deployed stock phrases to manage their slaves at law. They exhibited the same dexterity in commanding enslaved people using English legal jargon as they did in manipulating the environment to suit the needs of rice agriculture.

ENGLISH LAW'S TRAGEDY

Bonds of Empire reveals how English law ultimately served colonists' desire to command slave labor, but it also illustrates the tragic human consequences that their reliance upon English law set in motion. As a primary matter, the assumption that slaves were valuable things at law limited slave resistance. Enslaved people who struggled against their bondage not only found themselves checked by the coercive apparatus of the state, but also by more subtle legal practices that assumed they were property and by colonists who had learned by repeating these practices to treat them (and think of them) as mere things. When an Black mariner named Ned slipped away from his owners and hopped a ship bound for Great Britain in 1718, for example, he found himself condemned and sold in a Vice Admiralty Court, not hauled into a slave court.[58] When Henry Laurens's "likely" slave Sampson ran away in 1764, he faced not the lash, but the prospect of sale as his punishment.[59] Transactions and physical brutality answered resistance in plantation America, and in handling slaves as property under the watchful eye of the law, masters set limits for enslaved people's actions in pervasive and effective ways.

---

[57] Arthur Matthews to Samuel Hurst, Esq., March 1, 1742/1743, SCDAH.

[58] *Masters et al.* v. *Sloop Revenge*, November 19, 1718, South Carolina Vice-Admiralty Court Records, A-B vols., 276–300, Library of Congress, Manuscripts Division, Washington, DC.

[59] Henry Laurens to John & Thomas Tipping, December 4, 1764, *HLP*, vol. 4, 513–514.

In fact, historians have grossly underestimated the extent to which the routine and the mundane – litigation over property and debt, buying and selling, mortgaging and conveyancing – contracted rather than expanded space for slave agency. Forms as well as force policed freedom's boundaries. No matter how legally savvy slaves were, no matter how daring, the ubiquity of law in plantation society meant that it was nearly impossible for slaves to anticipate and counteract legal threats. Although nineteenth-century historians have shown that enslaved people might influence the outcome of a particular slave sale, the sheer variety of invisible legal obstacles that confronted slaves ultimately made it difficult for them to devise effective strategies for resistance. It was hard for an enslaved field hand to know whether or not she had been mortgaged or when a creditor might foreclose on that mortgage. A Black mariner could not anticipate when his ship might be hauled into a Vice Admiralty Court, and he might not know which colonial Vice Admiralty jurisdiction would determine his fate. Likewise, an owner's sudden death might result in a house slave's emancipation, or it might reveal the extent of a colonist's indebtedness, shattering that slave's family through a court-ordered sale. This is not to say that slaves did not resist, that resistance did not matter, or that enslaved people were not keenly aware that an encompassing legal regime held sway over their fates. Although this book takes as its subject the activities of white colonists, we also shall see evidence that slaves struggled against their bondage by running away, stopping work, and taking advantage of wartime disruptions to claim freedom for themselves and their families.[60] Nonetheless, in a place where slavery's laws were everywhere, enslaved people learned that freedom was only "unbound" where law could not follow.[61]

---

[60] A voluminous literature on slave resistance in South Carolina includes Peter Wood, *Black Majority: Negroes in Colonial South Carolina from 1670 through the Stono Rebellion* (New York: Random House, 1974); Jim Piecuch, *Three Peoples, One King: Loyalists, Indians, and Slaves in the American Revolutionary South, 1775–1782* (Columbia: University of South Carolina Press, 2013); Silvia R. Frey, *Water from the Rock: Black Resistance in a Revolutionary Age* (Princeton: Princeton University Press, 1991); Robert Olwell, "'Domestick Enemies': Slavery and Political Independence in South Carolina, May 1775-March 1776," *The Journal of Southern History* 55 (1989): 21–48; and Olwell, *Masters, Slaves, and Subjects*.

[61] As Christopher Tomlins has shown, it was only when a long and bloody civil war temporarily displaced law that colonial plantation America's slave regimes ceased to function. Tomlins, *Freedom Bound*, 569. See also G. Edward White, who argues that "law in America could not serve as a mechanism for transcending, or resolving, disputes about slavery because it had been enlisted on one side of those disputes. If law could not resolve the dispute, the only remaining options were force or the Union's dissolution."

Perhaps more important, the extensive replication of English institutions, forms, and procedures in plantation America contributed directly to the dehumanization of enslaved people. Historians have long puzzled over the capacity of colonists in plantation America to treat human beings as property, especially as they were entertaining broadening notions of natural rights. Indeed, slave owners persisted in treating slaves as things at law despite the fact that many colonists, particularly by the mid-eighteenth century, understood that enslaved people were human beings. Henry Laurens, for example, recognized the humanity of slaves when he lamented the fate of "three wretched human creatures call'd Negroes" who had been consigned to him, only to boast in the same letter that their sale was "the greatest Sale" he had ever made.[62] He also condemned the "inhumanity of seperating & tareing assunder" slave families, which he claimed he would "never do or cause to be done" except, of course, "in case of irresistable necessity."[63] Colonist Catherine Percy likewise thanked her male relation for his "care & attention" in attending to "the sale" of her "Negroes," expressing her "concern" for the slaves. But she also celebrated the fact that her human property had "more then doubled the interest" and "sold most extravagantly high."[64]

Laurens and Percy, like colonists throughout plantation America, oscillated between understanding the slaves they owned as human beings and as objects as it suited their economic interests. They did so without any enduring discomfort or concern, despite our expectation that they should have perceived treating people as property as a troubling contradiction. In fact, some historians have suggested that it *was* troubling; that as the eighteenth century progressed, slave owners grew increasingly conflicted over their ownership of human property; and that paternalism and its accompanying rhetoric helped to ease their psychological discomfort.[65] But when we watch what eighteenth-century slave owners did, not what they said, we see that they suffered no cognitive dissonance when they claimed property rights in people.

G. Edward White, *Law in American History: Volume 1: From the Colonial Years through the Civil War* (Oxford: Oxford University Press, 2012), 381.

[62] Henry Laurens to John and Thomas Tipping, Barbados, December 4, 1764, *HLP*, vol. 4, 513–514.

[63] Henry Laurens to Elias Ball, April 1, 1765, *ibid.*, 595–597.

[64] Catherine Percy to Barnard Elliot, October 5, 1778, Baker Family Papers, 11/537/10, SCHS.

[65] Eugene D. Genovese, *Roll, Jordan, Roll: The World the Slaves Made* (New York: First Vintage Books, 1976).

We are left to wonder why. The fact that slavery was ubiquitous in the early modern world partially explains why colonists suffered no qualms about treating people as property. As D. B. Davis has famously observed, it is antislavery rather than slavery that requires an explanation, so pervasive was the practice of slaveholding in the ancient, medieval, and early modern periods.[66] But the very nature of English law, far from puncturing this understanding of human slavery as normative, in fact, made it easier for colonists to dehumanize enslaved people. Indeed, the early modern English law that colonists brought with them to North America was a law of procedures and forms, of categories and catchphrases. It provided a vocabulary and a meta-language that seems at first glance to be inflexible but in practice was highly adaptable. As long as colonists could fit slaves into this preexisting linguistic framework, they could access a legal system that had evolved over time to suit the needs of a rapidly commercializing society. In fact, the logic of English law made it *necessary* for colonists to insert slaves into English legal categories and to deploy older procedural formulae if they hoped to maximize the value of their human property. In this sense, legal procedure functioned instrumentally in plantation America, giving colonists access to particular ways of proceeding at law that suited their desire to build wealth, accrue political power, and fashion themselves as elites within the broader British Empire. As was the case for nineteenth-century slave owners, legal procedure gave them practical access to different registers of empire-building, allowing them to treat slaves as capital investments while also constructing themselves through the buying and selling of human beings.[67]

At the same time, the language of English law was more than a mere tool for slaveholders bent on maximizing the value of their human property. It also performed an important psychological function, insulating colonists from the need to contemplate the moral consequences of initiating legal choices. Procedure in British plantation America served to reduce friction, in much the same way that Hannah Arendt found that "official-ese," clichés, and stock phrases allowed twentieth-century Nazi functionaries to participate in the mass murder of Jewish people without reflecting upon their actions. For Arendt, the repetition of empty phrases was "connected with an inability to think," and these phrases were the "most reliable of all safeguards" against "reality." Evil for Arendt was

[66] David Brion Davis, *The Problem of Slavery in the Age of Emancipation* (New York: Random House, 2014).
[67] Johnson, *Soul by Soul*, 88.

banal, and it appeared in the guise of categories, jargon, and bureaucracy.[68] In much the same way, when British colonists analogized slaves to things and when they classified enslaved people as property, they shielded themselves from the need to see slaves as simultaneously human beings and as objects as law, and from registering this as a contradiction. For British colonists, categories were placeholders, devoid of any intrinsic moral value. They deployed them instrumentally in order to fit slaves into a familiar English property law rubric. But when they did so, they also made it possible for themselves to participate uncritically in a genocidal economic system.

Legal categories and legal language did not merely function instrumentally in plantation America, nor did they simply act as a psychological balm. Rather, the language of law also constituted new social realities. As anthropologists, linguists, and legal theorists have begun to recognize, law is "the locus of a powerful act of linguistic appropriation, where the translation of everyday categories into legal language effects powerful changes."[69] In other words, the language of law possesses "dynamics of its own that contribute to social results."[70] Legal language "creates new meanings through its use in social context," and when we "only focus on the content (semantics) rather than the form (pragmatics) of speech, we miss a great deal about the creative function of language."[71] When colonists categorized slaves as chattel property, they not only smoothed over the apparent contradiction of treating people as things, they also created "a social reality that did not exist prior to the act of speaking."[72] Indeed, by calling slaves chattel, by treating Black people as things at law, colonists throughout plantation America constructed a legal world in which slaves were not just *like* things, they *were* things. Through the act of categorization, they rendered factual what had been a mere supposition – that people of African descent were less than human. Repeated over centuries, slotting slaves into English legal categories in turn foreclosed the possibility that enslaved people might be considered anything other than chattel, just as the classification of slaves as subjects in other imperial contexts ultimately

---

[68] Hannah Arendt, *Eichmann in Jerusalem: A Report on the Banality of Evil* (New York: Penguin, 2006), 46–47.

[69] Elizabeth Mertz, "Legal Language: Pragmatics, Poetics, and Social Power," *Annual Review of Anthropology* 23 (1994): 435–455

[70] *Ibid.*, 437.

[71] Elizabeth Mertz, "Language, Law, and Social Meanings: Linguistic/Anthropological Contributions to the Study of Law," *Law & Society Review* 26 (1992): 421–422.

[72] *Ibid.*, 422.

opened up space for negotiation and resistance.[73] Far from an item of antiquarian interest, then, English law's forms and procedures, not just its substance, matter tremendously in accounting for the dehumanization of Black people throughout the British Atlantic World.

****

Bonds of Empire follows colonists as they fit slavery into an English legal rubric, and it is therefore a book organized around legal words. From a modern perspective, these words are meaningless jargon – stock phrases like "chattel," "credit," "in rem," "equity." But to eighteenth-century colonists, they were the building blocks of a shared legal heritage, one that English people used to construct new legal systems across the globe. Just as colonists sought to transform the American environment into something that resembled their idealized notions of an English landscape, they deployed these words to create familiar legal cultures in America. They did so with alacrity, because they found that English law was flexible enough to accommodate their desire to impose legal order on what they perceived as an uncivil wilderness.

In each chapter, I examine one of these words in depth in order to explicate different facets of slavery's many laws. Chapter 1 emphasizes the relationship between English property law and slavery. I follow colonists as they sought to classify slaves as property and as they deployed their knowledge of English property law on a daily basis to manage slaves. Fitting slaves into an extant legal system that bifurcated property into real estate or chattels personal was an act with long-term practical consequences. American colonists – including those beyond plantation America – understood that each particular category unlocked different ways of proceeding at law that impacted their ability

---

[73] As Malick W. Ghachem shows, slaves in the French colony of San Domingue strategically invoked provisions of the Code Noir in asserting claims to freedom. The authors of the Code, which governed the behavior of both masters and slaves throughout the colonial period, "aimed to strike a balance between the view of the slave as outside the bounds of sovereign authority and an alternative view of the slave as a subject (however disfavored and mistreated) of absolute monarchy." Malick W. Ghachem, *The Old Regime and the Haitian Revolution* (Cambridge: Cambridge University Press, 2012), 58. This is not to say that slaves in British colonies were more submissive or less prone to rebellion than other slaves in Spanish America. Rather, the statutory law of slavery in British colonies provided slaves with fewer protections that could be used to hold masters accountable to royal oversight. Indeed, when imperial authorities did offer slaves the Crown's protection, particularly during the American Revolution, they eagerly seized upon these assurances. See, e.g., Piecuch, *Three Peoples, One King*, 68.

to buy and sell slaves and to shield them from creditors. Building upon customary practice in the transatlantic slave trade, South Carolina colonists treated enslaved people as chattel property, at first by custom and later via statute. Whereas most plantation colonies settled upon some mixture of chattel and real property when they determined how to classify their slaves, South Carolina colonists ultimately adopted pure chattel slavery in order to facilitate commercial transactions involving enslaved people and to expand their credit with British merchants. Treating slaves as a chattel property was economically beneficial for South Carolinians, but it had far-reaching cultural implications. Through close readings of legal forms, including marriage settlements, trusts, and wills, I also watch small acts of legal transformation, moments in which colonists analogized slaves to things. In these acts of legal transmutation, South Carolina colonists compared enslaved people to livestock and other valuable moveable objects, not because they believed them to be the same as those objects, but because they believed them to be the same at law. Nonetheless, these small acts of transformation had much larger consequences, giving motion and meaning to statutory schemes that allowed colonists to treat slaves as things.

In Chapter 2, I examine the specific legal consequences of colonists' decision to categorize slaves as chattels at law. Properly fit into an English law rubric, colonists in South Carolina and throughout plantation America transformed human beings into a dynamic form of capital that could be bought, sold, and financed with ease. As a practical matter, classifying slaves as chattel gave colonists access to a set of commercial forms and procedures that had coalesced to facilitate long-distance trading. Conditional bonds were among the most important of these, and I follow this legal form of debt as it became part of an expanding Atlantic commercial system. Originating in the Middle Ages, conditional bonds coalesced into a distinctive form that was easier to enforce in common law than other forms of debt. The enforceability of conditional bonds made them surprisingly portable as they traveled across the globe. Although this instrument had originated to suit the needs of an agrarian society, the conditional bond easily accommodated commercial ventures that assumed people could be property. The power of conditional bonds to hold debtors to account in colonial courts made them particularly useful in shoring up a trade that was built entirely upon credit. Ultimately, bonds became an unremarkable feature of commercial life in plantation societies like South Carolina and Jamaica, where creditors relied upon this much older instrument to secure a wide variety of commercial transactions.

Following conditional bonds across the Atlantic underscores English law's flexibility, even when it was embodied in seemingly rigid forms. We see a similar dynamic at work in Chapter 3, an examination of slave litigation in the Vice Admiralty Courts of colonial South Carolina and Jamaica. Following litigants of all sorts – including planters, merchants, and sailors – I show how they used centuries-old admiralty procedure to claim slaves and free Black sailors on ships as valuable prizes (commonly called in rem procedure). By comparing enslaved people to objects that could be seized and sold just like ships and cargo, these litigants convinced Vice Admiralty Courts to condemn and sell human beings for their benefit. The paper trail they left behind also provides a rare glimpse into the lives of free and enslaved Black mariners, showing how their commodification at English law's hands blunted the advantages that seafaring offered them. Although Black people who spent their working lives on water moved more freely through plantation societies than agricultural laborers, their voyages often brought them into contact with Vice Admiralty Courts, where litigants claimed them as property. In places where human beings were made things at law, the Vice Admiralty Court – a jurisdiction that specialized in seizing, appraising, and condemning things – demarcated the boundaries of slave agency even as it extended English law's reach.

In Chapter 4, I turn to another set of English legal procedures and categories that plantation colonists used to commodify enslaved people. Analyzing manuscript Chancery Court records, I show how colonists adapted the legal language of "equity" to claim enslaved people as property in the context of property and inheritance disputes. Equity in early modern England was pliable; it meant different things to different people. We conflate the term today with fairness, but in early modern England it was commonly associated with a grab bag of Western philosophical, legal, and political traditions, including "God's law, the public good," and "the king's conscience."[74] In places where people were deemed objects at law, however, equity opened up space for litigants to articulate property claims to human beings and to adjudicate complex inheritance cases involving slaves. Using procedures common to the English Court of Chancery and invoking familiar descriptions of equity as a legal concept, litigants in plantation colonies like South Carolina effectively transformed a court of the king's conscience into a slave court.

[74] Mark Fortier, *The Culture of Equity in Early Modern England* (Aldershot: Ashgate Publishing, 2005), 4.

British newcomers to South Carolina saw no irreconcilable tension between English law and the ownership of slaves, and in Chapter 5 I explore how administrative law in occupied Charlestown evolved to manage an increasingly mobile slave population. Rather than reforming colonial slave law, British administrators and military officers relied heavily upon colonial precedents as they balanced their need to maintain South Carolina's plantation economy against their desire to employ the labor of slaves in British army departments. Individual British administrators also learned to buy, sell, and argue over slaves, adopting slavery's legal language as they sought to supplement their incomes and build wealth. As they established their own plantations and confiscated the human property of people they called rebels, they, too, treated slaves as things on a daily basis, replicating local legal practices that did not appear from their perspective to be maladaptive. Consequently, the legal administration of occupied Charlestown tended to support rather than undermine slavery as an institution, despite growing antislavery sentiment in England.

I conclude with a preview of slave law in the early republic. Although independence transformed English subjects into American citizens, much about slave law remained the same; English law and English legal procedure continued to be useful for citizens living in a slaveholders' republic. Republican legal forms were not, in the end, significantly different from forms used under a monarchy, and this had far-reaching consequences. In particular, this legal continuity from the colonial period meant that the commodification of slaves not only continued, but also spread along with the expanding United States. Settlers in new plantation areas of the Deep South, who were steeped in a legal culture that valued tradition, modeled their slave laws on those of South Carolina and, therefore, on the language, practices, and precedents of English chattel slavery. The plantation society that they constructed, by hewing so closely to English legal forms, perpetuated the invidious legal fiction that people were things as a working reality in the slave South.

Taken together, *Bonds of Empire* asks us to rethink traditional narratives that link English law's extension overseas with the flowering of liberty. The rights-talk and liberal political ideology that we often associate with English law's proliferation across the globe obscures the fact that, in practice, English law was not a benign or even morally neutral force. When we move beyond the sweeping rhetoric that colonists so deftly deployed – when we look at what they did rather than what they said – a more insidious pattern emerges. In quotidian legal activities, in court rooms and private transactions, English law accommodated and indeed perpetuated slavery. The forms and procedures, the bonds and bills of sale, and Chancery petitions that gather dust in archives attest to this fact. Monuments to English law's enduring power to shape actions and mold realities, these documents and the words they bear failed to shed their potency even as Britain disavowed the transatlantic slave trade and, eventually, embraced emancipation. If we seek to understand the origins and persistence of American slavery, we must first look to them.

I

Chattel

In the last decade of the eighteenth century, South Carolina lawyer John Phillips painstakingly transcribed into his legal precedent book the proper form of pleadings for a case involving "[t]rover for a Negro."[1] This addition to his handwritten collection of legal forms and court decisions was one of many entries touching on litigation over enslaved people, including a sample writ of "[t]respass vi et ar[mis] for beating a slave," a writ of "trespass for killing a negro," and a form of declarations "to recover for an unsound Negro sold for a sound price." According to the formula Phillips followed, the plaintiff in a slave trover case – a lawsuit over the improper conversion of slave property – should first declare that he "was possessed of a certain Negro woman Slave" who was valued at "the price of – as of his own proper goods & chattels." He also should allege that the enslaved person subsequently came "into the hands" of the defendant, who "craftily & subtilly" converted the slave "to his own proper use" even though he knew that the slave was the plaintiff's property.[2] Having established that he owned the slave, that the defendant knowingly failed to return the slave, and that this willful act had resulted in damages, the plaintiff in such a case might request relief.

That Phillips created a precedent book like this is not surprising, nor does his interest in slave litigation shock, especially given the fact that he

---

[1] In this common law cause of action based on English legal precedents, the plaintiff complained in a plea of trespass on the case that the defendant had found his property and wrongfully converted it to his own use. J. H. Baker, *An Introduction to English Legal History*, 4th ed. (London: Butterworths Lexis Nexis, 2002), 399.

[2] John Phillips, Book of Precedents, 1788–1839, 34–400, 37, SCHS.

practiced in South Carolina, a Black-majority colony. What makes this particular entry in Phillips's precedent book noteworthy is the fact that he adapted the form to use in a case alleging trover for a horse. Indeed, it seems that he first made an exact copy of pleadings from litigation over a "Negro woman Slave" and only later edited his transcription, striking out "Negro woman slave" and replacing this phrase with "iron gray horse." When and why Phillips edited this entry is unclear, but his small act of dehumanization – substituting an animal for a person in a handwritten legal precedent book – encapsulates a larger process by which English property law, wielded by legally savvy colonists, transformed people into things throughout the British Atlantic World. In fact, when Phillips made this substitution, when he replaced one chattel with another that was to his mind legally identical, he repeated an act of analogy that had been performed countless times before by South Carolinians of all sorts as they managed their slaves. At the birth of a new nation and at the turn of a new century, Phillips drew upon a long history in which colonists cloaked the human tragedy of slavery in a distinctively English idiom of property law and inheritance. Using their knowledge of English property law to buy, sell, and devise slaves, these colonists exhibited the same dexterity in commanding enslaved people using the language of English property law as they did in manipulating the environment to suit the needs of rice agriculture.[3]

Historians have long understood that transforming people into property was Atlantic World slavery's defining characteristic, and have concluded that the dehumanization of slaves both in law and in daily life "was absolutely central to the slave experience." D. B. Davis, for example, has argued that "[f]rom antiquity, chattel slavery was modeled on the property rights traditionally claimed for domestic animals."[4] Eugene D. Genovese likewise has observed that slavery "rested on the principle of property in man," the idea that a slave was an "*instrumentum vocale* – a chattel, a possession, a thing, a mere extension of his master's will."[5] Similarly, for Philip Morgan, "masters thought of and acted toward" slaves "using the language of property."[6] Although historians are correct

---

[3] S. Max Edelson, *Plantation Enterprise in Colonial South Carolina* (Cambridge: Harvard University Press, 2006), 5.

[4] David Brion Davis, *The Problem of Slavery in the Age of Emancipation* (New York: Alfred A. Knopf, 2014), 11.

[5] Eugene D. Genovese, *Roll, Jordan, Roll: The World the Slaves Made* (New York: First Vintage Books, 1976), 3–4.

[6] Philip D. Morgan, *Slave Counterpoint: Black Culture in the Eighteenth-Century Chesapeake and Lowcountry* (Chapel Hill: University of North Carolina Press, 1998), 259.

to emphasize the property component of slavery, such a choice was not inevitable. In Spanish and French colonies, for example, an enslaved person was treated as an "inferior kind of subject" rather than "a special kind of property."[7] Although slaves in these colonies were bought, sold, and brutally exploited, they also could occasionally invoke the reciprocal bonds of allegiance and protection owed to them as subjects to make claims upon monarchs as people, not property. Relatively free from royal oversight when it came to making determinations about the status of slaves, English colonists chose a different path. They made a conscious decision to treat slaves not just as property at law, but as chattel property.

That momentous decision is one that can and should be placed in historical context. Despite the fact that "chattel slavery" has become an uninterrogated catchphrase used to describe the legal status of human property in British America and the United States South, the term had a distinct legal meaning, and perhaps more important, distinct legal and cultural consequences for both white colonists and enslaved people.[8] In English legal culture, defining something – or someone – as chattel property (i.e., moveable, personal property) endowed owners with a certain bundle of rights that allowed them to dispose of that property with little hindrance. Other types of property, especially real estate, conveyed a much more circumscribed bundle of rights. For colonists, then, classifying slaves as chattel property was a crucial first step in creating societies in which human beings could be transformed into moveable units of wealth, in which the slave became "a person with a price." This legal decision, in fact, was the sine qua non of an economic system that brought staggering riches to a few and untold suffering to millions more.

In this chapter, I examine the process by which colonists in South Carolina and throughout British America made critical determinations about how slaves should be treated as property at law. Throughout, I place their activities in an English legal context, examining how slave classificatory schemes endowed owners with particular rights and responsibilities. Colonists were keenly aware that their classificatory choices had serious consequences, and they made legal determinations about classifying slaves in order to maximize the value of the human beings that labored

---

[7] Elsa V. Goveia, "The West Indian Slave Laws of the Eighteenth Century," in *Caribbean Slavery in the Atlantic World: A Student Reader*, edited by Verene A. Shepherd and Hilary McD Beckles (Kingston, Jamaica: Ian Randle, 2000), 584.

[8] See, e.g., Morgan, *Slave Counterpoint*, 261; Winthrop D. Jordan, *White Over Black: American Attitudes Toward the Negro, 1550-1812* (Baltimore: Penguin, 1968), 98.

for their benefit. In expanding plantation colonies like South Carolina, treating slaves as chattel property helped to transform enslaved people into economic assets that they could transfer to other colonists and across generations. Classified as chattel, a slave became an investment whose value could be readily realized through sale, leasing, or borrowing in addition to a source of immediate labor. Chattel slaves could be attached by creditors and mortgaged to support the growth of plantations and mercantile enterprises. Likewise, they could be detached from the land they worked and forcibly transported to outlying plantations or frontier zones.

As colonists were well aware, decisions about how to classify slaves had significant legal consequences. But the choice to consider slaves chattel property was not merely a legal one; it also had profound cultural consequences. One of the most important of these was that making slaves legally equivalent to other types of moveable property invited colonists to compare slaves to livestock, which were also considered chattels under English law. Historians have long noted that colonists in plantation America analogized slaves to cattle, oxen, and other large farm animals, and recent work has made it clear that such analogies played a key role in dehumanizing enslaved people throughout the Atlantic World.[9] Showing that these analogies were rooted in a distinctively English legal heritage highlights the important role that English property law played in that process of dehumanization.

Indeed, taken together, statutory law and daily legal practice in South Carolina and other colonies reveal that the process of legal adaptation in plantation America was not fraught because there was no slave law in England. Rather, slave-owning colonists built an entire economic system upon the assumption that they could make slaves fit into an English property law rubric. English law provided the vocabulary, forms, and procedures that allowed colonists to treat slaves as things and to analogize people to livestock and other personal property on a daily basis. It was not a barrier to the development of slave societies; rather, English law made the dehumanization of slaves possible and even necessary by limiting colonists' choices when it came to slotting slaves into a preexisting property law rubric.

In making determinations about classifying slave property, colonists did not betray any concern with reconciling the humanity of slaves with

<hr />

[9] Jennifer L. Morgan, *Laboring Women: Reproduction and Gender in New World Slavery* (Philadelphia: University of Pennsylvania Press, 2004), 167.

their legal classification as things, in part because they were used to conventions of a legalese that required specialized language. Slave owners were less psychologically or morally conflicted about the "slave as thing" paradox than we might expect, and they could modulate between understanding the slave-as-human and the slave-as-property without much cognitive dissonance. English property law, in fact, encouraged a type of thinking that allowed and even required colonists to obscure the humanity of enslaved people if they wished to maximize their economic value. If colonists' legal choices lacked ideological content, however, documenting how they compared people to things also reveals that moments of legal analogy had distinct ideological *consequences*. In the aggregate, South Carolina colonists internalized these analogies, and they were layered atop preexisting beliefs about African racial inferiority. English law, then, encouraged a type of mechanical thinking that led to the dehumanization of Black people, with invidious and lasting consequences.

In "Adapting English Property Law," I briefly describe the law of property in England, and examine how colonists throughout plantation America adapted English property law to suit their needs as slaveholders. Because the process by which these colonists used English law to transform people into things is immediately visible in the slave codes passed by colonial assemblies, in "Societies with Slaves," I examine these codes to show how colonists throughout British America categorized enslaved people as property via statute. Despite the assumption that slaves always were considered chattel property, colonists carefully weighed different classificatory schemes, modulating between treating slaves as real estate and slaves as chattels in order to balance the commercial needs of colonial debtors and British merchants. Classifying slaves as real estate, for example, protected slaves from creditors, but at the cost of contracting credit that was based on the slaves' underlying value; treating slaves as chattel property subjected them to creditors' claims while making it easier for heirs to inherit enslaved people when slave owners died without a will.

In "Negroes, Goods, and Merchandizes," I examine the development of slave law in South Carolina, placing the colony's slave codes against a backdrop of property law administration in the colony. Moving from a customary legal regime in which slaves were treated as chattels de facto to a statutory law of slavery that codified customary practice, South Carolina colonists did not experiment with treating enslaved people as real estate. Deviating from West Indian precedents, slave law in South Carolina instead paralleled the legal trajectory of New England colonies like Massachusetts Bay, where familiarity with practices in the slave trade encouraged colonists to treat slaves as chattel property. Colonists eventually codified "pure" chattel slavery in the infamous Negro Act of 1740, an act that raised imperial administrators' suspicions but did little to change the actual practice of managing slaves in the colony. As I argue, enshrining chattel slavery in statute reveals South Carolina colonists as active participants in a broader imperial legal culture, one in which positive law was becoming an increasingly important source of binding legal authority.

The classification of slaves as chattel property in practice as well as at law in colonial South Carolina had decidedly tragic and long-lasting consequences for people of African descent. In this chapter's final section, I describe discrete moments in which colonists analogized slaves to other types of personal property in order to show that acts of categorization worked their own cultural violence. Most South Carolina colonists did not vocalize their mental calculations or even signal them, as Phillips did, by physically substituting the word "horse" for the word "slave." Nonetheless, in transactional documents and correspondence that supply our only evidence for daily legal practice, we can see that colonists frequently grouped slaves with other types of valuable personal property, including livestock. As D. B. Davis has shown, this sleight of hand, performed countless times over the course of a century and a half, fueled the growth of scientific racism in the late eighteenth and early nineteenth centuries.[10]

ADAPTING ENGLISH PROPERTY LAW

English property law, which provided the foundation for property law in the American colonies, divided property into real property and chattel property. Chattel property, also called personal or moveable property, included money, household furniture, clothing, debts, and livestock, while real estate typically denoted land.[11] Because land in England was central to economic, social, and political life, the law of property developed to provide significant protections for real property that did not apply to chattels. Specifically, unsecured creditors – those whose debts were not secured by land – could not attach a debtor's land upon his or her death,

---

[10] Davis, *The Problem of Slavery in the Age of Emancipation*, 32.
[11] Amy Louise Erickson, *Women and Property in Early Modern England* (London: Routledge, 1993), 23–24. Leases of land were considered "chattels real," "halfway between real and personal property." Although land in England could be held as freehold, copyhold, or leasehold property, only freehold property was considered to be real property. *Ibid.*, 24.

and real property descended to a debtor's heirs "free of all legal claims" of unsecured creditors.[12] Likewise, even when land was offered as security, the cost and procedural difficulties of obtaining a judgment against the debtor in court made seizing land used as security impracticable. In contrast, debtors could seize and sell personal property to satisfy debts even if that property had not been offered as security.[13] Land, unlike personal property, also could be entailed, which prevented heirs from dividing or alienating (selling) an estate, and ensured that land would pass intact from generation to generation.[14]

In England, "four separate but overlapping legal systems" administered legal disputes over real and personal property: common law, equity, ecclesiastical, and local courts (including manorial and borough courts).[15] These jurisdictions applied different rules in determining legal questions about the transmission of property, although over the course of the seventeenth century jurisdictional competition and Parliamentary statutes had the overall effect of standardizing property law administration. Roughly, the rules of property law that these courts followed created two distinct but overlapping regimes: one that addressed questions about marital property and another that governed the inheritance of real and personal property upon an individual's death.[16] Rules pertaining to marital property primarily concerned the ownership and transmission of married women's property (although courts also adjudicated questions about widowers' rights to land and chattels). At common law, a married woman was considered feme covert, subject to the doctrine of coverture, which stipulated that during marriage her legal identity was "covered" by that of her husband. As a result, a married woman could not make contracts in her own name; she could not make a will; she could not sue or be sued without her husband; and she forfeited control over her dowry and all personal property.[17] However, upon her husband's death she became entitled to a dower portion, which consisted of one-third of her husband's real property for life and one-third of his personalty outright.[18]

Although these legal rules deprived women of meaningful property rights in theory, individuals sought to mitigate coverture's deleterious

---

[12] Claire Priest, "Creating an American Property Law: Alienability and Its Limits in American History," *Harvard Law Review* 120 (2006): 388.
[13] *Ibid.*   [14] *Ibid.*, 419.
[15] Erickson, *Women and Property in Early Modern England*, 23.   [16] *Ibid.*, 24.
[17] *Ibid.* Widows and single women, however, could and did make wills.
[18] Carole Shammas, Marylynn Salmon, and Michael Dahlin, *Inheritance in America: From Colonial Times to the Present* (New Brunswick: Rutgers University Press, 1987), 25.

effects in practice, in part because property holders valued their daughters and cared for their maintenance and comfort, but also because they sought to protect familial wealth by shielding it from creditors. Of primary concern was protecting an heiress's property from an irresponsible or avaricious husband (particularly a husband who was a chronic debtor), and to prevent husbands from controlling valuable property after a wife's death. In response to these intergenerational concerns, over the course of the seventeenth and eighteenth centuries propertied families in England began to shield familial assets through marriage settlements, which conveyed property to trustees for the benefit of a woman in anticipation of her marriage. These settlements ensured that a husband could not access or dispose of his wife's property. Instead, a wife maintained control over her property (usually through trustees) during her marriage, thereby safeguarding familial wealth from her husband and his creditors and ensuring its transmission intact to the next generation. Married women could not dispose of their property via testamentary bequest at common law, a restriction that marriage settlements superseded by including stipulations authorizing a married woman to make a will despite her coverture. Although they were unenforceable at common law, marriage settlements were honored and litigated in equity courts, a jurisdiction that will be discussed more fully in Chapter 4.[19]

In addition to addressing questions about female property, English property law evolved to govern the transmission of property upon an individual's death. The question of overarching significance to family members and courts was whether a decedent died with or without a will (intestate). In contrast to Continental legal systems, where testamentary freedom was limited, by the end of the seventeenth century English men (as well as unmarried women and widows) could dispose of both personal and real property via will with few restraints.[20] The act of writing a will gave testators the power to "disinherit whomever they pleased," only subject to a widow's dower claim.[21] Writing a will also allowed a testator to choose an executor (or executrix), the person responsible

---

[19] Erickson, *Women and Property in Early Modern England*, 26.
[20] John E. Crowley, "Family Relations and Inheritance in Early South Carolina," *Histoire Social – Social History* 17 (1984): 35. However, as Carole Shammas has argued, it appears that merely one in four decedents in early modern England left a will, and wealth and testation were correlated: the propertied were more likely to make wills. Carole Shammas, "English Inheritance Law and Its Transfer to the Colonies," *The American Journal of Legal History* 31 (1987): 151.
[21] Shammas, Salmon, and Dahlin, *Inheritance in America*, 27.

for inventorying, managing, and distributing a decedent's estate to heirs, a process known as probate and overseen by ecclesiastical courts.[22]

For those who did not choose to make a will, the common law rules of inheritance governed the descent of real property. Under the "canons of descent," which had been followed since at least the thirteenth century, land descended by primogeniture (to the firstborn son), but in the absence of male heirs, daughters inherited jointly.[23] Over the early modern period, questions about the inheritance of intestates' personal property increasingly came to be governed by Parliamentary statute. Indeed, in the century immediately preceding the founding of the Carolina colony in 1670, a period of significant legal change in England, legislation rather than litigation or custom (with a few exceptions) controlled questions of inheritance. This trend culminated in a 1670 statute that gave intestates' widows one-third of a decedent's personalty (if the couple had issue) and provided for the equal inheritance of personal property by children.[24] Like testates' estates, intestates' estates were administered by ecclesiastical courts, which appointed an administrator (or administratrix) to manage, account for, and distribute the decedent's property to heirs at law. Parliament's resolution of what had previously been an anarchic system of intestate property distribution set an important precedent for colonists in South Carolina and in other colonies, who would primarily rely upon local legislation in delineating intestacy rules, and who would likewise use statutes to classify slaves as property for inheritance purposes.

The administration of English property law occupied significant institutional and mental space in early modern English legal culture. In fact, property law comprised the heart of English common law, which developed to provide litigants with a royal forum for adjudicating disputes over land.[25] Consequently, as English colonists began to settle in North America and the West Indies, adapting an English property law regime to suit colonial societies was of primary concern.[26] As Carole Shammas

---

[22] Erickson, *Women and Property in Early Modern England*, 27.   [23] *Ibid.*, 26.

[24] Shammas, Salmon, and Dahlin, *Inheritance in America*, 26.

[25] Baker, *An Introduction to English Legal History*, 15.

[26] As John McLaren, A. R. Buck, and Nancy E. Wright have argued, "[t]he use and regulation of property are central to an understanding of the history and culture of the settler colonies of the British Empire." John McLaren, A. R. Buck, and Nancy E. Wright, "Property Rights in the Colonial Imagination and Experience," in *Despotic Dominion*, edited by John McLaren, A. R. Buck, and Nancy E. Wright (Vancouver, Canada: University of British Columbia Press, 2005), 1.

has shown, colonies typically "followed one of two patterns," either delaying the passage of "any very detailed bill on inheritance" or "continually fiddl[ing] with specific provisions." In general, colonies with large dissenting populations (primarily Puritans and Quakers) deviated most dramatically from English precedents and changed their inheritance schemes frequently.[27] In contrast, colonies in the Chesapeake and Carolina Lowcountry, as Marylynn Salmon has argued, adhered to English legal precedents as closely as possible, largely for cultural reasons. According to Salmon, settlers in these colonies came to America "unwillingly" in the hopes of amassing large fortunes and succeeded "at the price" of "their dignity," and, in response, they mimicked English forms "as closely as possible" to compensate for their supposed feelings of cultural inferiority.[28]

As we shall see, however, slave-owning colonists' decisions to adhere to English legal forms and procedures also represented a practical acknowledgment that English property law provided a workable framework for thinking about and adjudicating disputes over land and, more importantly, slaves. In plantation colonies that relied upon slave labor, assembly members classified slaves as real estate or as chattel property to suit the needs of the planter class they represented, working with rather than discarding English property law forms and concepts in order to maximize the value of their human property. Scholars' assumptions that slaves were a novel form of property and that adapting colonial laws to suit slave societies was a fraught process are incorrect: watching colonists adapt English property law to suit their plantation economy reveals how seamless this process was as a practical and theoretical matter.

SOCIETIES WITH SLAVES

As South Carolina transitioned from a society with slaves into a true slave society in the late seventeenth century, colonists began to erect a legal infrastructure that organized and sanctioned the exploitation of enslaved Black and indigenous laborers.[29] They were not alone in this enterprise. In acts of legal genesis remarkable for their destructive creativity, colonists

---

[27] Shammas, Salmon, and Dahlin, *Inheritance in America*, 30
[28] Marylynn Salmon, *Women and the Law of Property in Early America* (Chapel Hill: University of North Carolina Press, 1986), 10.
[29] Ira Berlin, *Many Thousands Gone: The First Two Centuries of Slavery in North America* (Cambridge: Harvard University Press, 1998).

throughout the Atlantic World assembled legal systems that made it possible as a practical and theoretical matter to coerce labor in the New World. These systems were many-faceted and complex and ranged from the vernacular legal practices associated with slave trading to the slave codes promulgated by colonial assemblies. Although the "private" law of slavery – embodied in quotidian transactions and routine litigation – will occupy us in the coming chapters, the statutory law of slavery is perhaps the most striking aspect of colonial slave law. Promulgated by local legislatures, so-called slave codes authorized systems of enslaved and indentured labor and "validate[d] ... many customary elements of the legal relationship between white and black people in the colonial period."[30] We typically associate them with southern or West Indian colonies, but "each of the mainland colonies had at least the rudiments of a statutory law of slavery and nine of them had fairly elaborate slave codes," including New York, New Jersey, Pennsylvania, and Rhode Island.[31] Although slave codes varied from colony to colony, scholars have noted that most colonial assemblies engaged in "legal borrowing" as they drafted them with some codes – like the Barbados slave code – providing a template for a number of others.[32]

Slave codes have commanded significant scholarly attention and seem to show colonial legal deviance. Because "there was no slave law in England," American colonists appear to have generated slave codes "from scratch," drawing upon a wide variety of precedents to create a legal system that developed beyond the pale of English law.[33] This perception lingers despite recent efforts to uncover the English roots of slave codes, in part because the content of slave codes is viscerally shocking to modern sensibilities.[34] Slave

---

[30] As William Wiecek has shown, "by the time of the Revolution, each of the mainland colonies had at least the rudiments of a statutory law of slavery or race, and nine of them had fairly elaborate slave codes." William M. Wiecek, "The Statutory Law of Slavery and Race in the Thirteen Mainland Colonies of British America," *WMQ* 34 (1977): 258–259.

[31] *Ibid.*, 261–262.

[32] Bradley J. Nicholson, "Legal Borrowing and the Origins of Slave Law in the British colonies," *The American Journal of Legal History* 38 (1994): 38–54.

[33] Alan Watson, *Slave Law in the Americas* (Athens: University of Georgia Press, 1989), 62.

[34] Bradley Nicholson, for example, suggests that the law of slavery "was based on English legal traditions," although these traditions were outside of the common law. Specifically, England's "often brutal police law," developed in the sixteenth century as a response to the problem of "masterless men," provided a template for laws meant to control and police a lower stratum of people. While colonists did not transplant these policing laws "whole cloth," they did find portions of them useful in developing slave codes. Nicholson, "Legal Borrowing and the Origins of Slave Law in the British Colonies," 41. Robert Olwell likewise finds that "while inimitable in fact, the example of English criminal justice was nonetheless a very real presence in the mental worlds of South Carolina jurists" as

codes were bloody, and enshrined in law a regime of terror that was meant to coerce labor and prevent rebellion. Colonists relied upon cruel physical punishments – including whipping and branding – as well as an increasingly elaborate system of surveillance as they "mobilized the apparatus of coercion" to subjugate growing slave populations.[35]

In slave codes, the "limbs of 'Albion's Fatal Tree' that were unequal and brutal flourished," as Robert Olwell has shown. At the same time, "other branches that stressed due process and equality before the law withered."[36] Even as colonists legislated "new punishments" in the service of their expanding plantation economies, they simultaneously stripped enslaved people of the legal protections that white English men and women had come to expect as their birthright.[37] Although some codes sought to protect slaves against unduly harsh treatment, "[s]tatutory provisions directly or indirectly securing the rights of slaves were scanty." Slaves typically could not testify in court against whites, nor could they seek redress in colonial courts. Instead, slave codes instituted a separate criminal process for slaves, one in which colonists meted out a harsh brand of plantation "justice" without a jury.[38] As colonists made clear, these separate jurisdictions were justified and, indeed, necessary given the intrinsic inferiority of Black people Slaves were "Brutish" and "deserve[d] not" to "be tried by the Legal Trial of Twelve Men of their Peers or Neighbourhood," according to the Barbados Assembly. Due to "the Baseness of their Condition," their fate would instead be determined by justices of the peace and local freeholders, who tended to use slave trials to reclaim or reinforce their social standing within the neighborhood.[39] South Carolinians, too, insisted that "negroes and other slaves" were "generally of a barbarous and savage nature" and therefore were "unfit to be governed by the laws, customs and usages of England."[40] Previewing the language of scientific racism that would come to dominate planter

---

they crafted and interpreted slave legislation. Robert Olwell, *Masters, Slaves, and Subjects: The Culture of Power in the South Carolina Low Country, 1740–1790* (Ithaca: Cornell University Press, 1998), 61.

[35] Berlin, *Many Thousands Gone*, 115.   [36] Olwell, *Masters, Slaves, and Subjects*, 71.
[37] Berlin, *Many Thousands Gone*, 115–116.
[38] For slaves and testimony, see Miles Ogborn, "The Power of Speech: Orality, Oaths, and Evidence in the British Atlantic Word, 1650–1800," *Transactions of the Institute of British Geographers*, 36 (2011): 109–25.
[39] *The Laws of Barbados* (London, 1699), 160. For practice in South Carolina's slave courts, see Olwell, *Masters, Slaves, and Subjects*, 71 ff.
[40] "An Act for the Better Ordering and Governing Negroes and Other Slaves" (1735), *SAL*, vol. 7, 385.

discourse in the nineteenth century, they rationalized deviations from English precedents by insisting that people of African descent were beneath the protections enjoyed by British subjects, if not subhuman.

When colonists instituted draconian punishments for slaves and simultaneously deprived enslaved people of the legal protections that white men and women enjoyed as a matter of course, they exposed the "core contradiction of slavery" – "treating persons as things" – as a legal fiction.[41] Slaves themselves precipitated this reckoning. Reading slave codes against the grain reveals that enslaved people constantly challenged white structures of authority in both overt and subtle ways. In acts of resistance great and small, enslaved people refused to allow Britons to erase their humanity and, indeed, forced white colonists to acknowledge their humanity in law. For example, prohibitions against slave gatherings, the consumption of alcohol, and unauthorized travel reveal that slaves participated in these very human activities.[42] More importantly, they suggest that colonists believed that these activities posed threats to plantation regimes. Slave criminality and its punishment exposed the chattel principle's fictiveness in a visceral way that cannot but command our attention. Indeed, it is crucial to notice the ways that enslaved people exposed cracks in a legal system by forcing white colonists to reckon with their humanity. However, we cannot forget that the effort to erase slaves' humanity was Herculean and that the language of English property law was instrumental to this project. Slave codes were not entirely comprised of criminal or policing provisions. Alongside prohibitions against criminality, colonial assembly members also fit their human property into an English legal rubric that divided property into chattel property and real estate. Notably, they never moved beyond this rubric to treat an enslaved person as an "inferior kind of subject," as was the case in other European colonies, or write into law another category for enslaved people.[43] They did not jump the ruts of English property law's well-worn categories. Rather, they maneuvered within those categories, subtly expanding them to accommodate property rights in people. If the criminal and policing provisions in slave codes mark colonists as legal outliers, property law provisions in slave codes remind us that – like Britons throughout the globe – they maneuvered within a distinctively English legal idiom. As

---

[41] Morgan, *Slave Counterpoint*, 257.
[42] For a contemporary critique of enslaved people's sociability, see Letters of "The Stranger," September 17 and 24, 1772, *SCG*.
[43] Goveia, "The West Indian Slave Laws of the Eighteenth Century," 584.

we shall see, the very act of sorting slaves into English law's categories ultimately worked its own violence.

"NEGROES, GOODS, AND MERCHANDIZES"

Even as colonists cobbled the criminal and policing provisions of slave codes from a variety of legal sources, they sought to ground property rights in people in English law. From an early date, Britons framed their legal discourse about slaves in familiar commercial terms by treating the slave as saleable or moveable property. Although England lacked a statutory framework authorizing or regulating the possession of slaves, slave trading and slave owning were accepted practices in the seventeenth century, and English slave traders and factors developed ways of proceeding in trade that were recognized as binding legal custom.[44] Perhaps the most important of these mercantile customs was to regard slaves as chattel property or "merchandise" until they were sold.[45] The Royal African Company, which exercised a monopoly on the transport and sale of slaves from Africa to the Americas between 1672 and the close of the eighteenth century (although the company continued to trade into the 1730s), routinely considered slaves to be merchandise.[46] For example, in legal agreements between the company and ship captains slaves were grouped with other commodities and merchandise that could be bought and sold on the African coast. John Sperriford "of London Marriner and master of the Good Ship or Vessel called the *Fortune*" agreed with the Royal African Company in 1695 to "transport and bring Negroes Elephants Teeth and any other Goods Com[m]odities and merchandizes" from Africa "unto any of the English plantat[i]ons in America."[47] In the same year, Sam Kelly, master of the galley *Mary & Margaret*, also entered into a charterparty (a shipping agreement) undertaking to deliver slaves and other commodities and

---

[44] Goveia puts the case for revising the common belief that English law did not recognize slavery, noting that under both West Indian and English laws, "trading in slaves was a recognized and legal activity. Under both, there were provisions for regulating the mortgage of slaves and obliging their sale as chattels in cases of debt. This point is worth stressing. The idea of slaves as property was as firmly accepted in the law of England as it was in that of the colonies." Goveia, "The West Indian Slave Laws of the Eighteenth Century," 584.

[45] Baker, *An Introduction to English Legal History*, 475.

[46] Stephanie E. Smallwood, *Saltwater Slavery: A Middle Passage from Africa to American Diaspora* (Cambridge: Harvard University Press, 2008), 3.

[47] Articles of Agreement between the Royal African Company and John Sperriford, July 5, 1695, C111/184, TNA.

merchandise from the Angola region to the American colonies.[48] The wording of these agreements was nearly identical, suggesting that the company and its Court of Assistants used standard language in contracting with ship captains for the purchase and delivery of slaves bound for the Americas. Even at this early date, then, treating slaves as moveable property was routine legal practice among English slave merchants.

The grouping of slaves with other moveable property in legal documents reflected the imperatives of a commercial slave-trading system designed to dehumanize slaves. Stephanie Smallwood has described this system as one in which Africans were transformed into "human commodities" whose most important attribute was their "exchangeability."[49] Indeed, the Royal African Company paid slave-trading captains by the head, not by the ultimate sale price of slaves at their final destinations. This payment structure encouraged slave traders to perceive Africans not as human beings with individual qualities and characteristics, but as items that could be packed into the holds of ships. Associating slaves with merchandise in transactional documents was a natural outgrowth of a system of exchange in which slave traders reduced human beings to units of moveable property. When they conflated Africans with other types of fungible commodities like "Elephants Teeth," they made analogies that were readable in the context of a business that privileged calculation and valued enumeration in planning and conducting long-distance trade. This was a business in which traders filled their holds as quickly as possible with slaves.[50]

The decision to treat enslaved people as cargo or merchandise also made sense in an expanding commercial empire, one in which merchants and colonists increasingly relied upon preprinted transactional documents to manage long-distance trade. As we shall see in Chapter 2, these forms reduced transaction costs, making it easier as a practical matter for Britons to conduct business without a lawyer by simply filling in the blanks of a preprinted form. At the same time, the language in these forms disciplined commercial speech by forcing users to fit a wide variety

[48] Articles of Agreement between the Royal African Company and Sam Kelly, October 22, 1695, C111/184, TNA.
[49] Smallwood, *Saltwater Slavery*, 35.
[50] The Royal African Company traded to South Carolina into at least the 1720s. On August 30, 1720, Governor Francis Nicholson was instructed to "give all due Encouragement and Invitation" to the Royal African Company so the colony would have a "constant and sufficient Supply of Merchantable Negroes at Moderate Rates in Mony or Commodities" BPRO, vol. 8, 133.

of transactions – including transactions involving human property – into forms that would be honored in extant legal systems.

   We should not be surprised, then, to find that customary legal practices in the transatlantic slave trade provided early English colonists with workable precedents and that they took their cues from the merchants who had already found success in adapting familiar forms and practices to human trafficking. This was as true in New England as it was in plantation colonies. In the seventeenth and eighteenth centuries, slavery was not yet geographically confined to the area that would one day become the American South. Sanctioned by the Crown, slave trading was authorized and accepted by ordinary people who "told themselves and believed that even if enslaved people longed for freedom, their own personal enactment of slaveholding was permitted, protective, and unproblematic."[51] Early New England colonists, in fact, built upon the core principle that slaves were merchandise and wrote into slave codes an assumption that people could be property under English law. For example, the Massachusetts Body of Liberties (1641) often features in progressive narratives about the history of self-government and civil liberties, but the path-breaking document also recognized slave trafficking. While purporting to exclude slavery, the Body of Liberties sanctioned the enslavement of "lawful captives taken in just wars" and "such strangers" that were "sold" to colonists.[52] Building upon this precedent, the "Duke's Laws" in New York (1665) also recognized the buying and selling of slaves under certain circumstances.[53] Both of these early codes assumed that, when enslavement was legally justified, slaves might be bought and sold as goods or merchandise in keeping with customary practice in the slave trade. Even as they sought to prohibit slavery under most circumstances, these laws codified and legitimized the human trafficking that was already taking place in practice in New England ports.[54]

---

[51] Wendy Warren, *New England Bound, Slavery and Colonization in Early America* (New York: Liveright, 2016), 129.

[52] Massachusetts Body of Liberties, December 1641 in William H. Whitmore, *Bibliographical Sketch of the Laws of Massachusetts Colony from 1630-1686* (Boston: Rockwell and Churchill, 1890), 32–61. See also Wiecek, "The Statutory Law of Slavery and Race in the Thirteen Mainland Colonies of British America," 261; Warren, *New England Bound*, 34–35.

[53] Wiecek, "The Statutory Law of Slavery and Race in the Thirteen Mainland Colonies of British America," 261.

[54] According to Wendy Warren, "at a bare minimum at least nineteen documented trading voyages in the seventeenth century followed the telltale slaving route of New England to Africa to the West Indies and back." Warren, *New England Bound*, 45.

In New England and the Mid-Atlantic colonies, colonists continued to treat enslaved people as merchandise – or chattel property – despite the lack of specific statutory authorization from their assemblies.[55] Decidedly commercial in orientation and influenced by legal precedents in the slave trade, colonists in New England and the Mid-Atlantic assumed *arguendo* that enslaved people were merchandise and treated them as such. Into the eighteenth century, slave codes in these regions remained primarily concerned with drawing distinctions between white "Christian" servants and slaves and policing enslaved (and free Black) populations rather than defining what type of property slaves would be at law. For example, the Massachusetts Bay colony did not attempt to categorize slaves as a particular species property, although in wills, estate inventories, and bills of sale, "Negroes were listed in the same manner as bedsteads, china ware, guns, money, and horses." By 1675, slaves were also "placed in the same category" as other chattels, including "horses, sheep and swine," in tax rates.[56] Similarly, "even though colonial lawmakers never explicitly legalized race-based slave-holding" in Rhode Island, "they simply began legislating as if the institution were already in place."[57] Rhode Islanders may have been the "most deeply entrenched" in the slave trade; nonetheless, they did not seek to classify slaves via statute.[58] The same was true in New York and New Jersey. Although statutes declared that slaves were "property," neither colony explained what kind of property slaves would be at law.[59]

This lack of specificity did not extend to plantation America. In places where planters increasingly relied upon slave labor to produce commodities for Atlantic markets, colonists used slave codes to categorize enslaved people as property explicitly. Whereas New Englanders and Mid-Atlantic colonists were content to assume that slaves were chattel property in

---

[55] *Ibid.*, 112.

[56] Lorenzo Johnston Greene, *The Negro in Colonial New England, 1620–1776* (New York: Columbia University Press, 1942), 169–170.

[57] Christy Clark-Pujara, *Dark Work: The Business of Slavery in Rhode Island* (New York: New York University Press, 2016), 29.

[58] *Ibid.*, 28.

[59] "An Act for Regulating Slaves" (1702), *Acts of Assembly Passed in the Province of New York, from 1691–1718* (London, 1719), 59; "An Act for Preventing, Suppressing, and Punishing the Conspiracy and Insurrection of Negroes, and Other Slaves" (1712), *ibid.*, 14. For New Jersey, see an "Act for Regulating Slaves," *The Acts of the General Assembly of the Province of New-Jersey, from the Time of the Surrender of the Government in the Second Year of the Reign of Queen Anne, to this Present Time, being the Twenty Fifth Year of the Reign of King George the Second* (Philadelphia, 1752), 18–24.

keeping with mercantile practice, assemblies in plantation colonies began
to experiment with different classification schemes. As we have already
seen, English law bifurcated property into chattel property and real estate,
and each of these categories conveyed a different bundle of rights that
impacted masters' rights to sell, devise, and shield slaves from creditors.
Because they sought to maximize their legal rights to alienate but also to
shield their slave property from creditors' claims, assembly members in
plantation colonies often wrote into law an odd (from an English perspective) distribution of property rights. Legislators treated slaves as real
property in some circumstances (which technically ensured that eldest
sons would inherit both land and slaves in cases of intestacy), but also
deemed slaves chattel in order to expand credit with English merchants.
Although the overarching trend, at least in statutory law, was a shift from
classifying slaves-as-real estate to slaves-as-chattel, this move was halting
and contingent, as colonists responded to local economic conditions as
well as the realities of lawmaking in an imperial context. English property
law, which reified categories and forms, may have appeared rigid at first
glance, but in practice offered plantation colonists significant room to
maneuver.

The development of chattel slavery can seem inevitable when we view it
from a nineteenth-century perspective, but this was not the only option
available to colonists. As Thomas Morris has shown, "for one reason or
another rules of real property were applied in some instances in over one-
third of the jurisdictions that made up the slave south."[60] Morris's study,
which encompasses the nineteenth century as well as the colonial period,
disproves the assumption that legislators or judges understood slaves to be
exclusively chattel property from the beginning of the colonial period. In
fact, classifying slaves as real estate had a number of advantages over
"pure" chattel slavery, particularly in places where a planter's economic
success depended upon his ability to combine both land and slaves into
a productive unit. Because the laws of real property had evolved over time
to encourage intergenerational transfers of real estate, classifying slaves as
real estate allowed planters to annex their slaves to plantations and to
transmit them together to their heirs according to the rules of intestacy. In
other words, if a plantation owner died without a will, both his land and
slaves would descend to his heirs together. This offered significant advantages to planters in high mortality environments, who could ensure that

[60] Thomas D. Morris, *Southern Slavery and the Law, 1619–1860* (Chapel Hill: University of
    North Carolina Press, 1996), 64.

whole plantations, including an annexed labor force, would pass intact to their eldest sons according to the canons of descent.

Keeping plantations and slaves together (and therefore profitable) after a planter's untimely death also tended to protect widows, who were entitled to a one-third of an estate's proceeds for life. In high-mortality colonies like Virginia, the fate of widows deeply concerned assembly members, who feared that classifying slaves as chattel property might imperil their wives' financial stake in plantations. Writing to the Board of Trade in 1728, for example, Lieutenant Governor Gooch of Virginia explained that some Virginia colonists took "great exception" to an "act to explain and amend the act for declaring the negroe mulatto and Indian slaves within this Dominion to be real estate" on the grounds that the act did not sufficiently protect widows' dower rights to slaves.[61] This concern was linked to plantation colonists' awareness that classifying slaves as chattel or real estate impacted creditor-debtor relations. Under English law, these creditors could not attach real estate to satisfy outstanding debts. Classifying slaves as real estate, therefore, allowed colonists to shield their human property from unsecured creditors (that is, creditors who did not have a bond that listed the property that secured the debt). In Virginia and Jamaica, where indebtedness to English merchants was sometimes framed as a pressing problem, classifying slaves as real estate was tantalizingly attractive. Colonists in both places had direct experience with creditors, who "attached and sold all the slaves on an estate" in order to satisfy outstanding debts. This left the planters and his heirs with "bare land without Negroes to manure the same," which spelled financial ruin. To keep "plantations as viable working units," then, colonists who were anxious about indebtedness favored classifying slaves as real estate.[62]

This legal reclassification of slaves as real property concerned British merchants. Plantation colonists were not the most principled debtors, and their British creditors kept a weather eye out for any potential impediments that might impede their right to seize planters' most valuable assets.[63] In

[61] Gooch to Board of Trade, June 8, 1728, *CSP*, vol. 36.

[62] Richard S. Dunn, *Sugar and Slaves: The Rise of the Planter Class in the English West Indies, 1624–1713* (Chapel Hill: University of North Carolina Press, 1972), 241.

[63] "An Act for the Better Order and Government of Slaves" (1696), *Acts of Assembly, Passed in the Island of Jamaica: From 1681, to 1737, Inclusive* (London: John Baskett, 1738); Priest, "Creating an American Property Law," 421. Evidence from Antigua suggests that as late as the 1780s, some Antiguans treated their slaves as annexed to land. Frank Wesley Pitman argued that because Antiguan slaves were deemed annexed to land, they might be likened to serfs. Frank Wesley Pitman, "The Treatment of the British West Indian Slaves in Law and Custom," *The Journal of Negro History* 11 (1926): 616.

Jamaica, for example, courts often refused to attach slaves to satisfy creditors' claims, a trend that merchants found alarming. Virginia colonists were
also notorious for dodging their creditors, and merchants routinely complained about these practices until Parliament purportedly resolved the
problem with the 1732 Debt Recovery Act.[64] Abolishing "the legal distinctions between real property, chattel property, and slaves in relation to the
claims of creditors," the Debt Recovery Act made it possible for creditors to
seize slaves and even land in payment of debts, regardless of the way in
which colonial statutes classified assets.[65] No longer could colonists classify
their slaves as real estate (or reclassify them) in order to shield them from
creditors. The act was a decided victory for merchants, but plantation
colonists responded less favorably. Virginians, who were well aware that
the Debt Recovery Act would limit their ability to shield slaves from
creditors, "fiercely" resisted the legislation.[66] Likewise, Barbadians asked
the Board of Trade to declare that the act did not apply in the island. Failure
to do so, they charged, would result in the "compleat the ruin of the
inhabitants."[67] Plantation colonists may have overreacted to the Debt
Recovery Act, but their visceral response reveals that the classification of
enslaved people as property was more than merely a semantic issue. Like
their British creditors, slave owners understood that the power to categorize
allowed them to improve their position in commercial relationships in
places where financial success depended upon an ability to command
both labor and land. The Debt Recovery Act stripped them of this power,
leaving them vulnerable to the claims of British creditors. Viewed in this
light, colonists' reactions to the Debt Recovery Act begin to seem less like
hyperbole and more like a shrewd assessment of what they had lost.

Plantation colonists may have objected to the Debt Recovery Act, but
from an early date they too were aware of "the difficultys of making

---

[64] Priest, "Creating an American Property Law," 425. Representation of the President,
Council and Assembly of Barbados to Board of Trade, January 18, 1733, *CSP*, vol. 40.

[65] Priest, "Creating an American Property Law," 389. As Richard Sheridan explains, the
Debt Recovery Act prompted criticisms in England because it seemed to promote slave
auctions. In 1797, William Knox "pushed through a bill in Parliament ... to repeal as
much of the Credit Act as made Negroes chattels for the payment of debts." Richard
B. Sheridan, *Sugar and Slavery: An Economic History of the British West Indies,
1632–1775* (Baltimore: Johns Hopkins University Press, 1973), 289.

[66] Priest, "Creating an American Property Law," 425.

[67] This was because there was "but a very small currency of cash in this island," and
therefore if the "best sugar-work plantation[s]" were sold by outcry to satisfy creditors,
only English creditors would be able to afford to purchase them. Representation of the
President, Council and Assembly of Barbados to Board of Trade, January 18, 1733, *CSP*,
vol. 40.

a perishable thing governable by the ... rules of succession as lands of inheritance."[68] Classifying slaves as real estate may have allowed them shield slaves from creditors, but it was not a panacea. As a primary matter, treating slaves as real estate deviated from customary norms in the slave trade, as we have seen, and therefore made the rights and remedies of merchants and factors unclear when they unladed slaves in colonial ports. More importantly, classifying slaves as real property tended to contract credit. Because real property was difficult for unsecured creditors to attach, classifying slaves as real estate limited creditors' practical legal remedies when American creditors defaulted. As a result, English merchants were reluctant to extend much-needed credit to colonists when they were unable to attach their most valuable assets: their slaves. When Virginia colonists lamented that merchants only gave "credit according to the number of slaves they know a man is possess'd of," what they really meant is that merchants extended credit when slaves were available to attach.[69]

Aware of these limitations, assembly members in plantation colonies often wrote into law an odd (from an English perspective) distribution of property rights. Rather than limiting themselves to a binary choice – chattel or real estate – they modulated between treating enslaved people as chattel in some circumstances and real property in others. For example, although the 1698 Barbados slave code categorized slaves as "Estates Real, and not Chattels," the law specifically exempted merchants, factors, and agents: The slaves they imported to Barbados would be considered chattels until sold.[70] Virginia's 1705 slave code also declared slaves to be real estate for the purposes of inheritance, while allowing merchants, factors, and agents to treat slaves as chattels.[71] These exceptions codified customary practice in the slave trade and acknowledged that slave traders and factors required the maximum amount of legal flexibility in order to turn a profit on slave-trading voyages. They also reflected the fact that some (but not all) speculators in the

---

[68] Gooch to Board of Trade, June 8, 1728, *CSP*, vol. 36.

[69] Morris, *Southern Slavery and the Law*, 67. "An Act to explain and amend the Act, For declaring the Negro, Mulatto, and Indian Slaves, within this Dominion, to be Real Estate," William Waller Hening, *Statutes at Large: Being a Collection of all the Laws of Virginia, from the First Session of the Legislature in the Year 1619*, vol. 4, 225–226. Gooch to Board of Trade, June 8, 1728, *CSP*, vol. 36.

[70] "An Act Declaring the Negro-Slaves of this Island, to be Real Estates" (1668), *Acts Passed in the Island of Barbados, from 1643 to 1762, Inclusive* (London, 1764) (hereafter cited as *Barbados Acts*), 64–65.

[71] "An Act Declaring the Negro, Mulatto, and Indian Slaves within this Dominion, to be Real Estate" (1705), Hening, *Statutes at Large*, vol. 3, 333.

"Guinea" trade lacked the dynastic imperatives of colonists who sought to establish and transmit plantations and slaves to the next generation.

More importantly, plantation colonists – like British merchants – understood the broader financial implications of classifying slaves as real estate and specifically that treating slaves as real property contracted credit. As a result, assemblies classified slaves as real estate for inheritance purposes but allowed creditors to attach slaves in payment of debts. In 1672, for example, the Barbados assembly declared slaves to be "Chattels for the payment of Debts" but clarified that they would remain real estate "to all other intents and purposes."[72] Jamaica's 1696 slave code also considered slaves real property for the purposes of determining their descent upon an owner's death. In other words, English intestacy law would apply to slaves in the same way it applied to landed estates. However, slaves could be seized as chattels to satisfy creditors' claims until all of a decedent's debts had been paid. Only the slaves that remained after the payment of an owner's debts would descend as if they were land.[73] Assembly members in Virginia likewise adopted this modified approach. Following West Indian trends, in 1705 Virginia burgesses allowed creditors to seize slaves – otherwise treated as real estate – for payment of debts "as other chattels or personal estate may be."[74] Despite a statutory scheme that was generally protective of

---

[72] "A Declarative Act upon the Act Making Negroes Real Estate" (1672), *Barbados Acts*, 94. Priest, "Creating an American Property Law," 414.

[73] "An Act for the Better Order and Government of Slaves" (1696), *Acts of Assembly, Passed in the Island of Jamaica: From 1681, to 1737, Inclusive* (London: John Baskett, 1738).

[74] "An Act Declaring the Negro, Mulatto, and Indian Slaves within this Dominion, to be Real Estate" (1705), Hening, *Statutes at Large*, vol. 3, 334. The statute apparently created confusion about whether slaves could be entailed; however, this was resolved in a 1727 law that expressly authorized slave owners to entail their human property. Under this statute, executors and administrators could still seize slaves to pay the debts of the deceased, as was the case in earlier statutes, but only when the decedent's other personal estate was inadequate to pay those debts. Likewise, the statute provided some protection for wives' dower rights by maintaining that slaves "entailed and possessed by a husband in right of his wife could not be seized to satisfy his debts." Morris, *Southern Slavery and the Law*, 67. "An Act to explain and amend the Act, For declaring the Negro, Mulatto, and Indian Slaves, within this Dominion, to be Real Estate . . . ," Hening, *Statutes at Large*, vol. 4, 225–226. For a discussion of the practice of entailing slaves in Virginia, see Holly Brewer, "Entailing Aristocracy in Colonial Virginia: 'Ancient Feudal Restraints' and Revolutionary Reform," *WMQ* 54 (1997): 338–339. Brewer rebuts C. Ray Keim, "Primogeniture and Entail in Colonial Virginia," *WMQ* 25 (1968): 545–586. Analyzing wills from York County, Virginia, between 1715 and 1769, Morris has argued that most Virginians did not entail their slaves and that heirs who inherited slaves in fee tail could "dock" the entail easily. Morris, *Southern Slavery and the Law*, 71.

dynastic interests in land and slaves, Virginia's carve-out for creditors was a practical acknowledgment that in Virginia – as elsewhere in plantation America – credit was king.

CHATTEL BY CUSTOM

South Carolina's Commons House of Assembly passed its first slave code in 1691, and in this initial attempt to regulate slavery in the province, the assembly members followed West Indian precedents by stipulating that slaves should be freehold property (real property), except with regard to the payment of debts, in which case they should be "deemed and taken as all other goods and chattels."[75] However, the Lords Proprietors disallowed this law along with all other legislation passed during the gubernatorial regime of Seth Sothell, one of the infamous "Goose Creek" men who took control of the colony's government and later was recalled in disgrace by the Lords Proprietors.[76] For the next fifty years, statutory law in South Carolina remained surprisingly vague with regard to classifying slaves as property.[77] Indeed, colonists did not formally declare slaves to be chattels until 1740.[78]

In the absence of legislative guidance, South Carolinians followed customary mercantile practice and treated their slaves as chattel property. In early marriage settlement documents, slaves were listed with other personal property, and especially money, cattle, and household goods.[79] For example, in anticipation of Elizabeth Ashby's marriage to John Vinaridge, her family drew up a marriage settlement giving Elizabeth "separate use" of "all and Singular the Issue profits and increase of the negroes and other Slaves & all other the personal Estate whatsoever" without her husband's "hinderance." The assumption that slaves were personal estate was

[75] The law read: "[A]s to the payment of debts [negroes] shall be deemed and taken as all other goods and chattels . . . and all negroes shall be accounted as freehold in all other cases whatsoever, and descend accordingly." "An Act for the Better Ordering of Slaves" (1691), *SAL*, vol. 7, 343–344. This law is incorrectly dated to 1690 in *SAL*. See L. H. Roper, "The 1701 'Act for the Better Ordering of Slaves'," *WMQ* 64 (2007): 397, n. 1.

[76] Eugene Sirmans, "The Legal Status of the Slave in South Carolina, 1670–1740," *The Journal of Southern History* 28 (1962), 465.

[77] Although colonists continued to generate new slave legislation during this period, these codes primarily addressed concerns about policing the colony's expanding slave population. Between 1691 and 1740, colonists passed slave statutes (including minor revisions to older statutes) in 1693, 1695, 1696, 1701, 1712, 1714, 1717, 1722, and 1735.

[78] "An Act for the Better Ordering and Governing Negroes and Other Slaves in This Province" (1740), *SAL*, vol. 7, 397.

[79] Marylynn Salmon, "Women and Property in South Carolina: The Evidence from Marriage Settlements, 1730 to 1830," *WMQ* 39 (1982): 12.

reinforced later in the agreement, which also grouped Elizabeth's slaves with the rest of her "goods Chattles moneys or other personal Estate."[80] Slaves, Black as well as Native American, were also routinely included in South Carolina estate inventories, which only listed personal property. An early inventory dating to 1688, for example, included "one Indian woman named Francis," who was valued at £15 sterling.[81] And in slave-sale advertisements, South Carolina colonists called slaves "chattels," revealing that the term and its legal meaning were well understood from an early date. In 1735, for example, the *South Carolina Gazette* ran an advertisement for an estate sale of "all the Goods and Chattels" of the deceased, "consisting of Negroes, Household Goods and other Effects."[82] The phrase "Goods and Chattels" was a common trope, a piece of legal jargon with which colonists were familiar, and which appeared in a variety of places in conjunction with the word "negro" or "negroes." Elizabeth Ashby's marriage settlement included this grouping, but it also appeared in early colonial wills. In 1736, Jonathan Welden of Christ Church parish in Berkeley County left his "whole estate," including "both Negroes Horses and Cattle and all other my Goods and Chattels" to be shared equally among his wife and children.[83] Moses Wilson of Goose Creek also bequeathed his "well beloved" wife and her sons the residue of his estate, including his "Negroes Stock Goods Chattels & Estates."[84]

This de facto treatment of slaves as chattels parallels legal developments in New England, as we have already seen. Without discounting the many ways in with South Carolina's developmental trajectory diverged from that

---

[80] Articles of Agreement, February 9, 1729/30, Ball Family Papers, 33–83-1 (6) (oversized), SCHS. The agreement also empowered Elizabeth to devise her estate "both real and personal" by will.

[81] Roby Inventory, 1688, PROB 4/19619, TNA. See also Sirmans, "The Legal Status of the Slave in South Carolina, 1670–1740," 466–468.

[82] SCG, October 25, 1735, B3A3. Customary practice also dictated who would be deemed a slave. Enslaved people, according to assembly members in 1712, included "all negroes, mulatoes, mustizoes or Indians, which at any time heretofore have been sold, or now are held or taken to be, or hereafter shall be bought and sold for slaves." Moreover, "their children" also were "hereby made and declared slaves." "An Act for the Better Ordering and Governing of Negroes and Slaves" (1712), SAL, 7, 352. This language closely tracked that of earlier statutes (1691 and 1701). See Roper, "The 1701 'Act for the Better Ordering of Slaves'," for an extensive discussion of the 1701 act, which is located in manuscript at the British Library.

[83] Will of Jonathan Welden, July 26, 1736, ST 0505A, Secretary of State Recorded Instruments, Will books Vol. LL 1737–1747 S 213027, 12–14, SCDAH.

[84] Will of Moses Wilson, February 25, 1737/8, ST 0505A, Secretary of State Recorded Instruments, Will books Vol. LL 1737–1747 S 213027, 267–273, SCDAH.

of Massachusetts Bay or Rhode Island, these places shared a decidedly commercial outlook and an intimate familiarity with human trafficking. Dominated by an overlapping merchant and planter elite who did not shy away from discussing business affairs, South Carolina colonists engaged with the broader Atlantic marketplace, including the transatlantic slave trade.[85] Living "economic lives" that "shifted between production and exchange," South Carolina planters were connected to Atlantic mercantile life in a less attenuated way than their counterparts in Virginia, where the "tidewater gentry seemed disengaged from the details of Atlantic commerce."[86] This difference had significant cultural ramifications. Unlike other colonists in plantation America, and especially Virginia, South Carolinians "admitted the mundane world of production and exchange into polite society." They prided themselves on their commercial acumen and on their "commitment to business," which "became a normative standard around which elites oriented their values in the colonial era."[87] But South Carolina colonists' commercial orientation was also significant in that it bred familiarity with mercantile practice and particularly legal norms that governed daily practice in the slave trade, including treating slaves as chattel property.

Beyond these cultural reasons, South Carolinians may also have treated slaves as chattel property for the legal flexibility it conveyed. This may have seemed particularly important given the colony's rapid economic growth and, relatedly, its central role as a mainland slave importer by the middle of the eighteenth century. After a period of experimentation with a variety of commodities for export, the commercial production of rice accelerated at the turn of the eighteenth century and prompted South Carolina colonists to import larger numbers of enslaved Africans.[88] By 1740, the commercial production of rice and indigo in the colony had provided the foundation for an economy organized around increasingly diversified and far-flung plantation enterprises that relied heavily upon slave labor.[89] As a result, slaves made up an increasingly significant portion of colonists' wealth as the eighteenth century progressed. Slaves,

---

[85] Edelson, *Plantation Enterprise*, 174.

[86] *Ibid.*, 176, 177. Unlike Virginia and the West Indies, where commodity producers "tended to consign their staples for shipment to Europe," in South Carolina planters "sold almost all their rice and most of their indigo in town for an immediate return." *Ibid.*, 176.

[87] *Ibid.*, 174.

[88] Slave imports in South Carolina "rose markedly" in the 1720s and 1730s with importation rates nearly doubling in the 1730s. Morgan, *Slave Counterpoint*, 60.

[89] Edelson, *Plantation Enterprise*, 76, 111–112.

in fact, accounted for 40 to 50 percent of South Carolinians' movable property between 1720 and 1770, and this figure reached 68 percent in 1774.[90] By the middle of the eighteenth century, most colonists "had more wealth in slaves than land," and this made it particularly important to treat their human property in a way that would maximize colonists' ability to buy, sell, and move slaves to far-flung plantations.[91] Whereas in places like Virginia, classifying slaves as real estate kept land and labor together in a single productive unit that would descend intact down the generations, South Carolinians ensured a more equitable division of property upon death. Treating slaves as chattel property did this in two primary ways. First, it ensured that the children of South Carolina intestates would inherit the residue of personal property, including slaves, equally. Under the Intestates Estates Act, an English statute that South Carolina adopted in 1712, male and female children of intestates were entitled to inherit personalty equally.[92] This meant that – unlike colonies where slaves were real estate and would descend according to the canons of common law descent to the eldest son (primogeniture) – in South Carolina, daughters and sons alike would share in a decedent's enslaved property.[93]

In a high-mortality province like South Carolina, where colonists could not be sure of producing a surviving male heir, this was particularly important. Indeed, the interaction of disease, human actors, and the natural environment in the colony created a demographic profile that made it appear less like other mainland colonies and more like the British West Indies. Even by early modern standards, "which were nothing if not appalling," life in colonial South Carolina was "peculiarly fragile."[94] In the colony's "funereal lowlands," the white population "had difficulty sustaining itself naturally until the 1770s." Nearly one-third of the residents of who survived to the age of twenty died before they were forty, while the crude death rate in Charlestown among whites was "terrifically high: between 52 and 60 per thousand" between 1722 and

---

[90] Kenneth Morgan, "Slave Sales in Colonial Charleston," *The English Historical Review* 113 (1998): 907.

[91] Crowley, "Family Relations and Inheritance," 52.

[92] 22 and 23 C. 2, c. 10, adopted in *SAL*, vol. 2, 523 ff.

[93] Morris, *Southern Slavery and the Law*, 83. As John Crowley has argued, colonial South Carolina's property law represented an attempt to "take into account the legal status of slaves as personalty in the division of estates." Crowley, "Family Relations and Inheritance," 52.

[94] Peter A. Coclanis, *The Shadow of a Dream: Economic Life and Death in the South Carolina Low Country 1670–1920* (New York: Oxford University Press, 1989), 38.

1732.[95] Colonists were aware they were likely to die young and without male heirs, and although South Carolinians typically have been perceived as less dynastically minded than their counterparts in Virginia, they nonetheless sought to ensure the transmission of wealth, which increasingly took the form of slaves, through at least one generation. Treating slaves as chattel property made this possible, even when colonists failed to produce a surviving male heir.

Relatedly, chattel slavery also clarified any potential concerns about a widow's entitlement to slaves upon her husband's death. In South Carolina (as in England) widows were entitled to receive one-third of the residue of a decedent's personal property after debts had been paid.[96] Treating slaves as chattel, then, provided widows with increasingly valuable human property for their support. Whereas in England a "widow's interest in the landed estate was sufficiently compensated by maintenance for life from one-third of its income," for many South Carolina widows, returns from land could not provide adequate support.[97] At the same time, slaves-as-chattels also ensured that in South Carolina creditors could attach slaves, even when they were claimed by widows. Unlike land, personal property was subject to creditors' claims and funeral expenses before the residue could be apportioned as a widow's third, and as we have already seen, creditors were reluctant to extend credit when assets could not be attached. This, after all, had been the point of the Debt Recovery Act, which sought to prevent colonial legislatures from reclassifying slaves as real estate in order to shield them from creditors. For precisely this reason, assembly members in provinces where slaves were treated as real estate for some purposes passed laws that were creditor friendly, particularly when it came to

---

[95] *Ibid.*, 42.   [96] 22 and 23 C. 2, c. 10, adopted in *SAL*, vol. 2, 523 ff.

[97] The potential downside to South Carolina's intestacy scheme, however, was that a widow who remarried would take her deceased husband's slaves with her, which under the doctrine of coverture would become the property of her new husband and would no longer pass to her children upon her death. Slave owners could alter these "dangerous effects of intestacy" by writing a will that limited a wife's access to the estate. Salmon, *Women and the Law of Property*, 157. Wills were proved by the governor and council sitting as a Court of Ordinary. This court also had authority over the administration of intestates' estates. According to John Crowley, testation rates in colonial South Carolina were high, and testates usually comprised "between 40 and 50 percent of such listings as probated decedents, militiamen, and jurymen." As in England, wealthy decedents were more likely to leave a will. "Half of the testators with identifiable occupations were planters, one quarter were merchants, and another quarter were artisans and tradesmen. The proportion of widows varied between 8 and 19 percent." John E. Crowley, "The Importance of Kinship: Testamentary Evidence from South Carolina," *Journal of Interdisciplinary History* 16 (1986): 565–566.

widows' claims to slaves. Virginia burgesses, for example, worked hard to ensure that even though slaves were considered real property for the purposes of inheritance, creditors could still reach dower slaves.

South Carolina colonists arrived at a simpler solution. By treating slaves as chattel property, they ensured that creditors always and without question could attach slaves in the colony, even when those slaves were claimed by widows. Familiar with the needs of merchants and factors through their interactions with them in Charlestown and also by virtue of the fact that many South Carolina planters themselves were engaged in mercantile activities, slave owners crafted a customary legal regime that allowed them to maximize the availability of credit. Doing so was vital for colonists who increasingly relied upon credit to expand their plantation and mercantile enterprises. Indeed, the cycle of credit and debt in South Carolina relied upon the ready availability of this type of human capital, which was used to fuel the colony's geographic and financial expansion and helped make South Carolina's colonists the richest group on a per capita basis in North America on the eve of the American Revolution.[98]

THE "NEGRO ACT" OF 1740

In 1740, South Carolina finally enshrined the practice of treating slaves as chattel property in statute as part of a broader overhaul of the colony's laws. The Negro Act of 1740 extended and reinforced the colony's extant slave-policing regime.[99] Assembly members methodically eliminated slaves' ability to congregate, to move freely throughout the province, to access weapons, and to engage in marketing activities without permission. At the same time, they "stripped slaves of many of the individual protections customarily granted by the common law."[100] A legislative

---

[98] Slave mortgaging was a common practice in South Carolina as well as other plantation colonies, and colonists routinely risked slaves in order to fund purchases of additional land and slaves. As Russell Menard has shown, this type of plantation financing grew in tandem with the colony's increasingly prominent role as a commodity producer. During periods of prosperity, planters mortgaged slaves to finance the purchase of more slaves, which they hoped would allow them to participate more fully in South Carolina's bustling export economy. Slave mortgaging did not benefit great planters alone: many who engaged in this practice were "men of modest means" who used slave mortgages to help them build farms and accumulate wealth. Russell R. Menard, "Financing the Lowcountry Export Boom: Capital and Growth in Early Carolina," *WMQ* 51 (1994): 665.

[99] December 3, 1736, *Journal of the Commons House of Assembly* (*Journals*), November 10, 1736 – June 7, 1739, 30.

[100] Olwell, *Masters, Slaves, and Subjects*, 62, 66.

monument to the horrors wrought by the colony's participation in human bondage, the criminal and policing provisions in the act make it particularly worthy of notice. For our purposes, the Negro Act of 1740 is significant because it also codified chattel slavery in the colony, thereby distinguishing it from all other slave laws that preceded it and marking South Carolina's slave regime as different from others in plantation America.[101] In the Negro Act, assembly members specified that slaves would be "deemed, held, taken, reputed and adjudged in law, to be chattels personal, in the hands of their owners and possessors, and their executors, administrators and assigns."[102] Rather than stipulating that slaves would be considered chattel property in some cases and real estate for others, as was the case in Virginia and Britain's West Indian colonies, assembly members classified slaves as personal property "to all intents, constructions and purposes."[103]

The aberrance of this property law provision did not escape the attention of metropolitan legal authorities, including the Board of Trade's legal counsel, Matthew Lamb. Opining on the 1740 statue's legality, Lamb noted that the Negro Act was "[d]ifferent from all the Laws of the other Colonyes and Plantations" because it made "Negroes Chattells Personall," and he expressed concerns that the statute infringed upon the Debt Recovery Act. Although Lamb did not provide an elaborate explanation for his qualms about the Negro Act, it seems that he believed the Debt Recovery Act only authorized freehold slavery, not chattel slavery. Underlying this objection were deeper policy concerns about how classifying slaves as chattel property would impact imperial trade and defense, a point that the Privy Council repeated in 1751 when they rejected Virginia's bid to codify chattel slavery.[104] Classification schemes that "annexed Negroes to Land" had "increase[d] the Trade of Great Britain," "raise[d] the credit" of the colony, and "strengthen[ed] it in point of Defence," according to the Privy Council.[105] As a result, when Georgia sought to classify slaves as chattel property rather than real estate in 1766, they opined that the statute in

---

[101] First, assembly members reiterated that "all negroes and Indians ... mulattoes or mustizoes who now are, or shall hereafter be ... absolute slaves." Colonists also for the first time formally adopted the principle of *partus sequitur ventrem*, a civil law doctrine providing for the matrilineal heritability of slavery. Indeed, the 1740 act specified that the children of slaves would "follow the condition of the mother." "An Act for the Better Ordering and Governing Negroes and Other Slaves in This Province" (1740), *SAL*, vol. 7, 397.
[102] *Ibid.* [103] *Ibid.* [104] Hening, *Statutes at Large*, vol. 5, 432.
[105] *APC*, vol. 5 (London, 1908–1912), 138.

question was "of publick ill consequence" because it would hinder "the Cultivation and Improvement of Farms and plantations."[106] Despite Lamb's concerns, however, the 1740 Negro Act was never disallowed, largely due to the lobbying efforts of South Carolina merchants, and with a few minor alterations, the legislation remained in force throughout the colonial period.[107]

South Carolina's powerful lobby may have overridden Lamb's objections, but his critique points to a broader question: why did South Carolina codify chattel slavery in contravention of West Indian practices and against the wishes of the Privy Council? Unfortunately, the *Journals of the Commons House of Assembly* are silent on the matter. South Carolina's decision to classify slaves as chattel property seems to have occasioned none of the heated debates that played out in Virginia's House of Burgesses. From the beginning, it seems, assembly members assumed that the law would codify chattel slavery. Indeed, the final copy of the Negro Act echoes language that was present in its earliest iteration, including the classification of slaves as "Chattels Personal" and the codification of *partus sequiter ventrem*, the doctrine that declared that all children born of enslaved mothers were to be considered as slaves in the eyes of the law.[108] Assembly members also "agreed to" this provision without debate, according to the *Journals*.[109] Instead, the act's most controversial provisions related to the punishment of slaves, including whether slaves should be "[p]unished with Death for running off the Province" (no) and whether the "Publick" should "bear the Expences" for noncapital slave prosecutions (yes).[110] In the aftermath of 1739's Stono Rebellion, in which a group of slaves rose up along the Stono River and killed at least two dozen colonists, members offered additional amendments to the bill that restricted the movement and congregation of slaves, prohibited teaching slaves "to write," and other changes that

---

[106] *Ibid.*, 40–41.

[107] Matthew Lamb to Board of Trade, November 2, 1748, BPRO, vol. 23, 261. The board ultimately declined to take action "due to the intercession of Charles Town merchants, who often owned slaves and who enjoyed considerable influence with the Board of Trade." Sirmans, "The Legal Status of the Slave in South Carolina, 1670–1740," 472. For a discussion of the South Carolina lobby's influence, see Huw David, *Trade, Politics, and Revolution: South Carolina and Britain's Atlantic Commerce, 1730–1790* (Columbia: University of South Carolina, 2018), *passim*.

[108] *Journals*, December 13, 1737, 362.   [109] *Ibid.*, 364.

[110] *Journals*, January 26, 1737/8, p. 428. For additional debates, see pp. 429 ff, 511 (third reading).

reflected their concerns to prevent another slave insurrection.[111] However, the provision codifying chattel slavery remained the same.

This decision to codify chattel slavery in the Negro Act of 1740 is particularly puzzling, because enshrining customary practice in law did little to change the legal status quo in South Carolina. By 1740, colonists were already accustomed to treating slaves as chattel property in practice, as we have seen. As a result, classifying slaves as chattels would not have impacted inheritance patterns or South Carolina colonists' ability to access credit from English merchants, who already could attach slaves (regardless of classification) under the Debt Recovery Act. A purely instrumentalist perspective, then, fails to explain why South Carolina colonists finally chose in 1740 to clarify what had been a long-standing practice of treating slaves as chattels, when they had failed to do so multiple times before. Indeed, between 1691 and 1740, assembly members revised and reissued slave statutes numerous times without ever seeking to define enslaved people as property.[112]

Most recently, historians have analyzed the 1740 Negro Act to understand how South Carolina colonists perceived themselves as members of a broader British Empire, particularly given the fact that they owned human property. For Robert Olwell, the 1740 statute was a "cultural edifice," a law that "was both 'imagined' and constructed to reflect a metropolitan ideal."[113] Aware that the institution of slavery "engendered conflicts and incongruencies between the ideals and practices of English justice and its provincial counterpart," colonists drew upon English legal traditions in the Negro Act in order to recast their society as familiar.[114] Christopher Tomlins, too, has argued that in the Negro Act colonists signaled their "respect for English law" as part of a broader cultural performance in which they used a "discourse of legality" to serve their own self-interests.[115]

All of these things are true, but in describing the Negro Act of 1740 as a "cultural edifice," we cannot leave out the scaffolding. Not only did the substance of the Negro Act of 1740 imagine a more English South Carolina; the very act of codification marked South Carolinians as participants in a broader English legal culture, one in which statutes were increasingly eclipsing other sources of binding legal authority. This

---

[111] *Journals*, September 12, 1739–May 10, 1740, November 30, 1739, 68.

[112] Between 1691 and 1740, colonists passed slave statutes (including minor revisions to older statutes) in 1693, 1695, 1696, 1701, 1712, 1714, 1717, 1722, and 1735.

[113] Olwell, *Masters, Slaves, and Subjects*, 60.   [114] *Ibid.*, 61.

[115] Christopher Tomlins, *Freedom Bound: Law, Labor, and Civic Identity in Colonizing English America, 1580–1865* (Cambridge: Cambridge University Press, 2010), 450–451.

trend began with the English Reformation, as King Henry VIII sought to
ground his ecclesiastical authority in statute, and continued apace into the
eighteenth century. The volume of Parliamentary legislation increased
exponentially over the early modern period, according to Mark Knights.
Between 1660 and 1688, "parliament passed on average about 26 statutes
per session; between 1689 and 1714 this rose to 64 per session."[116] Not
only did Parliament produce more legislation; statutes became longer and
more elaborate with specific more preambles. Influenced by a shift in
mentalité, "humanist legislators" who were "confident in their ability to
improve things by the right use of power" sought to shape society through
statutes.[117] Many of these statutes touched upon criminal law or policing.
Over the early modern period, Parliament set criminal law on an increasingly draconian statutory footing, a trend that culminated in the infamous
Black Act of 1723.[118]

Colonists throughout the British Atlantic World, then, were part of an
imperial legal culture in which legislation increasingly defined the contours of society. In the eighteenth century, they accelerated this practice,
relying upon statutory law to "bring colonial jurisprudence more in line
with the standards of the metropolis."[119] The Negro Act of 1740 should
be viewed in this broader context. Nearly forty years before Chief Justice
Lord Mansfield claimed that slavery was "so odious" that it must be
grounded in "positive law." South Carolinians were aware that codification made chattel slavery legally legible to Britons across the globe.[120] The
purpose of the act was not to justify the institution itself. As the Negro
Act's preamble made clear, slavery had already been "introduced and
allowed" in "his Majesty's plantations in America." Rather, the act
aimed to specify and regulate the nature of the relationship between
masters and slaves in the province. In particular, assembly members
thought that the power of masters over their slaves "ought to be settled
and limited by positive laws" in order to keep slaves in "due subjection
and obedience," but without "exercising too great rigour and cruelty over
them."[121] As Robert Olwell has noted, "[t]he framers of the Negro Act

---

[116] Mark Knights, *Representation and Misrepresentation in Later Stuart Britain: Partisanship and Political Culture* (Oxford: Oxford University Press, 2005), 11–12.
[117] Baker, *An Introduction to English Legal History*, 207.
[118] Olwell, *Masters, Slaves, and Subjects*, 67. For a discussion of the "Black Act," see E. P. Thompson, *Whigs and Hunters: The Origin of the Black Act* (New York: Pantheon, 1975).
[119] Olwell, *Masters, Slaves, and Subjects*, 67.
[120] *Somerset v. Stewart* (1772) 98 Eng. Rep. 499, 510.   [121] *SAL*, vol. 7, 397.

made no apologies." Rather than justifying slavery as an un-English or aberrant institution, as had been the case in previous legislation, "the Negro Act sought to locate itself and slavery within the established practices of the metropolis."[122] This included codifying a "judicial system founded on the principle of racial caste" as well as a "larger legal and economic system based upon the primacy of property."[123] Although historians have emphasized the Negro Act's policing and criminal provisions, formally defining slaves as chattel property was crucial to this process of legitimation. The Negro Act not only demonstrated that South Carolina colonists conformed as much as possible to English criminal law, but also that they grasped the intricacies of the property law system that was at the heart of English law. Indeed, codifying property rights in people – and specifying what type of property slaves would be under English law – helped to mark the Negro Act of 1740 as a thoroughly English slave code.

"ALL THE NEGROES, CATTEL, [AND] HORSES"

Legislative and customary determinations about how slaves should be classified had significant legal ramifications. As we shall see in the chapters that follow, treating enslaved people as chattels for all purposes allowed South Carolina colonists to slot slaves into an extant English legal framework, complete with forms and procedures that allowed them maximize their value. Rather than creating sui generis a new legal system to accommodate their desire the hold property in people, colonists simply fit slave ownership into English property law's extant rubric. In custom and statute, slaves became yet another species of property that fit into the category "chattel."

Considering slaves to be chattel property, however, did not just create a legal ripple effect. Rather, it also had profound cultural consequences because it encouraged white colonists to compare slaves to livestock and moveable property in legal documents. Historians have long understood that colonists analogized slaves to livestock and that comparing slaves to animals played an important role in the dehumanization of enslaved people. Rooted in antiquity and fertilized by a Judeo-Christian worldview that posited an "almost unbridgeable gap between humans and animals," the animalization of "increasing numbers of outsiders" during the age of expansion removed the "inner human qualities that helped to protect an adult man or woman from being treated as a mere object – as opposed to

[122] Olwell, *Masters, Slaves, and Subjects*, 66. [123] Ibid., 69.

a moral 'center of consciousness'."[124] For Davis, the process of dehumanization "made slavery possible" by severing "ties of human identity and empathy." It allowed slave owners to overcome, albeit incompletely, the "problem of slavery," which was the "impossibility, seen throughout history, of converting humans into totally compliant, submissive chattel property."[125] Dehumanization, in fact, has primarily been seen as a psychological process, one in which conflating slaves with animals functioned to overcome the cognitive dissonance generated by treating people as property when they were, in fact, valued for their human capacities.[126] But dehumanization in British plantation colonies was first and foremost a legal process, an attempt to fit slaves within a familiar property law rubric in order to make this category of property instantly legible. As such, animal analogies demanded only a formal association of slaves and livestock within the well-worn pattern dictated by the law, not an explicit or ideological consideration of the comparison from first principles. Rather than reading colonists' dehumanizing language as reflecting a conflicted mental state, the grouping of slaves and livestock more often than not was a practical decision driven by twinned legal and economic imperatives.

South Carolina colonists, like those throughout plantation America, routinely described slaves using dehumanizing language. When Henry Laurens, who acted as a factor for British slave-trading merchants, intervened on behalf of a slave purchaser to request an abatement in price, he described the purchased slave in distinctly animal terms as a "Creature" and an "Idiot" who as "very Mauger & full of sores." Arguing on behalf of the "poor Industreous shoemaker" who now owned the defective slave, he suggested that even if the slave were "sound he would not be worth a Groat" given the fact that he was such "a Loathsome Carcass." According to Laurens, the buyer was "much to be pittied." Not only had he purchased a slave that "no one will take off of his hands at any rate," he was also forced to gaze upon "such an object in View that is shocking to human Nature."[127] Laurens's choice of vocabulary in referring to this particular enslaved person was not unusual. South Carolinians routinely referred to enslaved people in ways that suggested they were less than human, ranging from describing slaves as

---

[124] Davis, *The Problem of Slavery in the Age of Emancipation*, 22, 26, 13.
[125] *Ibid., passim.*
[126] "Slaveowners linked the reproductive lives of men and women to those of agricultural commodities in gestures that read as efforts to either establish distance from or to distinguish between their own struggles with 'increase'." Morgan, *Laboring Women*, 83.
[127] Austin & Laurens [Henry Laurens] to Robert & John Thompson & Co., April 20, 1757, *HLP*, vol. 2, 523–524.

"stock" (that is, as a form of productive capital) to summarily appraising female slaves along with their "issue and increase."[128] For example, describing his own slave, Nanny, Laurens characterized her as "a breeding Woman." Indeed, he expected that "in ten Years time" she would "double her worth in her own Children."[129] When colonists like Laurens deployed this type of language in connection with slaves, they engaged in a cultural practice that had become commonplace by the eighteenth century. As Davis and others have shown, slave owners in plantation America hearkened back to a much older discursive tradition when they analogized Africans to beasts, signaling their belief in the inherent inferiority of Black people by describing them as less than human.[130]

More than a cultural practice however, when English colonists grouped slaves with livestock, their linguistic choices also reflected their belief that slaves and livestock were similar from a legal perspective. Both were considered chattel property, and when colonists grouped them together, their decision to do so was driven in part because they recognized this fact. In fact, classifying slaves as chattel had practical legal ramifications that compelled colonists to associate slaves with livestock in transactional documents. For example, because slaves were not real estate, buyers could not assume that plantations would be conveyed along with the slaves who worked them. Colonists seeking to sell plantations, then, were required to stipulate whether slaves were included in a sale. As a result, sellers often grouped slaves with livestock and plantation equipment in conveyancing documents. For example, when William and Bridget Sereven sold Rene Ravenel a plantation in Berkley County, the sellers also included in the sale "one negro man named Jack one negro Woman named Bronka and one negro boy named Quashee and ye cart that belongs to ye said Plantation with all the working oxen their yokes and chains."[131] Peter Manigault, writing to David Deas, gave his correspondent "notice" that William Blake had purchased not only "Jasper's Barony" but also "all the Negroes Cattel Horses & all Stock whatsoever with the Plantation Tools & Provisions of every kind/merchantable Rice only excepted."[132] Detailing precisely what

[128] According to Jennifer Morgan, one-third of slave owners who "transferred enslaved women in their wills" between 1711 and 1729 used the term "increase." Morgan, *Laboring Women*, 138.
[129] Henry Laurens to Richard Oswald, London, October 16, 1767, *HLP*, vol. 5, 370.
[130] Davis, *The Problem of Slavery in the Age of Emancipation*, 11.
[131] October 15, 1708, William Cain Family Papers, 281.01.01.01(P) 01–14, SCHS.
[132] Peter Manigault to David Deas, May 1, 1771, Manigault Papers, Box 11/278/7, Peter Manigault Letterbook, 1763–1773, 149, SCHS.

personal property would be included in a real estate sale helped to ensure that a conveyance embodied the intent of both the buyers and the sellers and that the sale price accurately reflected the value of the property conveyed.

Because slaves were among a colonist's most valuable chattel property, testators also routinely listed them together with livestock in wills. As Lawrence Sanders Rowland has shown, slaves and livestock were the two most valuable types of personal property listed in colonial inventories from the Sea Islands of South Carolina.[133] In the period immediately prior to the colony's rice boom, livestock also "provided a source of income" and "represented the major form of wealth" in the colony.[134] Devising both livestock and slaves, then, was among a testator's most important final acts. In fact, South Carolina colonists associated testation with the possession of both slaves and cattle. Eliza Lucas Pinckney, who is best known for introducing commercial indigo planting in South Carolina, explicitly linked will making with the ownership of livestock and slaves. Pinckney spent one particularly slow social season learning "the rudiments of the law" from Thomas Wood's two-volume *Institute of the Laws of England*, and she explained to a correspondent that she used her newfound knowledge to provide legal services to her "poor Neighbors." These unfortunate individuals had "few slaves and Cattle to give their children" and consequently never thought of making a will until "they come upon a sick bed and find it too expensive to send to town for a Lawyer."[135] Pinckney's impression that colonists with slaves and cattle more typically wrote wills was correct. As John Crowley has shown,

[133] Lawrence Sanders Rowland, "Eighteenth Century Beaufort: A Study of South Carolina's Southern Parishes to 1800" (PhD diss., University of South Carolina, Columbia, 1978), 161.

[134] John Otto, "Livestock-Raising in Early South Carolina, 1670–1700: Prelude to the Rice Plantation Economy," *Agricultural History* 66 (1987): 21.

[135] Eliza Lucas Pinckney to [Miss Bartlett] [c. June 1742]. Elise Pinckney, ed., *The Letterbook of Eliza Lucas Pinckney, 1739–1762* (Columbia: University of South Carolina Press, 1972), 41. Far from doubting her own legal abilities, Pinckney believed that she had "done no harm" to these supplicants. Indeed, she had learned her "lesson very perfect" and knew "how to convey by will Estates real and personal." She "never forget in its proper place, him and his heirs for Ever, nor that 'tis to be signed by 3 Witnesses in presence of one another." Taking comfort in Doctor Wood's assurance that "the Law makes greater allowance for last Wills and Testaments presumeing the Testator could not have council learned in the law," she congratulated herself on a job well done. Nonetheless, Pinckney was willing to admit that her legal knowledge had its limits. As she confided to her friend, although a wealthy widow "teazed me intolerable to draw her a marriage settlement," Pinckney conceded that it was "out of my depth," although she did agree to act as one of the widow's trustees. *Ibid.*

testation in colonial South Carolina was "frequent," and "its likelihood increased with decedents' wealth."[136]

In their wills, South Carolina colonists typically devised their livestock and slaves in tandem. For example, in 1727 Dunkan MacGregror named his wife Mary his executrix and gave her one-third of all of his "Negroes Cattle and household goods."[137] Duncan McQueen of Pon Pon also left his "natural Son" John McQueen "one Negroe boy now at Savannah Town . . . together with half of Hogg's Horses and Mares about Savannah Town."[138] Likewise, Peter Gurry gave his "Beloved Wife" Marget one-third of the remainder of his estate, "that is to say Negro's horses Cattle and all what I posses except Lands."[139] More than a means by which planters "enacted a moral grammar through which they attained fluency in the practice of slaveownership," testation was a highly practical process. Colonists arranged their affairs in an economically logical way, listing their most valuable chattel property together when they made specific or general bequests of their residual estate.[140]

That the decision to group slaves with livestock was dictated by a perception of their comparable economic value is reinforced by the wills of tradesmen and mechanics. These testators typically grouped slaves not with cattle, as was the case for planter testators, but with their most valuable possessions – their tools. For example, William Linthwaite devised his wife "the use of" his "Negro Man named Lister and of all my shop Tools and other Instruments of my Trade" until his son came of age, at which point he would inherit "the said Negro Man Shop Tools & Instruments of Trade."[141] Hannah Gale, likely a blacksmith's widow, left her husband's tools to her daughters. They were to be "Equally Divided . . . Share and Share alike with the Negroes not herein mentioned."[142] The grouping of tools with slaves in these wills suggests that practicality more than ideology determined the ordering of personal property. Colonists associated slaves

---

[136] Crowley, "The Importance of Kinship," 565.

[137] Will of Dunkan MacGregor, February 15, 1726/7, Secretary of State Recorded Instruments; Will books Vol. LL 1737–1747 S 213027, 15, SCDAH.

[138] Will of Duncan McQueen, February 12, 1736, Secretary of State Recorded Instruments, Will books Vol. LL 1737–1747 S 213027, 22–24, SCDAH.

[139] Will of Peter Gurry, March 1, 1736/7, Secretary of State Recorded Instruments, Will books Vol. LL 1737–1747 S 213027, 43–45, SCDAH.

[140] Morgan, *Laboring Women*, 69.

[141] Will of William Linthwaite, April 8, 1739, Secretary of State Recorded Instruments, Will books Vol. LL 1737–1747 S 213027, 264–267, SCDAH.

[142] Will of Hannah Gale, November 25, 1735, Secretary of State Recorded Instruments; Will books Vol. LL 1737–1747 S 213027, 357–363, SCDAH.

with livestock not in the service of a broader psychological process that allowed them to ignore the humanity of slaves, but in order to rank their chattel property according to value and transfer it to the next generation. The legal process of handing down enslaved people as property focused practical attention on the ways in which slaves functioned to advance family wealth and diverted it from the ways in which people who were enslaved behaved like human beings.

***

Although the dehumanization of slaves occurred throughout the Americas, the economic and legal imperatives of English property law facilitated this process by making it advantageous and even necessary for colonists to group slaves with livestock. Whether they sought to identify property that would be conveyed in a plantation sale or to specify who would receive valuable chattel property upon their deaths, colonists associated slaves with livestock because they were legally identical and perceived to be of comparable value. Certainly, English colonists were not the only residents of the Americas who likened slaves to livestock. But English law gave them a particular incentive to do so. With its bifurcation of property into real estate and chattels, English property law provided no meaningful alternatives for colonists who sought to participate fully in a legal system that had already developed forms, procedures, and substantive law around this classificatory scheme. Categorizing slaves as chattels or real estate alone gave colonists access to this premade system, and colonists carefully weighed classificatory schemes with a full understanding that each conveyed different bundles of rights to slave owners.

In South Carolina, "pure" chattel slavery provided colonists with substantial flexibility in managing their slaves. This suited their needs as particularly active participants in a dynamic Atlantic economy, while also allowing them to accumulate and bring into production new and sometimes far-flung plantation acreage. Free from the restraints of entail, primogeniture, and dower claims to slaves, South Carolina colonists could move slaves to outlying plantations, sell them without encumbrances, and devise them to whomsoever they chose. While providing this flexibility, chattel slavery also created legal and economic incentives for colonists to group slaves with livestock. When John Phillips crossed out "Negro woman slave" and substituted this phrase with "iron gray horse," he did so in the context of a plantation society that had codified chattel slavery in a way that would have been recognized as legally binding by Britons across the globe. In a province where an enslaved person was legally identical to a horse or a cow, it is not surprising that colonists grouped slaves together with livestock in transactional documents or that a lawyer like Phillips would adapt English legal forms and procedures previously used to litigate over slaves to litigate over animals.

The decision to group slaves with livestock was in many ways a practical one, driven by the utility of doing so in the eyes of the law more than to address any qualms about the morality of holding property in human beings or to shore up legal distinctions between white and Black colonists. From the colony's beginning, these distinctions were readily evident; the degraded status of enslaved people in South Carolina did not require further explication. Rather, animal analogies were a natural outgrowth of a type of reasoning by analogy that was endemic of English common law thinking, one that required litigants, lawyers, and judges to constantly make comparisons between like and like.[143] If slaves were like livestock as a legal matter, then it followed that they should be grouped together in legal documents and indeed that the same documents used to litigate over animals could be used to litigate over human property. Viewed as a form of legal instrumentalism, a means by which slave owners categorized enslaved people as property in order to maximize their value, likening slaves to animals was a morally neutral act from the perspective of slave owners.[144]

If analogizing slaves to livestock was a morally neutral act from a slave owner's perspective, however, it had distinctly negative and long-lasting consequences for enslaved people. In the aggregate, livestock analogies generated in the colonial period reinforced and replicated stereotypes that inscribed animalistic qualities upon Black bodies. These stereotypes eventually were given the imprimatur of science, fueling the development of scientific racism in the late eighteenth and early nineteenth centuries and creating a "systematic way of institutionalizing" the dehumanization of slaves.[145] Ultimately, the institutionalized dehumanization of Black people became a justification not only for

---

[143] Patrick Nerhot, "Introduction," in *Legal Knowledge and Analogy: Fragments of Legal Epistemology, Hermeneutics, and Linguistics,* edited by Patrick Nerhot (Netherlands: Kluwer Academic Publishers, 1991), 1; Katja Langenbucher, "Argument by Analogy in European Law," *Cambridge Law Journal* 57 (1998): 481–521.

[144] For a discussion of the moral neutrality of instrumentalism, see Malick W. Ghachem, *The Old Regime and the Haitian Revolution* (Cambridge: Cambridge University Press, 2012), 8–9.

[145] Davis, *The Problem of Slavery in the Age of Emancipation*, 32.

enslavement per se, but also for day-to-day slave-trading practices that destroyed countless Black families. Through the workings of the internal slave trade and in the "epitome of bestialization," the slave auction, white slave owners drew upon a discourse of dehumanization as they expanded Westward and as they defended slavery from ever-louder critiques.[146]

As a practical matter, the codification of "pure" chattel slavery in the Negro Act of 1740 had invidious repercussions that extended far beyond the colony's borders. South Carolina's colonial slave regime, in fact, set a precedent for slave law in the Deep South as territories in the new United States engaged in their own project of legal borrowing. Just as mainland American colonies drew upon West Indian legal models in formulating a statutory law of slavery, so too did new Deep South slave societies look to South Carolina's slave law as an exemplar. Moving "from the eastern seaboard to the territories of Alabama, Mississippi, Arkansas, and Louisiana," planters "rapidly adopted" South Carolina's slave code "either in whole or in part." Indeed, South Carolina's slave law eventually became "the slave law of virtually all the newly formed territories."[147] This mass exportation included not only the colony's severe criminal and policing provisions, but also the codification of the "chattel principle" that suffused American life in the nineteenth century.

---

[146] *Ibid.*, 11.

[147] Sally E. Hadden, "The Fragmented Laws of Slavery in the Colonial and Revolutionary Eras," in *The Cambridge History of Law in America*, edited by Michael Grossberg and Christopher Tomlins, 3 vols. (Cambridge: Cambridge University Press, 2008), 1: 281. An exception to this trend was Kentucky, which adopted portions of its slave law from Virginia and North Carolina. *Ibid.*, 282. For a recent general treatment of the Western expansion of slavery, see Adam Rothman, *Slave Country: American Expansion and the Origins of the Deep South* (Cambridge: Harvard University Press, 2005).

2

Bonds

In 1779, South Carolina colonist Richard Bohun Baker sold fifty enslaved men, women, and children to William Henry Mills and Thomas Shepoe. The terms of the sale are unclear, largely because the only surviving evidence of the transaction is a conditional bond hidden among plantation records and other ephemera at the South Carolina Historical Society. Conditional bonds like the Baker bond were formal credit instruments that American colonists and Britons throughout the globe relied upon to secure their commercial transactions, from commodity sales to loan agreements. They were short, formulaic documents that worked by obligating debtors to pay a penalty if they defaulted on an agreement. Although merchants had used conditional bonds for centuries, their popularity grew in the early modern period as long-distance traders searched for new ways to raise capital and spread risks in transoceanic ventures. Conditional bonds recommended themselves in particular because they made it easy for creditors to recover liquidated damages in common law courts, and this assuaged their very real concerns about extending credit in long-distance transactions. By the eighteenth century, conditional bonds had become an entirely unremarkable part of early modern commercial life – the paper detritus of a bustling imperial economy.

The ubiquity of conditional bonds makes them easy to miss. Intercalated between papers that seem more historically significant, most bonds are jargon-ridden and disclose few details about the bargains they secured. Like other transactional documents that circulated throughout the early modern British Empire, they lull the reader into complacency with their formality, their blandness, and their lack of contextual information. Most consist of a few stock phrases that hang together in documents that remain maddeningly silent about the deals that inspired their creation. This is true for the Baker bond. On its face, there is little to distinguish it from any other conditional bond, or more importantly, to indicate that it secured the sale of human beings. It could have underwritten the sale of rice, sugar, or any other type of commodity. We only happen to know its provenance because nearly a decade later, Baker scrawled an explanatory note on the bond's back. As he contemplated his imminent death, the planter clarified that his wife owned "Nineteen of the fifty Negroes" that "the Bond was given for" and that these slaves should be "accounted for as hers on her Marriage Settlement."[1]

Baker's hastily scrawled note and the bond it explains are brief, but they gesture at a world in which colonists and merchants stretched familiar English legal forms to accommodate financial transactions to manage people as property. As we have already seen, plantation colonists sought to unlock the dynamic economic potential of their human property when they used local statutes to treat slaves as chattels rather than real estate. This seemingly minor act of categorization grafted property rights in people onto a broader legal culture that had never explicitly sanctioned slave ownership but nevertheless proved adept at handling the quotidian transactions that made it productive and profitable. It did so because it gave slave owners access to a set of commercial and legal forms that they could use to conduct routine transactions involving slaves. Short, formulaic, and increasingly available in print, these forms made it possible for Britons to buy, sell, and finance slaves in a way that conformed to English law and practice.

Many of these forms – including the conditional bond that Baker executed – were promises to pay, as paper debt radiated out across the Atlantic along with England's merchants. From the bills of exchange that facilitated their cashless transactions to the conditional bonds that secured them, long-distance merchants relied upon debt in various forms to finance their ventures. Set in motion in an expanding transatlantic economy, promises to pay became an integral part of a broader imperial debt economy that transformed public and private life in the early modern British Empire. As scholars have shown, an "unprecedented" system of public finance underwrote Britain's geopolitical ascendancy, making it possible for the state to meet its "ever-more ponderous burden of military commitments" in the eighteenth century.[2] Debt also accelerated commercialization, fueling the

---

[1] Conditional bond, Baker Family Papers, 1138.00, 11/535/33, SCHS.
[2] John Brewer, *The Sinews of Power: War, Money and the English State 1688–1783* (Cambridge: Harvard University Press, 1989), 38.

growth of institutions that have become synonymous with the financial revolution, including the stock market and a dedicated business press.[3] For individual men and women, debt bought access to the "Baubles of Britain" – from tea sets to the latest fashions – that flooded imperial markets in the eighteenth century. At the same time, debt's centrality in eighteenth-century life prompted nagging concerns about the consequences of financial dependence, as Britons on both sides of the Atlantic celebrated their empire of goods but also counted its costs.[4]

Scholars are right to characterize debt as an agent of change, but it is easy to forget that debt itself was also transformed by its engagement with empire. This was true when it came to debt's broader economic function. Passed from hand to hand through assignment, merchants and consumers treated paper debt as currency, using their credit instruments to purchase goods and meet their own financial obligations. This not only expanded commercial liquidity; repeated countless times, assignment also shifted debt's cultural meaning, stripping it of its moral connotations and recasting it as a purely financial matter. More importantly for our purposes, the merchants and colonists who relied upon debt to conduct cashless transactions long-pressed on its legal forms, asking them to accommodate new types of commercial activities and even new forms of property. In this chapter, I follow one particular legal form of debt – the conditional bond – on an odyssey that propelled it from its origins in the tumultuous commercial world of post-plague England to Richard Bohun Baker's Lowcountry plantation. Watching as merchants and colonists deployed this much older credit instrument in new commercial contexts underscores English law's astonishing portability, even when it was embodied in seemingly rigid legal forms. In fact, the conditional bond was useful in a variety of contexts because of its legal form rather than in spite of it. Conditional bonds were formal credit instruments, and in a legal system that privileged formal writings, bonds were easier to enforce than other forms of debt. With bond in hand, a creditor could sue a debtor at common law and expect to obtain a judgment in the bond's penalty amount. Its enforceability made the conditional bond a popular mechanism for strengthening agreements of all sorts. English merchants, seeking new ways to structure their long-distance transactions, found that they

---

[3] Nuala Zahedieh, *The Capital and the Colonies: London and the Atlantic Economy, 1660–1700* (Cambridge: Cambridge University Press, 2010), 81, 57, 83.

[4] T. H. Breen, *The Marketplace Revolution: How Consumer Politics Shaped American Independence* (Oxford: Oxford University Press, 2005), 81.

could rely upon conditional bonds to bring their far-flung debtors to account. On the coast of Africa, bonds proved equally useful to creditors in the slave trade, who harnessed their power to secure timely payments from slave purchasers. Slave-owning colonists, too, found much to admire in conditional bonds and made such ready use of them that they became an unremarkable feature of local commercial life.

As a practical matter, adapting conditional bonds to new commercial environments was simple. Bonds were short, formulaic documents that typically omitted substantive details about the bargains they secured. From a legal perspective, this information was irrelevant. Indeed, by executing a bond, parties purposefully created a new and separate obligation, one that gave them access to a remedy at common law. In case of default, then, creditors brought an action in debt to enforce the bond's penalty rather than "the underlying agreement" itself.[5] This silence seems insignificant at first glance, but it had subtle but far-reaching consequences as bonds crisscrossed the Atlantic. Vague as to the nature of the bargain, conditional bonds required little adaptation, and this meant that merchants and colonists could use them to secure commercial ventures of all sorts, including slave sales. As long as they adhered to the proper legal form – as long as bonds contained the necessary legal language and markers of authority – the type of the agreement that the bond secured was of little matter. Courts would continue to enforce these instruments without hesitation, and merchants would continue to accept them as a medium of exchange.

In a broader legal culture that elevated legal form over legal substance, the ease with which legal forms like bonds accommodated chattel slavery made it possible for slave owners to maneuver within an existing English legal framework rather than outside of it. Plantation colonists like Richard Bohun Baker were not legal outliers due to their reliance upon chattel slavery, in part because English law did not demand it as a practical matter. They slotted slaves into forms that had been designed with other chattels in mind, without encountering the practical difficulties that might otherwise have forced them to recognize chattel slavery as a legal aberration. We can imagine (although it is impossible to prove) that if conditional bonds had required slave owners to alter them significantly, it might have reinforced their broader concerns about the legal and cultural deviancy of their plantation societies. Instead, these forms precluded any need for critical inquiry

---

[5] J. H. Baker, *An Introduction to English Legal History*, 4th ed. (London: Butterworths Lexis Nexis, 2002), 324. Baker argues that this hindered the development of the law of contract. *Ibid.*

into the legal propriety of transactions involving slaves, even as it insulated colonists from contemplating the consequences of their actions.

Following conditional bonds, then, helps us to see plantation colonists as they saw themselves: as shared participants in a wider imperial legal culture rather than legal outliers because of their reliance upon slave labor. The ease with which colonists adapted legal forms like conditional bonds only reinforced this perception, sparing colonists from justifying the legality of transactions that presumed people could be property. At the same time, watching conditional bonds take root in plantation colonies reveals that the language of English law infused and defined the legal culture of slave societies, allowing colonists to order their lives and activities in a way that conformed to familiar legal norms. Plantation colonists drew legal authority from English law's categories and jargon, its forms and tropes, as we have already seen. But they also took full advantage of English law's studied silences, of moments when legal forms allowed them to ignore chattel slavery entirely. Silence, in fact, assumed a place of primacy in a broader rhetorical and commercial culture that was dedicated to upholding the legal fiction that people could be property. It reduced friction by allowing slave owners to ignore the humanity of the slaves that they commodified, to suppress the visceral reality that broke through in their own interactions with enslaved people. Plantation colonists may not have perceived their slaves as family members, as nineteenth-century slave owners liked to claim. Nonetheless, they understood that slaves were human beings, with their own personalities, desires, and emotions. When legal forms like conditional bonds allowed slave owners to avoid reckoning with chattel slavery's human toll, it freed them to buy and sell slaves without regard to the suffering that would inevitably result from their actions. English law's silences could bind, but they could also separate, sundering the ties of family and community that enslaved people worked so hard to forge.[6]

---

[6] This view of colonists' legal and economic behavior comports with recent scholarship on the nineteenth-century internal slave trade. Although unconcerned to reconstruct daily legal practice per se, slavery scholars of the post-Revolutionary period nonetheless have used economic transactions involving slaves to depict slave owners as market actors who zealously pursued profit maximization at the expense of enslaved families. On the whole, these scholars have illustrated that slave owners followed the "chattel principle," ascribing economic value to the bodies of their slaves and perceiving them as human capital that could be leveraged to suit their commercial needs. As this chapter shows, colonists fully understood the "chattel principle" long before the expansion of the internal slave trade, suggesting that there was less of a practical if not ideological break between pre- and post-Revolutionary slavery than many scholars have believed. Although the closing of the

The credit instrument that secured Baker's slave sale was not anomalous. Rather, it was one among a multitude of legal and transactional documents that circulated in England's early modern economy. The conditional bond that Baker executed, like many of these other documents, was a legal form of debt that merchants increasingly relied upon to secure their long-distance transactions. The enforceability of conditional bonds, above all, recommended them to England's long-distance traders, who struggled to collect debts in a complex commercial environment. When oceans separated creditors and debtors, conditional bonds guaranteed that common law courts would hold them to their obligations. As a result, merchants began to use conditional bonds to strengthen agreements of all sorts, from commodity sales to loans.

The legal advantages that made conditional bonds an ideal instrument for securing these transactions flowed from the bond's legal form, which I examine in depth in "Legal Bonds." At common law, a debt's enforceability depended upon its physical attributes as a legal document. Formal credit agreements like conditional bonds were generally easier to enforce in court than more informal credit arrangements like book debts. Because they were signed and sealed agreements, bonds could be used as dispositive proof of a debt's existence, while giving litigants access to a more reliable way of proceeding at common law. Rather than suing in covenant or assumpsit, bondholders could sue in debt on the bond itself and reliably obtain a judgment in their favor. As a result of this procedural felicity, bonds remained popular among creditors and debtors alike from the fourteenth century into the early modern period. Like other commercial and legal documents that enjoyed widespread popularity, bonds settled into a standardized form by the eighteenth century, and they were

international slave trade in 1807 certainly created a new, internal slave economy that differed in many respects from the transatlantic slave trade, when it came to viewing slaves as primarily economic investments and using their legal knowledge to act on that perception, colonial slaveholders did not differ greatly from subsequent generations. See, e.g., Walter Johnson, ed., *The Chattel Principle: Internal Slave Trades in the Americas* (New Haven: Yale University Press, 2004); idem., *Soul by Soul: Life inside the Antebellum Slave Market* (Cambridge: Harvard University Press, 1999); Michael Tadman, *Speculators and Slaves: Masters, Traders, and Slaves in the Old South* (Madison: University of Wisconsin Press, 1989); Steven Deyle, *Carry Me Back: The Domestic Slave Trade in American Life* (Oxford: Oxford University Press, 2005); Calvin Schermerhorn, *Money over Mastery, Family over Freedom: Slavery in the Antebellum Upper South* (Baltimore: Johns Hopkins University Press, 2011); Adam Rothman, *Slave Country: American Expansion and the Origins of the Deep South* (Cambridge: Harvard University Press, 2005); Joyce E. Chaplin, *An Anxious Pursuit: Agricultural Innovation & Modernity in the Lower South, 1730–1815* (Chapel Hill: University of North Carolina Press, 1993).

increasingly reproduced in print. This reduced transaction costs, but it also made it easier for colonists and merchants to adapt conditional bonds to new commercial contexts, as I show in "Debts Made Flesh." Following slave-trading merchants as they worked to improve profitability, I watch as they transformed conditional bonds into their legal instrument of choice for securing slave sales. Creditors in the slave trade were drawn to the bond's enforceability, which allowed them to extract timely remittances from colonists for the slaves that they bought on credit. When colonists struggled to pay for their slaves, bonds could hold them to account in colonial common law courts.

Although plantation colonists habitually complained about British creditors and their lending practices, they, too, recognized the procedural benefits that conditional bonds bestowed. In "Local Bonds," therefore, I follow slave owners as they relied upon conditional bonds in local transactions, from slave sales to loan agreements. As plantation colonists knew, the procedural benefits that conditional bonds bestowed reverberated differently in slave societies, where a successful suit entitled a creditor to seize and sell a debtor's slaves. This made the consequences of default potentially catastrophic for debtors, even as it complicated creditors' choices. Moreover, as I show in "Following Form," the increased availability of pre-printed bonds allowed aspiring slave-owners to reduce transaction costs, thereby deepening their commitment to chattel slavery. In "The Dance of Credit and Debt," I conclude by exploring the implications of insolvency for creditors and debtors in plantation societies. At moments of acute financial distress, the dual nature of chattel slavery – the fact that slaves were accounted financial assets and productive laborers – magnified the impact of conditional bonds. For creditors, the ability to attach slaves multiplied their options. They could choose to sell attached slaves, or they could put them work on their own plantations, benefitting from their labor as they waited for market conditions to improve. At the same time, debtors fought to maintain possession of their slaves, sometimes going to great lengths to avoid their creditors. From providing creditors with additional security to absconding with their slaves, debtors hoped to forestall the execution of judgments that would deprive them of their valuable human property. Conditional bonds seemed to place creditors in a more favorable legal position, but when we watch them interact with slave-owning debtors, their advantages disappeared in practice. More often than not, creditors and debtors reached non-litigated solutions, agreeing to leave debtors in possession of their land and slaves. Foregoing short-term gains in favor of a long-term debt collection strategy, creditors in particular bowed to the economic reality that they were more likely to recoup their losses by allowing slaves to continue laboring to service their owners' debts. Indeed, in moments of financial hardship, the dance of debt and credit in plantation colonies resembled what we find in other British places, but where it differed, it owed its peculiar steps to the presence of human property.

AN EMPIRE OF PAPER

When Richard Bohun Baker secured the sale of his slaves with a conditional bond, he generated a legal document with kinetic potential. Given the right conditions, this document could move across oceans and down the generations. It could be evaluated and discounted; it could be transferred or exchanged. It could be divorced entirely from the circumstances that surrounded its creation and become part of an empire built upon paper. Indeed, the Baker bond was one among countless other ephemeral byproducts of an eighteenth-century British Empire that was maritime, free, and decidedly commercial.[7] It joined stocks, bills of sale, bills of exchange, powers of attorney, insurance contracts, and other transactional documents in an ever-lengthening paper trail that made imperial commerce work.

This paper trail has its own history. It forms a vital part of a broader historical narrative about commercialization, one in which economic changes over the early modern period enabled Britain's rise as a global power. The so-called financial revolution was a complex and halting process, an evolutionary revolution that nonetheless produced a "radical transformation" of England's "financial system." One of its markers – and, simultaneously, its drivers – was the circulation of transactional documents on an unprecedented scale. Beginning with shares in joint-stock companies and extending to a wide variety of other commercial documents, bits of paper passed from hand to hand at a dizzying pace in the post-Restoration period. Most of these documents were not new: many had roots in medieval England or in the commercial practices of merchants from the Mediterranean or the Low Countries. Nonetheless, they acquired a more prominent position in the early modern economy, as they were repurposed to suit the needs of an increasingly mobile people.

---

[7] David Armitage, *The Ideological Origins of the British Empire* (Cambridge: Cambridge University Press, 2000), 8.

This was particularly true for the paper debt that underwrote colonial commerce. As a new generation of English merchants fanned out across the globe in the seventeenth century, they used debt to overcome the novel financial challenges posed by long-distance trading and especially the fact that these ventures "tied up capital for longer periods than usual."[8] Whereas overland and Continental trade could be conducted relatively quickly, the geographic realities of transoceanic commerce meant that investors might not see returns for months or even years.[9] This left them hard-pressed to meet their ongoing financial obligations and bereft of capital to invest in other potentially profitable enterprises. Debt provided a solution to this pressing liquidity problem. By using credit to purchase supplies and discharge their obligations, long-distance merchants could continue their business operations without awaiting the arrival and sale of distant commodities. The practical benefits of credit-based transactions were obvious to these merchants, and by the eighteenth century, they had refined an imperial commercial system that was built upon continuously circulating promises to pay.[10]

As shrewd merchants knew, promises to pay were not equal. Debt in early modern England assumed distinctive legal forms, which in turn shaped relationships between debtors and creditors when they bargained in the shadow of the law. The "role" that any given form of debt played in the economy hinged upon its enforceability, which in turn depended upon its formality.[11] Indeed, a debt's physical form was not a matter of mere aesthetics; it had distinctive legal and practical implications. Formal credit agreements – agreements that were written, signed, and sealed – were typically easier to enforce in common law courts than oral or unsigned written agreements like book debt.[12] This was a preference that stemmed from much older jurisdictional conflicts, as early medieval judges sought to elevate the king's central courts over local institutions. By requiring litigants to sue on a formal writing, common law judges hoped to capture the weightiest disputes over real property, which typically involved formal written agreements like deeds and charters.[13]

What began as a jurisdictional delimiter, however, hardened into a set of rules and assumptions that effectively "shut out" informal agreements

---

[8] Zahedieh, *The Capital and the Colonies*, 80, 83.   [9] *Ibid.*, 80, 83.   [10] *Ibid.*, 83.
[11] Bruce H. Mann, "The Transformation of Law and Economy in Early America," in *The Cambridge History of Law in America*, vol. 1, edited by Michael Grossberg and Christopher Tomlins (Cambridge: Cambridge University Press, 2008), 378.
[12] *Ibid.*   [13] Baker, *An Introduction to English Legal History*, 320.

"from the central courts."[14] Litigants could sue on informal agreements, but as a practical matter, common law courts were unlikely to enforce them. For example, the book accounts that early modern shopkeepers used to keep a running tally of purchases on credit were a staple of local commerce, but their informality meant that they were difficult to uphold in court.[15] Book accounts typically did not adhere to any prescribed format; they lacked an explicit promise to pay, and they were unsigned. Although creditors could present book accounts as evidence of a debt, courts tended to treat them as "merely a starting point" for discussion rather than dispositive proof of an obligation.[16]

This had practical consequences for early modern creditors and debtors, who entered into agreements with an eye toward enforceability. Denied formal legal relief, parties to informal agreements relied upon debt enforcement methods that flowed from intimate community connections, including personal persuasion and shaming.[17] These methods were effective in "insular local economies," where proximity bred familiarity and parties could call upon mutual friends and family members to broker disputes. However, they were "ill-suited" to the commercial realities of long-distance trade. Unlike the more intimate world of local commerce, transoceanic trade drew far-flung participants into an "increasingly complex web of multilateral exchanges."[18] Creditors and debtors – who found themselves connected by networks that spanned continents rather than towns – operated in circumstances of relative anonymity. Some knew each other only by reputation, if at all. In this relatively depersonalized commercial environment, debt collection methods that hinged upon personal or community connections were unlikely to be effective. England's long-distance merchants were well aware of this. They understood that when debtors defaulted, formal legal intervention was often the only way to hold them to account. As a result, long-distance merchants learned to avoid informal credit agreements and instead relied on forms of debt that courts of common law would enforce when necessary.

Above all, England's long-distance merchants made it a habit to structure their transactions using written credit instruments, including

---

[14] *Ibid.*

[15] James Oldham, *English Common Law in the Age of Mansfield* (Chapel Hill: University of North Carolina Press, 2004), 79.

[16] Bruce H. Mann, "Law, Legalism, and Community before the American Revolution," *Michigan Law Review* 84 (1986): 1419.

[17] Mann, "The Transformation of Law and Economy in Early America," 378.

[18] Zahedieh, *The Capital and the Colonies*, 80.

promissory notes, bills of exchange, and conditional bonds.[19] These were promises to pay that were in writing and signed by the debtor, and they carried interest.[20] Unlike informal credit agreements, they also featured "adornments," which could include the debtor's seal or signatures of witnesses. These markers of a document's authenticity enhanced its formality and therefore its value as evidence of an agreement. Although written credit agreements had long been a staple of European commerce, their enforceability ultimately recommended them to English merchants, who transformed them into the sine qua non of long-distance trade. From the bills of exchange that became their "workhorse," to the conditional bonds that secured countless transactions, long-distance traders deftly repurposed these much older legal forms in new commercial contexts.

As scholars have shown, written credit instruments proliferated in late seventeenth-century London, keeping pace with the rising "volume and value of colonial commerce." They gradually acquired a more prominent position in eighteenth-century life, along with other legal forms of debt that merchants used to finance their long-distance trading ventures. Scholars have thoroughly demonstrated debt's centrality to the eighteenth-century British Empire, and its far-reaching economic, political, and cultural implications. This was particularly true of written credit agreements, which began to acquire a commercial value that transcended their use in individual transactions. Because holders of these instruments could expect common law courts to enforce them, the instruments themselves gradually acquired value as a medium of exchange. By assigning their written credit instruments – or endorsing them over to another party – holders could treat promises to pay as currency, using paper debt to purchase goods or even discharge their own debts.[21] This was a common practice with bills of exchange, which merchants routinely assigned as early as the 1660s.[22] By the late seventeenth century, merchants and speculators had extended assignment to include a wide variety of other commercial documents, including bills, notes, bonds, insurance contracts, and receipts.[23]

Assignment was a relatively simple practice, but it had an outsized commercial impact. By transforming promises to pay into a vital source

---

[19] Mann, "The Transformation of Law and Economy in Early America," 378.

[20] The rate of interest was typically set by statute or in the instrument itself. *Ibid.*, 379.

[21] Zahedieh, *The Capital and the Colonies*, 57, 83.

[22] Oldham, *English Common Law in the Age of Mansfield*, 155. This practice was given official sanction in 1692, when the Court of King's Bench held that bills of exchange were assignable as a matter of law.

[23] Zahedieh, *The Capital and the Colonies*, 85.

of commercial liquidity, merchants and traders could continue meeting their financial obligations without depleting their capital.[24] As we have already seen, this was particularly important for long-distance traders, who operated in the context of capital scarcity, and therefore relied upon paper debt to conduct many of their transactions. Perhaps more importantly, as Bruce Mann has shown, assignment also heralded a broader conceptual shift. Repeated countless times, the assignment of paper debt taught Britons to treat credit instruments as "essentially fungible" commodities rather than the product of unique business arrangements. This is because in the context of assignment, the party who ultimately collects the debt will be a "distant supplier" rather than the original creditor.[25] In these circumstances of relative anonymity, value depends upon "certainty and predictability" of enforcement. Paper debt, after all, is only useful in an exchange to the extent that the party who holds the debt can collect it when it comes due. And in early modern England, enforceability flowed from an instrument's form rather than the substance of the underlying transaction, as we have already seen.[26] Assignment as practice, then, requires the depersonalization of debt. Before promises to pay can circulate in the economy as a medium of exchange, they must first be wrenched from their originating context.

The depersonalization of debt that assignment facilitated was "part of the social cost of commercialization," and it fundamentally realigned how Britons and their American counterparts understood debt and its role in their lives.[27] Indeed, between the seventeenth and nineteenth centuries, debt became an unremarkable part of commercial life rather than a signifier of failure, bankruptcy became a sign of misfortune rather than a defect of character, and creditworthiness became completely untethered from the intimate evaluation of communities.[28] These shifts marked the distance between a community-centered early modern economy and the radically depersonalized one that would succeed it, a world of arms-length transactions in which individuals enjoyed the fruits of commercialization in isolation. It would be a more economically efficient world, but it would also be a world in which debts of all sorts, even those incurred in slave trading, could quietly slip into broader circulation. In fact, the elevation of form

---

[24] *Ibid.*, 83.
[25] Mann, "The Transformation of Law and Economy in Early America," 380.
[26] Mann, "Law, Legalism, and Community before the American Revolution," 1423.
[27] Mann, "The Transformation of Law and Economy in Early America," 380.
[28] *Ibid.*, 394–395.

over substance that assignment required ultimately opened up space for written credit instruments to accommodate new commercial ventures and even new types of property without triggering any sustained inquiry into the legal or moral propriety of these adaptations. As long as debtors and creditors subscribed to the proper legal form, they could expect judges to honor their bargains and merchants to accept their instruments as a medium of exchange. Ultimately, it was the reification of form over substance that facilitated debt's most profound and far-reaching transformation: the unflinching addition of human beings to the category of financeable merchandise.

We can see this transformation most clearly when we watch how merchants and plantation colonists adapted one written credit instrument, the conditional bond, to the financial imperatives of chattel slavery. Born in the tumultuous commercial world of late medieval England, conditional bonds migrated across oceans along with England's early modern traders. When debtors defaulted on their obligations, bondholders could reliably collect liquidated damages in common law courts, and when default compounded into bankruptcy, they maintained priority over other creditors. This legal felicity recommended conditional bonds to merchants of all sorts, including slave traders. In the inherently risky commercial world of human trafficking, merchants deployed conditional bonds to hold their colonial factors to account, and factors in turn used bonds to squeeze payments from colonial debtors. As we shall see, the conditional bond's peculiar legal power to keep remittances flowing ultimately made them a ubiquitous part of commercial life in plantation America, where they became the preferred legal mechanism for securing slaves sales and a wide variety of other commercial transactions.

LEGAL BONDS

The conditional bonds that eventually inserted themselves into the very heart of plantation societies were similar in many ways to other instruments that long-distance merchants used to extend credit: they were written and signed promises to pay that carried interest. In practice, conditional bonds worked by obligating a debtor to pay the creditor a penalty sum, and they consisted of two main components. The first part – the obligation – specified a penalty amount (usually twice the sale price) that the debtor agreed to pay. The second part – the condition of defeasance – stated a condition that would void the obligation (typically the payment of the original amount by a certain date).[29] Although the conditional bond's language was technical, its overriding purpose was simple: to give creditors a legally enforceable way to collect predetermined liquidated damages at common law.

Conditional bonds had deep roots in medieval England, emerging as a mature legal instrument in the aftermath of the Black Death. In early bonds, the obligation and defeasance were executed in two separate instruments, but by the second half of the fourteenth century, they routinely appeared in one document. This development was apparently the result of chance rather than strategy, when an enterprising scribe made both bond parts fit onto his last piece of parchment.[30] Despite this unusual provenance, the Court of Common Pleas upheld the legality of the combined bond in 1356 and, more importantly, signaled its willingness to enforce penalties of all sorts. This represented a seismic shift in judicial attitudes. Whereas judges once hesitated to enforce penalties because they seemed usurious, the loss of nearly one-third of England's population in the Black Death removed these scruples. Thereafter, judges were more inclined to enforce conditional bonds and other instruments that helped to "preserve traditional society."[31] Late medieval judges typically assumed a "creditor-favoring stance," but they also made bonds more amenable to debtors by enforcing penalties only when they "were deserved."[32] As a result of this careful balancing of interests, the bond's popularity surged. Whereas litigation on penal bonds only "averaged about one case each year" between 1343 and 1356, bond litigation had become "common" by the 1370s.[33]

Conditional bonds sustained their popularity into the early modern period, and between the sixteenth and nineteenth centuries, bond litigation remained the most significant type of business in the Court of Common Pleas at Westminster.[34] The instrument's enduring appeal relative to other forms of debt stemmed from the fact that it sat astride early modern England's finely wrought credit hierarchy. As we have already seen, English common law privileged written agreements, which were

---

[29] Bruce H. Mann, *Republic of Debtors: Bankruptcy in the Age of American Independence* (Cambridge: Harvard University Press, 2009), 10. J. H. Baker also refers to this type of bond as a "common money bond." Baker, *An Introduction to English Legal History*, 324.

[30] Robert C. Palmer, *English Law in the Age of the Black Death, 1348–1381: A Transformation of Governance and Law* (Chapel Hill: University of North Carolina Press, 2000), 85.

[31] *Ibid.*, 91.   [32] *Ibid.*, 85.   [33] *Ibid.*, 82–83.

[34] Baker, *An Introduction to English Legal History*, 324.

easier to enforce than parole agreements (including unsigned and oral promises to pay). Conditional bonds provided creditors with an even higher degree of legal certainty. Because they were also sealed instruments, conditional bonds were technically considered deeds at common law. It was this seemingly minor distinction that ultimately gave bondholders advantages in common law courts.

These advantages were particularly important given the "unsettled" state of early modern commercial law.[35] English common law had evolved over centuries to resolve disputes over real property, but it struggled to keep pace with economic changes in the early modern period. The traditional forms of action that constrained litigants' choices had emerged to provide remedies for an agrarian rather than a commercial society. However, as the pace of commercialization accelerated in the early modern period, litigants increasingly found that their disputes fit uneasily or not at all into these older forms. Although tracing English common law's shift from property to contract oversimplifies a complicated process, it nonetheless captures an essential truth. The traditional forms of actions often proved unwieldy when it came to righting new kinds of wrongs.

The common law's limitations were glaringly evident when it came to contract law. Before Lord Mansfield began to align the common law with mercantile practice in the late eighteenth century, litigants faced limited procedural options. The older common law writs of covenant and debt, which traditionally governed interpersonal relations, were rife with "procedural and evidentiary constraints."[36] While covenant required evidence of a document under seal and only allowed a plaintiff to obtain specific performance, debt required "a sum certain" and evidence of "quid pro quo."[37] A plaintiff could avoid these pitfalls by using the newer and more flexible action of assumpsit, but this also had disadvantages, especially for merchant-plaintiffs. Because a lay jury rather than a merchant jury decided the issue of liability in assumpsit, the outcome of litigation remained uncertain.[38] Merchants, who were typically reluctant to entrust their fate to men unfamiliar with their customary practices, avoided assumpsit as a result.

Conditional bonds allowed litigants to make an end run around these procedural limitations, and this helps to explain their popularity. Because a bond was considered a deed, bondholders could avoid *covenant* and *assumpsit* and instead sue in debt on an obligation to enforce the bond

---

[35] Oldham, *English Common Law in the Age of Mansfield*, 83.   [36] *Ibid.*, 79.   [37] *Ibid.*
[38] *Ibid.*

itself. This gave them access to the more settled "law of deeds and conditions," in which bondholders almost always prevailed.[39] In this type of
action, courts considered a bond to be dispositive evidence of an agreement, and this left defendants with few viable defenses.[40] Victorious
bondholders were then entitled to collect the penalty amount, which the
court formally entered as a judgment. Because this procedural posture
made the outcome of litigation more certain (and more favorable to
bondholders), conditional bonds became a fixture of early modern commercial life. Merchants requested bonds to secure agreements of all sorts,
but they were particularly useful for securing debt agreements. Creditors
could ask debtors to execute a bond immediately upon reaching an
agreement, or they could request a bond when a debtor fell behind in
payments as additional security.

As was true for other commercial and transactional documents that
circulated in the early modern economy, the popularity of conditional
bonds encouraged their standardization as a legal form. From language to
layout, bonds settled into patterns that made them recognizable as distinctive document types. Late medieval bonds were handwritten in Latin,
and from differences in hand to subtle variations in language, they
reflected the individual circumstances of their making.[41] By the early
eighteenth century, however, these subtle differences had begun to fade.
Conditional bonds looked increasingly alike, and merchants throughout
the British Empire would have been able to identify a conditional bond
based upon predictable textual cues.

This was a process that the print revolution both reflected and accelerated. Although scholars of print culture have typically emphasized "works
of great learning, fastidious devotion or sophisticated entertainment," most
Britons interacted with less exalted printed texts, including legal forms and
financial documents.[42] The production of these quotidian documents –
including "bills of lading," "Bills of Sale, Bonds of all Sorts," and "blank
Law forms" – "soared" in the eighteenth century as printers sought to keep
pace with consumer demand.[43] Like many handwritten legal forms, printed
documents traced an overall arc of standardization. This was true for
conditional bonds. Although early printed bonds featured an italic-style

---

[39] Baker, *An Introduction to English Legal History*, 324.   [40] *Ibid.*, 324–325.
[41] *Ibid.*, 323.
[42] James Raven, "Why Ephemera Were Not Ephemeral: The Effectiveness of Innovative
Print in the Eighteenth Century," *The Yearbook of English Studies* 45 (2015): 56.
[43] *Ibid.*, 57–58.

type and Latin text, by the middle of the eighteenth century, they were usually block-set and in English. Printed conditional bonds also acquired a distinctive layout that mimicked the appearance of handwritten bonds on the page. Printers typically indented the first paragraph – which contained the recitation and the obligation – and set it off from the second paragraph – which described the bond's condition.[44] The end result was a document that was recognizable on sight as a conditional bond.

Taken together, printed legal documents like conditional bonds made it possible for merchants and financially savvy consumers to conduct routine transactions without a lawyer's aid. Printers supplied all of the relevant legal jargon, leaving purchasers with the relatively simple task of inserting details that were specific to their transactions. This reduced transaction costs and allowed consumers to take advantage of developments in fast-paced financial markets. More subtly, the "repeatability" and regular appearance of printed forms tended to enhance their "reputation and authority."[45] Print obscured the small distinctions – from handwriting to paper quality – that marked individual documents as different and opened up space for questions about their legal enforceability. From consistency of layout to standard typeface, the uniform appearance of printed documents reassured purchasers that they were authentic and enforceable, rather than the slipshod products of amateurs. This was particularly crucial for legal documents, which purchasers relied upon to accomplish specific tasks in a legal system that demanded outward conformity. Over time, this quest to convey authority through uniformity meant that credit instruments like bonds began to look more alike, which in turn made them easier to treat as a medium of exchange.

Although the seeming immutability of printed legal forms may have enhanced their authority, it is crucial to remember that printed forms never precluded "adaptability" or "resistance."[46] We often equate the fixity of printed legal documents with rigidity. After all, the very act of setting text in print seems calculated to freeze language in a specific historical moment. Nonetheless, the printed legal forms that circulated in the early modern economy remained open to adaptation and modification. This was particularly true for fill-in-the-blank bond forms, which seemed to invite purchasers to engage creatively with a document's text. Parties could insert lengthy descriptions in pre-supplied blanks, or they

---

[44] See, e.g., handwritten conditional bond, December 11, 1716; printed conditional bond, March 25, 1708, CLA/024/06 052, LMA.
[45] Raven, "Why Ephemera Were Not Ephemeral," 70. [46] *Ibid.,* 73.

could add or remove text. For example, the printer of a 1706 bond specified that payment should be made in "good and lawfull money of Great Britain." Nonetheless, one of the parties struck out "Great Britain" and replaced the phrase with "England," perhaps to signal an objection to the impending union of England and Scotland.[47] Alterations like this were minor, but parties could also make more substantive changes. For example, in a 1708 bond, an unknown individual altered the standard legal phrase, "Heires Executors Administrator[s] or Assignes," to read "Heires Executors or Administrator[s]."[48] This intervention fundamentally shifted the bond's meaning because it shielded assignees from the document's legal effect.

Despite the apparent rigidity of standardized legal forms like conditional bonds, then, they continued to provide early modern Britons with the same creative possibilities that we see with English law's other categories, tropes, and jargon. Visual uniformity may have conditioned consumers to see credit instruments as authoritative, but it could not entirely freeze them in place. In a legal system built upon the repetition of forms and language, individuals could always find room to maneuver within the margins. Conditional bonds in particular remained surprisingly responsive to changing commercial circumstances as they migrated across the globe. English merchants, who encountered new challenges financing long-distance trade, found that this older instrument could be adapted to suit their new and increasingly complex commercial ventures. Alongside the bills of exchange that facilitated cashless transactions, they relied upon conditional bonds to make long-distance trade possible and profitable. Because bonds gave creditors a reliable way to collect damages when debtors failed to pay, they helped creditors to offset their losses. This was particularly important in ventures that carried heightened risks for participants and therefore made default more likely.

Few commercial activities in the early modern world were as risky as slave trading. As the English merchants who sent ships to the coast of Africa learned, conditional bonds were ideally suited to secure transactions in a volatile trade that was financed entirely by credit. Creditors in the slave trade required their colonial factors to secure slave consignments with bonds, and factors in turn demanded conditional bonds from colonial purchasers. In colonial courts, the procedural advantages that bonds gave creditors in England were translated intact. Bonds continued to give

---

[47] Conditional bond, November 1, 1706, CLA/024/06 052, LMA.
[48] Conditional bond, September 1708, CLA/024/06 052, LMA.

creditors access to a more certain way of proceeding, one that avoided cumbersome procedural paths and resulted in a judgment for creditors. Nonetheless, the power of conditional bonds was magnified in plantation colonies, where they gave creditors access to a debtor's valuable human property.

DEBTS MADE FLESH

From the coasts of Africa to the swamps of the South Carolina Lowcountry, countless individuals engaged in practices that, taken together, transformed human beings into the early modern world's most valuable commodities. As a practical matter, commodification meant stripping Black people of their individual identities and recasting them as fungible property. This was a thoroughly scientific enterprise, and violence was its handmaiden. As Stephanie Smallwood has shown, slave traders methodically worked to "find the limits of human capacity for suffering," reducing life "to an arithmetical equation" in order to transform Africans into property. Violence in the slave trade was real and visceral, but it was also legally inflected. As we have already seen, English law's categories sundered meaningful human connections in the service of commodification by recasting slaves as chattel property. Slave traders on the Coast of Africa engaged in similar practices, fitting slaves into transactional documents by likening them to saleable goods. When traders grouped slaves with "Elephants Teeth" and "other Goods Com[m]odities and merchandizes," they not only commented on the relative value of slaves as economic assets. They also obscured the humanity of enslaved people and therefore facilitated their dehumanization.[49] Deployed in slave forts and on docks, the language of English law became an integral part of "the epistemological foundation on which the enterprise of commodification stood." It worked alongside a "body of lore" that traders on the coast of Africa developed to strip slaves of their individuality and reclassify them as objects that could be valued according to their physical characteristics.

The language of commodification, which owed so much to English law, followed enslaved people across the Atlantic in the transactional documents that allowed Britons to realize the fruits of commodification. The legal forms that merchants deployed in their routine commercial transactions

---

[49] Articles of Agreement between the Royal African Company and John Sperriford, July 5, 1695, C111/184, TNA.

made it possible as a practical matter to convert human beings into saleable goods. Although there is a tendency to isolate the transatlantic slave trade from other early modern commercial ventures, its participants directly benefitted from developments that we commonly associate with the financial revolution.[50] From the printed transactional documents that they used to buy and sell slaves, to the paper debt that they assigned as a medium of exchange, slave traders, factors, and plantation colonists were commercialization's foremost apostles. In their hands, these documents became an essential part of the "technology of colonization" that moved millions of Africans across oceans and that conveyed property rights in their bodies to colonial purchasers.

The conditional bond was among this technology's most important moving parts. From its medieval origins, the conditional bond migrated across oceans alongside a new generation of overseas merchants, who repurposed bonds to secure their long-distance transactions. Commodities trading in particular was vulnerable to countless manmade and environmental hazards: perishable agricultural commodities could rot, ships could flounder as a result of weather or war, and crops could catastrophically fail. Long-distance merchants also encountered "problems of trust and poor information" that increased their risks of misjudging a debtor's creditworthiness or incorrectly gauging local market conditions.[51] As scholars have shown, merchants sought to overcome these disadvantages in a number of ways. They built trusted trade networks of family members of coreligionists. They also demanded a constant flow of information from colonial correspondents, employing managers and agents to keep them apprised about a debtor's financial and physical health. More importantly for our purposes, they relied upon conditional bonds to secure remittances. When weather or war led to late payments or default, creditors in long-distance transactions could rely upon conditional bonds to hold their debtors to account.

England's long distance relied upon bonds to secure a wide variety of their commercial transactions, but they found them to be especially well suited to slave trading. Although a latecomer to the transatlantic slave trade, by the middle of the eighteenth century, Great Britain had become

---

[50] Kenneth Morgan suggests that we should see "[r]emittance procedures" in the transatlantic slave trade "in conjunction with the prevalence of credit transactions and cashless payment mechanisms in early modern international trade." Kenneth Morgan, "Remittance Procedures in the Eighteenth-Century British Slave Trade," *The Business History Review* 79 (2005): 718.

[51] Zahedieh, *The Capital and the Colonies*, 80.

"the world's leader" in human trafficking.[52] The private firms that dominated the slave trade in the eighteenth century ultimately transported more than two million enslaved people from Africa to British North America, the West Indies, and Spanish America.[53] As investors in the "Guinea" trade recognized, theirs was a "particularly risky form of maritime enterprise."[54] In addition to the hazards that were common to all long-distance ventures, slaving entailed risks that were unique to human cargoes. Enslaved people confined below decks did not passively accept their bondage: they resisted captivity in astonishingly varied ways, and sometimes violently. Slave revolts were far from uncommon, occurring on perhaps 10 percent of transatlantic slave ships.[55] Slaves also responded to the horrors of the Middle Passage by committing suicide or running away.[56] This was the case when two African slaves "ran away" soon after South Carolina colonist Henry Laurens purchased them. Although Laurens had paid £303 South Carolina currency "per head" for the men, running away depreciated their resale value, forcing Laurens to take the "best price" he could "obtain."[57]

Acts of resistance could spell tragic human consequences for captive Africans, but investors in the slave trade like Henry Laurens viewed them in more calculative economic terms, accounting for them as financial losses. The same was true for the diseases that stalked the decks of transatlantic slave ships, carrying off slaves and crewmembers alike. Perhaps as many as 20 percent of the Africans transported across the Atlantic in the eighteenth century died during the Middle Passage, while 40 percent "of cargoes experienced mortality levels above that benchmark."[58] Seasoned merchants and factors learned to expect these losses and accept them with aplomb. For example, when Laurens learned of a smallpox outbreak on two incoming slave ships, he handled the news with dignified resignation.

---

[52] Marcus Rediker, *Between the Devil and the Deep Blue Sea, Merchant Seamen, Pirates, and the Anglo-American Maritime World 1700–1750* (Cambridge: Cambridge University Press, 1989), 45.
[53] *Ibid.* [54] Morgan, "Remittance Procedures," 716.
[55] David Richardson, "Shipboard Revolts, African Authority, and the Atlantic Slave Trade," *WMQ* 58 (2001): 72.
[56] See Terri L. Snyder, *The Power to Die: Slavery and Suicide in British North America* (Chicago: University of Chicago Press, 2015).
[57] Henry Laurens to Joseph Brown, July 24, 1765, George C. Rogers, Jr., David R. Chesnutt et al., eds., *The Papers of Henry Laurens*, vol. 4, September 1, 1763–August 31, 1765 (Columbia: University of South Carolina Press, 1974), 658.
[58] Stephanie E. Smallwood, *Saltwater Slavery: A Middle Passage from Africa to American Diaspora* (Cambridge: Harvard University Press, 2008), 150.

After all, he observed, the "African trade" was "more liable to such Accidents than any other." This calm facade belied the constant vigilance that investors in the slave trade practiced in order to prevent losses. Laurens and his colleagues worked "to fortify themselves against every disappointment that the trade is Incident to," constantly seeking new ways to mitigate risks and reduce costs.[59]

Minimizing risks seemed particularly important to creditors given the fact that the transatlantic slave trade was not as profitable as scholars "once supposed." In the eighteenth century, ventures yielded returns of only 8 to 10 percent, significantly less than the average returns for sugar or rice plantations in the same period.[60] Slave merchants were keenly aware of these slim margins, and they dedicated themselves wholeheartedly to the "scientific enterprise" of profit maximization. As Stephanie Smallwood has suggested, the inhuman cruelties perpetuated on slave ships were one aspect of this larger project, as traders carefully explored "the limits up to which it is possible to discipline the body without extinguishing the life within."[61] Conditional bonds were another. Just as slave merchants relied upon "empirical evidence," technological innovations, and scientific observation in order to pack more Black bodies onto slave ships, they also seized upon the latest commercial and legal developments in order to increase profits, including the conditional bonds that facilitated other types of long-distance trade.[62] By bringing the full authority of English common law to bear on factors and purchasers, conditional bonds could mitigate the slave trade's most significant risk: the risk of default.[63]

Indeed, nearly every transaction in the transatlantic slave trade – from the Bristol docks to the slave pens – involved the extension of credit. The financial structure of the slave trade may have varied from colony to colony, but the reliance upon debt financing was universal. British merchants who sent ships to the coast of Africa consigned slave cargoes to colonial factors. In turn, colonial factors extended credit to colonial purchasers, ultimately remitting the proceeds back to Great Britain in bills of exchange or commodities.[64] This attenuated chain of remittances

---

[59] Austin & Laurens [Henry Laurens] to Wells, Wharton & Doran, May 27, 1755, *HLP* 1: 259.

[60] Morgan, "Remittance Procedures," 717.   [61] Smallwood, *Saltwater Slavery*, 36.

[62] *Ibid.*, 49.   [63] Morgan, "Remittance Procedures," 717.

[64] *Ibid.*, 719. Financed sales also benefitted slave factors, who could obtain higher prices when they offered credit. Factors discouraged specie purchases because the 5 percent discount traditionally offered for these transactions could operate to depreciate slave prices in the market as a whole. Sellers, then, incentivized slave sales on credit by offering

was vulnerable at every junction, but particularly at its end point. Slave purchasers in plantation colonies usually bought slaves on credit, often amassing significant debts in order to buy the laborers they required to produce commodities on a profitable scale. For example, in order to produce crops large enough to justify investing in a rice plantation, South Carolina planters required at least thirty workers. By the 1770s, these enslaved laborers could cost £40 a head, with planters purchasing as many as twenty or thirty slaves at a time.[65] The initial investment for aspiring sugar planters in Jamaica was equally "formidable." Planters needed to purchase not only land and expensive sugar processing equipment, but also hundreds of slaves. By the middle of the eighteenth century, "New Negroes" in Jamaica could cost as much as £30 per head, while "seasoned" slaves sold for up to 50 percent more.[66]

Although the start-up cost of producing commodities was daunting, aspiring planters nonetheless believed that purchasing slaves on credit was worth the risk. Newcomers to plantation colonies learned that planting offered the surest route to riches, and they contracted significant debts in order to purchase the land and slaves that could make their financial dreams a reality. For example, when Scots doctor William Murray discovered that "the only way of making an Estate quickly" in mid-century South Carolina was by planting, he "quit Physick" and bought a "very fine" plantation near Port Royal. He and his brother John immediately set out to buy "thirty very good Slaves" on credit and set them to work on the plantation producing indigo.[67] Murray expected to turn a quick profit on his venture,

---

terms that suited a buyer's needs, usually allowing purchasers up to twelve months to pay (with interest). Although these longer terms increased the chances that a buyer might default, the risk to the seller generally was outweighed by the opportunity to obtain a higher price and, thus, to remit more money to British slave merchants. An exception to the cashless payment system was the sale of slaves to Spanish and Portuguese colonies. *Ibid.*, 721.

[65] Philip D. Morgan, *Slave Counterpoint: Black Culture in the Eighteenth-Century Chesapeake and Lowcountry* (Chapel Hill: University of North Carolina Press, 1998), 36–37. Over the colonial period the number of large slaveholdings in the colony increased. Whereas in the 1720s only 12 percent of plantation units employed fifty or more slaves, by the 1770s 52 percent of units did so. *Ibid.*, 37, 40; John E. Crowley, "Family Relations and Inheritance in Early South Carolina," *Histoire Social – Social History* 17 (1984): 51. Kenneth Morgan notes that by the 1750s, South Carolina planters were purchasing slaves in lots of "twenty, thirty, and forty, though this had been previously uncommon in the province." Kenneth Morgan, "Slave Sales in Colonial Charleston," *The English Historical Review* 113 (1998): 913.

[66] Trevor Burnard and Kenneth Morgan, "The Dynamics of the Slave Market and Slave Purchasing Patterns in Jamaica, 1655–1788," *WMQ* 58 (2001): 209, 221.

[67] William Murray to John Murray of Murraythwait, May 27, 1755, GD219/288/9, SNA.

explaining to his mother in Scotland that local planters had cleared "a thousand pound sterling last year by their Crop." With hard work and skilled management, he had good reason to believe that his return on investment would be even more impressive.[68]

Murray never attained staggering riches as he had hoped, but his foray into planting nonetheless allowed him to "live pretty comfortably" later in life. When he decided to sell "the Plantation & Negroes," he was able to command a price that local planters "esteemed a good one[e]," turning a tidy profit on his planting venture by letting out the sale proceeds at 8 percent.[69] Murray's financial success, which was built upon buying land and slaves on credit, was not anomalous. Indeed, plantation colonists' faith in the wisdom of this financial strategy was largely well founded. Profitability in colonial South Carolina "varied from plantation to plantation," but a 10 to 15 percent return on investment was considered "a successful year." By the end of the colonial period, the "optimum" rate of return had climbed to an astonishing 15 to 20 percent.[70] South Carolina planters, in fact, expected field slaves to work off their purchase price in four years, with this number decreasing to less than two years by the 1770s.[71]

Sugar planting in Jamaica likewise produced "enormous returns," which often could exceed 14 percent.[72] Although the sugar economy favored larger planters, investing in slaves on even a small scale could be a sound financial decision. Thomas Thistlewood, a Jamaican overseer with few social connections, was able to attain "moderate" wealth and respectable social status in mid-century Jamaica by purchasing land and slaves on credit. As Trevor Burnard has shown, Thistlewood benefitted from Jamaica's booming sugar economy, which created an insatiable demand for slave laborers and drove slave prices upward. The price of slaves in Jamaica "jumped" an astronomical 145 percent between 1739 and 1775, making buying slaves on credit a wise choice "for white men from all social conditions."[73]

---

[68] John Murray to Mother, March 6, 1757, GD 219/287/12, SNA.

[69] William Murray to Mother, March 15, 1765, GD219/287/19, SNA.

[70] S. Max Edelson, *Plantation Enterprise in Colonial South Carolina* (Cambridge: Harvard University Press, 2006), 241. Philip Morgan suggests that the rate of return was "in excess of 20 percent." Morgan, *Slave Counterpoint*, 38.

[71] *Ibid.*

[72] Trevor Burnard, *Mastery, Tyranny, & Desire: Thomas Thistlewood and His Slaves in the Anglo-Jamaican World* (Chapel Hill: University of North Carolina Press, 2009), 64; see also Trevor Burnard, "'Prodigious Riches': The Wealth of Jamaica before the American Revolution," *The Economic History Review*, new ser. 54 (2001): 506–524.

[73] Burnard, *Mastery, Tyranny, & Desire*, 56, 41.

When plantation colonists like Murray and Thistlewood purchased slaves on credit, they both expected and hoped that a successful crop would allow them to meet their financial obligations.[74] As John Murray explained, "neat Crops" could "make every thing clear."[75] Despite this sunny optimism, however, the economic logic of purchasing slaves on credit could play out in a very different way. A host of factors beyond a planter's control might prevent him from making timely remittances to slave factors and other creditors. This was the case in the 1730s, when declining sugar prices and rice harvest failures left planters scrambling to meet their financial obligations.[76] Hurricanes and floods also "swallowed up dreams of bountiful rice harvests," while warfare depressed commodity prices and interrupted trade.[77] When crops failed or war halted transoceanic commerce, slave owners found themselves hard-pressed to pay their debts. For example, absentee colonist Ralph Izard had planned to discharge a bond that secured a slave purchase, but a poor rice harvest thwarted his plans. "[A]las! such is the uncertainty of Carolina Estates," his manager wrote, that Izard would "not make above half the Rice" he did the previous year.[78] Georgia planter Robert Baillie also struggled to meet the interest payments he owed to a slave seller because his "Crop did not turn out near so well" as he expected.[79]

When slave owners like Baillie and Izard encountered financial hardships, they typically prioritized their debts to slave factors before paying bills for dry goods.[80] Nonetheless, misfortunes both large and small could delay remittances to factors and set off a chain reaction among creditors. When British slave merchants hounded Henry Laurens to pay for a recent consignment of slaves, for example, he explained that "the extream backwardness" of slave purchasers had left him hard-pressed to meet his own obligations.[81] Perhaps "every body had concluded" that he "had no use for Money," he joked, or had even "combin'd" together to deprive him of cash.[82] Whatever the reason, late payments could have a domino effect on creditors, who often were left scrambling to pay their own debts.

---

[74] For an example of a handwritten bond, see GD237/10/1/14, SNA.

[75] John Murray to Mother, March 6, 1757, GD 219/287/12, SNA.

[76] Morgan, "Remittance Procedures," 733.   [77] Edelson, *Plantation Enterprise*, 102.

[78] Peter Manigault to Ralph Izard, September 6, 1769, Peter Manigault Letterbook, 1763–1773, Manigault Papers, Box 11/278/7, 100, SCHS.

[79] Robert Baillie to James Baillie, April 9, 1773, GD1/1155/72/4, SNA.

[80] John Murray to Mother, March 6, 1757, GD 219/287/12, SNA; Morgan, "Slave Sales in Colonial Charleston," 924.

[81] Henry Laurens to Smith & Baillies, *HLP* 4: 257.

[82] Henry Laurens to Joseph Brown, April 25, 1766, *HLP* 5: 120–121.

Wealthy creditors like Laurens were better able to absorb these losses than small planters like Robert Baillie. Moving from Jamaica to the Georgia Lowcountry in 1753, Baillie intended to set himself up as a dry goods merchant, but after making a poor showing, he sold his remaining stock and patented 500 acres on the Newport River.[83] Baillie decided to turn planter because he thought it was "by far the surest and most profitable way of Life." Because "the Land itself [was] Daily growing in Value, As Also the Negroes," a plantation was a safe financial bet. However, he was brought to the brink of financial ruin when he purchased slaves on credit, planning to pay for the slaves by calling in "a good Deal of Money due in this Province."[84] His faith in his debtors – who proved "very Backward in payment" – was misplaced, and he struggled to repay his own creditors as a result.[85] If Baillie's father had not intervened to provide financial assistance, he likely would have been forced to sell his "land & negroes" at "a great Disadvantage" in order to satisfy his debts.[86]

As merchants and colonists understood all too well, the financial consequences of late payments could ripple across oceans as well as colonial communities. This was the case when the slave-trading firm of Middleton, Liston, & Hope catastrophically failed in the 1760s. By all outward appearances, the firm seemed prosperous, but the death of partner Thomas Middleton laid bare the fact that its financial "[a]ffairs" were actually "upon the worst Footing." Creditors who picked through the firm's books were shocked by "the Immensity" of its debts, and they scrambled to secure the firm's remaining assets.[87] These included £25,000 owed to the firm by slave purchasers.[88] Although late payments for slaves were not

---

[83] Robert Baillie to James Baillie, November 18, 1753, GD1/1155/66/4, SNA.

[84] Robert Baillie to George Baillie, February 10, 1754, GD1/1155/66/5, SNA.

[85] Even shrewd financial managers could find themselves in this predicament, particularly during periods of economic contraction. In 1766, e.g., Henry Laurens complained, "I have receiv'd Mr. Dubourdeu's Note & if I knew where I would call for the Money for I was never so distress'd in my Life. It seems as if every body had concluded that I had no use for Money. It is certain that they have combin'd (by accident I suppose) not to pay me any this Year, say the past Winter." Henry Laurens to Joseph Brown, April 25, 1766, *HLP* 5: 120–121.

[86] Robert Baillie to George Baillie, May 25, 1754, GD1/1155/66/7, SNA.

[87] Peter Manigault to Robert Udney Janus & Co., July 21, 1767, Manigault Papers, Box 11/278/7, 56, SCHS; Morgan, "Remittance Procedures," 718.

[88] Henry Laurens to William Reeve, September 30, 1767, *HLP* 5: 323. In this complicated agreement, the debtors promised Henry Laurens and his creditor client that they would "surrender themselves & go to Jail, if those Creditors who have sued them & to whom Mr. H. Middleton stands as special Bail shall not drop their Actions & come in upon a footing with other Creditors & that in such case they must & will exclude them wholly.

solely responsible for the firm's collapse, these debts certainly played a role in a sequence of events that "ruined many poor People" from Charlestown to London.[89] Indeed, Middleton, Liston, & Hope's collapse had a negative cascading effect on creditors across the globe, who had bet on the credit-worthiness of far-flung debtors and lost.

For creditors in the transatlantic slave trade, conditional bonds were a legal mechanism that helped them to forestall the financial disaster that late payments threatened. They were part of a broader risk mitigation strategy, one that allowed creditors to shore up the chain of obligations that linked them together before it proved their undoing. In colonial courts, conditional bonds gave these creditors the same procedural advantages that they bestowed in England. Bondholders who sued their debtors in planta-tion colonies could avoid procedural obstacles, availing themselves of a more certain way of proceeding. In South Carolina, for example, colonists "developed a cumbersome, though theoretically sound, pro-debtor policy" that on the whole "obstructed" debt collection.[90] Although creditors could sue in assumpsit, this procedural posture ran the risk of entrapping them in protracted litigation. Debtors in assumpsit could postpone proceedings for months, and at the end of this frustrating process, a local jury would determine damages. Because these twelve men, good and true, were often debtors themselves, they were unlikely to favor creditors against their neighbors and friends.[91]

Creditors who sued in plantation colonies preferred a more certain legal path, one that conditional bonds opened for them. With bond in hand, a plaintiff in South Carolina could bypass assumpsit and instead sue in debt on the bond itself. Victorious bondholders could then obtain an "immedi-ate entry of a judgment," which they could satisfy by suing out a writ of execution and attaching a debtor's goods and chattels.[92] Crucially, this included a debtor's slaves, which creditors could attach and sell in order to offset their losses. Indeed, the fact that slaves were exposed to creditors' claims in plantation colonies made the stakes of debt collection significantly higher for creditors and debtors alike. Because enslaved people were finan-cial assets as well as productive laborers in plantation colonies, this

And such Creditors have all (one excepted) promised to discontinue their several actions." *Ibid.*, 325.

[89] Peter Manigault to [Robert Udney Janus & Co.], October 1, 1767, Manigault Papers, Box 11/278/7, 63, SCHS.

[90] William E. Nelson, *The Common Law in Colonial America, Volume II: The Middle Colonies and the Carolinas, 1660–1730* (New York: Oxford University Press, 2013), 72.

[91] *Ibid.*   [92] *Ibid.*

enhanced their value as collateral and multiplied a creditor's options. Creditors who obtained a judgment and sued out a writ of execution could always choose to attach and resell the slaves, gaining quick access to their market value. This could be a shrewd financial decision. Slaves sold in payment of debts commanded a good price in contrast to slaves sold for committing crimes, and they tended to appreciate in value despite price fluctuations over the course of the eighteenth century.[93] As a practical matter, this meant that creditors would reliably receive a valuable asset that they could sell to make good their losses.

Even when the value of slaves could not be made liquid through sale, though, creditors could still profit from their labor. When slave prices were depressed, creditors could instead choose to put slaves to work on their own plantations, waiting for market conditions to improve before exposing them to sale. Creditors who weighed the current price of slaves against their long-term value and found it wanting might decide this was a wiser course of action. For example, when the firm of Fabre & Price seized a plantation "with 20 Negroes independent of Children," they presented their creditor-client with two choices. Either the creditor could sell the slaves "for Cash & the Plantation at 1 2 & 3 Years Credit taking a mortgage on the Property," or he could use the slaves as laborers on the plantation. Fabre & Price ultimately recommended the latter option, suggesting that if their client "add[ed] 40 Hands to the 20" seized slaves, they could make "2 to 300 Barrells of Rice" before clearing unproductive swamp land, and "5 to 600 Barrells" after.[94] They advised their client to take a longer view, to forego immediate gratification, and instead bet that the price of rice and the price of slaves would continue to rise.

As creditors understood, conditional bonds maximized their flexibility to recoup losses when a debtor defaulted by giving them access to

---

[93] Laurens himself believed that debt slaves were a good bargain, and he specifically instructed his confederates in Jamaica to purchase them if they saw "a good opportunity." Henry Laurens to Richard Todd, September 23, 1767, *HLP* 5: 310. Between 1722 and 1775, "the (constant dollar) price of slaves increased at an estimated 1.45 percent per year, which is significantly different from the annual 0.82 percent increase in the Caribbean." David Eltis, Frank D. Lewis, and David Richardson, "Slave Prices, the African Slave Trade, and Productivity in Eighteenth-Century South Carolina: A Reassessment," *The Journal of Economic History* 66 (2006): 1057. Eltis, Lewis, and Richardson also found that the "real" slave price – a price deflated to account for export prices – "began to increase in the early 1740s" and more than doubled by the time of the American Revolution. *Ibid.*, 1060.

[94] Fabre & Price to Charles Goodwin and William Thomas, January 4, 1791, Add MS 85477, BL.

a debtor's slaves. These advantages were enough to prompt slave merchants, beginning with the Royal African Company, to require factors like Thomas Howard and Patrick Thompson, "of the Island of Barbados in the West Indies Merchants," to secure slave consignments with bonds.[95] Company agents and factors also required bonds from colonial purchasers, who typically paid cash, commodities, or other goods up front and secured remaining balances with bonds due in three, six, nine, or twelve months.[96] Conditional bonds even underwrote the relatively minor transactions that facilitated commercial activity aboard slave ships, securing loans to mariners and other extensions of credit.[97] For example, when Edward Elliott joined the *Africa* Galley as a "Chirgueon" in 1700, he borrowed 25 pounds "to provide himself" on the voyage and secured this debt with a conditional bond.[98]

By 1700, the Royal African Company had refined a system of credit-based slave trading, one in which conditional bonds secured nearly every financial transaction that linked forts on the African coast to purchasers in plantation colonies.[99] The practice of using conditional bonds continued into the eighteenth century, as private slave-trading firms came to dominate Britain's share of the transatlantic slave trade. In the 1730s and 1740s, conditional bonds became a particularly important component of a broader response to the problem of mounting colonial debts. As commodity prices declined and King George's War (1744–1748) set "insurance and freight rates soaring," the ensuing economic downturn made it difficult for plantation colonists in particular to pay their debts to British merchants.[100] The Debt Recovery Act of 1732 was one part of a broader effort to provide a remedy for British merchants and to prevent colonial debtors from avoiding their financial obligations.[101] As we have already seen, the act reflected the concerns of

---

[95] July 30, 1719 Affidavit, CLA/029/06/051, LMA.

[96] Jacob M. Price, "Credit in the Slave Trade and Plantation Economies," in *Slavery and the Rise of the Atlantic System,* edited by Barbara Solow (Cambridge: Cambridge University Press, 1991), 300. The Royal African Company itself also took out loans that it secured with bonds. By 1710, it had borrowed approximately 300,000 to 400,000. *Ibid.,* 301.

[97] Rediker, *Between the Devil and the Deep Blue Sea,* 125.

[98] Bill of Complaint and Answer in *Westmore v. Beadle,* 1701, CLA/024/07, LMA.

[99] Price, "Credit in the Slave Trade and Plantation Economies," 305.

[100] Stuart O. Stumpf, "Implications of King George's War for the Charleston Mercantile Community," *SCHM* 77 (1976): 169.

[101] Claire Priest, "Creating an American Property Law: Alienability and Its Limits in American History," *Harvard Law Review* 120 (2006): 389. As Richard Sheridan explains, the Debt Recovery Act prompted criticisms in England because it seemed to promote slave auctions. In 1797, William Knox "pushed through a bill in Parliament . . . to repeal as much of the Credit Act as made Negroes chattels for the payment of debts."

merchants, who operated in a credit-based transatlantic economy, that colonists had used (or might use) local statutes to reclassify slaves as real estate and therefore limit their ability to seize them in payment of debts. Whereas colonial factors previously had been unable to seize real estate – including slaves categorized as real estate – after the passage of the act they now could seize most types of colonial property. Debts, including those incurred for buying slaves, also would be secured by bonds, which could be sued upon in colonial courts.[102]

Ultimately, the act "tightened up" credit practices in the slave trade and led to a greater reliance on conditional bonds in South Carolina. Because slave factors could be assured a legal remedy against colonial debtors, British slave-trading firms began to require factors to enter into contracts obligating them to remit two-thirds of a sale's proceeds within one year and the remainder within two years. In turn, Charlestown-based factors sought more guarantees from purchasers in the form of a conditional bond.[103] Changing commercial practices in the slave trade also reinforced an economic logic that drove the use of bonds. Even as Parliament debated the Debt Recovery Act, British slave merchants themselves were already tightening their credit practices in response to the economic downturn. The result was the "guarantee" or "bills in the bottom system," which began in the West Indies and migrated to Charlestown. When a slave-trading vessel returned to England, colonial factors were increasingly expected to remit whatever commodities they had received from slave purchasers, along with bills of exchange drawn on the factor's own surety for the balance. The point of this overhaul was to make factors legally accountable for sending remittances to London-based slave merchants and at the same time to shift the burden of extending credit from British merchants to colonial slave factors. Unsurprisingly, factors responded to increased financial pressure by requiring slave purchasers to execute conditional bonds. In South Carolina, these typically were due in eighteenth months, which allowed a planter ample time to profit from the next year's crop. However, if he failed to pay, the factor expected a debtor to execute a bond due in another year, which carried a 10-percent penalty.[104] Jamaican factors also required their purchasers to

---

Richard B. Sheridan, *Sugar and Slavery: An Economic History of the British West Indies, 1632–1775* (Baltimore: Johns Hopkins University Press, 1973), 289.

[102] Morgan, "Remittance Procedures," 720.

[103] Price, "Credit in the Slave Trade and Plantation Economies," 311.

[104] *Ibid.*, 311, 313.

execute a conditional bond, a practice that was common by the 1760s. As one Jamaican explained to his correspondent, who was "a Stranger to ye Guinea Trade," slave buyers there also gave the local "Guinea Factor" a "Bond payable in Two or Three Months" in order to secure their sales.[105]

Taken together, the widespread reliance on conditional bonds reinforced the slave trade's most vulnerable junctures by guaranteeing factors legal remedies and therefore increasing pressure on debtors to pay for their slaves on time. Colonial planters may have found the Debt Recovery Act and the tightening of credit practices in the slave trade "deeply offensive," but these changes worked in their favor. British merchants and colonial factors responded to these more creditor-friendly conditions by expanding credit in plantation colonies.[106] Colonists, in turn, took advantage of improving economic conditions in the 1740s to purchase even more enslaved laborers on credit.[107]

LOCAL BONDS

If plantation colonists ultimately benefited from the overhaul of credit practices in the slave trade, they were also aware that conditional bonds were far from a metropolitan innovation, their grievances notwithstanding. In fact, planters and merchants had long relied upon conditional bonds to secure local slave sales, realizing their procedural benefits decades before the Debt Recovery Act's passage. It is often easy to miss the use of bonds in local slave sales. Just as conditional bonds in England did not typically describe an underlying transaction, bonds used to purchase slaves are difficult to distinguish from those that secured other types of agreements, as we have already seen with the Baker bond. Nonetheless, court records, correspondence, and other evidence reveal that slave owners relied upon conditional bonds to secure local slave sales from an early date. In 1718, for example, Landgrave Thomas Smith executed a conditional bond in order to secure his purchase of "Twenty Eight Negroe Slaves" from Richard Beresford, who happened to be the province's chancellor. Smith had purchased the slaves in exchange for "Twenty

[105] Anonymous to John Fisher, June 22, 1763, LMA; Morgan, "Remittance Procedures," 739.
[106] Price, "Credit in the Slave Trade and Plantation Economies," 309; Morgan, "Remittance Procedures," 720.
[107] Priest, "Creating an American Property Law," 434.

Three hundred and Sixty Barrells of Tarr," and he sought relief in South
Carolina's Chancery Court after Beresford threatened to "sue execution"
in the Court of Common Pleas and attach his "goods and chattels."[108]

Smith sought a reprieve in Chancery because he, like other colonists,
feared the remedy that bonds provided to creditors – the power to attach
and sell personal property, including slaves. Indeed, conditional bonds
were a particularly effective way to pressure slave owners to pay their
debts, and they remained a staple of local commercial life into the eighteenth century. Like colonial factors, plantation colonists relied upon
bonds to secure intercolonial slave sales. As we have already seen,
Richard Bohun Baker used a conditional bond to secure the slave sale
that opened this chapter. Ralph Izard also executed a conditional bond to
secure a purchase of slaves from colonist William Henry Drayton.[109] And
Henry Laurens routinely required purchasers of his own personal slaves to
give a bond as security. This was the case in 1764, when Laurens ordered
his agent to sell a slave "named Abram" "for ready Money or upon Bond
& security with Interest." According to Laurens, Abram had made "some
pernicious connexions" in Charlestown, which he feared would have
a "very bad effect upon the manners" of his other slaves.[110] Laurens
sold a runaway slave named Sampson in 1765 for similar reasons, and
he structured the transaction in a similar way. His agent, Joseph Brown,
was to sell Sampson "to a safe hand for the best price" possible and to
send "the proceeds in Money or Bond."[111]

Plantation colonists like Laurens relied upon conditional bonds to
secure slave sales in their capacity as individual slave owners, but institutions in plantation colonies also expected slave purchasers to execute
bonds. As nineteenth-century historians have clearly demonstrated, chattel slavery benefitted groups and institutions beyond white southern slave
owners, from churches to schools. This trend had colonial antecedents.
Indeed, colonial courts in plantation colonies were particularly active in
selling slaves. South Carolina's Vice Admiralty Court, for example, routinely condemned and sold slaves that were found aboard enemy ships or
pirate vessels. When colonists purchased slaves in court-ordered sales,

[108] *Landgrave Thomas Smith v. Richard Beresford and Richard Splatt,* August 15, 1720,
Chancery Case Papers, 1700–1791, Court of Chancery Bundle 1717–1720, No. 17,
S142001, 260, SCDAH.
[109] Peter Manigault to Ralph Izard, September 6, 1769, Peter Manigault Letterbook,
1763–1773, Manigault Papers, Box 11/278/7, 100, SCHS.
[110] Henry Laurens to George Dick, June 1764, *HLP* 4: 298–299.
[111] Henry Laurens to Joseph Brown, June 28, 1765, *HLP* 4: 645.

they executed conditional bonds in order to ensure that they complied with the terms of payments. This was the case in 1739, when John Parish bought "three Negro Men Slaves Names Francis Quaro and Quash" and secured his purchase with a bond. Requiring a bond in this case proved farsighted: Parris defaulted on the debt and returned the slaves to the court, which sold the three men yet again.[112]

Colonial courts and individual colonists relied upon conditional bonds to secure their slave sales, but bonds were also useful in securing other transactions. Regardless of the nature of the underlying agreement, conditional bonds gave creditors access to a colonist's slaves, and this enhanced their value as security in a wide variety of commercial contexts. For example, colonists used conditional bonds to secure loan agreements, including an agreement that Anne Rowsham's husband made before he was "barbarously murdered Intestate" by "the Indians."[113] Conditional bonds also secure sales of commodities and other goods, like the cabinets that Jamaican merchant Joshua Wright ordered from a London firm in 1715.[114] Finally, colonists used conditional bonds to secure their real estate sales. For example, when merchant John Rose purchased "warfes & Stores with 340 Acers of land" in South Carolina – "the Most Valueable purchase" he had made since he "lived in this Cuntry" – he secured the balance due with a conditional bond at 8 percent interest.[115]

Because conditional bonds were ubiquitous in the commercial life of plantation societies, they were also ubiquitous in death. Bonds make a regular appearance in colonial estate records, where they were accounted as part of a decedent's personal property. For example, when Henry Laurens's father died in 1747, his inventory enumerated bonds and notes along with slaves and dry goods.[116] Conditional bonds also feature prominently in disputes over decedents' estates, as supposed heirs clashed over their conflicting claims to a relative's personal property. For example, in 1719, George and Mary Flood asked South Carolina's Chancery Court to force Mary's stepmother to account for her late father's "goods and

---

[112] January 23, 1739, South Carolina Vice-Admiralty Court Records, 1736–149, C–D vols., photostats of originals, AC4205, Box 4, 262, LOC.

[113] *Anne Rowsham v. Robert Dewes, Executor of William Rowsham, Sr.*, filed June 7, 1717, in Anne King Gregorie, ed., *Records of the Court of Chancery of South Carolina, 1671–1779* (Washington: American Historical Association, 1950), 204.

[114] Conditional bond, March 25, 1715, CLA/024/06/052, LMA.

[115] John Rose to Uncle [Mr. Charles Irvine], Charlestown October 6, 1753, Rose Letters, LOC.

[116] Inventory of John Laurens, recorded September 12, 1747, *HLP* 1: 369–381.

Chattles," which were "of very Considerable Value." The decedent's estate included "Money Bonds Bills, promissory Notes," and "book debts," in addition to "Negroes Houshold Stuff" and "Plantation Tools."[117] South Carolina colonist Sarah Fenwicke also died with a "very Considerable Personal Estate" for her relatives to divide, including "Debts due for Rent, Arrear and By Bonds, Judgments, Mortgages, and other Securities, and by Simple Contract."[118] And Jamaican colonist, Thomas Ashburne, claimed a share of his father-in-law's personal estate, including his "Specialties and other securities."[119]

When plantation colonists died with accounts due, their heirs squabbled over who should have the right to them. Debts – especially conditional bonds – seemed worth the fight because they conveyed access in life as well as in death to a legal process that could result in the attachment of a debtor's slaves. As a result, plantation colonists aggressively laid claim to the bits of paper that memorialized a decedent's debts. Indeed, estate litigation in plantation colonies reveals the extent to which slave owners' wealth was built on paper, amassed as they bought the lives and suffering of countless enslaved people on credit.

FOLLOWING FORM

Given the widespread use of conditional bonds and other forms of paper debt in plantation America, it is not surprising that colonists there eagerly availed themselves of the standardized and printed bond forms that began to drift across the Atlantic in the eighteenth century. As we have already seen, printed blank law forms were available to London merchants and consumers by the early eighteenth century, who used them to facilitate low-cost commercial transactions and take advantage of fast-paced markets. These forms were a boon to Britons throughout the globe, but they were particularly helpful for slave-owning colonists. Indeed, the day-to-day activities of managing plantations and slaves required plantation colonists to conduct countless routine commercial and legal transactions.

---

[117] *George and Mary Flood* v. *Johanna Baker, Administratrix of Thomas Baker*, filed July 23, 1719, in Gregorie, ed., Records of the Court of Chancery of South Carolina, 252.
[118] *Elizabeth and Mary Clapp* v. *Hugh Hext, Executor of Fenwicke*, filed September 23, 1728, Court of Chancery Bundle 1721–1735 Nos. 1–13, No. 8, Oversize; S142001, SCDAH.
[119] *Ashburne* v. *Archbould*, April 14, 1711, Chancery Court Papers, REF 1A/3/5, JNA. A "specialty" was another way to refer to a sealed instrument, which included conditional bonds.

They bought and sold slaves and commodities, hired out slaves and plant-ations, wrote wills, administered estates, penned bills of exchange, drafted powers of attorney, and negotiated agreements of all sorts. Although wealthier colonists could avail themselves of skilled legal practitioners, many colonists conducted these tasks themselves, becoming legal experts in order to reduce their transaction costs. Henry Laurens, for example, preferred to transact his own business without going to "the trouble & expence" of a lawyer, vowing "never ask" for professional legal help where he could "possibly avoid it."[120] Eliza Lucas Pinckney likewise may have demurred that the "cramped phrases" of English legal treatises gave her trouble, but in reality she was an accomplished legal draftswoman. As she giddily confided to a friend, she had already "made two wills" and knew "how to convey by will Estates real and personal," all without forgetting to add "in its proper place, him and his heirs for Ever."[121]

Pinckney and Laurens were among South Carolina's most elite planters, but their legal acumen was typical of slave-owning colonists from less-privileged financial backgrounds. These ordinary men and women eagerly sought practical legal information, especially when it facilitated low-cost transactions involving slaves. Some achieved a remarkable degree of legal proficiency in this regard. For example, when colonist Arthur Matthews prevented the Provost Marshal from seizing "Some Negros" that had been mortgaged to him, he was certain that he had conformed "in all Cases as the Law Directs in Relations to Negros under Mortgage." Satisfied – according to his own interpretation of the law – that his actions had been proper, he even dared the marshal to try again. The "[g]entlemen that has Directed you to Sease right or wrong may Com on Me for the Slaves," he threatened, but Matthews would "[d]efend them" until he was "[s]attisfied."[122]

We do not know whether Matthews successfully prevented the officer from taking the mortgaged slaves, but his hastily scrawled letter betrays his acute awareness of how the law of credit and debt worked in practice. Other South Carolina colonists displayed an equally impressive command of the basics of legal drafting, relying on templates to guide them as they wrote wills, contracts, bills of sale, and powers of attorney. For example, planter David Anderson drafted an agreement with his overseer, Paul

---

[120] Henry Laurens to James Donnam, July 4, 1763, *HLP* 3: 487.
[121] Eliza Lucas Pinckney to [Miss Bartlett] [c. June 1742], Elise Pinckney, ed., *The Letterbook of Eliza Lucas Pinckney, 1739–1762* (Columbia: University of South Carolina Press, 1972), 41.
[122] Arthur Matthews to Samuel Hurst, Esq., March 1, 1743, S205002, SCDAH.

Villepontoux, in which the two men "[c]onsent[ed] & agree[ed]" to "[p]lant Corn Rice &c. Jointly" and to divide the crop fairly. Villepontoux also wrote his own agreements, copying them by hand into his plantation diary in order to maintain an accurate record. In 1775, for example, he "agreed with Mr. Peter Harison to over See" two plantations "for the Consideration of Two hundred Pounds Currency per year to begin from the Date hereof." The arrangement entitled Villepontoux to an "[e]qual Share for Four negroes of all produce Sent to market or Sold off the plantation." He also could claim "half the Hoggs Raised on the plantation" but only "after allowing for or paying for half the old Stock to be Valued by indifferent persons."[123]

Villepontoux's use of legal terms (or terms that sounded legal) – including "[c]onsideration," "hereof," and "indifferent persons" – is striking, but not unusual. When plantation colonists drafted their own legal documents, they often included stock phrases or legal jargon. They may have believed that this language was necessary to accomplish their legal objectives, whether based upon previous experience or advice gleaned from practical law manuals. Others may have deployed legal language to make their documents sound more formal and therefore more authoritative. For example, when Elizabeth Elliott disposed of her assets in a letter to her children, the document in no way resembled the formal wills typical of Lowcountry planters. Nonetheless, Elliott's tone and word choice conveyed formality, as befit a document that she hoped would command respect at the hour of her death. Elliott left all of her money – located "in a jugg" in her "[c]losett up Stair" – to her four daughters, directing that it should "be equally divided as they all agree between themselves" as "[p]ockett money for their own use." She only lamented that she did not have "more" to leave them.[124] In this brief letter, Elliott frankly and poignantly acknowledged her humble financial circumstances. At the same time, she deployed formal, legal-sounding words like "equally divided" and "for their own use," perhaps to burnish the otherwise depressing reality that she did not have much to give. She understood on some level that these words would command the reader's respect and ensure that her wishes were honored when she was no longer present to enforce them.

Although Elliott may have lacked a formal legal education, she and countless plantation colonists like her were "legal literates" who displayed

---

[123] Allston Family Papers, Box 1164.01, 12/6/26, Paul Villepontoux's Book, 1774–1777, February 1 or 7, 1775, SCHS.
[124] Elizabeth Elliott, January 4, 1760, Baker Family Papers, 11/537/4, SCHS.

a surprisingly deep understanding of their colony's "laws and legal process." They managed their commercial affairs without a lawyer's aid, and they also grasped the enduring power of English law's language – its ability to command respect, unlock remedies, and direct action.[125] Indeed, plantation colonists understood that legal tropes and catchphrases had legal resonance, even if they lacked a distinctive legal meaning. Whether they deployed legal language properly or not, they placed their abiding faith in its transformative power. Proper legal words could accomplish impressive legal feats, changing mere suggestions into binding commands. And if they did not, they at least imparted a veneer of respectability to quotidian activities, cloaking their actions and directives in the majesty of law. This logic was powerful, and it flowed almost inexorably from the fact that plantation colonists were part of, not separate from, a wider Anglo-American legal culture. This was a culture that reified form, imbuing the proper combination of legal words with near-magical powers to bind and compel. When plantation colonists used terms like "consideration," we cannot know whether their linguistic choices were deliberate. Nonetheless, their inclusion of these terms suggests their immersion in English law, in its wash of words and sounds. Ordinary colonists may not have precisely grasped the legal meaning of these words, but they certainly understood their cultural power.

Plantation colonists' reverence for the language of English law reached its logical conclusion in the printed legal documents that helped them to reduce transaction costs and avoid costly errors that could result from poor draftsmanship. In printed legal forms, plantation colonists encountered English law's operative words, packaged and presented in a way that seemed to remove all doubt and uncertainty. By simply purchasing a form and filling in the blanks, every colonist could be his own lawyer. South Carolina's slaveholders were especially precocious in embracing the print revolution's legal byproducts. Printed legal forms like conditional bonds began to appear in the province as early as the 1720s, and by the 1730s, colonists could buy blank bonds and other law forms of local provenance. Indeed, the colony's first printer, Eleazar Phillips, Jr., printed and sold them from his Charlestown storefront to consumers eager to transact their routine business without a lawyer's aid.[126]

---

[125] Mary Sarah Bilder, "The Lost Lawyers: Early American Legal Literates and Transatlantic Legal Culture," *Yale Journal of Law and the Humanities* 11 (1999): 60.

[126] See, e.g., three printed writs of attachment for the body issued in name of George II, July 1, 1740, Balzano Collection, 110.20 (Misc. MSS), SCHS; see, e.g., conditional bond, February 1, 1754, TP Ravenel, 12/316/7, SCHS.

It is difficult to know with any certainty how often plantation colonists used printed bonds to secure their transactions. The instruments themselves are scattered throughout the globe in court records, personal correspondence, estate accounts, and ephemera, and this makes them difficult to find, much less count. However, it does seem that South Carolina colonists used printed and handwritten bonds interchangeably, oscillating between the two forms for reasons that remain unclear. Richard Bohun Baker, for example, relied upon both printed and handwritten bonds to conduct his commercial affairs. In 1761, he used a printed bond form to secure an agreement with Benjamin Smith and Miles Brewton, and he again relied upon a printed bond in 1776.[127] However, the bond that secured the 1779 slave sale that opened this chapter was drafted by hand. We can surmise that Baker wrote out this particular bond because the Revolutionary War made it difficult to procure printed legal forms. In most instances, though, it is nearly impossible to determine why a colonist used one medium or another, or even if they made a conscious choice. Projecting our modern conviction about the superiority of print on the past, we might assume that colonists preferred printed legal forms when they were available. However, the fact that handwritten bonds continued to circulate through the end of the colonial period in places like South Carolina suggests a more complicated reality. Colonists may have considered printed legal forms problematic for a variety of reasons, including the fact that they were as vulnerable to mistake and manipulation as the handwritten forms they never fully replaced. Indeed, printed legal forms were not perfect instruments, as we have already seen. Henry Laurens learned this sobering lesson in 1764, when a debtor "filled up" a blank bond form "contrary" to his advice, and with total disregard *"to a form"* that Laurens *"gave him* for that purpose." It seems that Laurens had carefully orchestrated the drafting process from start to finish, coaching the debtor about what to write and providing him with a template to follow. Despite these considerable efforts, the debtor still managed to disappoint his expectations. Rather than stipulating repayment in a form of currency that Laurens preferred, he included a payment method of his own choosing.[128]

As Henry Laurens and other colonists discovered, even printed legal documents could fail to bind when debtors refused to follow form.

---

[127] January 5, 1761, Baker Family Papers, 1138.00, 11/535/18, SCHS; June 19, 1776, Baker Family Papers, 1138.00, 11/535/25, SCHS.
[128] Henry Laurens to William Hodshon, February 24, 1764, *HLP* 4: 180–181.

Standardized and printed legal forms remained open to acts of creativity, agency, and even resistance in plantation colonies, just as they did in England. Nonetheless, printed legal documents offered significant advantages to colonial slaveholders, despite these drawbacks. In fact, the timing of their appearance in South Carolina suggests an intimate and complicated relationship between printed legal forms and the colony's booming slave economy. Blank bond forms began to appear in the colony just as credit practices in the slave trade began to change, and likely in order to satisfy increased demand for the bonds that factors increasingly required to secure slave purchases on credit. The proliferation of bonds forms into the 1740s, in turn, made it easier for plantation colonists of all sorts – not just creole elites – to take advantage of improving credit conditions and invest in slaves. Because printers included all of the operative legal language, even colonists with little legal knowledge could use printed bond forms to buy slaves, and they could reliably expect these forms to be legally binding. Giving more colonists access to the Black bodies that would become their most significant form of wealth and the key to their pre-Revolutionary economic success, printed conditional bond forms worked in the long term to deepen colonists' commitment to chattel slavery.

More subtly, printed legal forms like conditional bonds also may have helped to insulate slave owners from contemplating the consequences of their actions. If standardized legal forms like conditional bonds reduced transaction costs, they also reduced friction, effectively absolving parties from scrutinizing their choices. These documents required little critical inquiry from the colonists that benefitted from them, because they made it relatively simple for parties to fill-in-the-blanks while ignoring the substance of any given transaction. In a legal system in which adherence to form was of paramount importance, this made practical sense, but it also meant that there was little incentive for slave-owning colonists to pause and consider whether English legal forms *should* accommodate human property. As a matter of law, these forms *could* accommodate human property.

This was a desirable consequence of the decision to classify slaves as chattel property from the perspective of slave owners. By making slaves personal property, plantation colonists bought themselves access to Britain's Empire of Paper, including the host of legal and commercial documents generated by the commercial and print revolutions. As long as colonists adhered to the form of these forms, neither courts nor other colonists would scrutinize their quiet acts of adaptation. Neither did slave owners themselves. Preprinted conditional bonds and other printed law forms that circulated in slave societies therefore challenge common characterizations about the consequences of print's expansion in the eighteenth century. Whereas the proliferation of print traditionally has been viewed as a positive force for the development of a broader public sphere, wider access to printed legal forms also facilitated the sale of slaves, serving the practical needs of slaveholders or aspiring slaveholders.[129]

[129] For a generally positive view of print's role in early New England's religious and political culture, see David Hall, *Worlds of Wonder, Days of Judgment: Popular Religious Belief in Early New England* (Cambridge: Harvard University Press, 1990) and Stephen Innes, *Creating the Commonwealth: The Economic Culture of Puritan New England* (New York: Norton, 1995). On the role of print in facilitating the growth of transatlantic merchant networks, see Peter E. Pope, *Fish into Wine: The Newfoundland Plantation in the Seventeenth Century* (Chapel Hill: UNC Press, 2003). For the function of print during the imperial crisis and in the development of American nationalism, see David Waldstreicher, "Rites of Rebellion, Rituals of Assent: Celebration, Print Culture, and the Origins of American Nationalism," *Journal of American History* 82 (1995): 37–61. See also Nathan O. Hatch, *The Democratization of American Christianity* (New Haven: Yale University Press, 1989) for the influence of print in early republic religious expansion. But see Clare Lyons, *Sex among the Rabble: An Intimate History of Gender and Power in the Age of Revolution, Philadelphia, 1730–1830* (Chapel Hill: UNC Press, 2006) for a discussion of the role of print in curtailing female agency in early republic Philadelphia.

For a discussion of the link between rising literacy rates and London crowd politics in early modern England, see Tim Harris, *London Crowds in the Reign of Charles II: Propaganda and Politics from the Restoration until the Exclusion Crisis* (Cambridge: Cambridge University Press, 1987). Harris, however, also helpfully reminds scholars of the enduring importance of oral culture in the growth of early modern England's public sphere. Tim Harris, "Understanding Popular Politics in Restoration Britain," in *A Nation Transformed: England after the Restoration*, edited by Alan Houston and Steve Pincus (Cambridge: Cambridge University Press, 2001), 125–153. An analysis of literacy's expansion and its connection to the "decline of magic" is contained in Keith Thomas, *Religion and the Decline of Magic* (New York: Scribner, 1971). Christopher Hill approvingly links the growth of political radicalism to increased access to print in *The World Turned Upside Down: Radical Ideas during the English Revolution* (London: Temple Smith, 1972). Kevin Sharpe, in *Remapping Early Modern England: The Culture of Seventeenth-Century Politics* (Cambridge: Cambridge University Press, 2000), explains how the growth of print culture helped to democratize royal words. But see Kevin Sharpe, *Reading Revolution: The Politics of Reading in Early Modern England* (Yale: Yale University Press, 2000), which depicts print as ambivalent, both extending and mediating royal authority. Mark Knights links the expansion of print culture to the development of political parties and the construction of a "public" in *Representation and Misrepresentation in Later Stuart Britain: Partisanship and Political Culture* (Oxford: Oxford University Press, 2005). And Linda Colley discusses the importance of print to the eighteenth-century British Empire in *Britons: Forging the Nation: 1707–1837* (Yale: Yale University Press, 1992).

THE DANCE OF CREDIT AND DEBT

When Richard Bohun Baker secured his slave sale with a conditional bond, the transaction was unlikely to provoke interest. By the final decades of the eighteenth century, conditional bonds had become an unremarkable part of commercial life in plantation colonies, where they secured slave sales and wide variety of other commercial transactions. The conditional bonds that plantation colonists used were identical to their English antecedents, in form as well as content, and creditors asked their colonial debtors to execute conditional bonds for the same reasons that creditors required them of English debtors: because bonds provided a legally enforceable way of holding debtors to account. Across thousands of nautical miles, bonds proved to be remarkably resilient, retaining their power to give creditors legal remedies in common law courts across the globe.

Although following conditional bonds across the Atlantic illustrates that the forms and practices of English law easily accommodated chattel slavery, watching creditors and debtors interact in planation colonies also reminds us that chattel profoundly shaped creditor-debtor relations on the ground. Conditional bonds in South Carolina looked the same as conditional bonds in England, and they were used to accomplish similar objectives, but they reverberated differently in practice. The dual nature of human property – the fact that slaves were both productive laborers and financial assets – profoundly shaped the legal choices of creditors and debtors who bargained in the shadow of a law that assumed people were property.

At first glance, conditional bonds seemed to favor creditors in plantation colonies by giving them access to a debtor's slaves. As we have already seen, the ability to attach slaves gave creditors the flexibility to sell slaves or put them to work on plantations, depending upon the specific economic circumstances. Creditors appreciated this flexibility, but they also understood that enslaved people were not a perfect form of security. Indeed, the very characteristics of human property that made slaves appealing to creditors also made them a risky form of collateral. Plantation colonists may have classified slaves as chattel property, compared them to livestock, and slotted them into English legal forms, but in their daily lives they were confronted with tangible evidence that human property was different. As a primary matter, slaves themselves constantly belied the legal fiction inherent in chattel slavery by running away in order to preempt their attachment and sale. It was difficult for enslaved people – who were denied access to important legal information – to navigate the dense web of creditor-debtor relationships in plantation societies. Nonetheless, slaves developed resistance strategies and protected themselves and their families when they could, whether by running away to avoid sale or shaping the conditions of sale.

Enslaved people stole themselves, but debtors also thwarted their creditors when insolvency loomed. Slave-owning colonists proved particularly adept at maneuvering within a legal reality in which the physical possession of slaves often could prove more significant than judicial fiat. Indeed, conditional bonds technically gave creditors access to a debtor's slaves, but this remedy was meaningless when debtors concealed slaves or moved them beyond the law's reach. As a result, insolvent colonists used fair means and foul to prevent the attachment of their slaves. Jonathan Atcheson, for example, tried to "carry off every one" of his slaves in the middle of the night, to the horror of his creditors.[130] Andrew DeLavillette, a Georgetown merchant who owed "a large Sum" of money to the firm of Austin & Laurens, also escaped with his thirty slaves to the West Indies. Acting "a very ungenerous part," DeLavillette slipped out of the province and sailed to Antigua, where the law and Henry Laurens were unlikely to reach him.[131] Spanish Florida and the South Carolina backcountry (which lacked courts until the early republic period) were particularly popular destinations for debtors, who found that blurred jurisdictional boundaries worked to their advantage. Fabre & Price were concerned that one planter might "fly" with his slaves "over to the Spaniards or Perhaps over the blue Mountains" if they pressed him too hard for payments. The backcountry, they complained, had "become a fashionable resort" for indebted planters, who retreated west in order to avoid their obligations. When slave owners expected an "executi[on] against them," they would "decamp with all their movables 4 to 500 Miles back," where they could buy land "for a Trifling consideration" and live "at ease & Freedom so far as to keep their Creditors at defiance."[132]

Creditors and their agents like Fabre & Price were aware that they could bid "farewell to any Recovery of Debts" when debtors absconded with their slaves.[133] Although a South Carolina statute authorized

---

[130] James Mickie to Sir Alexander Nisbet, March 29, 1747, GD237/1/154/3, SNA.
[131] Austin & Laurens [Henry Laurens] to Robert Stuart, April 28, 1756, *HLP* 2: 174–175.
[132] Fabre & Price to Charles Goodwin and William Thomas, January 4, 1791, Add MS 85477, BL.
[133] *Ibid.*

creditors to attach any "money, goods, or chattels" that remained in the province after debtors fled, these sorts of remedies would have been of limited practical utility when colonists took their most valuable moveable property with them. The advantages that conditional bonds gave them ran up against the practical reality that their legal remedies were limited in plantation colonies. Because slaves were moveable property that could also be moved beyond the law's reach, it was relatively simple for debtors to prevent creditors from realizing the benefits that conditional bonds technically bestowed. As a result, creditors often stood to benefit more from reaching an agreement with debtors who were willing to assign their possessions (including their outstanding debts) in exchange for a discharge. These types of private agreements were "the Mode" in plantation colonies like South Carolina, and bondholders and judgment creditors usually were paid before unsecured creditors. For example, when Middleton, Liston, & Hope failed, the firm's creditors agreed to pay bondholders and judgment creditors before the simple contract creditors, who were unlikely to recover anything.[134] When South Carolina debtor Samuel Peronneau died in 1768 much to the "Surprize of every Body," his contract creditors knew that they would not see a shilling, because Peronneau departed the world "without enough to Satisfy his Judgment Creditors," who would claim priority.[135] Certainly, conditional bonds did not guarantee payment. Nonetheless, they entrenched creditors at the top of the colonial debt hierarchy, giving them at least some chance of recovering their losses in non-litigated settlements. This, in turn, increased pressure on bondholding creditors to avoid litigation and its risks.

In fact, creditors and debtors alike preferred to resolve their disputes in a way that left debtors in possession of their slaves. When debtors fell behind in payments, the creditor's first step was not a lawsuit, but a demand of additional security that typically took the form of a slave mortgage. As scholars have shown, plantation colonists mortgaged slaves for various reasons, including to secure preexisting debts.[136] This was

---

[134] Henry Laurens to William Reeve, September 30, 1767, *HLP* 5: 324. For a discussion of this bankruptcy, see also Morgan, "Remittance Procedures," 726.

[135] Peter Manigault to Isaac King, December 20, 1768, Peter Manigault Letterbook, 1763–1773, Manigault Papers, 11/278/7, 87, SCHS.

[136] See, e.g., Bonnie Martin, "Slavery's Invisible Engine: Mortgaging Human Property," *The Journal of Southern History* 76 (2010): 817–866; Russell R. Menard, "Financing the Lowcountry Export Boom: Capital and Growth in Early Carolina," *WMQ*, 3rd ser. 51 (1994): 659–676; David Hancock, "'Capital and Credit with Approved Security':

particularly common in the West Indies, where mortgages constituted "the last stage in the ontogeny of debt: book debt, bond, judgment mortgage." When West Indian debtors failed to discharge their conditional bonds, they could offer their creditors a mortgage of land, slaves, or some combination of both in order to "forestall action on the judgment."[137] South Carolina debtors used slave mortgages to secure their preexisting debts less frequently, but the practice was far from unusual.[138] For example, when a debtor failed to discharge his bond, Henry Laurens asked him to secure the debt "by Mortgage or personal security." In this case, Laurens directed his agent to accept delivery of "as many Negroes," as the agent thought, were "worth the Amount of said principal Ballance."[139] In 1747, colonist Jonathan Atcheson likewise agreed to mortgage all of his slaves in order to better secure his creditors.[140]

Demanding a slave mortgage at the first sign of trouble was a wise decision because it improved a creditor's chances of seizing slaves as opposed to other, less-valuable personal property, if a debtor defaulted. As Henry Laurens knew, mortgages also allowed creditors to specify which slaves (or their collective value) would serve as collateral, listing enslaved people by name. This reassured creditors that if a debtor defaulted, they could attach slaves with a value that roughly equaled the amount of the loss.[141] Slave mortgages could be an effective way, then, for creditors to increase pressure on their debtors to pay their debts on time. But stiffening a bond with a mortgage also benefitted debtors, allowing them to put off the day of reckoning and continue feeding hopes that the next crop would finally clear their debts. This strategy bought debtors valuable time to profit from the labor of mortgaged slaves, which ultimately improved their chances of extracting themselves from their financial predicaments. In pleading with their creditors to keep plantations and slaves intact, debtors relied upon the argument that doing so was in the creditor's best interest as well as their own. As Robert Baillie explained, he

Financial Markets in Montserrat and South Carolina, 1748–1775," *Business and Economic History* 23 (1994): 61–84.

[137] Price, "Credit in the Slave Trade and Plantation Economies," 325.
[138] Russel Menard has found that mortgages securing a preexisting debt made up only 5 to 9 percent of mortgages in South Carolina. Menard, "Financing the Lowcountry Export Boom," 674.
[139] Henry Laurens to Roger Moore, December 14, 1747, *HLP*, vol. 1, 89–90. Laurens also obtained a mortgage of a Mr. Dunlap's slaves in 1762. Henry Laurens to William Smith, October 30, 1762, *HLP* 3: 144.
[140] James Mickie to Sir Alexander Nisbet, March 29, 1747, GD237/1/154/3, SNA.
[141] Mann, *Republic of Debtors*, 15.

could "reimburse" his creditors if he kept his slaves, but without them, he would "remain poor" and unable "to pay [his] debts."[142]

Creditors tended to agree with this assessment. Just as debtors understood that slaves were the primary means by which they could satisfy their creditors, creditors knew that attaching slaves could be financially counterproductive, inhibiting rather than hastening the collection of debts. As a result, they often chose to leave the debtor in possession of his land and slaves, hoping that a planter could produce crops that would allow him to service interest if not repay the principal. When Thomas Walter assigned "a small plantation of 15 Negroes" to his creditors, for example, Peter Manigault urged his client to allow Walter to keep his slaves. Although his client technically had a legal right to attach and sell the slaves, Manigault nonetheless advised that it would be "best to let him keep them ... in his Possession until the Crop of Indigo is made." If the crop was a good one, Walter's creditors stood to gain more from this arrangement than by selling the slaves immediately.[143] Likewise, when the mercantile house of Dacosta & Farr failed, Manigault took an assignment of the firm's debts on behalf of his clients, but hesitated to seize the remainder of the firm's assets, including "Household Goods & Slaves." The debtor had rightly pointed out to Manigault that if his creditors allowed him to keep his property, he would "one Day or other be able to pay" them, but if they "distress[ed] him now," they would "loose" their "[m]oney irrecoverably."[144]

Henry Laurens was similarly dubious of the benefit of attaching slaves. Rather than seizing the slaves of William Butler, who "had about 60 Negroes with some Land but all under Mortgage," Laurens and Butler's other creditors ultimately decided to keep "the Estate together allowing him a small maintenance for the management of it." They hoped that this would allow Butler, whom the creditors knew "to be a good Planter," to produce a crop that could satisfy at least some of their demands.[145] Laurens likewise urged the creditors of Andrew Fesch, who had "near Sixty Slaves of the Companys in his possession," to "wait untill the Crop is made" before acting against him.[146] Creditors and their colonial agents understood that

[142] Robert Baillie to George Baillie, February 10, 1754, GD1/1155/66/5, SNA.
[143] Peter Manigault to Isaac King, September 6, 1771, Manigault Papers, 11/278/7, 162–163, Peter Manigault Letterbook, 1763–1773, SCHS.
[144] Peter Manigault to Sarah Nickleson & Co., Manigault Papers, 11/278/7, 16–17, Peter Manigault Letterbook, 1763–1773, SCHS.
[145] Austin & Laurens [Henry Laurens] to Gidney Clarke, June 30, 1756, *HLP* 2: 235–237.
[146] Henry Laurens [Austin, Laurens, & Appleby] to Henry Bouquet, September 7, 1761, *HLP* 3: 80–82.

the law technically favored them and that they could obtain a judgment against their debtors if they took their cases to court. Nonetheless, when a debtor's assets included slaves, they urged caution and accommodation rather than litigation. Privileging slaves as laborers over slaves as commodities, they ultimately chose long-term productivity over short-term liquidity.

We can see the extent to which the presence of slaves shaped the choices of debtors and creditors alike as we watch South Carolina colonist Peter Manigault pursue two particularly wily debtors on behalf of his English clients. Richard and Archibald Stobo were brothers who owed money to London merchants Isaac King and Sarah Nickleson. Although the nature and amount of their debt are unclear, for nearly five years, they led Peter Manigault on a merry chase as they avoided his attempts at debt collection. Educated at the Inns of Court, Manigault was one of several South Carolinians who built a profitable side business managing the estates of absentee colonists and collecting debts owed to British merchants.[147] The Stobo brothers first appeared in Manigault's letterbook in 1765, by which point they already had been "amusing" him "for some Time." Their refusal to pay Manigault's clients or to come to an agreement ultimately prompted him to "take Writs against them" and put their debts in suit in South Carolina's Court of Common Pleas. Rather than allowing their property (or themselves) to be taken, however, the Stobos began keeping to their house in order to dodge the people Manigault had employed "with the Offers of a great Reward to take them." Manigault and his hired men could not apprehend the Stobos, it seems, because they had become experts in "keeping close." This was a strategy debtors used to avoid being served with a writ of attachment or a writ of execution.[148] Because "the law everywhere prohibited sheriffs and constables from forcibly entering a person's dwelling to serve a writ on the occupant," debtors could dodge legal process by hiding out in their homes, often for years at a time.[149] This, it appears, is precisely what the Stobos did with great aplomb, only making appearances "when the Courts of Justice were

---

[147] Bruce Mann has traced the emergence of professional debt collectors to the early republic, contrasting debt collection that "was more clearly becoming a business" with the "personalized, polite duns of pre-Revolutionary" debt collectors. By at least the 1760s, however, prominent South Carolina merchants and lawyers advertised their services as debt collectors for hire. Mann, *Republic of Debtors*, 32.

[148] Peter Manigault to Sarah Nickleson & Co., March 25, 1765, Manigault Papers, 11/278/7, 16–17, Peter Manigault Letterbook, 1763–1773, SCHS.

[149] Mann, *Republic of Debtors*, 26–27. Creditors and their agents could not force their way inside a home, although they could "enter through an open or unlocked door, climb through an unsecured window, or trick their way inside." *Ibid.*, 27.

shut up" or on Sundays when writs could not be served. Afterward, they dutifully retired to their "Lurking Place" where Manigault and his spies could not reach them.[150]

For the Stobos, keeping close was a desperate act, but it also was part of a larger strategy to force their creditors to come to a better accommodation. Although Richard Stobo (Archibald died while they were still keeping close) would not allow Manigault to take him, he nonetheless was in frequent communication with his frustrated pursuer, suggesting terms for an accord. In August 1766 he offered Manigault "£2000 Sterling for a Discharge or to assign his Books," an offer that Manigault refused because he could not "depend upon anything he says."[151] But Stobo continued to hold out, using the occasion of his brother's death to secure a "Protection for a few Months" from the Chancery Court. As Manigault complained, under the court's protection Stobo was allowed to walk "publicly about Town," and he dared "not arrest him."[152] Stobo's tactics ultimately worked: worn down chasing the wily debtor, Manigault accepted his "[o]ffer to pay two thousand pounds Sterling in four Years, & give good Security." Even though Manigault knew that Stobo was "not worth a half penny" and that he likely would "fly off as before," he nonetheless "closed with the Offer provided the Security is good."[153]

The fact that Richard and Archibald Stobo were slaveholders inspired these Herculean efforts at both debt collection and avoidance. Indeed, it seems that Richard Stobo originally decided to "keep close" in order to avoid being served with a writ of attachment "upon which his Negroes were all [to be] taken." Manigault, too, acted aggressively to preserve his clients' interests when he realized that there were judgment creditors who would also take the "Negroes & must be first satisfied."[154] For Stobo, keeping close until his creditors agreed to accept a bond and security (which likely would take the form of a slave mortgage) would allow him to retain his slaves, whose labor was his only way of repaying his creditors. For Manigault, the knowledge that Stobo's slaves would be taken to

---

[150] Peter Manigault to Sarah Nickleson & Co., May 14, 1766, Manigault Papers, 11/278/7, 35, Peter Manigault Letterbook, 1763–1773, SCHS.

[151] Peter Manigault to Sarah Nickleson & Co., August 12, 1766, Manigault Papers, 11/278/7, 41–43, Peter Manigault Letterbook, 1763–1773, SCHS.

[152] Peter Manigault to Isaac King, October 21, 1768, Manigault Papers, 11/278/7, 80–81, Peter Manigault Letterbook, 1763–1773, SCHS.

[153] Peter Manigault to Isaac King, April 28, 1770, Manigault Papers, 11/278/7, 120, Peter Manigault Letterbook, 1763–1773, SCHS.

[154] Peter Manigault to Sarah Nickleson, May 18, 1765, Manigault Papers, 11/278/7, 18–19, Peter Manigault Letterbook, 1763–1773, SCHS.

satisfy other creditors prompted him to conclude an agreement with Stobo despite his initial reservations. Although the accommodation they ultimately reached was less favorable than Manigault hoped, it at least gave his clients a secured interest in Stobo's property before his slaves were taken.

This arrangement recognized the reality that when debtors were insolvent, creditors often stood to benefit more from reaching an agreement with debtors rather than suing them. Manigault, although trained as a lawyer – or perhaps because of it – avoided lawyers and litigation, considering law "the Ratio ultima of Scoundrels." Instead, he sought to negotiate with debtors rather than sue them.[155] In his desire to avoid lawyers and litigation costs, Manigault was not unlike creditors elsewhere in mainland America, who realized that the cost of debt litigation outweighed its potential benefits. As Bruce Mann has noted, creditors in northern colonies also preferred "nonlitigated resolutions," understanding that lawsuits could "set in motion a train of events that were not necessarily to their advantage." Lawyers were expensive, and the pace of justice was slow.[156] Nonetheless, litigation, which brought with it the threat of attachment or imprisonment, was an especially risky proposition for creditors when a debtor's assets included slaves. Just as slave-owning debtors understood that slaves were the primary means by which they could satisfy their creditors, creditors knew that attaching slaves could be financially counterproductive, inhibiting rather than hastening the collection of debts. As a result, they often chose to leave the debtor in possession of his land and slaves, hoping that a planter could produce crops that at least would allow him to service interest if not repay the principal.

CONCLUSION

When colonists like the Stobo brothers took extreme measures to elude their creditors (or to force them to reach an accommodation), their actions marked them as part of a broader English legal culture. Like colonists in other provinces, plantation colonists avoided legal process and generally eluded their creditors, displaying a degree of legal literacy that can be surprising from a modern-day perspective. Colonists in plantation America, however, maneuvered in the shadow of law that treated people as things, and this shaped their decisions in profound ways. Debtors like

[155] Peter Manigault to Ralph Izard, [1765], Manigault Papers, 11/278/7, 22–25, Peter Manigault Letterbook, 1763–1773, SCHS.
[156] Mann, *Republic of Debtors*, 20.

Richard Stobo and Robert Baillie, for example, operated with an eye toward shielding their human property from creditors, knowing that slaves were both their most valuable assets and the only means they had of extricating themselves from debt. For creditors like Arthur Matthews, who declared that he would defend slaves mortgaged to him against all other creditors, the knowledge that a debtor owned slaves likewise influenced legal behavior in times of financial hardship. These creditors were forced to decide whether to recoup losses immediately by attaching and selling slaves or, alternatively, to allow debtors to retain their slaves in the hopes that this would result in larger remittances.[157]

English law made these types of choices possible. Legal forms, including conditional bonds, allowed slave traders and plantation colonists to conform their transactions involving human property to English law and practice with little effort. In fact, watching them deploy conditional bonds to secure slave sales reveals just how little – not how much – adaptation was required to create a moral economy in which what mattered most was "satisfying" other white colonists. The form of these forms, it turns out, mattered tremendously to white colonists as well as to the slaves they commodified. If the language of English property law provided a way for colonists to think about and talk about slaves, the silences that colonists encountered in legal forms like bonds insulated them from contemplating the tragic human consequences of their actions. Obscuring the humanity of enslaved people, forms like conditional bonds ultimately freed colonists to subordinate the desires of slaves to their own economic needs, to layer all other priorities atop the lives and aspirations of enslaved people. We should view these forms, then, as an integral part of slave law. Certainly, slave law was a creature of statute. But it was also a law of seemingly insignificant everyday transactions. It was a law built in the aggregate as colonists bought, sold, and mortgaged slaves, and as they used centuries-old legal language to do so. On a daily basis, in fact, it was the quotidian stuff of credit and debt and buying and selling that made slavery work. Plantation colonists understood this. They knew that slave law not only organized relationships among masters and slaves, but also among buyers and sellers, planters, and British merchants. The paper trail that these colonists left in their wake reveals the contours of an economy in which capital, realized in the bodies of enslaved people and documented on scraps of paper, connected them to Britons the world over.

[157] Arthur Matthews to Samuel Hurst, Esq., March 1, 1743, SCDAH.

3

In Rem

In 1718, South Carolina colonists Richard and Catherine Tuckerman laid claim to a "Negro Man named Ned" who had been captured on a ship belonging to the infamous pirate Stede Bonnet. At the Vice Admiralty Court in Charlestown, the Tuckermans detailed the twisting path by which Ned, whom they hired out to a ship's captain as a diver, was taken – not once, but twice – by buccaneers as he sought to escape from servitude on a Britain-bound snow. Buried in a compelling story of violence on the high seas, the Tuckermans' claim to their human property not only included a "prayer" that the judge would declare them Ned's owners; they also asked the court to sell the "notorious Renegade" at public auction. Using the imperial state's legal apparatus to great effect, the Tuckermans ultimately obtained their desired result: the court ordered Ned to be appraised and sold.[1]

Ned's maritime travels, which brought him from Charlestown to New England to the Bahamas and then back again, were not uncommon. Although New World slavery is often taken as a shorthand for agricultural labor on plantations, Great Britain's blue water empire was a more polychromatic space than we might expect. Scholars have recently begun to appreciate that Black mariners and watermen were ubiquitous in the British Atlantic World: enslaved and free sailors pumped bilges on

---

[1] *Masters et al.* v. *Sloop Revenge*, November 19, 1718, South Carolina Vice-Admiralty Court Records, A–B vols., 276–300, Library of Congress, Manuscripts Division, Washington, DC. Unless otherwise noted, I have dated cases based upon the first record entry in the Vice Admiralty Court's Minute Books. Special thanks to Kevin Dawson for sharing his insights about this particular case, and more generally about the lives of enslaved free divers like Ned Grant.

transatlantic merchant vessels, translated for the crews of slave ships, and fought in naval military engagements around the globe. Colonists and merchants alike also relied upon local Black pilots to guide their vessels into treacherous harbors, and they used enslaved watermen to transport commodities and shuttle foodstuffs between scattered plantations. Whether piloting sloops over the Charlestown bar, working as hired laborers on merchant vessels, or fishing off the coast of Jamaica, slaves were omnipresent along early America's waterways and coasts.[2]

For these enslaved maritime workers, setting sail presented new possibilities for autonomy and agency. Although seafaring was considered a "contemptible occupation for white men," it could be an "occupation of opportunity for slaves" and free Blacks.[3] The lack of oversight aboard ship meant that Black sailors could move about more freely than plantation laborers, while skilled maritime slaves like Ned often leveraged their talents to build "semi-independent lives of privileged exploitation."[4] Despite the advantages that maritime labor offered, however, Black sailors and divers also encountered significant obstacles when they plied the deep. Early modern mariners were by no means color blind, as scholars have noted, and racial hierarchies persisted on the forecastle as well as in the fields.[5] More importantly for our purposes, the law of slavery also stubbornly followed people of African descent on their voyages. The legal categories, procedures, and assumptions that would soon become a hallmark of race-based New World slavery were not landlocked. Instead, they migrated downriver and across oceans, infusing the worldview of those who labored at sea and mingling with a multitude of older customs and laws that governed maritime life.

---

[2] Michael J. Jarvis, "Maritime Masters and Seafaring Slaves in Bermuda, 1680–1783," *WMQ* 59 (2002): 585–622; W. Jeffrey Bolster, *Black Jacks: African American Seamen in the Age of Sail* (Cambridge: Harvard University Press, 1998); Marcus Rediker, *Between the Devil and the Deep Blue Sea, Merchant Seamen, Pirates, and the Anglo-American Maritime World 1700–1750* (Cambridge: Cambridge University Press, 1989); Kevin Dawson, *Undercurrents of Power: Aquatic Culture in the African Diaspora* (Philadelphia: University of Pennsylvania Press, 2018); Kevin Dawson, "History below the Waterline: Enslaved Salvage Divers Harvesting Seaports' Hinter-Seas in the Early Modern Atlantic," *International Review of Social History* 64 (2019): 43–70. For the life of Charlestown pilot Thomas Jeremiah, see William R. Ryan, *The World of Thomas Jeremiah: Charles Town on the Eve of the American Revolution* (Oxford: Oxford University Press, 2010) and J. William Harris, *The Hanging of Thomas Jeremiah: A Free Black Man's Encounter with Liberty* (New Haven: Yale University Press, 2009).
[3] Bolster, *Black Jacks*, 4.   [4] Dawson, "History below the Waterline," 43.
[5] Bolster, *Black Jacks*, 3.

Few of these legal assumptions were as significant as the treatment of slaves as chattel property. As we have already seen, classifying enslaved people as chattel property was a crucial first step in creating societies in which human beings could be transformed into moveable units of wealth, in which the slave become "a person with a price."[6] In part, this was because treating slaves as chattels had practical legal consequences. Properly categorized as chattel, slaves could be slotted into bills of sale, mortgages, trusts, and conditional bonds. Litigants also found that they could substitute slaves for other moveable property in common law causes of action or in Vice Admiralty litigation, where they routinely analogized enslaved people to marine cargo. In this chapter, then, I move beyond plantation America's shores to trace how the legal logic of chattel slavery projected out into the Atlantic Ocean along with the people who traversed it. The idea that human beings could be treated as things at law was not limited to plantation colonists or southern slaveowners. Rather, it shaped the quotidian legal activities of Britons throughout the Atlantic World. This becomes clear when we sift through the claims of the countless sailors, captains, and merchants who brought their disputes to colonial Vice Admiralty Courts, which governed life on British naval and merchant vessels. Sitting without juries and following procedures that derived from European civil law, these courts were spread across the British Empire, from Bermuda to Bombay. They applied a body of substantive law that had emerged over centuries to meet merchants' need for speedy dispute resolution and sailors' demands for fair pay and protection. With a broader jurisdiction than admiralty courts in England, their judges decided an assortment of suits touching on maritime life, including mariners' wage claims, prize cases, breaches of shipping contracts, torts, petty crimes, and violations of the Navigation Acts. They differed in fundamental ways from colonial common law courts, but most of all because colonial Vice Admiralty litigants could sue things, usually ships and their cargoes. In fact, it was the courts' in rem (against the thing) jurisdiction that made them especially attractive to litigants living in transient maritime communities where individuals were difficult to locate and hold to legal account. As a result, although American revolutionaries maligned Vice Admiralty Courts as venues that infringed on the rights of the accused during the imperial crisis of the 1760s and 1770s, they provided

---

[6] Walter Johnson, *Soul by Soul: Life inside the Antebellum Slave Market* (Cambridge, MA: Harvard University Press, 1999), 2.

much-needed legal mechanisms for securing property in a global maritime economy.[7]

Vice Admiralty Court records offer an unparalleled glimpse into the working lives of individuals who might otherwise be lost to history, from enslaved divers like Ned to countless jack tars who plied the Atlantic. In deposition testimony, witnesses sketch a vivid picture of life in the age of sail, one that was characterized by violence and instability, but also by shipboard camaraderie and esprit de corps. They reveal a world in which Black and white crewmembers often worked side by side and in which the exigencies of life at sea worked to subvert the racial hierarchies that historians might expect to find. Enslaved divers like Ned could build lives of relative comfort for themselves and their families, leveraging their talents to insulate themselves from the unremitting subjugation that characterized life on plantations. Free and enslaved sailors of African descent were promoted above white mariners on the basis of merit, and the linguistic talents of African translators won them positions of prestige and power among a slave ship's crew. Their stories remind us that Atlantic World slavery was astonishingly complex and defy our attempts to fit master-slave relationships into reductive stereotypes.

More importantly for our purposes, watching these liminal figures navigate the legal boundary between slavery and freedom as they crisscrossed oceans is important because it draws our attention to the boundary itself. This line was taut in some places and slack in others. Slave codes empowered white Britons to coerce slave labor with physical force, but ships' masters and captains routinely mitigated the law's severity when

---

[7] The best most recent study of a colonial Vice Admiralty Court is David R. Owen and Michael C. Tolley, *Courts of Vice Admiralty in Colonial America: The Maryland Experience, 1634–1776* (Durham: Carolina Academic Press, 1995). Studies of Vice Admiralty Courts in other jurisdictions include Carl Ubbelohde, "The Vice Admiralty Court of Royal North Carolina," *North Carolina Historical Review* 31 (1954): 517–528; Dorothy S. Towle, ed., *Records of the Vice-Admiralty Court of Rhode Island 1716–1752* (Washington, DC: The American Historical Association, 1936); A Stone, "The Admiralty Court in Colonial Nova Scotia," *Dalhousie Law Journal* 17 (1994): 363–429; C. Hough, ed., *Reports of Cases in the Vice Admiralty of the Province of New York and in the Court of Admiralty of the State of New York, 1715–1788* (New Haven: Yale University Press, 1925); G. Reese, ed., *Proceedings in the Court of Vice-Admiralty of Virginia 1698–1775* (Richmond: Virginia State Library, 1983); L. Wroth, "The Massachusetts Vice Admiralty Court and the Federal Admiralty Jurisdiction," *American Journal of Legal History* 6 (1962): 347–367; E. Aldrich, "Admiralty Jurisdiction, and the Admiralty Courts of New Hampshire during the Colonial and Revolutionary Period, and the Period since the Adoption of the Constitution of 1783–1784," in *Proceedings of the New Hampshire Bar Association* (1909–1910), 31–62.

confronted with the reality of Black agency. As the shore receded from view, the resistance strategies of enslaved and free people of color stayed in the hands of white Britons, who relied upon skilled Black laborers for their livelihoods and their lives.

If resistance at sea could check the more coercive aspects of slave law, however, the classification of slaves as chattel property constituted a near-impermeable boundary. Reified in positive law and absorbed into the language of imperial commerce, white Britons internalized the "chattel principle" – the notion that monetary value inhered in the bodies of Black people.[8] In quotidian acts of economic exchange and in litigation that assumed people could be things, they imbued the letter of the law with motion and meaning as they transformed human beings into the Atlantic World's most valuable commodities. This objectification at the law's hands was more difficult for enslaved people to counter, as Vice Admiralty records reveal. Although Black maritime laborers sometimes avoided being checked by the coercive apparatus of the state, they remained vulnerable to the property claims of white Britons who had learned to treat them (and think of them) as mere things. Transactions as well as physical brutality answered resistance in British America, and in categorizing slaves as property, white Britons set limits for enslaved people's actions in effective ways. Attending to the Vice Admiralty Courts and their work, then, also prompts us to reassess our basic assumptions about slave law – what it was and how it worked. With a few exceptions, historians have typically emphasized the criminal law of slavery, conflating slave law with the slave codes promulgated by colonial assemblies.[9] Vice Admiralty litigation, however, returns our gaze to the

[8] Johnson, *Soul by Soul*, 2.
[9] In *Many Thousands Gone*, e.g., Ira Berlin focuses entirely on the ways in which "planters mobilized the apparatus of coercion in the service" of their new labor regime, while David Barry Gaspar emphasizes the harsh physical punishments meted out to slaves in colonial Jamaica. Ira Berlin, *Many Thousands Gone: The First Two Centuries of Slavery in North America* (Cambridge, MA: Harvard University Press, 1998), 115; David Barry Gaspar, "'Rigid and Inclement': Origins of the Jamaica Slave Laws of the Seventeenth Century," in *The Many Legalities of Early America*, edited by Christopher L. Tomlins and Bruce H. Mann (Chapel Hill: University of North Carolina Press, 2000), 78–96; William M. Wiecek, "The Statutory Law of Slavery and Race in the Thirteen Mainland Colonies of British America," *The William and Mary Quarterly*, 3rd ser. 34 (1977): 258–280. Likewise, studies of the culture of power in plantation America privilege the criminal dimension of slave law, suggesting that slave courts and the apparatus of terror surrounding the execution of slaves allowed whites to project their authority over enslaved people and even each other. Robert Olwell, *Masters, Slaves, and Subjects: The Culture of Power in the South Carolina Low Country, 1740–1790* (Ithaca, NY: Cornell University Press,

"private" law component of slave law, revealing that the classification of slaves as chattel property played a powerful role in shaping legal choices for Britons in the age of sail. Certainly state-sanctioned violence and the threat of physical brutality omnipresent in slave codes were key components of a legal culture that Europeans erected to exploit enslaved labor, but this legal culture also worked quietly to dehumanize and commodify enslaved people.

Crucially, the language of English law – its categories and procedures – facilitated this process of dehumanization. In fact, Vice Admiralty litigation shifts our gaze from substance to procedure in accounting for the development of slave law in the British Atlantic World. Seeking to profit from the bodies and labor of Black people, white Britons drew upon a formalistic English legal culture in which procedure was a site of innovation and legal fictions were ubiquitous. We can see this process at work in Vice Admiralty litigation. Although English admiralty law had developed over centuries to allow European sailors and merchants to seize cargo and ships, Vice Admiralty litigants, lawyers, and judges extended the courts' in rem jurisdiction to include slaves found on captured vessels. Analogizing slaves to other types of marine property, they slotted enslaved people into ready-made forms and procedures, bringing Black bodies before the court as objects that could be condemned, appraised, and sold. In fact, the in rem process that distinguished admiralty jurisdictions from common law renders the process of transforming people into property highly visible to historians. In places where human beings were considered things at law, the Vice Admiralty Court – a jurisdiction that specialized in seizing, appraising, and condemning things – provided a time-tested procedure for litigants who wished to claim people of African descent as property.

This stretching of *res* as a legal category to include enslaved people was a gradual process, and it largely lacked ideological content. When white Britons compared enslaved people to marine property, they did so in order to profit from a global economy in which slaves were valuable commodities. Nonetheless, repeated time and again, these moments of legal analogy had profoundly ideological consequences. The litigants, lawyers, and judges who characterized slaves as *res* ultimately created "a social reality that did not exist prior to the act of speaking."[10] By calling slaves chattel,

---

1998), 100; Vincent Brown, *The Reaper's Garden: Death and Power in the World of Atlantic Slavery* (Cambridge, MA: Harvard University Press, 2008), 131–144.

[10] Elizabeth Mertz, "Language, Law, and Social Meanings: Linguistic/Anthropological Contributions to the Study of Law," *Law & Society Review* 26 (1992): 422.

by treating Black people as things at law, white Britons in Vice Admiralty Courts and elsewhere constructed a legal world in which slaves were not just *like* things, they *were* things for the purposes of proceedings and judgments. Through the act of legal categorization, they rendered factual what had been a mere supposition – that Black people were less than human.

***

In "Law Adrift," I briefly describe the evolution of the colonial Vice Admiralty Court system after 1696, placing the courts within the broader context of early modern maritime law. I then turn to a discussion of admiralty jurisdiction and procedure, distinguishing colonial Vice Admiralty Courts from the common law courts that scholars more typically emphasize. Here, I focus on the courts' in rem jurisdiction, which as a procedural matter allowed litigants to bring marine property to the courts' attention. In "The Chattel Principle in an Age of Sail," I examine slave litigation in the Vice Admiralty Courts of South Carolina and Jamaica, Great Britain's two most profitable plantation colonies and British America's largest slave-trading entrepôts. From colonists to sailors to the king, litigants in these colonies asked Vice Admiralty Courts to acknowledge their property rights in human beings. Although Eugene Genovese has suggested that courts repeatedly "tripped over the slave's humanity," I have found instead that litigants and judges did not pause to consider the humanity of slaves, nor did they betray any cognitive dissonance in treating enslaved people as property.[11] Rather, they seamlessly analogized slaves to other types of marine property using centuries-old admiralty procedures, as I show in "*Dom. Rex v. 3 Negro Men Slaves* and the Language of Admiralty." Their activities helped make it possible, in ideological as well as practical terms, to treat enslaved people as property.

In "Policing the Trade," I examine how Vice Admiralty Courts contributed to the dehumanization of Black people in a more subtle but no less significant way: by acting as a regulatory body for the transatlantic slave trade. As British merchants dominated the transatlantic slave trade over the course of the eighteenth century, Vice Admiralty judges increasingly found themselves called upon to resolve complex disputes about life on slave ships, including wage claims and allegations of shipboard

---

[11] Eugene D. Genovese, *Roll, Jordan, Roll: The World the Slaves Made* (New York, NY: First Vintage Books, 1976), 29.

brutality. Overall, these judges worked to protect mariners who labored in the notoriously harsh "Guinea" trade. They did so based upon the commonplace assumption that sailors were incapable of protecting themselves. The mariners who appear in Vice Admiralty records, however, reveal this assumption to be entirely false. In fact, sailors were savvy actors who used their legal knowledge to benefit from the global slave economy. They understood that slaves were valuable commodities, they ruthlessly claimed enslaved people as property, and they expected to reap the rewards of Britain's rising commerce in African slaves.

If Vice Admiralty Courts favored the claims of white sailors, this deference did not extend to maritime laborers of African descent. I conclude by focusing upon the human beings that found themselves trapped by a legal system in which even the most skilled Black mariners were treated as people with a price. Their stories elucidate the real risks of life at sea for individuals like Ned, who were always subject to the property claims of avaricious Vice Admiralty litigants. Indeed, the specter of commodification haunted all sailors of African descent, whether they were enslaved or free, because the equation of black skin with legal objectification meant that even free Blacks might be recast as property. At the same time, however, Vice Admiralty records reveal that Black sailors were no less legally savvy than their white counterparts. Faced with capture and sale, some used their knowledge of English law to shape more positive outcomes. Occasionally, their strategies were successful, and they slipped through law's interstices. For the most part, however, the legal logic of chattel slavery proved inescapable; for every triumph, there were many more tragedies.

LAW ADRIFT

Although early modern cartographers, writers, and travelers often associated oceans with lawlessness and violence, many early modern Europeans in fact understood that the seas were "variegated spaces transected by law."[12] Vessels themselves were considered "islands of law," and their captains enjoyed quasi-regal authority to discipline crewmembers and maintain order aboard ship.[13] As these ships moved across oceans, they projected municipal law beyond Europe's shores, marking out corridors

[12] Lauren Benton, *A Search for Sovereignty: Law and Geography in European Empires, 1400–1900* (Cambridge: Cambridge University Press, 2010), 105.
[13] *Ibid.*, 112.

of sovereignty for the monarchs they served. In turn, ships and their crews maneuvered across expanses of water that were overlaid with other, competing sources of legal authority, including municipal law, customary law, the law of nations, royal proclamations, and statutes. There was no singular maritime law, per se. Rather, ocean-goers of all sorts – from captains to jack tars to pirates – strategically invoked various legal sources in their disputes with each other and with land-based authorities.[14] As Mary Sarah Bilder has described with regard to the transatlantic constitution, maritime legal regimes were constituted by "arguments" rather than "answers."[15]

For sailors on English (and later, British) ships, colonial Vice Admiralty Courts were the most important institutions in the "complex tangle of jurisdictional strings" that tied together the early modern maritime legal order.[16] Before 1763, when the financial burdens of the Seven Years' War prompted a reorganization of the colonial Vice Admiralty system, these courts adjudicated cases at the water's edge throughout the British Empire. Most were created in the late seventeenth century as part of a broader effort to centralize imperial administration and enforce the Navigation Acts.[17] These were a series of Parliamentary statutes promulgated in the seventeenth century in order to prevent the Dutch from engrossing colonial trade. In general, the acts aimed to "promote shipping, increase customs revenues, and monopolize trade with the colonies."[18] They stipulated that ships engaged in colonial trade must be owned by English subjects and built in England or English colonies. Shipmasters and at least three-quarters of the crew also had to be English subjects, and enumerated commodities were to be unloaded and reloaded in England (with a duty paid) prior to being transshipped to other countries.[19]

---

[14] *Ibid.*, 112–113.

[15] Mary Sarah Bilder, *The Transatlantic Constitution: Colonial Legal Culture and the Empire* (Cambridge, MA: Harvard University Press, 2008), 4.

[16] Benton, *A Search for Sovereignty*, 161.

[17] With the exception of Jamaica (1662), Maryland (1694), and New York (1696), most colonies erected Vice Admiralty jurisdictions (courts with commissions issued directly from the High Court of Admiralty) after 1697. Owen and Tolley, *Courts of Admiralty*, 26; 20.

[18] *Ibid.*, 102.

[19] An excellent description of the Navigation Acts and the colonial trade system can be found in Nuala Zahedieh, *The Capital and the Colonies: London and the Atlantic Economy, 1660–1700* (Cambridge: Cambridge University Press, 2010), 35–55. See also Owen and Tolley, *Courts of Admiralty*, 102–103. As Michael Jarvis has shown, enslaved Bermudian mariners owned by British subjects constituted British subjects for the purposes of the Navigation Acts. Jarvis, "Maritime Masters," 598.

Governors took an oath to uphold the Navigation Acts, and they received financial incentives for successful prosecutions.[20] Nonetheless, enforcement in the American colonies was lax. Many governors lacked the political power to target offenders, and the Naval Officers appointed to monitor compliance were poorly paid.[21] Even more problematically, common law juries in colonial seaboard communities refused to convict local violators, who also happened to be their friends, neighbors, and business associates. As a result, in 1696 Parliament gave jurisdiction over Navigation Acts violations to colonial Vice Admiralty Courts, and in 1697 the Privy Council authorized the creation of new courts in colonies where they did not yet exist.[22] Decidedly royal courts, these jurisdictions "derived their authority from the king, conducted their proceedings in the king's name, and were presided over by a judge whose commission under warrant from the crown was issued directly from the High Court of Admiralty."[23]

The Vice Admiralty Courts' procedures more than anything else set them apart from other colonial jurisdictions. As institutions derived from European civil law rather than English common law, admiralty courts in the British Isles and the American colonies tried cases without juries, which made them vulnerable to criticism in England during the

---

[20] Owen and Tolley, *Courts of Admiralty*, 107; 104. There is reason for thinking that these financial incentives sometimes worked. In South Carolina, e.g., governor James Glen worked tirelessly behind the scenes to have the ship *Vrouw Dorothea* condemned for Navigation Acts violations. Writing as the case wound its way through a particularly lengthy and complicated appeals process, Glen observed that "there can be no doubt but that I was very desirous that the Vessel and Cargo should be Condemned." Indeed, he "was fully convinced that there had been a flagrant breach of the Laws of Trade." He was even more certain that the Governor of Jamaica, who first captured the vessel, was not entitled to compensation. After all, according to Glen, "vigilantibus non dormientibus &ca." James Glen Letterbook, GD45/2/1, [1751–1752], 141, SNA.

In a 1729 case, the master of the ship *St. Antonio*, libeled for violating the Navigation Acts, challenged the court's authority to apply the Navigation Acts to non-British subjects. In his answer, the respondent argued that "if he hath Comitted any Offence against the Laws of Great Britain that is not Malum in Se or contrary to Jus Gentium." The court was unpersuaded however, and the ship was condemned. *Thomas Gadsden Collector of Customs v. St. Antonio*, June 30, 1729, South Carolina Vice Admiralty Court Minute Books, A–B vols., 563.

[21] Zahedieh, *The Capital and the Colonies*, 38

[22] Helen Crump, *Colonial Admiralty Jurisdiction in the Seventeenth Century* (London: Longmans, Green and Co., 1932), 1–2; Charles M. Andrews, *The Colonial Period of American History*, 4 vols. (New Haven: Yale University Press, 1938), 4: 226.

[23] Charles M. Andrews, "Introduction," in *Records of the Vice-Admiralty Court of Rhode Island 1716–1752*, edited by Dorothy S. Towle (Washington, DC: The American Historical Association, 1936), 17.

seventeenth century and in the mainland American colonies immediately
prior to the American Revolution.[24] (This was also precisely the reason
why they were chosen to adjudicate Navigation Acts violations.) Practice
in these courts also differed from common law proceedings. Whereas
common law witnesses testified in open court, in a typical admiralty
trial a judge issued a final decree based upon written testimony alone.
This testimony took the form of answers to interrogatories (questions
propounded to witnesses) or depositions (sworn written statements).[25]

   More importantly for our purposes, Vice Admiralty Courts could
proceed in rem (against the thing) whereas common law courts typically
proceeded in personam (against the person).[26] As in other admiralty
jurisdictions, libelants (plaintiffs) in colonial Vice Admiralty Courts
could libel (sue) things, generally ships and their cargoes.[27] A suit com-
menced when the libelant, represented by a proctor (attorney) (or in the
case of the Crown the Advocate General), filed a libel (a complaint) setting
out the facts of the case and asking for relief. The court then issued
a warrant to the Vice Admiralty Court's marshal to arrest the libeled
ship and/or cargo. Crucially, the owner of the arrested ship (the respondent) could then file a stipulation that substituted security in place of the
vessel. This meant that the ship could immediately return to sea without
having to await the outcome of a trial. If the libelant prevailed, the court
either ordered the ship sold or the security forfeited.[28] Courts also

---

[24] Admiralty jurisdictions in England also proved unpopular because admiralty courts
   deprived other courts of potentially lucrative business. This included not only courts of
   common law, but also manor and borough courts. The fourteenth-century Ricardian
   statutes that limited admiralty jurisdiction to the body of the counties specifically refer-
   enced the encroachment of admiralty jurisdiction on "diverse franchises." 13 R. 2 c.5,
   1389. For colonists' complaints about Vice Admiralty Courts in the 1760s and 1770s, see
   David S. Lovejoy, "Rights Imply Equality: The Case against Admiralty Jurisdiction in
   America, 1764–1776," WMQ 16 (1959): 459–484.

[25] Owen and Tolley, *Courts of Admiralty*, 17. In disputes over captured prize ships, interrogatories often adhered to a formula that was meant to elicit testimony about the nature
   of the ship's cargo, the crew members' places of origin, and the ship's owner, making the
   records in these cases particularly interesting sources for social history.

[26] It was possible to proceed in personam in colonial Vice Admiralty Courts, particularly in
   criminal cases. These usually were initiated with a warrant to arrest the body of the
   defendant. See, e.g., *Joseph Powell v. William Lyford*, January 3, 1763, South Carolina
   Vice Admiralty Minute Books, E–F vols., 494–500, NARA.

[27] A libelant might also choose to libel the cargo alone. See, e.g., *Parcel of Brandy*,
   September 25, 1717, South Carolina Vice Admiralty Minute Books, A–B vols.,
   126–137, LOC.

[28] Owen and Tolley, *Courts of Admiralty*, 15. In the case of a contumacious respondent,
   Vice Admiralty judges also had the power to attach and condemn any of the respondent's

generally provided an opportunity for those financially interested in a ship or its cargo, including sailors, to claim their respective share of a ship or the goods it transported.

Vice Admiralty procedures provided a number of advantages to litigants, many of whom were busy merchants or peripatetic mariners. In fact, they were tailor-made to suit a maritime empire in which people maneuvered outside of traditional communities that provided judicial oversight and mechanisms for conflict resolution. More streamlined than common law suits, there were no requirements to adhere to the forms of action in Vice Admiralty litigation. This lessened opportunities for delay, which was important for ship owners anxious to return their vessels to the course of commerce. Remedies, too, made the Vice Admiralty Court friendly to merchant and mariner litigants. For example, the requirement that respondents provide security prior to trying a libel helped to ensure that claims would be satisfied even if a ship sailed off to a foreign port.[29] Finally, deposition and interrogatory evidence was uniquely well suited for mariner or merchant witnesses. Rather than requiring these individuals to appear in court, Vice Admiralty judges issued commissions to take depositions or interrogatories, even to witnesses in other colonies.[30] This written evidence, as a practical matter, also was easier to translate than in-court testimony. In fact, colonial Vice Admiralty Court records reveal the linguistic diversity of early modern maritime communities, as witnesses and litigants were nearly as likely to be Spanish, Dutch, or French speakers as they were to be English speakers.[31]

---

maritime property within the jurisdiction. Maritime attachment, although once available to the High Court of Admiralty, "fell into disuse" in England. More like an action in personam, it had been attacked by common law judges over the course of the seventeenth century. *Ibid.*, 17.

[29] *Ibid.*, 16.

[30] In a 1747 South Carolina case, e.g., the Court issued commissions to two New York merchants and one "Counsellor at Law" to interview "material Witnesses" residing in New York. *William Walton* v. *William Yeomans*, September 28, 1747, South Carolina Vice Admiralty Minute Books, C–D vols., NARA.

[31] The Vice Admiralty Court in South Carolina employed foreign merchants living in Charlestown to translate written depositions or answers to interrogatories. These individuals also might be called upon by the court to translate ship's papers, including customs documents, instructions, letters of marque, captains' logs, and bills of lading. In the case of the *Ju Vrouw Anna*, a Jamaican prize case, the court used a jeweler from Kingston, Jamaica, to translate Dutch documents. *Ju Vrouw Anna*, October 4, 1747, Records of the High Court of Admiralty and Colonial Vice-Admiralty Courts, TNA, HCA 49/60.

Although their procedures mimicked practice in English admiralty jurisdictions, the colonial Vice Admiralty Courts enjoyed a substantially broader jurisdiction than these older courts.[32] In part, this was because their authority to try Navigation Acts cases was a jurisdiction unknown to admiralty courts in England.[33] The courts also exercised jurisdiction in

---

[32] Owen and Tolley, *Courts of Admiralty*, xiv; According to Crump, "The victory of the common lawyers came with the civil wars, but under the Restoration admiralty courts gained ground in the colonies, though the High Court of Admiralty at London lost almost all business save prize." Crump, *Colonial Admiralty Jurisdiction*, 141. See also Andrews, *Colonial Period*, 4:228. The High Court of Admiralty had original jurisdiction in maritime causes and prize cases. It also could appoint commissioners to sit as courts of *oyer* and *terminer* to try (with a jury) felonies on the high seas. England's local Vice Admiralty Courts "looked chiefly after marine business," but not trade violations. *Ibid.*, 4:223.

[33] Owen and Tolley, *Courts of Admiralty*, 4–5. In England, violations of trade laws were tried in the Court of Exchequer or by barons of the exchequer in the counties. Andrews, *Colonial Period*, 4:223. Although after a period of confusion the Board of Trade ultimately decided that the Vice Admiralty Courts in the colonies exercised a concurrent jurisdiction to enforce the Navigation Acts with common law courts, in many colonies Navigation Acts cases comprised a significant portion of the court's docket. Owen and Tolley, *Courts of Admiralty*, 7. Actions to enforce Parliamentary statutes forbidding colonists from cutting marked white pine trees (which were used by the royal navy) were an exception to this rule. Ubbelohde, "The Vice-Admiralty Court," 16.

The colonial Vice Admiralty Courts also were largely unrestricted by Parliamentary statutes, and particularly the two statutes of Richard II that limited the High Court of Admiralty's jurisdiction to things "done upon the sea" but not "within the bodies of the counties." Indeed commissions from the High Court of Admiralty endowed some colonial Vice Admiralty judges with the authority to try torts that occurred in waters *infra corpus comitatus* (within the body of the county). Owen and Tolley, *Courts of Admiralty*, 138–139. South Carolina is an important exception to this as the colony specifically incorporated Parliamentary statutes limiting admiralty jurisdiction to the body of the counties, including 13 R.2 c.5, 1389, "What Things the Admiralty and His Deputy Shall Meddle," and 15 R.2 c.3, 1391, "In What Places the Admiral's Jurisdiction Doth Lie," in "An Act to Put in Force ..." (1712), *SAL*, vol. 2, 445–470.

Colonial Vice Admiralty courts also largely avoided the jurisdictional competition that resulted in the limitation of admiralty jurisdiction in England. Although the High Court of Admiralty enjoyed a resurgence under the Tudors, during the seventeenth century common law judges and lawyers eroded the court's jurisdiction. Using writs of prohibition, Sir Edward Coke in particular "demanded that admiralty jurisdiction be confined to the open sea only and that the courts be prohibited from dealing with cases arising within the waters of the realm, that is, within rivers as far as the first bridge that impeded navigation." Andrews, *Colonial Period*, 4:224; Owen and Tolley, *Courts of Admiralty*, 3. Andrews has found evidence of writs of prohibition issuing to Vice Admiralty Court judges in some of the American colonies. "The writ was made use of probably in all the colonies at one time or another, but we have no certain evidence of its exercise in Maryland, Virginia, and Antigua. Of the other colonies illustrations are few from Bermuda and Barbados. But in Massachusetts, Rhode Island, New York, Pennsylvania, and the two Carolinas, prohibitions were frequently employed." Andrews, *Colonial Period*, 4:263.

two other types of cases: prize and instance. After each declaration of war, the High Court of Admiralty issued prize warrants to Vice Admiralty Court judges, which gave them the authority to condemn ships and cargo that were captured by naval vessels or privateers.[34] Both military necessity and commercial demands for speedy condemnation of vessels made it particularly important for colonial Vice Admiralty Courts to act in cases of prize. In fact, prize ships could not be legally sold prior to condemnation, a process that produced a certificate that could be used as a title deed. Especially in the West Indies, where ships were needed during times of war, it was impractical to require captors to sail their ships to England for condemnation prior to reregistering them and returning them to the Caribbean theater.[35]

Acting in their capacity as prize judges, Vice Admiralty judges applied the law of nations rather than maritime law.[36] Prize warrants, in fact, specifically directed judges to proceed "[a]ccording to the Course of Admiralty & Laws of Nations," and the letters of marque and reprisal issued to privateers, which Vice Admiralty judges read as part of a prize case record, routinely urged captains not to "attempt any thing against the Laws of Nations."[37] In adjudicating these prize cases, which could become quite complex, judges also were required to interpret and balance other sources of law, including treaties, proclamations regarding the distribution of prize money, declarations of war, and Parliamentary statutes.

Vice Admiralty Courts also exercised instance jurisdiction, which was litigation brought on the "instance" of the plaintiff against a vessel and/or its cargo. In instance cases, judges applied maritime law, sometimes called the law merchant, which differed significantly from law applied in the

---

[34] Prize warrant, June 5, 1756, South Carolina Vice Admiralty Court Minute Books, E–F vols., 115, NARA.

[35] This need for a jurisdiction that could quickly condemn prizes accounts for the early establishment of a Vice Admiralty Court in Jamaica. Crump, *Colonial Admiralty Jurisdiction*, 97. Not surprisingly given their geographic location, the adjudication of prize claims formed an important portion of the business of West Indian Vice Admiralty Courts, and particularly the Jamaican Vice Admiralty Court. In fact, Ubbelohde thought that "[p]rize cases comprised more than one-third of the litigation before the American vice-admiralty courts in the years 1702 to 1763," although the empirical basis for this conclusion is unclear. Ubbelohde, "The Vice-Admiralty Court," 17.

[36] Owen and Tolley, *Courts of Admiralty*, 11.

[37] Prize warrant, June 5, 1756, South Carolina Vice Admiralty Court Minute Books, E–F vols., 115, NARA. Instructions accompanying letters of marque and reprisal issued to William Asserre & Joseph Prews, November 22, 1739, South Carolina Vice Admiralty Court Minute Books, C–D vols., 279, LOC.

common law courts. An amalgam of Roman law and "procedures developed by merchants in European ports of the Mediterranean, Atlantic Coast, North Sea, and Baltic," maritime law facilitated international commerce by ensuring that ships could be returned to sea quickly.[38] It evolved to spread risks among merchants, to reward those who hazarded life and limb to save marine property, and to limit the liability of ship owners. Instance suits included mariners' claims for unpaid wages, claims for salvage (retrieving a ship or cargo that had been captured, beached, or wrecked), and bottomry bond suits in which captains borrowed against the value of their vessels in foreign ports. The courts' instance jurisdiction also extended to maritime contracts for ship supply and repair, marine insurance, charter party cases, and claims brought by sailors that a ship was unfit for sea.[39] Finally, as a part of their instance jurisdiction, Vice Admiralty Courts heard cases involving torts and petty crimes committed on the high seas.[40] In sum, this court operated in ways that were designed to facilitate the ceaseless movement that made transatlantic commerce possible, while preserving the liberties of subjects far from English shores.

THE CHATTEL PRINCIPLE IN AN AGE OF SAIL

Because South Carolina and Jamaica were vitally important commercial nodes within the British Atlantic World, their Vice Admiralty Courts were bustling jurisdictions. South Carolina's surviving records from 1716 to 1763 include 139 cases, a run that compares favorably with that of Maryland's Vice Admiralty Court.[41] Moreover, between 1716 and 1749, the court's caseload nearly doubled, an increase in business that tracks South Carolina's growth as a commodity exporter over the first half of the eighteenth century [see Tables 3.1 and 3.2]. Because Jamaica's Vice Admiralty records are in a poor state of preservation, it is difficult to similarly quantify the court's business. From what case files remain, though, it is clear that Jamaica was among the most important prize jurisdictions in North America.

---

[38] Owen and Tolley, *Courts of Admiralty*, 6–7.

[39] In these cases, courts had the authority to arrest the ship, order it surveyed, and either certify the vessel as fit or have it condemned and sold. This is precisely what happened in the 1716 case of the snow Rochdale, which South Carolina's Vice Admiralty judge condemned after her mariners protested "against the Wind and Seas" for damaging the vessel beyond repair. *In re Snow Rochdale*, November 13, 1716, South Carolina Vice Admiralty Court Minute Books, A–B vols., 1–19, LOC. Unfit ships typically were sold for the benefit of the owners.

[40] Owen and Tolley, *Courts of Admiralty*, 12–14.   [41] See *Ibid., passim.*

TABLE 3.1 *South Carolina Vice Admiralty Court business by jurisdictional basis, 1716–1763*[42]

	Prize	Navigation Act Violations	Instance	Piracy	Unknown	Total
1716–1732	8	7	13	2	1	31
1736–1749	24	4	25	0	3	56
1752–1763	24	4	20	2	2	52
Total	56	15	58	4	6	139
Percent of Total Cases	40.29%	10.79%	41.73%	2.88%	4.32%	

TABLE 3.2 *South Carolina Vice Admiralty Court instance business, 1716–1763*

	Mariners' Wages	Salvage	Crimes and Torts	Unfit Ship	Damaged Goods	Unknown	Total
1716–1732	8	2	2	1	0	0	13
1736–1749	11	3	4	4	2	1	25
1752–1763	4	0	4	11	1	0	20
Total	23	5	10	16	3	1	58
Percentage of Total Cases	16.55%	3.60%	7.19%	11.51%	2.16%	0.72%	
Percentage of Total Instance Business	39.66%	8.62%	17.24%	27.59%	5.17%	1.72%	

Jamaican Vice Admiralty appeals to the Lords Commissioners of Prize Appeals far exceeded those from any other colony, although appeals from New York and Antigua also were common.[43] This is unsurprising given Jamaica's strategically important location between the British West Indies

---

[42] See Note on Methodology, p. 158.

[43] A body that consisted of members of the Privy Council, the Commissioners heard prize appeals from the colonial Vice Admiralty Courts as well as the High Court of Admiralty. Appeals from colonial Vice Admiralty Courts ran in instance matters to the High Court of Admiralty in London. Further appeal could be taken to the High Court of Delegates. In

and Spanish America, and the fact that the Caribbean experienced near-constant warfare in the eighteenth century.[44] As imperial powers grappled over access to Spanish trade and to increasingly lucrative sugar islands, Jamaica's Vice Admiralty Court became a clearinghouse for captured ships that could be condemned and refitted for action in the West Indies.

In both South Carolina and Jamaica, the assumption that people of African descent were valuable commodities shaped litigants' claims. Sailors, merchants, and Crown officials took advantage of the Vice Admiralty Courts' in rem jurisdiction to claim enslaved people as property, and they used the courts to profit from the transatlantic slave trade. In South Carolina, more than 21 percent of Vice Admiralty cases between 1716 and 1763 included claims to slaves as property or the regulation of life on transatlantic slave ships, and between 1716 and 1732 cases involving slaves comprised above 35 percent of the court's business. These cases were distributed across the court's docket, and could arise in the context of instance, prize, or Navigation Acts litigation [Tables 3.3 and 3.4]. More than half of these cases involved claims to slaves as property, as litigants vied to assert property rights in Black on ships, who were typically mariners [Table 3.3].[45] The Jamaican Court also routinely heard cases involving slaves, which included claims to enslaved people as property and a wide variety of cases brought by mariners on transatlantic slave ships.

Vice Admiralty litigation over slaves, which scholars have largely ignored, reflected the fact that South Carolina and Jamaica experienced economic booms in the eighteenth century that were bound up in colonists' growing ability to command slave labor. Both were colonies in which planters and merchants successfully leveraged the value of enslaved people to fuel economic growth.[46] Viewing enslaved people as economic investments as well as a source of labor, they used the value inherent in the bodies of enslaved people to expand their plantations and businesses. Indeed, litigants in both South Carolina and Jamaica understood that

prize cases, appeals ran to the Lords Commissioners of Prize Appeals. On appeal, the case was tried de novo.

[44] Crump, *Colonial Admiralty Jurisdiction*, 97.

[45] Although the South Carolina Court's records are surprisingly complete, they have not yet been systematically analyzed, likely because they remain unpublished. It seems that Charles Andrews reviewed these records, but aside from occasional citations to decisions, he never produced a detailed analysis of the court's business.

[46] Russell R. Menard, "Financing the Lowcountry Export Boom: Capital and Growth in Early Carolina," *WMQ* 51 (1994): 669–670; Daniel C. Littlefield, "The Slave Trade to Colonial South Carolina: A Profile," *South Carolina Historical Magazine* 101 (2000): 110–111.

TABLE 3.3 *South Carolina Vice Admiralty*
cases involving slaves, 1716–1763

Case Type	Number
Claims to slaves as property	17
Cases involving slave ships	10
Other*	3
Total	30
Percentage of Total Cases (139)	21.58%

* This category includes one case brought by a "a free
Negro Man," presumably for unpaid wages. See *Thomas
Ware vs. John Millar*, June 29, 1749, South Carolina
Vice Admiralty Court Minute Books, C–D vols., NARA.
I also have included a claim to a ship containing convict
and indentured servants, largely because these servants
were libeled in precisely the same way as slaves. See *In re
the Eagle Galley als. The New Yorks Revenges Revenge*,
December 17, 1718, South Carolina Vice Admiralty
Court Minute Books, A–B vols., 380–412, LOC.

TABLE 3.4 *South Carolina Vice Admiralty cases involving slaves over time*

Date Range	Number of Cases Involving Slaves	Total Number of Cases in Date Range	Percentage of Cases in Date Range Involving Slaves	Percentage of Total Slave Cases
1716–1732	11	31	35.48%	36.67%
1736–1749	11	56	19.64%	36.67%
1752–1763	8	52	15.38%	26.67%
Total	30	139		

slaves were valuable as commodities as well as laborers. John Stevens
explained it well. When his ship ran aground at the Charlestown bar in
1717, he was carrying two male slaves valued at £500, a female slave
worth £200, a head of rum appraised at £150, and muscovado sugar
worth a mere £40.[47] The slaves on board the *Diamond* were by far the

[47] *John Stevens Master and Owner of the Sloop Diamond v. Joseph River, Richard Rivers,
James Denford & Alexander Spencer of Berkeley County Planters*, December 18, 1717,

most valuable property in her hold. This is why Stevens was so discon-
certed, as he told the court, when Berkeley County planters Joseph Rivers,
Richard Rivers, Joseph Danford, Alexander Spencer, and "Divers other
Confederates" took a canoe out to the vessel and carried away "all the
Singular the Negros Goods and Merchandizes."[48] The alleged thieves had
offered to pay for the rum, but for Stevens, this was no satisfaction.[49] "It
was not the rum that he matter'd," he told them, "but the negroes which
he Expected to have account of."[50]

Although colonists claimed slaves in colonial Vice Admiralty Courts,
they were not the only individuals who understood that slaves were
valuable commodities. Despite the fact that many sailors had never visited
a rice or sugar plantation, they were nonetheless aware that slaves were
likely to be the most valuable cargo on a captured ship. As a result, when
merchant or naval vessels captured a prize, their crews asked Vice
Admiralty Courts to award them any slaves found aboard. In Ned's
case, for example, the captors of the ship *Revenge* initially brought the
litigation and asked the court to grant them "all & Singular The Negroes
Goods and Merchandizes aboard the Same."[51] This included ten slaves,
who were identified by name in an attached schedule.[52]

The captors of the *Revenge* were not alone. Other crews claimed
enslaved people on prize ships, including the crew of the Sloop of War
Movil Trader, who libeled the Spanish Prize *Nuestra Senora de Candelaria*
and "all & Singular the negro & Indian Slaves Goods & Merchandizes
found on board," and the sailors of the Sloops of War *Hornett* and *Port
Royal*, who libeled a slave ship that had been captured with a cargo of slaves
bound from Surinam to Cap Francois.[53] In 1778, the crew of the *Porcupine*
asked the Jamaican Vice Admiralty Court to condemn the "[c]argoe
apparel and furniture and also the Nergroe Mulatto and other Slaves on
board" the schooner *Abigail* "for the Use of the Captors."[54] And in perhaps
one of the largest and most complicated slave claim ever litigated in

---

South Carolina Vice Admiralty Court Minute Books, A–B vols., 195, LOC. These prices
   are likely in South Carolina currency, not in pounds sterling.
[48] *In re Sloop Diamond*, 195.   [49] *Ibid.*, 204.   [50] *Ibid.*, 203–204.
[51] *In re Sloop Revenge*, November 19, 1718, South Carolina Vice Admiralty Court Records,
   A–B vols., 277, LOC.
[52] *Ibid.*, 230.
[53] *In re Nuestra Senora de la Candelaria*, South Carolina Vice Admiralty Court Minute
   Books, A–B vols., 413–421, LOC; *In re De Jonge Isaac*, October 28, 1758 (date of
   capture), Records of the High Court of Admiralty and Colonial Vice-Admiralty Courts,
   TNA, HCA 45/5.
[54] *In re the Abigail*, February 16, 1778, HCVA 302/286–308, JARD.

Jamaica, the judge sorted through voluminous testimony in order to determine which navy crews were entitled to the slaves captured in Fort Fernando de Omoa, a Spanish Fort in the Bay of Honduras, when it fell to the British navy during the American Revolution.[55]

Even the Crown libeled slaves in Vice Admiralty Courts. In *Dom. Rex v. 3 Negro Men Slaves*, South Carolina's Advocate General argued that three slaves taken on the high seas by the crew of the ship *Pool* belonged to the king "as Right & Perquisite of Admiralty."[56] This case reveals the Crown's active involvement in human trafficking, but more importantly, it illustrates how easily the forms and practices of the Vice Admiralty Court were adapted to accommodate new kinds of property, and especially human property. In this case and in other disputes over slaves, litigants and judges substituted slaves for ships and other kinds of marine property that centuries-old admiralty procedure permitted litigants to sue, attach, and sell. The extension of the court's in rem jurisdiction to slaves in this case and in others like it benefitted not only the king and wealthy colonists, but also sailors, many of whom angled for their share of slaves as property using this venue as well.

DOM. REX V. 3 NEGRO MEN SLAVES AND THE LANGUAGE OF ADMIRALTY

In June 1736, the crew of the Pink *Pool* spotted three slaves in a canoe "about Ten Leagues distance from the Island of Cuba."[57] The slaves had run away from their masters and were in poor physical health – Boatswain Henry Wright testified that they had been subsisting on nothing but "[s]tinking beef and bread" since their escape.[58] Despite their sorry state, however, the *Pool*'s captain, Richard Wall, recognized a windfall when he saw one. He did what most other clever mariners would do in this situation: He brought the men aboard and set about trying to profit from his good fortune. Wall's plans were disrupted at

---

[55] Affidavit of Patrick Bourke, January 31, 1780, *Advocate General et al. v. Indigo Quick silver and other Goods and divers Negroe Slaves*: HCVA 302/391–403, JARD.

[56] *Dom. Rex v. 3 Negro Men Slaves*, July 28, 1737, South Carolina Vice Admiralty Court Minute Books, C–D vols., 149, LOC.

[57] *Ibid.*, 148–149. The crew believed that they were slaves because "[o]ne of the said negroes spoke English" and told them "they were all Slaves." Affidavit of Boatswain Henry Wright, August 3, 1737, *Ibid.*, 154.

[58] Affidavit of Boatswain Henry Wright, August 3, 1737, *Dom. Rex v.3 Negro Men Slaves*, 154.

every turn. He first tried to sell the slaves but failed to reach an agreement with his potential buyer over the terms of payment. After this disappointment, bad weather forced the ship into the Charlestown harbor, where Wall became increasingly anxious. He was aware that if royal officials discovered the slaves, they could be confiscated as perquisites, or *droits*, of Admiralty. Typically, the Admiralty was entitled to one-tenth the value of wrecks, prizes, royal fish, "derelicts," and abandoned ships "within its jurisdiction."[59] Because Wall had found the slaves adrift on the high seas, he feared that they might be considered derelict or abandoned property that was subject to the Admiral's claims.

Wall might have decided at this point to bow to the inevitable and haul his ship and the three slaves into a Vice Admiralty Court, where he likely would be rewarded for his pains. Instead, he panicked, and he pressured the crew to conceal the slaves. While riding out the storm, he ordered his sailors not to disclose that the "three Negroes were taken up at Sea," and he set the slaves to "hard Labour in pumping" water from the ship's hold.[60] Unfortunately for Wall, this secrecy was all in vain. The slaves were discovered, and the *Pool*'s captain found himself under arrest. In the litigation that followed, South Carolina's Advocate General argued that the slaves belonged to the King of England "as Right & Perquisite of Admiralty," just as Wall had feared.[61]

From this opening salvo through the case's resolution, the fact that the slaves at issue were valuable commodities shaped the litigation. As we have already seen, Wall concealed the slaves because he understood that they were valuable, and he anticipated that others would dispute his right to them. The king's representatives also prosecuted the case because they had an expectation that the three slaves would fetch a good price in the Charlestown market. For the court's deputy receiver, Benjamin Whitaker, the three enslaved people were no different from an abandoned or wrecked vessel: They were valuable objects that could be sold to enrich the king's coffers and to line the pockets of his officials in South Carolina.

More important for our purposes, all of the parties in the case assumed that the slaves could be fit into admiralty law's forms and procedures and treated like any other *res*. Wall, for one, believed that a Vice Admiralty

[59] Towle, ed., *Records of the Vice-Admiralty Court of Rhode Island*, 31, n. 4.
[60] Mariner Charles Watkins agreed that the captain "gave Strict Orders" to the crew not to reveal the presence of the slaves or that they "were taken up at Sea." Affidavit of mariner Charles Watkins, August 3, 1737, *Dom. Rex v. 3 Negro Men Slaves*, 155. Affidavit of Boatswain Henry Wright, August 3, 1737, *Dom. Rex v. 3 Negro Men Slaves*, 154.
[61] *Dom. Rex v. 3 Negro Men Slaves*, 149.

Court would consider the slaves to be derelicts or abandoned property, and this is precisely why he sought to hide them from royal officials. The deputy receiver came to the same conclusion, and he proceeded on the assumption that it was procedurally possible to claim the slaves as rights of Admiralty. Most striking, the Vice Admiralty Court's secretary slotted the slaves into a caption – or case name – that experienced English proctors would have immediately recognized, except in this case, "3 Negro Men Slaves" appeared in place of a ship's name.[62]

For his part, the judge proceeded in this case just as he would have in any other libel. He first sought to ensure that the slaves' owners were given proper notice of the proceedings, issuing four proclamations that invited anyone "claiming or pretending to claim any Right Title or Interest in the said Three Negro Men Slaves" to come forward.[63] This was standard practice in Vice Admiralty litigation. He also issued a warrant of appraisal directing several Charlestown merchants to "view examine and well and faithfully Appraise" the three slaves.[64] Warrants of appraisal in Vice Admiralty cases were also de rigueur; judges issued them in most cases in order to ascertain the value of libeled property. It was not unusual for judges to follow the form of ship appraisal warrants when they issued warrants to appraise slaves. In 1740, for example, the court ordered "Othniel Beale Ebenezer Simons and Isaac Beauchamp of Charles Town Merchants" to appraise a ship "lying in the harbour of Charles Town" and also to value "certain Spanish Goods and Merchandizes and Two Indian and One Negroe Slaves lately taken and Seized."[65] With no apparent concern that the property being appraised was, in fact, human, Vice Admiralty judges routinely brought slaves before the court as objects that might be condemned, valued, and sold.

---

[62] See also *Boseaven* v. *Spanish privateer called the St. Joseph las Animas alias Le Pearl and four Negroes*, May 2, 1740, South Carolina Vice Admiralty Court Minute Books, C–D vols., 340, LOC; *Jones* v. *Spanish Goods and Slaves*, July 1, 1740, South Carolina Vice Admiralty Court Minute Books, C–D vols., 352, LOC; *Owners Officers and Sailors of the Galley Isabella versus Sloop lately retaken and her contents, and also against three Spanish Slaves lately taken in the Ship Patience*, September 10, 1747, South Carolina Vice Admiralty Court Records, 1736–1749, C–D vols., 424; *Advocate General et al.* v. *Indigo Quick Silver and Other Goods and Divers Negroe Slaves*, January 1780, JARD, HCVA 302/391–403; *In re 20 Negro[es] and Other Slaves*, December 29, 1780, JARD, HCVA 302/638.

[63] *Dom. Rex* v. *3 Negro Men Slaves*, 149.   [64] *Ibid.*, 151.

[65] *Jones* v. *Spanish Goods and Slaves*, July 1, 1740, South Carolina Vice Admiralty Court Minute Books, C–D vols., 352, LOC.

The parties in *Dom. Rex v. 3 Negro Men Slaves* also fit the slaves at issue in the case into admiralty law's much older substantive categories. We have already seen that the deputy receiver claimed the three slaves as *droits* of Admiralty, but Captain Wall also argued that he was entitled to salvage for rescuing the slaves. The term "salvage" was rooted in an assumption that the "salved" property was, in fact, property. Here, however, Wall applied it to human beings. Hauled before the judge to justify concealing the three slaves from the court, Wall attempted to preserve his last chance to profit from this ill-fated venture. He disclaimed "any Right or property" in the slaves, but he humbly asked the court to deduct his salvage costs "out of the said Negroes" because he had been at great expense in their feeding and upkeep.[66] The judge eventually satisfied his demand: he awarded Wall salvage from the proceeds of the court-ordered slave sale.[67]

This commodification continued through the case's resolution. Judge Lewis declared that the slaves were perquisites of Admiralty, but he hesitated to sell them at first. He planned to delay the sale for a year and a day in order to provide any potential owner with an opportunity to claim them.[68] However, the deputy receiver urged the court to "expos[e]" the slaves "to Publick Sale" immediately. Rather than going to the expense of feeding the slaves, he argued, the court could simply hold the sale proceeds in the event an owner came forward. Whitaker also insisted that it would be "difficult and hazardous" to keep the slaves in the colony, presumably because the three men were proven runaways. Finally, he expressed a very real fear that the slaves were "[s]ubject to Mortality." If they died before they were sold, no one would profit from Wall's find, including the judge.[69]

Whitaker's reasoning here is the exception to the rule that litigants in Vice Admiralty cases typically did not acknowledge the humanity of enslaved people. By urging the judge to sell the slaves at public auction, Whitaker treated the three men as marketable commodities. On the other hand, he also advocated for their immediate sale based upon his concern that they posed a flight risk or might succumb to sickness. Both of these reasons acknowledged the reality that the slaves were, in fact, human beings. As scholars have shown, when slaves ran away or died, it forced white Europeans to reckon with their actions. Whitaker gestured at this, but what is striking here is that his gesture ultimately served a more mercenary goal. Indeed, Whitaker reminded the judge that these slaves

---

[66] *Dom Rex v. 3 Negro Men Slaves*, 153.   [67] *Ibid.*, 161.   [68] *Ibid.*   [69] *Ibid.*, 163.

were human beings, not out of any humanitarian concern, but because he hoped to preserve their value at the time of sale. The judge found this argument compelling. Although the court's final decree has not survived, other case records show that the court ultimately sold the three slaves to colonist John Parris for £302 SC currency. This sale benefitted all of the parties involved in the case, with the obvious exception of the enslaved men. The king received his perquisites. The court's officers, including the Judge and Marshal, took a cut, and Captain Wall collected £60 for his trouble. It was less than he might have made had he sold the slaves himself, but better than emerging from the ordeal empty-handed.[70]

This outcome is a reminder that individuals of all sorts reaped the benefits of chattel slavery and the legal apparatus that buttressed it. As *Dom. Rex v. 3 Negro Men Slaves* makes clear, Vice Admiralty litigants, whether sailors or sovereigns, took advantage of procedures that allowed them to claim slaves just as they would ships or cargo. As we have already seen, plantation colonists routinely compared slaves to other types of movable property, and especially livestock, in other contexts. That a similar process occurred in Vice Admiralty Courts suggests that analogizing people to things was a more widespread practice than previously has been acknowledged, and that these types of analogies were in many cases legally inflected. Vice Admiralty litigants and judges treated slaves like marine property in pleadings because both were, at law, chattel property that might be brought before the court. Law's language provided a useful template that they deployed for practical reasons to claim valuable human property. It disciplined and channeled their speech, making the choice of these analogies a natural and logical one rather than one that triggered disquiet or cognitive dissonance. In one way, then, watching litigants as they maneuvered in Vice Admiralty Courts reveals that the language of law was rigid. Preexisting categories left litigants with few linguistic alternatives that would have accomplished their objective of successfully claiming slaves in court. At the same time, however, Vice Admiralty cases like *Dom. Rex v. 3 Negro Men Slaves* reveal that legalese was also astonishingly flexible. Older categories may have persisted, but their meaning could be expanded and changed. Although the terms of Vice Admiralty practice appeared to be set, they in fact were infinitely variable, as colonists and judges adapted age-old forms to suit their desire to treat Black people as property that could be libeled, condemned, and sold.

---

[70] *Ibid.*, 264. Parris never fulfilled the terms of his bond. In subsequent litigation, the court ordered Parris's executors to return the slaves, who were sold yet again.

POLICING THE TRADE

We have already seen how Vice Admiralty Courts litigants adapted admiralty procedures to claim enslaved people as property. In this way, they thrust the economic benefits of chattel slavery beyond the shores of plantation America and out into the Atlantic. At the same time, the courts and their litigants also contributed to the commodification of Black people in a less direct but no less significant way: by regulating life on transatlantic slave-trading ships. The appearance of Guinea ships over the horizon was a commonplace event in South Carolina and Jamaica, and the mariners who worked aboard them routinely asked local Vice Admiralty Courts to adjudicate their claims at voyage's end. In fact, watching these courts in action shows that they worked to satisfy mariners' expectations about the payment of wages and the administration of shipboard discipline. Although scholars have rightly noted that nineteenth-century Vice Admiralty Courts and their judges "embarked on an unprecedented experiment in international humanitarian intervention" in order to end the slave trade, their predecessors actively facilitated Britain's commerce in slaves.[71]

By 1740 Great Britain was "the world's leader in carrying human cargoes," and British ships transported approximately 2 million Africans into slavery between 1740 and 1807.[72] As British merchants engrossed the transatlantic slave trade over the course of the eighteenth century, they "required a steadily growing number of maritime workers."[73] Life on a slave ship, however, was unattractive even by the notoriously low standards of eighteenth-century sailors. As Marcus Rediker has noted, "[s]eamen disliked the African trade more than any other, and their reasons are not difficult to discern."[74] Mortality rates were high: sailors on slave ships "died in roughly the same horrendous proportions" as their cargos.[75] Mutiny was also common. As sailors lingered on the coast of Africa for months at a time procuring cargoes, some reached the breaking point and took over the vessel. This was true of mariner Benjamin Sumpton, who turned "Pirate and Rebell," imprisoned the ship's Chief Mate, and persuaded the crew to mutiny.[76] In 1766,

---

[71] Jenny S. Martinez, *The Slave Trade and the Origins of International Human Rights Law* (Oxford: Oxford University Press, 2011); Tara Helfman, "The Court of Vice Admiralty at Sierra Leone and the Abolition of the West African Slave Trade," *Yale Law Journal* 115 (2006): 1122.

[72] Rediker, *Between the Devil and the Deep Blue Sea*, 45.   [73] *Ibid.*, 46.   [74] *Ibid.*
[75] *Ibid.*, 47.   [76] *Rex* v. *Benjamin Sumpton*, February 1756, HCVA 101, JARD.

mariners on the slave ship *Venus* also mutinied off the African coast, while in 1770 William Floyd murdered a fellow crew member and led a revolt on his ship at "Callabar."[77] Incidents like these did little to enhance the reputation of mariners in the slave trade, who were among the Vice Admiralty Courts' most avid consumers of justice.

Many who sailed on slave ships used the courts to hold physically abusive captains to account. Although maritime discipline was notoriously harsh in the eighteenth century, Vice Admiralty judges provided a forum for determining when punishments were excessive. In *King v. Harrison*, for example, the South Carolina Court was asked to determine whether a shipboard lashing was severe enough to result in the death of a crew member on a slave ship.[78] John Dobb, master of the snow *Old Ann*, was accused in the Jamaica Vice Admiralty Court of whipping to death a mariner under his command, while Captain Ralph Lowe, "not having the feare of God before his Eyes but being moved and Seduced by the Instigation of the Devil," allegedly starved one of his crewmembers to death.[79]

Accused ships' officers occasionally won these cases, especially when they could prove that sailors were mutinous. Mutinies and slave revolts, which were commonplace in the Guinea trade, disrupted the flow of Atlantic commerce and created instability in the slave trade.[80] As a result, Vice Admiralty judges did not hesitate to punish alleged mutineers or to uphold captains' rights to discipline mutinous sailors. For example, in 1753, mariner James Littman asked the South Carolina Vice Admiralty Court to arrest Peter Bostock, master of the ship *Prince George*, for chaining him and beating him "with force and arms" on a voyage to the River Gambia.[81] Littman sought monetary damages, but the master argued that his actions were justified. He countered that the sailor was, in fact, a notorious drunk who was "very abusive to this Defendant & to the rest of the Officers." More seriously, Littman made "behaved himself in a very disorderly & mutinous mannor & threatened to carry away the

[77] *Rex* v. *John Wait*, April 15, 1766, HCVA 101/30, 32, JARD; *Rex* v. *William Floyd*, November 1770, HCVA 101/34, JARD.

[78] *King* v. *Joseph Harrison*, June 22, 1758, South Carolina Vice Admiralty Court Minute Books, E–F vols., 45–52, NARA.

[79] *Rex* v. *William Ainsworth*, March 1, 1758, HCVA 101/14–16, JARD; *Rex* v. *Ralph Lowe*, April 28, 1755, HCVA 101/5, JARD.

[80] Rediker, *Between the Devil and the Deep Blue Sea*, 48–50.

[81] *James Littman* v. *Peter Bostock*, September 19, 1753, South Carolina Vice Admiralty Court Minute Books, E–F vols., 52, NARA.

Boat."[82] In this case, the judge found the captain's explanation convincing, and he dismissed the libel because "putting the Actor in Irons upon the Coast of Gambia" was "[j]ustified" by his "[t]urbulent & unruly behavior."[83]

Although officers could occasionally prevail over their crews in litigation over punishments, sailors usually won Vice Admiralty wage suits. Most mariners were wage laborers, and they signed labor contracts on shore that "formalized and mediated the relations among owners, captain, officers, and crew."[84] These agreements could vary, but they typically stipulated the length of the voyage and how much the sailor would be paid. Sailors expected that captains would adhere to their promises, but when they failed to do so, they sought the aid of Vice Admiralty Courts.[85] Mariners typically brought wage claims by libeling their ship, and if they won their case, the Vice Admiralty judge could order the ship sold to satisfy back wages. The case of the *Ludlow* (1717) was typical. The *Ludlow*'s crew had contracted to sail from London to Guinea, where they planned to acquire "a Cargoe of Negro Slaves." From there, they agreed to travel to Barbados, Charlestown, and finally Virginia, unlading the slaves as they traveled from place to place. But upon landing in Charlestown and "finding Negroes" were "a very good price," the *Ludlow*'s captain deviated from the plan: He decided to sell the rest of the cargo at Charlestown rather than proceeding to Virginia as contracted. The *Ludlow*'s crew objected on the grounds that they had not signed on for this route; they requested their back wages and asked to be discharged from service.[86] Although the captain refused, the Vice Admiralty judge sided with the sailors and ordered the captain to pay their wages in Carolina money proportionately to British pounds, not in substantially devalued local currency.[87]

---

[82] *Ibid.*, 50.

[83] *Ibid.*, 54. See also *John Harvey, John Heslom, Richard Robbins, John Parry and George Ferguson, Mariners, versus John Ebsworthy, Master of the Brigantine Seaflower*, August 14, 1738, South Carolina Vice Admiralty Court Minute Books, C–D vols., 169–184, LOC. In this case, John Harvey claimed that the master of the *Seaflower* "with force and arms ... did beat wound and evilly entreat so that of his life it was dispaired and did also encourage the slaves on board the said vessel to beat him the said John Harvey." *Ibid.*, 177.

[84] Rediker, *Between the Devil and the Deep Blue Sea*, 117.   [85] *Ibid.*, 117; 119.

[86] *Mariners of the Fly Brigantine against the Fly Brigantine and against the owners*, November 9, 1717, South Carolina Vice Admiralty Court Minute Books, A–B vols., 158, LOC.

[87] *In re Ludlow*, May 23, 1717, South Carolina Vice Admiralty Court Minute Books, A–B vols., 64, LOC.

The crew of the *Ludlow* held their captain and his employer to account for failing to adhere to an agreed-upon route. Other mariners on transatlantic slave ships sued for wages when voyages were unprofitable. Captains in the Guinea trade did not always oversee successful voyages, but sailors nonetheless expected to be paid. This was true for the crew of the *Fly*, who libeled their ship for the payment of wages owed for a disastrous voyage to Africa. The mariners had agreed to sail "from London to Guinea for a Cargoe of Negroes," and then "from Guinea to Carolina." On the African coast, however, a series of misfortunes caused them to deviate from their expected route. A number of sailors died of illness, and the rest barely managed to escape from a group of "Country Negroes," who planned "to rise and Come on board them." Although the crew learned of the attack in time, they nonetheless fled with only "part of their Cargoe of Negroes on board." This meant, of course, that the voyage was a financial failure. Without a full contingent of slaves to sell, it was unlikely that the captain and his employers would turn a profit. Presumably for this reason, the captain failed to pay the crew as promised, and they asked the Vice Admiralty judge for relief.[88]

Vice Admiralty Courts typically favored mariner-libelants like the crews of the *Ludlow* and the *Fly*. As a procedural matter, they made it relatively simple for sailors to initiate suits. Crews could join together to libel a ship, which limited individual litigation costs and made adjudicating cases faster.[89] Judges also could arrest vessels to secure mariners' wage claims, and upon the sale of a condemned ship, they preferred wage claims ahead of all other creditors when proceeds were distributed.[90] Moreover, they "did not hesitate" to sell merchant vessels in order to satisfy wage claims.[91] This was partly because Vice Admiralty judges "recognized the indispensability of maritime labor to the orderly movement of commodities," which in the eighteenth century included slaves.[92] But it also reflected contemporary assumptions about sailors as a social class. Most early modern Britons believed that mariners were incapable of making

---

[88] *Mariners of the Fly Brigantine against the Fly Brigantine and against the owners*, November 9, 1717, South Carolina Vice Admiralty Court Minute Books, A–B vols., 158, LOC.

[89] Generally, sailors would execute, en masse, a power of attorney authorizing a local merchant or their ship's captain to prosecute a case on their behalf. The attorney would then appoint a proctor to bring the libel. This type of collective advocacy was also used by mariners to collect prize money due to them upon the condemnation of a ship.

[90] Owen and Tolley, *Courts of Admiralty*, 2–3. Owen and Tolley have found that in Maryland, wage cases brought by seamen were won "without exception." *Ibid.*, 11.

[91] Rediker, *Between the Devil and the Deep Blue Sea*, 119.   [92] *Ibid.*

rational decisions and therefore in need of heightened legal protection. Sir William Scott, a High Court of Admiralty judge, encapsulated this view when he proclaimed that the "common mariner" was "easy and careless, illiterate and unthinking" and that he had no "resources," whether "in his own intelligence" or "experience in habits of business."[93] Mariners constantly gave the lie to this characterization, however. As Laura Benton has shown, many sailors were savvy legal actors. They were familiar with customary legal norms that structured life on the high seas, and they "actively engaged in imaginative legal posturing, rehearsing stories that might serve to establish actions as legal in judicial forums."[94] We have already seen how Richard Wall concealed slaves from the court in *Dom. Rex v. 3 Negro Men Slaves* because he understood that the Vice Admiralty Court might declare them to be perquisites of Admiralty. Wall was familiar enough with admiralty practice to assess the consequences that would follow if royal officials discovered the slaves. Mariners who labored on transatlantic slave ships were equally astute. In Vice Admiralty litigation, they revealed that they, too, could navigate the dense web of legal arrangements that organized early modern maritime life. Most importantly for our purposes, they understood that slaves were valuable, and they used the courts to profit from their commodification.

This is especially clear in *Worsdale v. Barry*, a case that merged concerns about the financial organization of slave-trading voyages with questions about the ownership of slave property. In this 1729 litigation, the mate of an Africa-bound snow, Nicholas Worsdale, claimed that the ship's captain, Thomas Barry, had denied him his rightful commission for the sale of slaves in Charlestown. According to Worsdale, he was entitled to "a Reward (according to Custom) One Moiety of Four Pounds for every One Hundred & Four Pounds for which the said Negroes should be sold in Carolina."[95] But in order to deprive him of his "said Priviledge and Liberty," Barry detained him on the ship, presumably to prevent him from knowing how many slaves were sold.

Although most sailors contracted for wages, officers on slave-trading vessels like Worsdale and Barry signed more complicated compensation agreements. Some, like Worsdale, were entitled to a bonus for each slave

---

[93] H. Bourguignon, *Sir William Scott, Lord Stowell, Judge of the High Court of Admiralty* (Cambridge: Cambridge University Press, 1987), 5–7.

[94] Benton, *A Search for Sovereignty*, 113.

[95] *Worsdale v. Barry*, August 26, 1729, South Carolina Vice Admiralty Court Minute Books, A–B vols., 610–665, LOC.

delivered alive to their final destination. Others were allowed "to carry one or more Africans as privilege, taking the slave's fare and provisions from the ship's stores."[96] To determine how much Barry owed Worsdale, then, the Vice Admiralty judge first had to calculate how many slaves were subject to commission and how many were privilege slaves. Barry revealed that a number of officers on the ship were investing in the bodies of African slaves. He testified that fifteen of the slaves "were his Own Property, purchased with his own Private Goods." Another slave "belonged to the second mate of the Said Snow name of Charles Smith," while yet another "belonged to George Rocks Master of a Ship lost on the Coast of Africa."[97] These officers viewed the enslaved people that they transported as part of a larger compensation package that included payment in various forms. As a result, they kept close tabs on their "privilege" slaves, and identified individual slaves as property in ways that courts would recognize.

For example, Barry, like most mariners who worked the transatlantic slave trade, identified his enslaved property by branding them. He told the court that knew which slaves were his because he had "caused [them] to be markt for his own proper use and account . . . branding them on the right Shoulder with a bowl of a Tobacco Pipe."[98] Historians have interpreted slave branding as a practice that revealed that masters perceived their slaves to be human. Jennifer Morgan, for example, has argued that a slave was "branded 'like' an animal in order to humiliate, not because she was an animal and was insensate."[99] In marking his "privilege" slaves with a tobacco pipe, however, Barry was engaged in a practice that speaks less to his understanding of slaves as human and more to his legal acumen. By branding his slaves, Barry was adhering to customary slave trade practice, a source of authority that not only the South Carolina Vice Admiralty Court, but courts throughout the British Atlantic World – and even judges in Westminster – recognized.

In fact, in a 1768 Court of Exchequer dispute over a captain's privilege slaves, the barons of the Exchequer issued interrogatories in order to discover whether there was "any known Custom or usage in cases between Captains or Masters of Ships and their Owners or Merchants in the African Trade from Bristol with respect to the Masters privilege of

[96] Rediker, *Between the Devil and the Deep Blue Sea*, 119.
[97] *Worsdale v. Barry*, 617–618.   [98] *Ibid.*, 664.
[99] Jennifer L. Morgan, *Laboring Women: Reproduction and Gender in New World Slavery* (Philadelphia: University of Pennsylvania Press, 2004), 105.

Negroes." Interviewing several Bristol-based mariners, the court learned that it was typical for captains to mark their privilege slaves, and that a ship's master earned "four pounds of every One hundred and four pounds after the factor has deducted five pounds p[er]cent from the gross Sales of the Cargo." By marking his privilege slaves, then, Barry was following a set of customary legal norms that were familiar to sailors who traversed the globe. And by claiming his four-pound commission on slave sales, the same number that a Bristol sailor quoted to the barons of the Exchequer, Worsdale revealed himself to be conversant in the standards and practices of the same legal culture.[100]

Although it is tempting to read Worsdale's and Barry's actions for their ideological content, these were first and foremost attempts to conform their individual actions to widely accepted legal practice, all in the pursuit of economic advantage. Because they were legally savvy, both mariners could predict that judges would rule in their favor if they adhered to widely recognized customs, and they conformed their practices accordingly. Their choices lacked independent, idiosyncratic content – they were not actions behind which stood fraught or complicated intentions – and instead reflect adaptations on a microscale to legal norms in the slave trade that touched even the most humble British subjects.

BLACK MARINERS IN PERIL ON THE SEA

Despite clear evidence that mariner-litigants were sophisticated legal actors, Vice Admiralty Courts nonetheless continued to favor them. This heightened protection, however, did not extend to Black people who labored at sea. In fact, court records reveal that Black seafarers were particularly vulnerable to condemnation or sale. The commodification of Black bodies throughout the Atlantic World meant that any person of African descent might be libeled as property in a Vice Admiralty Court. This is especially evident in early prize litigation over the contents of pirate ships, which often included claims to Black or Native American slaves found aboard. Litigated just as Great Britain's blue water empire began its steep geopolitical ascent, these cases offer snapshots of shipboard life at the turn of the eighteenth century. They reveal an astonishingly polychromatic world, one in which the racial hierarchies that we might expect to find are disrupted. It is a world in which – to a greater extent than was true on

---

[100] *John Lean v. Edward Nichols et al.*, Depositions Taken at Bristol, April 18, 1768, TNA E134/8Geo3/East9.

land – free and enslaved Black laborers could leverage their formidable skills to build lives of relative prosperity for themselves and their families. Nonetheless, we also encounter a world that was rife with risk. Liminal figures like Ned navigated a perilous course between slavery and freedom, relying upon various strategies to avoid commodification. Although some successfully resisted attempts by white Britons to claim them as property, others learned that freedom was only "unbound" where law could not follow.[101]

At the beginning of the eighteenth century, piracy had become a particular problem in the North American southeast and Caribbean, and the governors of Virginia and South Carolina engaged in serious efforts to eradicate buccaneers from the southeast coast of the American mainland. This local "war against pirates" was part of a broader imperial campaign that culminated in a series of sensational piracy trials, including the trial and execution of Stede Bonnet in South Carolina.[102] High-stakes litigation over pirate ships and their contents often followed the capture and criminal conviction of pirates as captors claimed these ships and any slaves found aboard them as prizes, or claimed a percentage of their value as "salvage." In the libel of Stede Bonnet's ship *Revenge*, for example, the captors asked Judge Nicholas Trott to condemn the ship and "all & Singular The Negroes Goods and Merchandizes aboard the Same."[103] These included a number of "Negroes, vizt. Prince Francois Sampson Yellow belly Mingo Tony Peter Ned Little Mingo a Negro Boy Ruby an Indian," whose combined value would have brought the captors (including William Rhett, Trott's son-in-law) a significant salvage fee.[104]

As we have already seen, South Carolina colonists also asserted claims to individual slaves on the *Revenge*, asking the court to return their human property. For example, Stephen Beaden, a South Carolina colonist, claimed that he was the "Sole Owner" of Peter, whom Bonnett had "piratically" taken off a "shallop called the Golden Fleece."[105] Catherine and Richard Tuckerman also argued that they were the rightful

---

[101] As Christopher Tomlins has shown, it was only when a long and bloody civil war temporarily displaced law that colonial plantation America's slave regimes ceased to function. Christopher Tomlins, *Freedom Bound: Law, Labor, and Civic Identity in Colonizing English America, 1580–1865* (Cambridge: Cambridge University Press, 2010), 569.

[102] Robert C. Ritchie, *Captain Kidd and the War against the Pirates* (Cambridge: Harvard University Press, 1986), 25; 235–236.

[103] *In re Revenge*, South Carolina Vice Admiralty Court Minute Books, A–B vols., 276, LOC.

[104] *Ibid.* [105] *Ibid.*, 290–291.

owners of Ned Grant, an enslaved diver discovered aboard Bonnett's ship. As Catherine explained, she had hired the "Notorious Renegade" out to one "Captain Barrett," who employed him as a salvage diver on the "Bahama Wrecks" off the Coast of Cape Canaveral. While working this favorite haunt of pirates and salvagers, Ned was captured by a "Captain Burgess," but he somehow escaped to New England, where he boarded a snow bound for Great Britain. Soon thereafter, however, Ned's luck ran out. Captured yet again – this time by Bonnett – Ned returned to the Bahamas and likely continued to work as a diver until 1718, when Bonnett was finally captured on the Cape Fear River.[106]

In Vice Admiralty records, Ned's story is mediated by the white colonists who claimed him as property. Nonetheless, even the Tuckermans' version of events allows us to draw some conclusions about his working life. As a free diver – a diver who could submerge for extended periods of time using only the air in his lungs – Ned was a highly skilled and, therefore, valuable slave. In an age when most white Europeans could not swim, divers of African descent like Ned were capable of diving more than 90 feet deep and holding their breath for two to four minutes. Perfecting their talents from a young age, they trained their bodies to withstand the taxing physical and psychological demands of deep diving.[107] These skills won Black divers renown throughout Europe as early as the sixteenth century, as Miranda Kaufmann has shown, and monarchs and merchants alike relied upon their expertise to extract wealth from the ocean floor.[108] As white Britons extended their reach across the Atlantic, the demand for Black divers' talents only increased. Indeed, the "thousands of ships" that "sank in the western Atlantic" tempted salvagers with the prospect of quick riches, and they used enslaved divers to "fish" upon the Spanish wrecks that crowded the Caribbean's dangerous shipping lanes.[109] Whether diving for pearls or salvaging artillery from sunken vessels, enslaved divers transformed these "hinter-seas" into zones of wealth production. At the same time, their exploits had the potential to provide their owners and contracted employers with a life-changing economic windfall.[110]

---

[106] Many thanks to Kevin Dawson for helping to identify the correct geographic location of the Bahama Wrecks.

[107] Kevin Dawson, "Enslaved Swimmers and Divers in the Atlantic World," *The Journal of American History* 92 (2006): 1346.

[108] Miranda Kaufmann, *Black Tudors: The Untold Story* (London: Oneworld Publications, 2017).

[109] Dawson, "History below the Waterline," 44.   [110] For this term, see *ibid.*

As Kevin Dawson has shown, the talents and irreplaceability of enslaved divers placed them atop the British Atlantic World's skilled labor hierarchy. Unlike skilled slaves on land, who could be replaced at any time with skilled white craftsmen, Black divers performed work that white Europeans simply could not. As a result, owners and contract employers sought to motivate divers through a mixture of financial compensation and privileged treatment rather than physical force.[111] For example, most divers received a share of goods salvaged in addition to wages, and whereas most slave gangs labored from dawn until dusk, divers "spent less than two hours a day underwater."[112] Checked by a fear of injuring these irreplaceable workers, white Britons avoided punishing divers in a way that might cause bodily harm. Indeed, divers were not typically subject to the day-to-day brutality, sanctioned by law, that coerced labor on plantations. They also could avoid "the churning whirlpools of verbal and physical abuse that punctuated the daily experiences of sailors and agricultural slaves."[113] This elevated status was hardwon. Although white Britons used financial and social privileges to exploit divers' skills, divers "did not passively wait for white authority to bequeath privileges."[114] Rather, they were cognizant of their irreplaceability, and they maneuvered within this reality to shape labor conditions. Divers carefully safeguarded their knowledge in order to protect their status, in some cases "creating semi-fraternal orders that precluded slaveholders from appropriating and propagating their aquatic fluencies."[115] Likewise, they actively resisted changes to customary working arrangements, utilizing work slowdowns to stoppages to register their disapproval. Whereas these resistance strategies earned slaves on land severe physical punishment, they were often effective at sea, where fear stayed the hand of white Britons.[116]

The working lives of these skilled Black maritime laborers underscore slavery's astonishing variety even as they upend our expectations about racial hierarchies in the early modern Atlantic World. As W. Jeffrey Bolster has reminded us, Black seafaring experiences cannot be reduced to "the image of manacled ancestors crammed aboard slave ships."[117] Enslaved people were not merely acted upon by white Britons. Rather, many took advantage of their positions aboard ship to construct lives of

---

[111] Dawson, "History below the Waterline," 42–43.   [112] *Ibid.*   [113] *Ibid.*, 58.
[114] *Ibid.*, 57.   [115] *Ibid.*, 60.
[116] Dawson, "Enslaved Swimmers and Divers in the Atlantic World," 1347.
[117] Bolster, *Black Jacks*, 2.

relative comfort for themselves when we compare their experiences to those of enslaved people toiling on plantations. In examining their working lives, it is important to recognize moments of agency and to identify the conditions that gave Black seafarers advantages as they resisted enslavement. It is equally important to isolate the particular aspects of slave law that Black maritime workers successfully mitigated. What we discover is that skilled maritime laborers were especially adept at checking slave law's physical brutality. As land receded into the horizon, so too did the conditions precedent for coercively disciplining Black bodies. At the same time, the yawning distance between land and sea created space for resistance and negotiation that skilled maritime laborers exploited to their benefit.

The chattel principle, however, was more difficult to elude. The presumption that Black people were property translated across oceans, imperiling the lives that individuals like Ned built for themselves. In fact, the very talents that gave skilled slaves leverage over whites at sea – that allowed them to avoid physical punishment and to enjoy relative economic prosperity – exposed them to danger by increasing their value as property. Ned learned this to his detriment. Indeed, it is not a coincidence that pirates, colonists, and court officials alike pursued Ned and claimed him as a prize. His diving talents made him exceedingly valuable, and this created incentives for white Britons of all sorts to treat him as property in Vice Admiralty litigation. Even at sea, the chattel principle worked an inexorable logic, transforming human beings of great skill into property in the eyes of the law.

This was true even when Black maritime workers were known to be free people, as we can see in *King v. Harrison*, a 1758 South Carolina Vice Admiralty Court case. In this rare felony prosecution, the gunner of the slave ship *Rainbow* accused Captain Joseph Harrison of murdering a sailor named Comer. Multiple witnesses linked Comer's death to a whipping administered by a "Negro Fellow call'd Dick," who worked as the ship's translator.[118] Although the litigation turned on whether the lashing was excessive, court records also reveal an underlying concern to uncover why Harrison allowed a Black man to whip a white sailor. What emerges from the trial records is a snapshot of the precarious life that Dick led as a free African maritime worker. A "[f]ree Negro Man," Dick had been hired at "Benein" in order to serve "as a Linguist" who could help

[118] *King v. Joseph Harrison*, June 22, 1758, South Carolina Vice Admiralty Court Minute Books, E–F vols., 46, NARA.

Captain Harrison communicate with his enslaved cargo.[119] It seems that some of the *Rainbow*'s white mariners understood that Dick's job was important to their success. Because he could communicate with the slaves aboard, Dick could help to detect and prevent a slave revolt during their voyage. This meant "that his living onboard the said Snow was of great Consequence to the Interest of the Voyage." Nonetheless, court records also reveal that some mariners, including Comer, resented the fact that Dick occupied a position of authority on the ship. Comer expressed his anger by harassing Dick, and in particular by threatening him with enslavement and sale. Witnesses confirmed that he relentlessly taunted Dick, saying that he "was bought as a Slave by Capt. Harrison and wou'd be sold at the West Indies" and that "he was no better than a Slave, and wou'd be Sold as Such."[120]

According to first mate John Dawson, Dick took these insults seriously, and he used his unique position aboard the ship to register his discontent. "Dick grew Sulky," according to Dawson, and he convinced the slaves below deck to refuse their food. More seriously, he also encouraged the slaves to revolt. According to Dawson, Dick incited the slaves, who became restless as a result and "wou'd be under no Command as formerly." They remained "in this humour ... for two days."[121] Although this protest certainly would have caught Captain Harrison's attention, Dick also complained to the captain directly about Comer's behavior, going so far as to "demanded Satisfaction" of the white sailor. Harrison at first demurred, and he advised Dick that "he could give him no Satisfaction" because he had "no power to beat any white Person on board." However, Dick refused to accept this answer. He continued to pressure Harrison, who finally authorized Dick to whip Comer "at two different times about three or four and twenty Lashes" in order "to prevent insurrection" aboard the ship.[122]

As the only person on board who could communicate with the *Rainbow*'s enslaved cargo, Dick's linguistic talents made him an asset to the captain and crew. They also endowed him with the power to make or break the voyage. If Dick chose to encourage a slave revolt, Captain Harrison and his crew might end their journey in a watery grave rather than spending their profits in the West Indies. Dick reminded Captain Harrison of this reality, and in a power shift that is shocking from the modern perspective, Harrison allowed Dick to beat a white man. Certainly, the fact that he did so with impunity is noteworthy.

[119] *Ibid.*, 49.   [120] *Ibid.*, 49–50.   [121] *Ibid.*, 49–50.   [122] *Ibid.*, 49–50.

Underscoring the diversity of Black work experiences in the Atlantic World, Dick's life at sea also reveals that skilled Black maritime workers could ascend shipboard power hierarchies based upon their talents. In acts of resistance great and small, they forced white Britons to cede power and to acknowledge their humanity.

Nonetheless, Comer's insults and Dick's response to them also remind us that Dick had much to fear. In a different context, his skin color would be sufficient to transform him from a free person into a person with a price, despite his considerable talents. Dick knew this, and this helps to explain his increasingly severe response to Comer's taunts. Encouraging a hunger strike and, finally, wielding the lash himself, Dick reaffirmed his authority and his personhood, creating a world in which Black was over white, if only for the span of a voyage. As his story shows, the chattel principle had deep undercurrents. Indeed, the categorization of slaves as chattel property in law and practice shaped the world that Dick and Comer inhabited, and it channeled their actions even before Comer's death became the subject of litigation. In Vice Admiralty Court records, we find evidence of inverted racial hierarchies that Black laborers skillfully exploited to check the more coercive aspects of slave law. At the same time, though, we also find the limits of resistance in law's very language.

This is not to suggest that Black maritime workers never jumped the ruts of a legal system that assumed they were chattel property. Against formidable odds, a few Black mariners adopted successful legal strategies. One of the most effective was to change the terms of the debate by claiming to be subjects of the Crown. Today, the term "subject" lacks a salient legal connotation. In the early modern Atlantic World, however, subjecthood was an enduringly powerful legal concept that encapsulated how individuals were linked to a sovereign. In general, the term connoted the reciprocal bond – called *ligeantia* – between a monarch and those born within his or her dominions. According to Sir Matthew Hale, a seventeenth-century English jurist, *ligeantia* implied "faith between the governor and governed": The subject gave the monarch allegiance and in turn received protection. At the heart of subjecthood, then, was an understanding that subjects owed allegiance to monarchs and monarchs offered protection to subjects.[123] This seems straightforward, but in reality it was much messier. At one level, subjecthood was visceral. Subjects owed their allegiance to the actual body of the king, which they were obligated to

---

[123] Sir Matthew Hale's *The Prerogatives of the King*, ed. D. E. C. Yale (London: Selden Society, 1976), 59.

protect just as the king protected the bodies of his subjects.[124] Nonetheless, subjecthood was as much a mystical bond as a physical one. For example, being born in the king's dominions did not automatically make one a subject; "faith and truth," which were "qualities of the mind and soul of man," were also needed. This meant that all sorts of people "might be brought into the benefits of subjecthood," as Paul Halliday has shown.[125]

Although enslaved people were never formally granted the protection of British subjects, people of African descent nonetheless persistently claimed this status into the nineteenth century. In the context of Vice Admiralty litigation, such a claim could mean the difference between freedom or condemnation. In fact, because British naval vessels or privateers were prohibited from capturing ships owned or crewed by British subjects, one strategy for avoiding capture altogether was for mariners on a ship to claim that they were British subjects (whether this was true or not). This included Black mariners. For example, when the ship *Royall Fancy* was captured as a prize during the Seven Years' War, "Six White Men Mariners & One Negro ... declared themselves English Subjects" and insisted that there were "no French subjects on board."[126] Displaying a keen understanding of maritime law, these crew members managed to avoid condemnation and sale by claiming subjecthood. For the Black sailor on board, the stakes of such a strategy were even higher: claiming British subjecthood might have ultimately saved him from public auction.

Similarly, in the remarkable 1747 case *Isabella v. 3 Slaves*, events took a surprising turn when the three slaves claimed as property petitioned the court as free subjects of the King of Spain. "Manuel Barnadina & Gabriel Joseph two Indian men & Manuel Stephens a Negro Man Subjects of the King of Spain" had been captured aboard the ship *Patience* and libeled in the South Carolina Vice Admiralty Court. We can only imagine the judge's surprise when he received a petition from the alleged objects in the case. In it, they insisted that they were free men and subjects of the King of Spain, and they asked the judge to interrogate witnesses on their behalf. The judge agreed, and a witness corroborated that they were, in

---

[124] Paul Halliday, *Habeas Corpus: From England to Empire* (Cambridge, MA: Harvard University Press, 2010), 70.

[125] *Ibid.*, 202.

[126] *Peter McIntosh et al. v. Sloop Royall Fancy*, May 2, 1760, South Carolina Vice Admiralty Court Minute Books, E–F vols., 304–305, NARA.

fact, "[f]ree Men and that their Fathers and Mothers were also Free."[127] Based upon this evidence, the court decreed the men "to be free Persons." He also ordered the captors in the case to pay costs "on account of their having prosecuted the said three Persons and accordingly by their Defending their Freedom & Liberty as aforesaid."[128] As subjects of the King of Spain who could definitively prove their free status, these three men became visible to the court as persons, not as property. And as persons at law, they were not liable to condemnation according to the terms of letters of reprisal and marque issued to the captors.[129]

The cases of the *Isabella* and the *Royal Fancy* are exceptions that prove the rule rather than evidence of a pattern of successful litigation by people of African descent in colonial Vice Admiralty Courts. They reveal a legal system that acted against powerful interests, but only under certain discrete circumstances, and only on behalf of those deemed persons in the eyes of the law. In fact, the ease with which courts adjudicated cases involving slaves indicates that individual positive results for Black sailors never challenged chattel slavery as a practice, and slaves claimed during the course of a Vice Admiralty trial were overwhelmingly likely to be condemned as property. Nonetheless, these cases do suggest that Black maritime laborers may

---

[127] *Owners Officers and Sailors of the Galley Isabella versus Sloop lately retaken and her contents, and also against three Spanish Slaves lately taken in the Ship Patience,* September 10, 1747, South Carolina Vice Admiralty Court Minute Books, C–D vols., 430, LOC.

[128] *Ibid.,* 431.

[129] As a private ship of war, the *Isabella's* activities technically were limited by the specific terms of her captain's commission of marque and reprisal. Although in this particular case the commission does not seem to have survived, others issued during the course of the War of Austrian Succession suggest that privateers were only authorized to seize Spanish property, and specifically ships and cargo. Because "several unjust Seizures had been made and Depredations carried on in the West Indies by Spanish Guarda Costas," the king authorized private ships to be fitted out to capture "[s]hips Vessels and Goods belonging to the King of Spain his Vassals and Subjects." Allowing Englishmen to take this property would provide "[r]eparacion and Satisfaction for his injured Subjects." Commission of marque and reprisal, November 22, 1739, South Carolina Vice Admiralty Court Minute Books, vols. C–D, 276–277, LOC. Manuel Barnardina, Gabriel Joseph, and Manuel made a credible case that they were not property and therefore not subject to confiscation. Although the Vice Admiralty Court might have chosen to disregard their evidence, in this case the judge honored their claims as persons and as subjects of the Spanish King, producing a result consistent with the law of nations. See also David Barry Gaspar, "'Subjects to the King of Portugal': Captivity and Repatriation in the Atlantic Slave Trade," in *The Creation of the British Atlantic World,* edited by Elizabeth Mancke and Carole Shammas (Baltimore: Johns Hopkins University Press, 2005), 93–115.

have discovered at least one effective strategy for resisting their commodification in Vice Admiralty Courts. By claiming subjecthood, Black litigants invoked an alternative legal discourse, one that allowed them escape the classifications of a legal system erected upon the proposition that people could be things. In other words, by shifting the terms of the debate, they made it possible for white Britons to recast them as people rather than property at law. They, too, transformed a much older legal category into a site of innovation and resistance, invoking subjecthood to assert their humanity and rebut the legal fiction inherent in chattel slavery.

Their success was unusual. Nonetheless, it lays bare the power of legal language to shape outcomes for Black people. Although the coercive power of law manifested in slave codes commands our attention with good reason, we cannot forget that forms as well as force policed freedom's boundaries. As we have seen, enslaved people who struggled against their bondage not only found themselves checked by the coercive apparatus of the state, but also by more subtle legal practices that assumed they were property, and by Britons who had learned by repeating these practices to treat them (and think of them) as commodities. When colonists classified slaves as chattel property, they did so in order to access a fully formed legal system that allowed them to maximize the value of their human property at law. Nonetheless, this decision had far-reaching and invidious effects, because law's role in the British Atlantic World was not merely instrumental. Legal language also worked as actor and agent, refracting and creating new legal and social realities. As anthropologists, linguists, and legal theorists recently have begun to recognize, law is "the locus of a powerful act of linguistic appropriation, where the translation of everyday categories into legal language effects powerful changes."[130] In other words, the language of law possesses "dynamics of its own that contribute to social results."[131] When Britons categorized slaves as chattel property, they created "a social reality that did not exist prior to the act of speaking."[132] They constructed a legal world in which slaves were not just *like* things, they *were* things. As a practical matter, this act of categorization, repeated countless times, effectively foreclosed other "trajectories of possibility" for people of African descent.[133] It made it "just a tiny bit

---

[130] Elizabeth Mertz, "Legal Language: Pragmatics, Poetics, and Social Power," *Annual Review of Anthropology* 23 (1994): 441.

[131] *Ibid.*, 437.   [132] Mertz, "Language, Law, and Social Meanings," 422.

[133] Robert W. Gordon, "Critical Legal Histories," *Stanford Law Review* 36 (1984): 112.

more unthinkable" and "a tiny bit more difficult to imagine something altogether outside the scope of familiar possibilities," that slaves could be treated as human beings at law or in reality.[134] In the *Isabella* and the *Royal Fancy* cases, we can see the broad contours of an alternative trajectory, one that took as a starting point the humanity of Black people rather than their objectivity. Appearing before the court as subjects not objects, Black litigants effectively counteracted the dehumanization that D. B. Davis has said was "absolutely central to the slave experience."[135] It is impossible to know whether a more systematic attempt to bring slaves within the protective mantle of subjecthood would have resulted in significant structural changes for people of African descent. Nonetheless, the fate of these litigants offers a tantalizing glimpse of a world that might have been if law's language had provided Black people with more room to maneuver.

NOTE ON METHODOLOGY

The embedded tables are based upon an analysis of the entirety of South Carolina's surviving Vice Admiralty Court Minute Books, which run from 1716 to 1763. These records are housed in manuscript form at the National Archives Southeast Regional Authority and in photostats at the Library of Congress.

Cases that I have identified as slave cases do not include litigation where the cargo of a ship is unknown or unstated. If a case's records include appraisals or cargo inventories without specifically enumerating slaves, I have assumed that no slaves were at issue. This means I likely have underestimated the total number of slave cases in colonial South Carolina. Indeed, the court register's practice changed in the 1730s and 1740s, and in this period case records often omit the substantive documents that would enable me to determine whether any slaves were at issue. In the case of the *Vrouw Dorothea*, for example, the South Carolina records do not enumerate enslaved cargo, but appeals records show that there was, in fact, a slave being consigned on the ship.

In assessing the court's business, I have included a distinct category for piracy even though these cases technically were not heard by the Vice

---

[134] *Ibid.*, 111.
[135] David Brion Davis, *The Problem of Slavery in the Age of Emancipation* (New York, NY: Alfred A. Knopf, 2014), 11.

Admiralty Court. My rationale for this is that the court's register included these cases in his record, and that the court heard one trial (without a jury) in which the libel complained of both piracy and murder. Prize claims to pirate ships are categorized as prizes and allegations of mutiny are classified as crimes.

4

Equity

In her 1714 bill initiating legal process in South Carolina's Chancery Court, Christian Arthur invoked the power of equity jurisdictions like Chancery to provide legal solutions for those "altogether remediless" under "the strict rules of the Common Law." Describing the court as the only place where the "matters and frauds" she outlined in her bill might be "remeadied and redressed," she characterized Chancery as a venue in which the unique circumstances of litigants would be taken into account, a place where the rigor of the common law would be mitigated to produce a just and equitable result.[1] Simultaneously a justification for jurisdiction and a description of equity law, Arthur's language would have resonated with equity judges in Great Britain and throughout the British Atlantic World. Indeed, her bill closely mapped predominant early modern views of equity as both a concept and as a legal process, and adhered to familiar characterizations of Chancery as a court that could "correct Mens Consciences for Frauds, Breach of Trusts, Wrongs and Oppressions," a jurisdiction that could "soften and mollify the Extremity of the Law."[2]

If Arthur couched her claim in familiar language, however, the substance of her bill would surely have been novel to the Lord Chancellor sitting in Westminster. Whereas the English Chancery Court was accustomed to adjudicating land inheritance cases and business disputes

---

[1] *Christopher Arthur, By Christian Arthur, His Prochien Amie and Guardian, v. John Gough*, December 8, 1714, Chancery Case Papers, 1700–1791, Court of Chancery Bundle 1700–1716, Nos. 1–17, No. 10, Oversize, S142001, South Carolina Department of Archives and History, Columbia, South Carolina.
[2] *The Earl of Oxford's Case* (1615), 21 Eng. Rep. 486.

involving traditional debt instruments, Arthur asked the South Carolina Court to determine legal title to an estate that consisted "chiefly of Negro Slaves."[3] Indeed, in this complicated estate litigation, Arthur and the executor of her brother's will sparred over the ownership and management of a plantation and its enslaved labor force. Whereas Arthur accused the executor of wasting the estate by selling or mortgaging "all or the greatest part of the hands and Negroes," the executor complained that Arthur herself had irreparably damaged the plantation by allowing the "[c]attle and hoggs to destroy the Crops" and by "secreting the Negroes and hindring them from their work."[4]

In placing questions about human property before the South Carolina Chancery Court, Christian Arthur was not alone. South Carolina colonists, in fact, routinely claimed enslaved people not only in law, understood as common law, but also in equity, asking the Chancery Court to recognize property interests in people and to facilitate the transfer of familial wealth in the form of slaves. Using procedures common to English equity courts and invoking familiar descriptions of equity, Arthur and litigants like her transformed the South Carolina Court of Chancery into a slave court. In this court, equity law and procedure – which had evolved to suit the needs of landholders in early modern England – opened up space for litigants to articulate complicated claims to land *and* enslaved people, claims that assumed that "[r]eal Estate would not be Capable of any Improvement" without a labor force.[5]

For these litigants, taking disputes over slaves to Chancery had distinct advantages. Whereas at common law complainants were constrained by traditional forms of action, Chancery procedures gave South Carolina colonists an opportunity to claim enslaved people when evidence had been destroyed, when relatives conspired to conceal slaves, or when witnesses could not be located. And whereas common law venues could only provide monetary damages, in Chancery aggrieved colonists could request equitable remedies. They could request the specific performance of a slave-hiring contract, for example, ask the chancellor to prevent a party from removing specific slaves from the province, or demand a court-administered sale of slaves to pay outstanding debts. Using the relative openness of Chancery bill procedure to tell their complicated stories, they

---

[3] Answer of John Gough, December 20, 1714, *Arthur* v. *Gough*, Chancery Case Papers, 1700–1791, Court of Chancery Bundle 1700–1716, Nos. 1–17, No. 10, Oversize, S142001, SCDAH.

[4] *Ibid.*; Answer of John Gough, December 20, 1714, SCDAH.   [5] *Ibid.*

asked the court to intervene and adjudicate the space between the customary and legal. In doing so, they lay bare the dense web of arrangements and
assumptions involving human property that made their plantation economy work and the court's role in perpetuating those arrangements.

Despite the fact that claims to enslaved people comprised a significant
percentage of cases heard by South Carolina's Chancery Court – more
than 40 percent of all litigation – scholars have ignored this important
business just as they have failed more broadly to investigate colonial
chancery courts. Although early modern English historians have acknowledged the importance of English equity jurisdictions into the eighteenth
century, early American historians have neglected colonial equity courts
or have dismissed them as unimportant when compared to common law
venues.[6] Most recently, for example, G. Edward White has argued that
colonial chancery courts were insignificant because "they did not assume

---

[6] There has been no systematic study of litigation in colonial South Carolina's Chancery
Court, although John Edker Douglass provided an overview of the court in his dissertation,
"The Creation of South Carolina's Legal System, 1670–1731" (PhD diss., University of
Missouri-Columbia, 1984). Anne Gregorie and J. Nelson Frierson also provide useful
introductions to Chancery practice in South Carolina in their edited volume of court
records. Anne King Gregorie, ed., *Records of the Court of Chancery of South Carolina,
1671–1779* (Washington: American Historical Association, 1950). For a discussion of the
shortcomings of this edition, see Notes on Sources and Methodology, infra. William
Nelson briefly discusses South Carolina Chancery practice in William E. Nelson, *The
Common Law in Colonial America, Vol. II: The Middle Colonies and the Carolinas,
1660–1730* (New York: Oxford University Press, 2013), 72–73.
   Nineteenth-century legal historians, and particularly Hendrik Hartog, have attended to
equity law in the early republic and antebellum United States, emphasizing the role of
equity judges in the development of American family law. Hartog primarily has empha-
sized practice in New York's Chancery Court. Hendrik Hartog, *Man and Wife in America:
A History* (Cambridge: Harvard University Press, 2002). For equity courts in England, see
Amy Louise Erickson, *Women and Property in Early Modern England* (London:
Routledge, 1993), 114–128; David Lemmings, *Professors of the Law: Barristers and
English Legal Culture in the Eighteenth Century* (New York: Oxford University Press,
2000), 150–202; Henry Horwitz and Patrick Polden, "Continuity or Change in the Court
of Chancery in the Seventeenth and Eighteenth Centuries?," *Journal of British Studies* 35
(1996): 24–57; Mark Fortier, *The Culture of Equity in Early Modern England* (Aldershot:
Ashgate Publishing, 2005), 59–86.
   An important exception to this general trend has been the work of colonial gender
historians. Tracing the legal history of female property ownership in early America, for
example, Marylynn Salmon has found that equity courts, which could enforce marriage
settlements, benefitted women. Salmon's work, however, relies largely upon a reading of
marriage settlements and nineteenth-century Chancery cases, not colonial litigation
records. Marylynn Salmon, *Women and the Law of Property in Early America* (Chapel
Hill: University of North Carolina Press, 1986), 11. See also Marylynn Salmon, "Women
and Property in South Carolina: The Evidence from Marriage Settlements, 1730–1830,"
WMQ 39 (1982): 655–685; Carole Shammas, Marylynn Salmon, and Michael Dahlin,

the English role of providing a clear alternative to the procedures of the common-law courts."[7] Lawrence Friedman has offered a similarly dismissive characterization of colonial chancery practice, suggesting that because equity courts sat "only in the capital," equity law, "unlike the common law, was not brought to the town square and the village, where everybody had access."[8] Whether insisting that chancery courts lacked a clear institutional identity or depicting them as unpopular and elitist jurisdictions, scholars tend to gloss quickly over equity courts in their haste to reconstruct the activities of common law lawyers, judges, and litigants.

This lack of attention to chancery stems in part from the fact that older institutional legal histories primarily emphasized developments in the New England colonies, most of which did not establish separate equity courts. Indeed, Puritan settlers carried with them a hostility to the Court of Chancery in England. Rather than establishing separate equity jurisdictions, they created common law courts that also administered substantive equity law.[9] Equity courts also remain relatively understudied because the commingling of executive, legislative, and judicial functions in early America makes them difficult to see. In royal colonies like South Carolina and Jamaica, for example, governors and council members served in a judicial capacity as chancery judges, and early equity records often appear in council journals rather than as a distinct run of litigation documents. Non-common law courts in early America did not conform to

---

Inheritance in America from Colonial Times to the Present (New Brunswick: Rutgers University Press, 1987), 7.

[7] G. Edward White, *Law in American History: Volume 1 From the Colonial Years Through the Civil War* (Oxford: Oxford University Press, 2012), 82.

[8] Lawrence Friedman, *A History of American Law*, 3rd ed. (New York: Touchstone, 2005), 21. This may have been true for colonial New England, but in South Carolina, the colony's major jurisdictions were located in Charlestown. Charlestown's central role in the colony's legal life meant that colonists were required to travel to town not only to litigate in equity, but also at law.

[9] Neither Connecticut nor Massachusetts had equity jurisdictions, for example. As Marylynn Salmon has noted, the lack of equity institutions in Puritan-dominated colonies was a natural outgrowth of seventeenth-century English political conflicts over the High Court of Chancery. Although "Puritan legal reformers in England did not succeed in abolishing" the court, "in America the Puritans got what they wanted." Substantive equity law in the New England colonies was administered in the courts of common law. Salmon, *Women and the Law of Property in Early America*, 11. For an analysis of the "gravitational pull" of New England in early American legal histories, see Sally E. Hadden and Patricia Hagler Minter, "Introduction," in *Signposts: New Directions in Southern Legal History*, edited by Sally E. Hadden and Patricia Hagler Minter (Athens: University of Georgia Press, 2013), 2.

a modern conception of the separation of powers, and this has obscured their important role in colonial society. Finally, the criticism of equity courts lodged by mainland American colonists in the run-up to the American Revolution and the subsequent abolition of many equity courts in the early republic has created the misimpression that these courts were neither widely utilized nor significant.[10] Certainly American colonists, including those in South Carolina, criticized chancery courts for their costliness and dilatory procedures, and hostility to these courts was "fairly widespread in the eighteenth century." These criticisms, however, were not novel, nor were they a distinctively colonial phenomenon. In fact, American complaints about Chancery echoed those of Britons who characterized the eighteenth-century English Chancery Court as an "elaborate racket in the administration of the law," a worthy predecessor of the unwieldy institution later ridiculed in Charles Dickens's *Bleak House*.[11]

In this chapter, I reconstruct the business of South Carolina's Chancery Court, arguing that despite colonists' complaints about equity law and its administration, Chancery was an institutionally distinct jurisdiction that was particularly useful for colonial slave owners. By piecing together the court's docket through an analysis of surviving manuscript litigation records (which scholars have ignored in favor of a substantially incomplete printed edition), I show that the South Carolina Chancery Court, unlike English Chancery, maintained a steady business throughout the colonial period largely because it offered a meaningful alternative to the colony's common law jurisdiction, the Court of Common Pleas.[12] Indeed,

---

[10] Lawrence Friedman argues that Chancery Courts were unpopular because they were "closely associated with executive power, hence, with the English colonial masters." Friedman, *A History of American Law*, 21.

[11] *Ibid.*; Lemmings, *Professors of the Law*, 186.

[12] Chancery records from South Carolina survive in three forms: in entries in the Grand Council Journals, in miscellaneous manuscript case papers from 1700–1791, and in minute books (which summarize actions that the court took on particular cases). The Littleton Griswold Fund of the American Historical Association underwrote the preparation of an edited volume of a portion of South Carolina's Court records. Although a useful resource, this edited volume does not accurately reproduce the extent of Chancery materials available. Rather, the edited volume contains only the court's minute books from 1721–1736; 1737–1766; 1770–1774, as well as case papers from 1700–1720. This printed edition also includes a summary of cases from 1767 to 1770 based on a calendar prepared in 1933 for the South Carolina Bar Association. These papers were lost after the South Carolina courthouse was remodeled.

This chapter is based upon a reading of the entirety of the court's manuscript case records from 1700 to 1780, which are original litigation materials rather than summaries or accounts of proceedings. The AHA edition includes these records from 1700 to 1720, but the South Carolina Department of Archives and History holds hundreds of

whereas business in England's Chancery constricted over the course of the eighteenth century, litigation in South Carolina's Chancery Court held steady because the court continued to be useful to slave-owning litigants. With the capacity to bring before itself voluminous evidence of complicated and customary transactions involving slaves, the court was an attractive venue for colonists engaged in business enterprises and joint planting ventures. Likewise, in a province where a volatile subtropical climate frequently led to the destruction of important legal records, Chancery offered a venue where disputes over slaves could be litigated even when documentary evidence was lacking. Chancery procedure, in fact, was well suited to meet the needs of colonists living in places where climate inhibited record keeping.

Finally, and perhaps most importantly, Chancery continued to attract South Carolina litigants because it was the only local venue with the capacity to sort through complicated inheritance disputes involving real as well as personal property. As in England, Chancery practice in South Carolina primarily revolved around estate disputes; however, in South Carolina, many of these disputes concerned the ownership of enslaved people. Crucially, slaves that were claimed in the context of South Carolina estate disputes frequently belonged to widows and daughters, and men typically sued alongside their wives to collect their bequests. The South Carolina Chancery Court was in practice a slave court that operated to transfer women's wealth in the form of enslaved people to husbands.

Beyond proving the relevance and even existence of functioning equity jurisdictions in early America, attending to South Carolina's Chancery Court provides an opportunity to reassess the place of plantation colonies in the British Atlantic legal world. In fact, understanding South Carolina's jurisdictional map as complex and varied – not just populated by common

---

manuscript case records that were omitted from the printed edition, and upon which I rely here. Most surviving case records include at least a bill; some also contain replications, masters' reports, interrogatories, and decrees. Few records are complete.

Because Chancery did not proceed by writ, categorizing the court's business is difficult and necessarily unscientific. Categories, in fact, can overlap. For example, many inheritance disputes also concerned an estate's debts. Lease disputes also could be business disputes. In hard cases, I have assigned categories by identifying the legal question that seemed to be of the greatest import to the complainant. I arrived at the figures in the table mentioned later by counting discrete cases – duplicates have been omitted. In assessing the number of slave cases in Chancery, I erred on the side of undercounting. Indeed, I have only counted cases where slaves are specifically mentioned and have not included broader claims to "personal estate," which likely included claims to slaves.

law institutions – helps us to see South Carolina colonists as engaged participants in a broader Anglo-American legal culture rather than as figures who strained to fit the legal aberration of slavery with an English legal tradition whose institutions have seemed predisposed to encourage liberty. Like Britons across the globe, South Carolina colonists drew upon a legal source culture that was dynamic and complex, and not immune to influences from so-called rival legal systems that derived from Continental legal practice, including Chancery.[13] They operated in legal environments where jurisdictional diversity was the norm, and where venues beyond common law courts offered meaningful alternatives. These included not only chancery courts, but also ecclesiastical courts, admiralty courts, and extra-judicial means of dispute resolution. South Carolina colonists, then, experienced a legal topography that was variegated, not flat, one that opened up opportunities for formulating sophisticated legal strategies, for forum shopping, and for interacting with different types of law.[14]

---

[13] Christopher Tomlins, *Freedom Bound: Law, Labor, and Civic Identity in Colonizing English America, 1580–1865* (Cambridge: Cambridge University Press, 2010), 188.

[14] For recent work on the importance of non-common law institutions and concepts in colonial environments, see *Ibid.*, 6–7; Lauren A. Benton, *A Search for Sovereignty: Law and Geography in European Empires, 1400–1900* (Cambridge: Cambridge University Press, 2009), 32–33; Ken MacMillan, *Sovereignty and Possession in the English New World: The Legal Foundations of Empire, 1576–1640* (Cambridge: Cambridge University Press, 2006), 7–14; and Lisa Ford, *Settler Sovereignty: Jurisdiction and Indigenous People in America and Australia, 1788–1836* (Cambridge: Harvard University Press, 2010), 5–6. These works are a natural extension of an English legal historiography which has moved from assuming English legal exceptionalism to acknowledging the importance of the *ius commune* in England. T. F. T. Plucknett, "The Relations between Roman Law and English Common Law down to the Sixteenth Century: A General Survey," *The University of Toronto Law Journal* 3 (1939): 24–50; M. Sarfatti, "Roman Law and Common Law: Forerunners of a General Unification of Law," *International Comparative Law Quarterly* 3, no. 1 (1954): 102–115; R. C. van Caenegem, *The Birth of the English Common Law* (Cambridge: Cambridge University Press, 1973); Ralph V. Turner, "Roman Law in England before the Time of Bracton," *The Journal of British Studies* 15 (1975): 1–25; Charles Donahue, Jr., "Ius Commune, Canon Law, and Common Law in England," *Tulane Law Review* 66 (1992): 1745–1767; R. H. Helmholz, "Continental Law and Common Law: Historical Strangers or Companions?," *Duke Law Journal* 6 (1990): 1207–1228; David J. Seipp, "The Reception of Canon Law and Civil Law in the Common Law Courts before 1600," *The Oxford Journal of Legal Studies* 13 (1993): 388–420; R. H. Helmholz, *The Ius Commune in England: Four Studies* (Oxford: Oxford University Press, 2001).
   In this chapter, I follow Hendrik Hartog in his use of the term "jurisdictional diversity" to describe legal environments in which litigants can avail themselves of different courts. Hartog refers narrowly to the forum choices available to litigants in the nineteenth-century United States as a result of the layers of judicial structures created under an American federal system. Hartog, *Man and Wife in America*, 310.

South Carolina's variegated legal landscape lays bare slavery's profound impact on legal practice in the colony. South Carolina colonists experienced legal institutions in a way that placed them within the mainstream of British legal experience, but they used those institutions for different ends. South Carolina colonists deployed equity law first and foremost to meet their needs as slave owners operating in a high-mortality plantation environment, and this helps to account for litigation patterns that differed from those in English Chancery. Whereas evidence from English Chancery litigation reveals a shift from country-based litigation over land to town-centered business litigation over the course of the eighteenth century, South Carolina colonists overwhelmingly and consistently used Chancery to litigate over land and slaves in the context of inheritance disputes over female property. In a society in which women's property often took the form of slaves and in which high mortality rates among white settlers inhibited traditional wealth-building strategies, Chancery provided a convenient venue for managing, distributing, and reassembling familial wealth across generations.

In "A Culture of Equity," I briefly describe the development of equity as a concept and as a legal process in early modern England, concluding with an examination of practice and procedure in the English Court of Chancery. I then turn to a discussion of the South Carolina Chancery Court and its institutional history, suggesting that although the South Carolina Court closely mimicked Chancery in Westminster, it also differed in important respects. In South Carolina, for example, the governor and members of the council sat as equity judges. Moreover, the South Carolina Court entirely lacked a Latin side, which in England proceeded according to common law. Next, I examine in depth the business of South Carolina's Chancery Court, drawing upon an analysis of 127 cases heard between 1700 and 1780. These cases reveal a vibrant jurisdiction that entertained a variety of causes, but primarily heard colonists' disputes over estates. In "An Equitable Slave Court," I turn to an examination of slave litigation in South Carolina's Chancery Court, following colonists as they fought over enslaved people in the context of business, debt, and inheritance disputes. Although slave litigation set South Carolina's Chancery Court apart from English Chancery, in claiming slaves South Carolina colonists took advantage of time-worn English Chancery procedures even as they drew upon a discourse of equity that was familiar to Britons the world over.

Colonists most typically claimed slaves in the context of inheritance suits over female property, and I conclude by examining the role of women in Chancery slave litigation. As a direct consequence of South Carolina decedents' relatively liberal provisions for widows and daughters, women comprised a surprisingly high percentage of named litigants in equity suits. Suing with their husbands, they sought to claim inheritance (usually in the form of slaves) from estate executors and administrators. The frequent appearance of women in Chancery proceedings, however, does not suggest that South Carolina's Chancery Court was a proto-feminist institution. Rather, the court helped to reinforce patriarchal social structures in the colony by providing a legal mechanism by which husbands could claim valuable property in right of their wives. At the same time, Chancery records reveal that in practice some South Carolina widows wielded significant authority over land and slaves. Following colonists as they exhaustively detailed the perfidy of propertied widows shows that administratrices and executrices often took control over slaves on behalf of themselves and their children. Their refusal to surrender valuable human property resulted in protracted interfamily struggles in which colonists revealed the extent to which slave ownership shaped their expectations about inheritance.

A CULTURE OF EQUITY

Early modern England, according to Mark Fortier, had a "culture of equity." Indeed, "equity" as a term and as a concept enjoyed "widespread use," not only in law, but in religion, politics, and literature, so much so that it constituted "one of the key ideas in general currency." Equity was pliable; it meant different things to different people, and it was not distinctively English. Rather, equity was "thousands of years old," meandering to the British Isles "from Athens, from Rome, from the Holy Land, from Wittenberg and Geneva."[15] William West, writing about the origins of equity, rooted it firmly in religion, as did many early modern writers. "God," he wrote, "is the efficient cause of Equitie."[16] Put another way by a complainant in England's Chancery Court, "equity speaks as the Law of God speaks." Presumably, his adversary, who sought to "silence Equity," also sought to silence God.[17] Equity's intellectual pedigree, however, was more complicated, and West and other writers also acknowledged that it

[15] Fortier, *The Culture of Equity*, 1–3.
[16] William West, *The Second Part of Symboleography* (London, 1601), 175, Early English Books Online, Chadwyck-Healey, https://eebo.chadwyck.com
[17] *The Earl of Oxford's Case* (1615), 21 Eng. Rep. 486.

derived from "[t]he Law of Nature, the Law of Nations, and good man[n]ers."[18] In fact, equity was commonly associated with a grab bag of Western philosophical, legal, and political traditions, including "natural law, fundamental law, God's law, the public good, the king's conscience, the individual (Christian) conscience, or reason."[19]

As a legal concept, equity was an inseparable part of law. Equity was law's "life, spirit and intention." Whereas the letter of the law "resembleth the flesh," equity was the "reason, the Soul" of law.[20] Law and equity were fused together. Yet equity also maneuvered externally to law, outside and above it. "Laws covet to be ruled by equity," according to Christopher St. German, and equity's task was to correct for law's inability to track the variability of human experience. Equity was necessary, in fact, because "[m]ens Actions are so divers and infinite, That it is impossible to make any general Law which may aptly meet with every particular Act, and not fail in some Circumstances."[21] Equity, then, assessed and accounted for unique circumstances, and it adjusted for factors unforeseen by fallible human legislators. Capturing the mutable, mystical quality of equity in early modern English legal thought, St. German invoked the prince's prerogative power to intervene miraculously in individual cases when the letter of the law became divorced from its soul. Indeed, equity was "a right wiseness that considereth all the particular circumstances of the deed" but which, according to St. German, was also "tempered with the sweetness of mercie."[22]

For most early modern legal thinkers, the intended object of this miraculous intervention was the common law, a set of procedural and substantive laws associated with the superior courts of common law in England: the Court of King's Bench, the Court of Common Pleas, and the Exchequer of Pleas. Common law in these three courts developed over the early modern period to encompass complicated legal procedures, including a writ system that limited a subject's remedies, and a formalized structure of pleading by which parties came to "issue," a legal question to be decided. Practice in common law courts was technical and constrained, and common law judges' scrupulous application of rules meant that litigation in these venues could produce results in individual cases

[18] West, *Symboleography*, 175.   [19] Fortier, *The Culture of Equity*, 4.
[20] West, *Symboleography*, 175–176.
[21] *The Earl of Oxford's Case* (1615), 21 Eng. Rep. 486.
[22] Christopher St. German, *The Dialogue in English between a Doctor of Divinity and a Student in the Laws of England* (London, 1660), 27, EEBO.

that seemed unjust. Equity law, then, worked to undo hardships created by common law and the judges who administered it. Indeed, "Equity," according to eighteenth-century legal treatise writer Thomas Wood, "[a]bat[ed] the Rigour of the common Law." It considered "the Intention" rather than the "[w]ords of the Law," and it was tasked with "[e]xerting Power in Cases wherein the Subject is without Remedy in the Courts of Common Law."[23] Equity judges, deciding cases based upon a full consideration of the facts and the dictates of conscience, would "supply the defects" of law when the "rigor of general rules" was "hard upon individuals."[24]

Although equity as a concept could be pliable, it also referred to a set of distinctive practices and procedures that emerged around the Court of Chancery in Westminster.[25] In this court, the most important of England's equity courts, a judgment "obtained by Oppression, Wrong and a hard Conscience" would be set aside, "not for any error or defect in the Judgment, but for the hard Conscience of the Party."[26] Overseen by a chancellor who derived his authority from his possession of the Great Seal, the Chancery Court exercised jurisdiction on two different "sides" of the court by the eighteenth century. The first, called the Latin or ordinary side, proceeded "according to the Laws and Statutes of the Realm." Process was issued under the Great Seal in Latin and "according to the Common Law."[27] Reflecting Chancery's medieval origins as the administrative center of the king's household, the Latin side heard litigation relating to Crown property and Crown appointees. With "[j]urisdiction to Hold Plea of Scire Facias for Repeal of the King's Letters Patents," the Latin side also could hear actions "[b]y or Against Any Officer" of the court.[28] Likewise, the Latin side entertained petitions "seeking redress against the Crown," and was responsible for issuing "all commissions of charitable uses, bankrupts, sewers, lunatics."[29] Appeals from the Latin side by writ of error were heard in King's Bench.[30]

---

[23] Thomas Wood, *An Institute of the Laws of England* (London, 1720), 789.

[24] Sir William Blackstone, *Commentaries on the Laws of England*, 4 vols. (Chicago: University of Chicago Press, 1979), 3: 60.

[25] Other courts that proceeded in equity were the Court of Star Chamber, the Court of Requests, and regional councils.

[26] *The Earl of Oxford's Case* (1615), 21 Eng. Rep. 487.

[27] Wood, *An Institute of the Laws of England*, 787–788.   [28] *Ibid.*, 788.

[29] *Ibid.*, 789. J. H. Baker, *An Introduction to English Legal History*, 4th ed. (London: Butterworths Lexis Nexis, 2002), 101. In order to issue these commissions, the court was always open, unlike common law jurisdictions, which were only open during four yearly terms.

[30] Wood, *An Institute of the Laws of England*, 789.

More important for our purposes, the chancellor also exercised equitable jurisdiction on the English side of Chancery (the "Extraordinary Court"). The chancellor's English jurisdiction (so called because bills were written in English) grew out of his authority as the preeminent member of the king's council. In this capacity, he heard bills of complaint from aggrieved subjects who alleged "interference with the common law," and he dispensed justice where a common law remedy was unavailable or where the strict application of common law might work a hardship in an individual case.[31] Chancery practice developed over time to give chancellors the flexibility required to decide cases "according to Equity and Good Conscience."[32] Indeed, legal process that was streamlined (in principle if not always in practice), in the vernacular, and avoided the technicalities of the common law writ system allowed chancellors access to all of the facts of the case. Without concern for "the blinkers of due process," for "[f]orm or Mispleading," or for the possibility of creating harmful precedents, chancellors weighed these facts and ruled accordingly.[33]

When compared to process in common law venues, where the "possibilities of technical failure were legion," legal process on the English side of Chancery was simple.[34] Complainants (plaintiffs) were not required to seek an original writ, which was necessary to begin a common law action. Instead, they could initiate process through a bill, which detailed in English (not in Latin, as with common law writs) the specific nature of the complaint and the relief sought. Bill procedure provided litigants with an opportunity to explain fully the unique circumstances of a case without the constraints of adhering to formulaic common law writs. It also allowed litigants to demand relief where no writ – and therefore no remedy – was available at common law. For example, if a litigant entered into a parole (oral) contract, he was without a common law writ and therefore without a remedy in a common law court. In Chancery, however, the court would consider all the circumstances outlined in the complainant's bill rather than refuse to enforce the contract merely because it was oral. Chancery, then, acknowledged that neither

---

[31] Baker, *An Introduction to English Legal History*, 101. Although at first chancellors referred these bills to other jurisdictions for adjudication, eventually the chancellor began to issue decrees providing novel remedies. These decrees were not precedential – they bound only parties to the suit – and indeed, the English side of Chancery was not considered a court of record like King's Bench or Common Pleas.

[32] Wood, *An Institute of the Laws of England*, 794.

[33] *Ibid.* Indeed, the Court of Chancery was not a court of record whose decisions were binding on other parties: a decree (decision) in Chancery bound only the parties. Baker, *An Introduction to English Legal History*, 104.

[34] *Ibid.*, 102.

prescriptive written law nor common law could not adequately capture the complexity of human behavior and provided remedies for those who could not find justice elsewhere.

Uninhibited by the restraints of common law procedure and substance, the chancellor could do any number of things that could not be done at common law. In Chancery, relief might be "[g]iven For or Against an Infant, notwithstanding His Minority; For or Against a Married Woman, notwithstanding her Coverture." Likewise, complainants could sue to correct "[a]ll frauds and Deceits for which there is no remedy at Common Law" and "All Breaches of Trust and Confidence."[35] The court also recognized and enforced trusts, a legal mechanism that gave landowners greater control over their property, but which were not enforceable at common law.[36] In all of these matters the court could grant equitable relief, whereas common law courts might only assess monetary damages. Because justice in Chancery was not viewed in strictly monetary terms, judges could narrowly tailor remedies to suit the needs of individual litigants who might not otherwise be made whole by an award of damages.

Flexibility and ease of process in the English side of Chancery continued throughout the course of litigation. Adhering to Continental civil procedure rather than common law procedure, Chancery did not require litigants to conform to strict forms of common law pleading. Rather, the chancellor, presiding without a jury, issued a decree based upon on all of the facts described in the written record. This record could include written testimony in the form of affidavits, oaths, and responses to interrogatories, all of which were elicited and recorded by chancery masters.[37] Significantly, chancellors also possessed enforcement mechanisms that ensured cases moved swiftly to resolution. After the filing of a bill, for example, chancellors issued subpoenas directing respondents to answer allegations "under pain of" a monetary fine. If a respondent refused to answer, chancellors also could order the attachment of property, or in extreme circumstances direct the contumacious respondent to be taken "to Fleet Prison."[38] Chancellors

---

[35] Wood, *An Institute of the Laws of England*, 792–793.

[36] Over the fifteenth and sixteenth centuries, Chancery's jurisdiction over uses and, later, trusts helped to attract litigants. Baker, *An Introduction to English Legal History*, 251–252.

[37] As in other jurisdictions that derived procedures from civil law, witnesses in Chancery suits typically did not provide in-court testimony.

[38] Wood, *An Institute of the Laws of England*, 795–796. The chancellor's arsenal of subpoenas included subpoenas to make better answer; to reply, to rejoin; for witnesses to testify; for publication of depositions; to hear judgment; and to bring in writings.

also could issue injunctions, which ordered common law tribunals to stay proceedings pending the outcome of Chancery litigation, and they could hold parties in contempt for failing to adhere to final decrees.

Flexibility of process and the availability of effective enforcement mechanisms helped to attract litigants to Chancery in the fifteenth and sixteenth centuries, even as these procedural advantages elicited heated criticism from common law judges. By the eighteenth century, however, this relative flexibility had begun to harden as the court developed its own substantive and procedural rules.[39] Partly as a result of this, but also in keeping with broader litigation trends in all of the Westminster Courts, Chancery suffered a "truly massive decline in litigation" in the eighteenth century. By 1750, the number of bills filed in Chancery had been reduced to one-fifth the number of bills filed in 1700–1701.[40] The court's reputation likewise began to suffer, and over the course of the eighteenth century, Chancery became synonymous with dilatory and expensive process. Although the court once attracted litigants with its speedy and economical adjudication of complicated cases, the multiplication of interlocutory business (motion practice) made Chancery expensive and sluggish.[41] Indeed, complaints about the cost of Chancery litigation "increased during the early eighteenth century," and most barbs were aimed at "creeping administrative and procedural growth."[42]

Despite these criticisms, Chancery continued to offer advantages to litigants. Equity "remained more flexible than the common law" because it could still take into account "individual circumstances." Likewise, the court continued to be the only recourse for litigants seeking to resolve disputes involving trusts, which common law courts could not recognize, and which had become a popular means by which wealthy Britons protected landed inheritance. Indeed, for litigants with sufficient resources, Chancery remained an attractive venue, and eighteenth-century treatise writers insisted that the court was still effective in "[a]bating the Rigour of the common Law" and offering relief "in Cases wherein the Subject is without Remedy in the Courts of Common Law."[43] In fact, despite Chancery's eighteenth-century slump, these treatise writers characterized Chancery as the most important court in Westminster. For Wood, writing early in the eighteenth century, the "[j]urisdiction and Power of This

[39] Baker, *An Introduction to English Legal History*, 110.
[40] Lemmings, *Professors of the Law*, 184. As Lemmings notes, despite this fact, Chancery remained "an excellent place of employment for barristers."
[41] *Ibid.*   [42] *Ibid.*, 185.   [43] Wood, *An Institute of the Laws of England*, 789.

Court of Equity" was of "vast Extent." In fact, "almost All Causes of Weight and Moment, First or Last, have Their Determination here."[44] William Blackstone, supplanting Wood as the century's most important treatise writer, agreed, calling Chancery "the court of the greatest judicial consequence." For Blackstone, this was particularly true with respect to disputes over property, in which Chancery was "by much the most important of any of the king's superior and original courts of justice."[45]

EQUITY IN THE WILDERNESS

Although historians largely have ignored colonial chancery courts, English settlers and colonial projectors – particularly in southern and Caribbean colonies – reproduced an English legal landscape by establishing equity jurisdictions that provided an alternative to common law courts. Virginia and Maryland had equity jurisdictions, for example, as did the West Indian colonies of Barbados, St. Christopher, Antigua, and Jamaica. In Carolina, too, the Lords Proprietors expected that their fledgling province would maintain a functioning equity jurisdiction from an early date. Drawing upon the extensive powers granted to them under their 1665 charter "to award process, hold pleas, and determine, in all the said courts and places of judicature, all actions, suits, and causes whatsoever," they outlined plans for a "Chancellor's Court" in the Fundamental Constitutions of Carolina.[46] This court would consist of "one of ye proprietors & his six councillers," who would possess the "seal of ye Palatinate" and would have jurisdiction over all commissions, grants, and treaties with Indians. Consonant with accepted understandings of English Chancery as a court of conscience, they also gave the court jurisdiction over cases involving the "law of liberty of conscience, & all disturbances of [th]e publique peace upon pretence of religion."[47] This Chancellor's

[44] *Ibid.*, 792.   [45] Blackstone, *Commentaries*, 3: 46.
[46] "Charter of Carolina," June 30, 1665, Yale Law School, The Avalon Project, http://avalon .law.yale.edu/17th_century/nc04.asp.
[47] John Locke, First Draft of Fundamental Constitutions of Carolina, July 21, 1669, The National Archives, Kew, United Kingdom, PRO/24/47/3. That Anthony Ashley Cooper sought to establish a court of Chancery in Carolina, his pet project, is not surprising given his legal background. Indeed, in October 1672, Charles II named Cooper Lord Chancellor of England, and in this capacity he not only presided over numerous suits in Chancery, but also initiated a series of legal reforms meant to streamline procedure. The legal historian W. S. Holdsworth remarked that these reforms were "a complete code of procedure: and they show that Shaftesbury was quite able to appreciate the principles which should underline the procedure of the court, and the main evils against which it was necessary

Court, however, was never established. By the time that the first Carolina colonists embarked for the New World in 1669, it was already clear to the Proprietors that the elaborate administrative structures prescribed in the Fundamental Constitutions, including its court system, could not be fully implemented.[48] Nonetheless, during the early proprietary period Carolina did maintain a functioning equity jurisdiction, which was overseen by the governor and the Grand Council.

A 1721 Commons House of Assembly statute prescribed the institutional structure that South Carolina's Chancery Court retained, with minor modifications, throughout the colonial period.[49] The court consisted of the governor, who sat as chancellor, aided by a majority of the members of the royal council. A master, appointed by royal commission, reviewed complaints and made written recommendations to the Chancery judges.[50] The court also had an official register who signed writs, kept

---

to guard." W. S. Holdsworth, *A History of English Law*, 14 vols. (London: Methuen & Co., 1924), 6: 615. K. H. D. Haley, *The First Earl of Shaftesbury* (Oxford: Clarendon Press, 1968), 311.

[48] In a set of instructions to Carolina in July 1669, the Proprietors noted: "In regard ye number of people w[hi]ch will at first be sett downe at Port Royall, will be soe small, together w[i]th want of Landgraves & Cassiques, that it will not be possible to putt o[u]r Grand Modell of Governm[en]t in practice at first." "Copy of Instruccons Annexed to Ye Commission For Ye Govern[men]t & Councell," July 27, 1669, L. Cheves, ed., *The Shaftesbury Papers* (Charleston: Home Press, 2010), 119–120.

[49] "An Act for Establishing a Court of Chancery in This His Majesty's Province of South Carolina," (1721), in *The Statutes at Large of South Carolina*, edited by Thomas Cooper and David J. McCord, 10 vols. (Columbia: A. S. Johnston, 1836–1841), 7: 163–165. South Carolina's 1776 state constitution altered the chancery court's structure, stipulating that the court would consist of the "Vice President of the Colony and Privy Council." The court was again altered in 1778, when the lieutenant governor replaced the vice president. When Charlestown surrendered to the British in 1780, pending Chancery cases were discontinued, but were reopened after the American Revolution. Gregorie, ed., *Records of the Court of Chancery*, 8.

[50] The form of a master's commission to Alexander Cramahe read: "To Alexander Cramahe Gent: I reposing Special Trust and Confidence in your Loyalty Integrity and Ability have Constituted and assigned and by these Presents Do Constitute Authorize and Assign you the said Alexander Cramahe to be Master of our Court of Chancery in our Province of South Carolina. To Have hold Exercise & Enjoy the said Office of Master of our said Court of Chancery During our pleasure and your Residence within our said province Together with all and Singular the Rights, Salaries fees profits priviledges and Emoluments thereunto Belonging or in anywise appertaining." July 2, 1734 (Recorded July 8, 1734), Anne Gregorie Papers, 28/17/3, South Carolina Historical Society, Charleston, South Carolina.

This position, it seems, was not particularly lucrative. As Governor Robert Johnson wrote to the Duke of Newcastle on the death of Chancery Master Theophilus Gregory, although the place required "a great deal of Attendance," it was "triffling as to the Income and Profits, the greatest part of it depending on the allowance of ye Assembly will think fit

official records of court proceedings, and issued written interrogatories to witnesses.[51] According to the 1721 statute, the register also was responsible for providing notifications of all causes scheduled for hearing by tacking a list of cases "at the public watch-house in Charlestown."[52] Both the master and register were legally obligated to live in Charlestown and to perform their jobs personally "on pain of being removed from their respective offices."[53] This stipulation reflected the centrality of Charlestown in South Carolina's legal culture. Unlike Virginia, where a county government system meant that colonists could access courts closer to home, South Carolinians seeking to litigate their disputes were forced to travel to Charlestown to avail themselves of common law, vice admiralty, chancery, or ecclesiastical courts. Indeed, the critical mass of legal institutions in Charlestown and their relative absence in the hinterland well into the 1760s has led William Nelson to call the town a "city-state."[54]

The 1721 statute endowed the Chancery Court with significant powers, giving the chancellor and judges the authority to "have, exercise and use the same jurisdiction ... in granting and issuing forth all original and remedial writs and other process whatsoever, and in hearing, adjudging and determining all causes and suits in equity, in as full and ample manner as any chancellor, or court or courts of chancery, in America, can, may or ought to do."[55] It likewise directed the court to adhere as closely as possible to the "known laws, customs, statutes and usages of the Kingdom of Great Britain, and also as near as may be, according to the known and established rules of his Majesty's high court of chancery in South Britain."[56]

If colonists hoped the court would conform as closely as possible to English precedents and procedures, however, it fell short of this standard in significant respects. Perhaps most importantly, the blending of gubernatorial and judicial duties in Chancery marked South Carolina's Court – as well as other colonial Chancery Courts – as different from English

---

to Annex to it." Robert Johnson to the Duke of Newcastle, August 7, 1734, Records in the British Public Record Office Relating to South Carolina, 1663–1782, edited by W. Noel Sainsbury, 36 vols., Emory University, Woodruff Library, Atlanta, GA, 17: 4. Nonetheless, the position could be a powerful one. Indeed, the master determined "which cases were heard by the court and when." Douglass, "The Creation of South Carolina's Legal System," 266.

[51] *Ibid.*, 261, 266.   [52] *SAL*, 7:164.   [53] *Ibid.*, 164.
[54] Nelson, *The Common Law in Colonial America, passim.*   [55] *SAL*, 7:163.
[56] *Ibid.*, 165.

Chancery. And as was true in other colonies, an overlapping colonial judiciary and its attendant administration concerned South Carolina colonists. For example, after the overthrow of proprietary government in 1719, South Carolina's revolutionaries immediately sought to separate the Court of Chancery from the Grand Council, putting the court on an independent statutory footing and creating a chancellor who could be removable only by the king.[57] Their reforms were short-lived, however, and the 1721 statute returned the court to its previous configuration.[58] Nicholas Trott, South Carolina's most important legal figure in the early eighteenth century, also complained that Chancery lacked clearly defined administrative positions. "The Officers of Register and Examiner in Chancery have been usually granted to the same Person," he lamented, while "the Masters office has some times been annexed to the Secretary's office, at other times to the Office of Clerk of the Council."[59] Imperial administrators might be forgiven for ignoring Trott's complaints, however, given that he not only served as the Chief Justice of the Court of Common Pleas, but also as a Chancery and Vice Admiralty judge. In fact, during Trott's tenure in office, it was said that there were "no appeals but from himself to himself."

South Carolina's Chancery Court also did not have a Latin side. Despite the 1721 statute's expansive language, South Carolina's Chancery judges never believed they were "authorized ... to issue any

---

[57] Douglass, "The Creation of South Carolina's Legal System," 155; see also Friedman, *A History of American Law*, 21.

[58] This reconfiguration never received the Crown's approval. Scott Douglas Gerber, *A Distinct Judicial Power: The Origins of an Independent Judiciary, 1606–1787* (Oxford: Oxford University Press, 2011), 210–211. Colonists in other provinces where governors acted as chancellors echoed these complaints. In Jamaica, for example, the governor and council, empowered by royal commission, comprised the colony's Chancery Court. There, the governor's authority over the chancery court concerned colonists who were worried that governor retained too much power over property litigation, a mainstay of colonial chancery courts. As one early eighteenth-century Jamaican pamphleteer complained, the governor of Jamaica was "not only CAPTAIN GENERAL and Commander in chief of that Island." He was "likewise CHANCELLOR." This engrossing of governmental and judicial functions posed a danger, according to this pamphleteer, for colonists keen to secure their property. *The Groans of Jamaica Express'd in a Letter* (London, 1714), vi–vii, ECCO.

[59] Nicholas Trott, "Observations on the Present State of the Courts of Judicature In his Majesty's province of South Carolina" (1730), South Carolina Court Records, 1730–1788, AC 1399, Library of Congress, Manuscripts Division, Washington, DC. J. Nelson Frierson, "Introduction," in *Records of the Court of Chancery of South Carolina, 1671–1779*, edited by Anne King Gregorie (Washington: American Historical Association, 1950), 12.

Original Writ," nor did they extend "their Jurisdiction any farther than hearing and determining Causes and Suits in Equity." As Trott lamented, "[t]here is no plea or Petit Bag side, nor any officer appointed or properly invested with a Power to issue writs Original or remedial, Commissions, or other process."[60] Judges instead consistently refused to exercise Latin side jurisdiction. They believed that doing so "would be like erecting a new Court of Judicature not before erected or established in this Province," which was prohibited by the governor's instructions. As a result of this significant and extended exercise in judicial restraint, the governor and councilors confined themselves "to the hearing of Causes in Equity only" until 1746, when a statutory revision formally precluded the possibility of Latin side jurisdiction.[61]

For defenders of the royal prerogative like Trott, the lack of a Latin side in Chancery was highly problematic. Without a Latin side (or a Court of Exchequer, which Trott desired), there was no legal means by which the king could enforce his rights in South Carolina, and Trott cited numerous instances in which the lack of Latin jurisdiction had infringed on "the prerogative of the Crown." For example, the members of the Chancery Court had never "taken upon themselves to hold plea of Scire Facias to the Kings Patent or Grant." This was particularly troublesome when land was "granted by several Patents to several Persons," or when "the King or his Governor" was "deceived by false Suggestion" into granting land. In these circumstances, which Trott suggested were commonplace, the Crown lacked a judicial mechanism for retracting duplicative patents.[62]

Similarly, without a Latin side the Crown could not collect its feudal incidents, which were payments or obligations that subjects owed the Crown.[63] Chancery could not issue commissions "for taking Inquest of Office on forfeitures in Case of Treason or felony or Escheats upon failure of Heirs General or Special," for example, which in England were "within the Ordinary Jurisdiction of the Court of Chancery."[64] As colonist and

---

[60] *Ibid.*, 1.

[61] *Ibid.*, 2–3. "An Act to Impower his Excellency the Governor, or the Commander-In-Chief of this Province for the time being, and a majority of the Members of his Majesty's Honorable Council who shall be in this Province, to hold a Court of Chancery; for repealing the First and Ninth Paragraphs of [the 1721 act] ... and for preventing the Discontinuance of Process, and the Abatement of Suits in the Courts of Justice" (1746), *SAL*, 7:191.

[62] Trott, "Observations," 3.

[63] William Stubbs, *The Constitutional History of England in its Origin and Development*, 6th ed., 3 vols. (Oxford: Clarendon Press, 1903–1906), 1: 47.

[64] Trott, "Observations," 3.

judge Benjamin Whitaker observed, the court's refusal to issue commissions "to take Inquisitions" or to "[t]o enter into Lands Escheated" made it "impossible but that a failure of Justice in many cases must happen."[65] Perhaps more importantly, it meant the loss of revenue that could be used to fund the government.[66]

In addition to lacking a Latin side, the South Carolina Chancery Court was technically restricted in its ability to grant injunctions, a type of equitable remedy granted by the English Chancery Court to stay common law proceedings pending the outcome of equity litigation. The 1721 Act specifically limited the availability of injunctive relief, stipulating that injunctions could not be issued "of course, or by surprise." Injunctions, in fact, would only be granted when requested in the bill of complaint, and when opposing parties were provided with at least two days' notice. This provision was a direct response to colonists' concerns that writs of injunction issued too freely under the proprietary government, and that this had infringed upon the colony's common law jurisdiction, the Court of Common Pleas.[67]

While Assembly members clearly sought to limit the availability of injunctive relief, it is less certain whether this statutory restriction was scrupulously followed. Court records, in fact, show that Chancery litigants continued to request injunctions throughout the colonial period.[68] In 1713, for example, Benjamin Schenckingh asked the court to issue a writ of injunction "for the Staying of process at the Common Law against" him in a debt dispute.[69] John Moore also requested an injunction staying common law proceedings for failure to perform a contract.[70] Anecdotal evidence suggests that the court occasionally granted these requests. When Peter Manigault sought to enforce a judgment against perpetual debtor Richard Stobo, for example, he complained that the Court of Chancery had "granted" Stobo "a Protection for a few Months." As the frustrated Manigault noted, Stobo "now walks publicly about Town And I dare not arrest him."[71]

---

[65] Benjamin Whitaker to Henry McCulloh, February 3, 1742/3, transcription in Anne Gregorie Papers, 28/17/3, SCHS.

[66] *Ibid.*   [67] Gregorie, ed., *Records of the Court of Chancery*, 54.

[68] Douglass, "The Creation of South Carolina's Legal System," 262.

[69] *Edward Holmes v. Benjamin Schenckingh, Executor of Berringer*, February 12, 1713, SCDAH; Gregorie, ed., *Records of the Court of Chancery*, 95.

[70] *John Moore v. Benjamin Godin and Benjamin De La Conseillere*, February 18, 1716, Chancery Case Papers, 1700–1791, Court of Chancery Bundle 1700–1716, Nos. 1–17, No. 13, Oversize, S142001, SCDAH.

[71] Peter Manigault to Isaac King, October 21, 1768, Manigault Papers, Box 11/278/7, 80–81, Peter Manigault Letterbook, 1763–1773, SCHS. See also Nelson, who argues

Early practice in South Carolina's Chancery Court likewise differed from English Chancery practice. The court's venue set the tone, as judges met for hearings in a local tavern. This casual setting appalled Assembly members, who thought it a "disgrace to the Country & even Scandalous [tha]t [the]e most publick Courts of Judicature Should be held in a Tavern as they now are."[72] The court's informal atmosphere was matched by the poor quality of early legal representation. Indeed, the 1721 statute complained that "divers unskillful persons" acting as solicitors "in the courts of law and equity" had done "unspeakable damage" to their clients by misfeasance.[73] Gradually, however, practice in the court began to conform more closely to English Chancery practice.[74] Improvements in the colonial bar help to account for this. After 1721, for example, only solicitors who were formally admitted to practice by the chief justice of the Court of Common Pleas tried Chancery cases, and many of these practitioners had received a legal education at the Inns of Court in London.[75] Given this educational background, they "possessed not only a detailed understanding of chancery procedure but also fairly extensive knowledge of equity law," and they closely adhered to the "jurisdiction and procedure of the English Court of Chancery."[76]

As in England, process in South Carolina's Chancery Court began when a solicitor filed a bill of complaint with the register of the court, who then issued a subpoena to the respondent (defendant) directing him to answer the bill. The respondent could answer the bill, or he could allege that the bill was deficient in some way. When the respondent finally answered, the complainant had an opportunity to respond to the answer (a replication), to which the respondent could again reply with a rejoinder. Litigants also could file exceptions to the pleadings, which were the

that the court frequently granted injunctions. Nelson, *The Common Law in Colonial America*, 72.

[72] A. S. Salley, ed., *Commissions and Instructions From the Lords Proprietors of Carolina to Public Officials of South Carolina, 1685–1715* (Columbia: Historical Commission of South Carolina, 1916), 270.

[73] *SAL*, 7:173. [74] Douglass, "The Creation of South Carolina's Legal System," 259.

[75] *Ibid.*, 260. South Carolinians maintained a distinction between "solicitors" and "counselors" that tracked the distinction in English legal practice between "barristers" and "solicitors." Frierson, "Introduction," 15.

[76] Douglass, "The Creation of South Carolina's Legal System," 255–256; Gregorie, ed., *Records of the Court of Chancery*, 36. Court records suggest that litigants and their solicitors understood that proceeding in equity was distinct from proceeding at common law. They invoked Chancery jurisdiction in cases of fraud and collusion, where witnesses could not be located, where written evidence was lacking, and, perhaps most importantly, where there was no common law remedy.

equivalent of demurrers at common law. They also might choose to examine witnesses through written interrogatories, even if those witnesses were located outside of the province.[77] After the completion of written discovery, the court – often on the recommendation of the master in complicated cases – would issue a final written decree, which could be appealed to the Privy Council if the value of the case exceeded £300 sterling.[78]

Just as the South Carolina Court's procedures resembled English Chancery practice, so too did colonists' complaints about the price and pace of eighteenth-century Chancery litigation echo those of Britons in the metropole. South Carolinians, in fact, were outspoken critics of Chancery, lamenting the court's costliness and dilatoriness. In advising two English merchants to rethink their plans to bring a Chancery suit in South Carolina, for example, Henry Laurens explained that an equity suit would be lengthy and costly. "This Court," he explained, "is here as in all other places as much reputed for its costliness & delay as it is reverenc'd for its equity."[79] Peter Manigault likewise commented on the court's penchant for delay, advising his clients that he was "afraid a Chancery Suit" was "unavoidable," and this unfortunately meant that "[d]elays which are the Delight of some Folks" also would be inevitable.[80] Manigault advised another client that a Chancery suit would be "attended with a great Expence" and recommended that it should therefore be avoided.[81]

Few complete Chancery Court case records survive, but those that do suggest that colonists' complaints about equity law and its administration may have matched reality. For example, *Executors of Baker v. Executors of Jenys* lingered from 1739 until 1750, while *Durand v. Guichard* dragged on from 1742 to 1753, lengthy suits even by English Chancery standards. These delays may have stemmed from the multiplication of motions and interlocutory appeals (appeals taken before the conclusion of litigation), as was the case in England, or the fact that colonial governors

[77] In 1743, for example, a commission issued to take examinations in Bristol and Liverpool in the complicated business dispute *Samuel Wragg* v. *Joseph Wragg*. June 16, 1743, Balzano Collection, 110.20 (Misc. MSS), SCHS.

[78] *SAL*, 7:165. This statute required the appellant to provide double security. Losing appellants were required to pay the costs of the suit. During the proprietary period, appeals ran to the governor and council, or by petition to the Lords Proprietors. Few appeals were taken to the king and council prior to 1768. Frierson, "Introduction," 15.

[79] *HLP* 4:546.

[80] Peter Manigault to Isaac King, undated [spring 1771], Manigault Letterbook, 152.

[81] Peter Manigault to Dr. John Delahow, March 2, 1772. *Ibid.*, 175.

and council members typically lacked legal training.[82] More concretely, it seems clear that Chancery litigation in South Carolina was protracted because the court had difficulty maintaining a quorum – under the 1721 statute, a majority of the council. "[M]any of the [Council] Members," James Glen complained, "were frequently absent from the Province," and this occasioned delays in Chancery that sometimes lasted "many years." Indeed, the court's business was "entirely at a stand" when enough council members could not be located, and delays occasioned by the lack of a quorum had led to "a total failure of Justice" on a number of occasions.[83] As a result of the "Cries of the Suitors for dispatch," the Assembly amended the 1721 statute. After 1746, Chancery could sit with a majority of council members *actually resident* in the colony rather than a majority of all council members.

THE BUSINESS OF EQUITY

Despite colonists' complaints about Chancery, which reflected evident problems with the court's administration, the jurisdiction remained busy throughout the colonial period [Table 4.1]. Overwhelmingly, South Carolina's Chancery Court adjudicated complex disputes over inheritance. In fact, between 1700 and 1780, 47 percent of the court's business involved disputes over decedents' estates, which included both real and personal property. Moreover, the number of inheritance cases litigated in Chancery nearly doubled over the course of the colonial period, an increase that roughly tracks developments in English Chancery[84] [Table 4.1]. Henry Horwitz and Patrick Polden have argued that the decline of church courts (which typically heard estate disputes) rather than changing rates of testation accounts for an expanding estate business in English Chancery, but it is difficult to determine whether a similar phenomenon was at work in South Carolina.[85] Although South Carolina did have a Court of Ordinary – charged with adjudicating cases relating to wills and inheritance – its records are too incomplete to determine whether Chancery engrossed the Court of Ordinary's business over time.[86] We do know, however, that rates of testation in South Carolina did not significantly change over the colonial period; other factors, therefore, must account for increased inheritance litigation

---

[82] Frierson, "Introduction," 11.   [83] October 10, 1748, BPRO, 23:218.
[84] Horwitz and Polden, "Continuity or Change," 35.   [85] *Ibid.*, 39.
[86] South Carolina Court of Ordinary records only survive for the period 1771–1775.

TABLE 4.1 *South Carolina Chancery Court cases by type, 1700–1780*

	Inheritance	Business Disputes	Debt	Land Disputes	Marital Causes	Other	Unknown	Total
1700–1730	17	8	10	7	0	4		46
1731–1760	17	5	6	0	2	1	1	32
1761–1780	25	6	6	8	0	1	3	49
Total	59	19	22	15	2	6	4	127
Percentage of Total Cases	46.5%	15.0%	17.3%	11.8%	1.6%	4.7%	3.2%	100.0%

in Chancery.[87] One possible explanation is that as South Carolina colonists became wealthier over the course of the eighteenth century, the expense of estate litigation in Chancery became more economically justifiable. Indeed, as Peter Coclanis has shown, the mean total wealth of inventoried white decedents in South Carolina grew from £416.79 sterling in the period 1722–1726 to £862.71 sterling in the period 1757–1762. Given this pattern, the financial stakes for heirs may have become high enough to drive more litigants into Chancery even while testation rates remained static.[88]

As in English Chancery, the number of debt cases in South Carolina also fell over the colonial period, although South Carolina's Chancery Court did not experience the same proportional decrease in debt suits as the English Court.[89] Indeed, disputes over debt were the second most litigated type of case in South Carolina, comprising 17 percent of the court's business, and although the number of debt cases declined by almost one-half between 1700 and 1731, litigation over debt remained steady between 1731 and 1780 [Table 4.1]. Horwitz and Polden have suggested that the greater availability of equitable remedies in common law courts explains the sharp decrease in English Chancery debt cases in the early modern period. Similarly, the evolution of more streamlined common law debt collection procedures may have driven litigants from Chancery to South Carolina's common law jurisdiction, the Court of Common Pleas.[90] Over the course of the eighteenth century, attorneys in Common Pleas began to bypass the complicated procedural maneuvering that typically accompanied common law debt cases. In particular, debtors could appoint an attorney to "confess judgment" of a specific amount that they owed to a creditor rather than forcing creditors to sue out a writ of inquiry.[91] Combined with the lower cost of litigating at

---

[87] John E. Crowley, "Family Relations and Inheritance in Early South Carolina," *Histoire Social – Social History* 17 (1984): 40n.

[88] Peter A. Coclanis, *The Shadow of a Dream: Economic Life and Death in the South Carolina Low Country 1670–1920* (New York: Oxford University Press, 1989), 89. The size of plantation units and the number of slaves per household also grew. John J. McCusker and Russell R. Menard, *The Economy of British America, 1607–1789* (Chapel Hill: University of North Carolina Press, 1991), 182. The number of slaves per household in St. George's Parish, for example, grew from 8 in 1720 to 24 by 1741. *Ibid.*, 182.

[89] Horwitz and Polden, "Continuity or Change," 35.   [90] *Ibid.*, 38–39.

[91] Nelson, *The Common Law in Colonial America*, 72. As part of a broader debt collection strategy, creditors might request that a debtor confess judgment, which the creditor could then choose to execute at a later date. This effectively provided the creditor with security

common law, this procedure may account for the decline in debt cases in South Carolina's Chancery Court.[92]

If expanding inheritance litigation and contracting debt litigation in South Carolina's Chancery Court roughly mimicked litigation patterns in English Chancery, in other significant respects the South Carolina Court's business differed. Chancery in South Carolina, for example, did not experience a substantial increase in business litigation, while the number of business cases in English Chancery nearly tripled between the seventeenth and nineteenth centuries.[93] Instead, business disputes occupied a meager 15 percent of the South Carolina Chancery Court's docket, and the number of cases heard by the court remained steady between 1700 and 1780 [Table 4.1]. At first glance, this is surprising. Indeed, historians have characterized South Carolina colonists as particularly engaged participants in a wider Atlantic economy, and we might expect that as elite colonists expanded their businesses and plantations over the course of the eighteenth century, commercial disputes in Chancery would increase.[94] One possible explanation for this unexpected result is that the cost of bringing a suit in Chancery was only justifiable in the most valuable cases, which typically were disputes over estates, not contract disputes. Likewise, litigants may have hesitated to bring disputes over contracts to deliver commodities – which had fluctuating prices – to a court notorious for delay.

Jurisdictional competition also may account for the relative lack of business litigation in South Carolina's Chancery Court. Indeed, just as an increasingly sophisticated common law debt practice may have attracted litigants to Common Pleas, so too did Common Pleas provide remedies that appealed to litigants in business cases. As William Nelson has

---

for the debt. James Mickie explained this process to a Scottish correspondent: "What I mean by Confessing a Judgment," he explained to a Scottish correspondent, "is this I have brought an Accon for Breach of Covenant (for not Paying the money wch you advanced for you could not Sue the Bond wch was not due nor in my Possession) and on this a Judgment is confessed in order to give you a preference on the arrears of the Estate for the Satisfaction of Sunderlands Bond." James Mickie to [Sir Alexander Nisbet], March 7, 1745, GD237/1/154/2, Scottish National Archives, Edinburgh, Scotland, United Kingdom.

[92] According to Nelson, the greater availability of printed legal forms over the course of the eighteenth century also may have "streamlined the debt collection process" while providing creditors with written instruments on which to sue in Common Pleas. Nelson, *The Common Law in Colonial America*, 72.

[93] Horwitz and Polden, "Continuity or Change," 35.

[94] See S. Max Edelson, *Plantation Enterprise in Colonial South Carolina* (Cambridge: Harvard University Press, 2006), 174–186.

observed, by the eighteenth century Common Pleas had a thriving writ system that gave potential litigants access to a number of ways to proceed at common law. Available writs included "writs of debt, trespass, and assumpsit" in addition to "actions of account, covenant, detinue, eject-ment, replevin, and trover, as well as qui tam actions."[95] With a variety of common law remedies from which to choose, business litigants were more likely to seek relief in the less-expensive Court of Common Pleas unless they required equitable remedies or faced evidentiary problems that pre-vented them from suing at common law.

Finally, whereas in England the number of trust cases increased signifi-cantly in the early modern period, the South Carolina Court heard a statistically insignificant number of trust disputes.[96] Trusts were equit-able estates that were recognized in equity law but not in common law, and they emerged in England primarily to provide "an escape from the inflexible certainty of the legal rules of succession." For example, they allowed a landowner to "provide for younger sons, daughters, bastards, remote relations, or charities" by conveying an estate to trustees for the use of beneficiaries rather than by passing legal title directly to heirs.[97] In the English Chancery Court, the most significant type of litigated trust was a marriage settlement, which conveyed property to trustees for the benefit of a woman, usually in anticipation of her marriage.[98] The relative lack of trust litigation in South Carolina reflects the fact that marriage settlements in the province were uncommon. As Marylynn Salmon has shown through a quantitative analysis of marriage settlements between 1785 and 1810 (a period during which all settlements were recorded and reli-able census data exists), only "1–2 percent of marrying couples created separate estates" through marriage settlements. In fact, settlements "were far from the common occurrence that some historians have believed, at least in South Carolina," where only the wealthiest female colonists had separate estates.[99]

---

[95] Nelson, *The Common Law in Colonial America*, 70.
[96] Horwitz and Polden, "Continuity or Change," 35. In fact, I have only located one dispute over a marriage settlement in South Carolina's manuscript case records, although Salmon suggests there may be several more cases based upon an examination of the court's printed minute books.
[97] Baker, *An Introduction to English Legal History*, 252.
[98] Horwitz and Polden, "Continuity or Change," 34.
[99] Salmon, "Women and Property in South Carolina," 663. Salmon also found that marriage settlements "most often included slaves, money, cattle, and household goods, but not land." *Ibid.*, 665.

Despite Chancery's obvious deficiencies, colonists nonetheless found the jurisdiction useful and, in some cases, indispensable for resolving their disputes. An English legal heritage may have predisposed them to embrace jurisdictional diversity, but Chancery's procedures also made it particularly well suited for colonists who hoped to resolve their lengthy and complicated disputes over slaves, and especially disputes over inheritance. Not only did Chancery bill procedure open up space for colonists to explain their often-convoluted claims, the court's willingness to accept oral evidence and to painstakingly trace title to slaves back over generations merged with their legal needs. In a place where records frequently were destroyed and in which undocumented customary arrangements often organized plantation life, colonists continued to seek justice in Chancery even if its pace was slow.

AN EQUITABLE SLAVE COURT

The single most important difference between Chancery practice in England and South Carolina was that 41 percent of all cases heard by the South Carolina Chancery Court involved slaves. Indeed, South Carolina colonists routinely used their local equity court to litigate claims to enslaved people, primarily in the context of inheritance disputes (65 percent) [Table 4.2]. Cases involving slaves, however, were spread across the entirety of the court's docket between 1700 and 1780, as colonists also argued over slaves in business disputes (19 percent), debt litigation (12 percent), and conflicts over leases (2 percent) [Table 4.3]. The ubiquity of slaves in Chancery proceedings reveals their centrality to South Carolina's economy. More importantly, slave litigation in Chancery shows that slave owners found the procedures of equity as much as its substance useful when they asked the court to adjudicate their complex cases. Taking advantage of bill procedure and deploying the language of equity uncritically, they sought legal recognition for the most inequitable of practices.

Business disputes over slaves in Chancery took a variety of forms. Some colonists litigated over contracts in which one party promised to deliver goods or provide services to another party. In these cases, slaves typically appeared as laborers, rather than as the property objects of colonists' claims. In 1716, for example, John Moore asked the court to relieve him of a contractual obligation to make pitch, which he could not perform because it had "pleased god to Vissitt this Province with an unhappy Warr with the Infidell Indians." As he explained to the court, during the Yamasee War his "Slaves and Servants hire were Cutt off, and Driven

TABLE 4.2 *South Carolina Chancery Court cases involving slaves, 1700–1780*

		Percentage of Total Cases
1700–1730	22	17.3%
1731–1760	10	7.9%
1761–1780	20	15.8%
Total	52	40.9%

TABLE 4.3 *South Carolina Chancery Court slave cases by type, 1700–1780*

		Percentage of Slave Cases	Percentage of Total Cases
Inheritance	34	65.4%	26.8%
Business Dispute	10	19.2%	7.9%
Debt	6	11.5%	4.7%
Leases	1	1.9%	0.8%
Other	1	1.9%	0.8%
Total	52	100.0%	40.9%

from theire plantations," and along with Moore they did not dare return for "fear of theire lives." Consequently, if he were "compelled to performe the Strictness of such his Contract or Agreement," he would "be a verry, great Sufferer," particularly as the price of pitch had "vastly Risen" in the interim. Because "the hand of god" prevented his performance, holding him to his agreement "would be Contrary, to Equity and good Conscience."[100]

Litigants in Chancery also sparred over slave hiring contracts and plantation leases, revealing the extent to which renting land and slaves remained a significant practice despite historians' emphasis on the importance of fee simple ownership in plantation economies. Slave and plantation hiring not only provided a source of income for colonists with slaves they could not put to work. It also gave less-wealthy colonists access to

[100] *John Moore v. Benjamin Godin and Benjamin De La Conseillere*, filed February 18, 1716, Chancery Case Papers, 1700–1791, Court of Chancery Bundle 1700–1716, Nos. 1–17, No. 13, Oversize, S142001, SCDAH.

land and labor for a lower cost, thereby removing barriers to entry for poor whites who aspired to slave and plantation ownership. These rental arrangements often were customary or unwritten, and hiring cases were brought in Chancery rather than Common Pleas because colonists lacked written records. For example, in 1715 John Kincaird, a "Berkley County planter," sued in Chancery over a parole (oral) plantation lease that entitled him to use "[e]leven Negroes and one Indian slave (vizt) Jack. Jacko. Quaminash. Boson. Tony. Prince. Cudjo. Pussaugh. Moll. Doll. Hannah and Guay an Indian." Although Kincaird and the plantation owner intended to memorialize their agreement, the owner was killed in the Yamasee War before it could be reduced "into writeing." Lacking any proof of the lease, Kincaird was subject to harassment from the heir, who "dayly" threatened to "take away the said negroes" and to "cut down take and carry away the Crop now growing."[101] Similarly, Jamaican merchant William Hawett brought a suit in Chancery because, "being an Aged man," he had "lost or Mislaid" letters outlining the terms of a plantation management agreement with Elizabeth Moore. Hawett alleged that Moore had agreed to take "care of the Negroes and Stock" on one of his South Carolina plantations and to "[i]mprove the same to the best Advantage and Live on the Same For the space of Sevean years" in exchange for an annuity. However, Moore had never "returned ... one penny of the Encrease or profitts of the said Farme." Instead, she had wasted the property and had caused Hawett's "Negroes on the said Plantation to be Attached" when the annuity was not paid.[102]

Similar cases appeared on the Jamaican Chancery Court's docket, where colonists routinely asked judges to settle complicated disputes about the nature of slave and plantation hiring agreements. For example, in 1711 cabinet maker Andrew Blanchard responded to a complaint that he had failed to pay for the services on an enslaved man named Sampson. Blanchard flatly denied the existence of a hiring agreement, insisting that "he never desired to hire or ever did hire the Complts said Negro named

[101] *John Kincaird* v. *Mathew Beard*, October 1715, Chancery Case Papers, 1700–1791, Court of Chancery Bundle 1700–1716, Nos. 1–17, No. 11, Oversize, S142001, SCDAH.

[102] *William Hawett* v. *Thomas Moore and Wife*, filed November 9, 1716, Chancery Case Papers, 1700–1791, Court of Chancery Bundle 1700–1716, Nos. 1–17, No. 17, Oversize, S142001, SCDAH. Elizabeth, for her part, admitted that she had attached the slaves "in order to recover the Arrears of her said Annuity," but only after discovering that she had been written out of Hawett's will, the old man "being more carefully and watchfully guarded by his Dependants than the Golden Fleece." Answer filed March 7, 1717.

Sampson." Instead, he claimed that he had agreed to take on Sampson as an apprentice rather than a laborer soon after he arrived in Jamaica. For nearly "[t]welve months," Blanchard "tooke particular care and paines to Instruct the said Negroe Sampson," who under his tutelage became "a very good work man." It was only at this point, according to Blanchard, that the complainant demanded compensation. As Blanchard explained, this arrangement made little sense. He "could work severall Negroes of his own" and therefore did not require Sampson's services, despite the enslaved man's talents. More importantly, he would never have agreed to "give wages for the hire of [Sampson]" and "undertake to teach a Negro as well."[103]

Cases like Hawett's and Blanchard's lay bare the widespread but largely hidden customary economic system by which planters created working arrangements that hinged on transferring and selling slave labor. In a place where small-scale business deals involving slaves were made informally, Chancery could give legal force to a wide variety of undocumented arrangements. The court's bill procedure made this possible. Colonists described in detail the contract they hoped the court would enforce, and explained why they lacked written evidence of their agreements. But written discovery, in the form of depositions and interrogatories, also gave the court access to evidence of local custom, which judges used to adjudicate disputes over slave and plantation leases. Indeed, parties could propound interrogatories to witnesses inquiring about local slave hiring customs, which the court could then take into account in formulating a decree. For example, complainant John Brown sued in Chancery to recover costs he incurred providing medical treatment for "fifteen Negroe and Indian" hired slaves. He also asked to be compensated for money he had expended capturing these slaves when they ran away, an apparently frequent occurrence. In this case, witnesses were asked to answer questions about when colonists like Brown were entitled to recompense. "What is the Custom of South Carolina when Slaves are hired with a Plantation for a Term of Years by Lease?" Was it customary "to Allow for Sick or Black Days or run away Days of said Negroes in Such case or not?" One witness suggested that when slaves were hired by the year, they were not allowed "[s]ick or Black days" unless that was part of the contractual agreement. The respondent in the case agreed, suggesting that there was a "[w]ide Difference in the Case where Slaves are lett per Week or Month and where they are leased for years." Whereas the "[s]ick

---

[103] *Blanchard v. Thurgar*, March 26, 1711, Jamaica Chancery Records, JARD, REF 1A/3/5.

Days or Physick be Sometimes allowed where Slaves are hired per Week or Month," this was because "[s]laves lett per Week or Month are lett at Rack Rates to witt at double the price at what they are generally leased." In this case, she argued, because the renter received a bargain rate of "[t]wo hundred Pounds per Annum" for the lease of a plantation and "[f]ifteen Negroes and Indians Slaves," the complainant was not entitled to collect medical costs.[104]

The Chancery Court's ability to inquire into these complicated customary practices made it an invaluable resource for colonists who sought a narrowly tailored solution to their particular problems. These colonists expected and received justice that took into account local and customary assumptions about how slave and plantation hiring should work, and who should bear the potentially significant costs of caring for sick slaves. Far from an insignificant or powerless jurisdiction, Chancery in South Carolina was a venue in which an elaborate system of customary management and exchange, centered on the hiring of slaves and plantations, was adjudicated, and in which those who sought to violate this system were called to account. By providing a mechanism for interrogating and upholding customary practices, the court in turn encouraged the elaboration of a practical law of slavery, one in which the value of a slave-as-property was not fixed at a sale price, but modulated according to a renter's labor needs in any given season.

Just as the court's procedural flexibility made it a useful venue for inquiring into and adjudicating the terms of customary arrangements, so too did this flexibility make it ideal for resolving complex business disputes over slaves. South Carolina's Chancery Court, and particularly the master in Chancery, could pick through voluminous correspondence and financial accounts in order to unravel even the most complicated business arrangements. Disputes over joint planting ventures and copartnership agreements could be particularly vexing and were well suited for disposition Chancery. Indeed, litigants could ask the court to review articles of agreement as well as extensive financial documents in order to determine how a firm's assets and debts should be allocated. For example, when Kinsey Burden and Richard Moncrief, two Charlestown-based carpenters, fought over the dissolution of their partnership in 1773, they asked the court to determine whether Burden should be compensated because Moncrief had breached his contractual obligation to pay for hired slave

---

[104] *John Brown* v. *Eleana Wright*, Answer filed February 16, 1717, Chancery Case Papers, 1700–1791, Court of Chancery Bundle 1717–1720, Nos. 1–8, No. 1, S142001, SCDAH.

labor. Burden alleged that in articles of copartnership Moncrief had agreed to "pay for one able white Man or two negroe Men" to complete "[h]ouses and Buildings and all other Carpenters and Joiner's Work," an obligation he had allegedly failed to perform.[105]

In these complicated copartnership disputes, questions about allocating assets typically were combined with allegations of fraud, which justified Chancery jurisdiction. In 1770, for example, three partners in a planting venture clashed over the sale of a plantation when the partnership was dissolved. Specifically, they squabbled over whether one of the partners had caused "some Cattle, one Negroe Boy, and a few Horses to be moved to Georgia" with "an Intent or Design . . . to injure or defraud" another partner.[106] Similarly, in a dispute involving a slave-trading firm, Samuel Wragg alleged that his brother and copartner Joseph Wragg had mismanaged the firm's assets and concealed accounts. While the Britain-based Samuel Wragg toiled to "procur[e] and mak[e] Consignments of Negroes and other Commodities" to his brother, Joseph had contracted "large Debts" in South Carolina by "making purchases, carrying on Expensive Buildings, & Decorations And in private Adventures in the way of Trade."[107] Allegations of fraud like Wragg's placed colonists' claims squarely within the court's ambit, echoing not only contemporary justifications for English Chancery jurisdiction, but also an older early modern equitable discourse. They also reveal a world in which the resident planter presiding over enslaved workers on a single plantation was only one possibility among the variety of economic arrangements that mobile slave labor, organized in a customary legal framework, encouraged to generate wealth.

In addition to litigating a wide variety of business concerns involving slaves in Chancery, colonists also litigated over enslaved people in the context of debt disputes. As we have seen in Chapter 2, South Carolina colonists primarily purchased slaves on credit, structuring their purchases with debt instruments like conditional bonds and mortgages.[108] When

[105] *Kinsey Burden* v. *Richard Moncrief*, Bill filed [January 23, 1773], Chancery Case Papers, 1700–1791, Court of Chancery Bundle 1770–1779, Nos. 1–16, No. 3a, S142001, SCDAH.

[106] *Jonathan Williamson* v. *James Thompson and Robert Thompson*, Answer filed June 30, 1770, Chancery Case Papers, 1700–1791, Court of Chancery Bundle 1767–1769, Nos. 1–16, No. 16, SCDAH.

[107] *Samuel Wragg* v. *Joseph Wragg*, Bill filed March 2, 1742, Chancery Case Papers, 1700–1791, Court of Chancery Bundle 1721–1735, No. 12, S142001, SCDAH.

[108] Kenneth Morgan, "Remittance Procedures in the Eighteenth-Century British Slave Trade," *The Business History Review* 79 (2005): 715–749; Bonnie Martin, "Slavery's

a debtor defaulted on a loan, creditors could sue on these instruments in the Court of Common Pleas. Occasionally, though, written instruments were lost or damaged, which caused some litigants to seek relief in Chancery. In 1701, for example, Jamaican merchant Jacob Mears sued Charles Town merchant Simon Valentine for debts incurred purchasing "[w]heat flower, Indico, Negroes, Sugar, and such like Comodities" because he could not prove the debts with a written instrument. The unlucky Mears apparently lost all of his business records in an earthquake which had "[i]ndiscriminately Swallowed up" the house where "he allwaies kept his books of Accounts."[109]

That Chancery provided relief for litigants like Mears who lacked written records helps to explain its continuing appeal in colonies where climate, military conflict, and natural disasters made record keeping difficult. Historians have noted that climate had profound implications for material life and provincial identity formation in the Greater Caribbean region, but natural disasters and climatological factors also had significant *legal* ramifications.[110] None was more important than the destruction of legal records, not only because these records memorialized important agreements and proved title to property, but also because their mere physical existence allowed colonists to sue in common law courts. By offering colonists an alternative venue, one that did not require legal documentation, Chancery became particularly useful to legal consumers like Mears who operated in harsh new world environments.

Even when colonists retained records, the Chancery Court's ability to offer injunctive relief made it an appealing court of last resort for debtors who could not pay for their slaves and found themselves sued in Common Pleas. In Chancery, these colonists could describe in great detail the circumstances that had prevented them from discharging their obligations, and could ask the court to stay proceedings. Thomas Smith, for example, sought injunctive relief in Chancery when his creditors sued him

Invisible Engine: Mortgaging Human Property," *The Journal of Southern History* 76 (2010): 817–866; Russell R. Menard, "Financing the Lowcountry Export Boom: Capital and Growth in Early Carolina," *WMQ* 51 (1994): 659–676; David Hancock, "'Capital and Credit with Approved Security': Financial Markets in Montserrat and South Carolina, 1748–1775," *Business and Economic History* 23 (1994): 61–84.

[109] *Jacob Mears v. Simon Valentine*, August 26, 1701, Chancery Case Papers, 1700–1791, Court of Chancery Bundle 1700–1716, Nos. 1–17, No. 2, Oversize, S142001, SCDAH.

[110] Matthew Mulcahy, *Hurricanes and Society in the Greater British Caribbean, 1624–1783* (Baltimore: Johns Hopkins University Press, 2005), 2–3. Jack P. Greene, *Imperatives, Behaviors and Identities: Essays in Early American Cultural History* (Charlottesville: University of Virginia Press, 1992), 13–67.

in Common Pleas for failing to deliver "[t]wenty Three hundred and Sixty Barrells of Tarr" in payment for "[t]wenty Eight Negroe Slaves." Smith claimed that he had discharged the debt by delivering the tar, but that the respondents had failed to collect the tar in a timely manner.[111] It was unjust, he argued, for the Court of Common Pleas to penalize him under these circumstances, and he asked Chancery to intervene and enjoin the attachment of his property. As we have seen in Chapter 2, preventing the attachment of property, and particularly slaves, was an important goal for South Carolina debtors like Thomas Smith. Not only did the attachment of slaves mean the loss of valuable economic assets; without slaves, debtors like Smith could not hope to repay their creditors. By providing a means to stop the attachment process, Chancery gave debtors one last opportunity to thwart their creditors and to continue to use their slaves productively to discharge outstanding debts.

Just like business litigants in Chancery, debt litigants also relied upon allegations of fraud, conspiracy, or collusion in order to justify Chancery jurisdiction. Jacob Yorkson's framing of his quest to redeem his mort-gaged slave from Grace Buckley reveals the extent to which it was import-ant for litigants to position themselves as victims in Chancery pleadings. Finding himself short of money, Yorkson borrowed twenty-six pounds from Buckley, securing his debt with the mortgage of "one Negroe boy named Robin." According to Yorkson, when the debt came due, he offered Buckley payment, but she refused to take it, saying that "it would be a great kindness to her" to allow Robin to continue working "till she was capable and had an opportunity of buying one in his Room." Year after year, Yorkson offered to discharge the mortgage and retrieve Robin, but year after year, Buckley convinced him to let her keep the slave "with fair Speeches." Yorkson eventually grew suspicious that Buckley would "take Advantage of his Mortgage and of his not Redeeming the said Negroe," suspicions that proved correct. As he explained to the court, Buckley had combined with "divers Persons unknown to your Orator," and now she gave out that he had "forfeited his Negroe by not Complying with his Mortgage." Indeed, she refused to "deliver up" Robin, for whom he had been "offered Three hundred pounds." Calling upon the court to exercise jurisdiction, Buckley, like other South Carolina colonists and,

---

[111] *Landgrave Thomas Smith v. Richard Beresford and Richard Splatt,* August 15, 1720, Chancery Case Papers, 1700–1791, Court of Chancery Bundle 1717–1720, No. 17, S142001, SCDAH.

indeed, like English litigants in Chancery, claimed that Yorkson's actions were "contrary to all Equity and Good Conscience."[112]

Whether they positioned themselves as victims of fraudulent defendants, the Lowcountry's subtropical climate, or simply bad luck, colonists took advantage of equity procedures to lay claim to slaves. Free to launch into a lengthy explanation of their grievances, they called upon the court to craft a remedy that suited their individual circumstances, even when they lacked documentary evidence to substantiate their claims. They did so using a much older equitable discourse, one that they wielded uncritically as they fought over enslaved people. Indeed, for colonists like Buckley, the phrase "Equity and Good Conscience" was an empty one, a mere catch phrase that granted him access to Chancery Court, its substantive law, and most importantly, its procedures.

WOMEN AND SLAVES IN CHANCERY

When written evidence was lacking, when business affairs were complicated, and when individuals conspired to defraud South Carolina colonists, Chancery provided a venue in which litigants might seek relief in cases involving slaves. Overwhelmingly, however, South Carolina's Chancery Court was a resource for colonists who litigated claims to slaves in the context of inheritance disputes. Indeed, 65 percent of all Chancery inheritance cases in South Carolina involved claims to slaves as personal property [Table 4.3]. In some of these cases, litigants asked the court to perform administrative tasks, including dividing personal property or granting executors permission to sell a decedent's slaves. For example, Benjamin Godin's executors sought relief in Chancery because they did not have "[c]ash in hand Sufficient to discharge the Several pecuniary Legacies bequeathed by" Godin, and they asked the court for the "[l]iberty to Sell the Negroes and other of the personal Estate of the said Deceased."[113] The executors of John St. John also asked the Chancery Court to divide "several negroes" belonging to St. John's estate, which had not originally been included in the estate's inventory.[114] Aside

[112] *Jacob Yorkson v. Grace Buckley*, August 6, 1719, Chancery Case Papers, 1700–1791, Court of Chancery Bundle 1717–1720, No. 15, S142001, SCDAH.
[113] *Executors of Benjamin Godin, deceased*, December 18, 1749, Chancery Case Papers, 1700–1791, Court of Chancery Bundle 1736–1760, Nos. 1–21, No. 10, S142001, SCDAH.
[114] *Elizabeth Beatty, Executrix of John St. John and Others v. Lambert Lance, Executor of John St. John*, April 20, 1767, Chancery Case Papers, 1700–1791; Court of Chancery Bundle 1763–1766, Nos. 1–12, No. 4, S142001, SCDAH.

from the fact that inheritance disputes like this were within Chancery's jurisdictional orbit, as a practical matter the court was better suited to craft individual solutions to the vexing problem of dividing human property than Common Pleas. The court could order slaves to be sold and divide the proceeds, which it occasionally did. But because Chancery had potentially unlimited access to accounts, witness testimony, and voluminous pleadings, judges also were able to make informed decisions about the relative value of slaves and how they should be allocated among creditors and heirs.

Chancery's capacity to bring before itself a complete record of an estate also benefitted heirs who were concerned that executors were mismanaging plantations and slaves. Indeed, complainants in Chancery frequently alleged that executors wasted estates, and particularly that they improperly disposed of enslaved property through sales and mortgages. As we already have seen, Christian Arthur complained that her brother's executor, John Gough, had wasted the estate by selling and mortgaging "all or the greatest part of the hands and Negroes" to the detriment of her minor son, who was heir at law. Not only did Arthur want the court to prevent Gough from continuing to waste the estate; she also asked the court to compel Gough to produce estate accounts. She wanted to know "[w]hat goods and Effects either in goods Merchandizes Negroes and Slaves or bond persons he has sold or disposed off ... [a]nd what Negroes or hands belonging to the said reall Estate he has mortgaged and sold and upon what account." This type of request was typical. Because chancellors had the authority to compel testimony and to bring important financial documents into the court's record, Chancery was a useful place for remote heirs to gain a more accurate picture of an estate's financial footing. In this case, Arthur's prodding produced an admission that Gough did, in fact, mortgage ten slaves, but he denied that he "[s]old any of the Negros or Slaves" or mortgaged any additional slaves without Arthur's permission.[115]

In her request for additional information about the management of her brother's plantation, Arthur's claim was typical. So too was the fact that Arthur, a female, was a named party to the case. In fact, between 1700 and 1780, 52 percent of all South Carolina Chancery cases included named female litigants. This percentage was even higher in Chancery litigation over slaves (65 percent) [Tables 4.4 and 4.5]. The high incidence of female

---

[115] *Christopher Arthur, By Christian Arthur, His Prochien Amie and Guardian, v. John Gough,* filed December 8, 1714, Chancery Case Papers, 1700–1791, Court of Chancery Bundle 1700–1716, Nos. 1–17, No. 10, Oversize; S142001, SCDAH.

TABLE 4.4 *South Carolina Chancery Court cases with named female litigants, 1700–1780*

		Percentage of Total Cases
1700–1730	22	17.3%
1731–1760	19	15.0%
1761–1780	25	19.7%
Total	66	52.0%

TABLE 4.5 *South Carolina Chancery Court slave cases with named female litigants, 1700–1780*

		Percentage of Slave Cases
1700–1730	14	26.9%
1731–1760	7	13.5%
1761–1780	13	25.0%
Total	34	65.4%

litigants in South Carolina's Chancery Court is striking when contrasted with the number of named female litigants in English Chancery. Horwitz and Polden, for example, found that women comprised only 18.8 percent of all named Chancery litigants in 1627 and 30.6 percent in 1818/19.[116] Amy Louise Erickson arrived at slightly different figures, determining that women comprised 17 percent of litigants in Chancery between 1558–1603 and 26 percent between 1613–1714.[117] Whichever figures one chooses to credit, women in South Carolina were much more frequently named in Chancery suits than were women in England.[118]

The high incidence of named female litigants across all South Carolina Chancery business reflects women's significant role in colonial South Carolina's economic life, in turn a result of negative demographic conditions in the province.[119] High mortality in South Carolina inhibited family formation even as it made traditional estate management strategies impractical. Significantly, the "cultural preference for adult, male heirs

[116] Horwitz and Polden, "Continuity or Change," 45.
[117] Erickson, *Women and Property in Early Modern England*, 115.   [118] *Ibid.*, 115.
[119] Coclanis, *The Shadow of a Dream*, 38, 42.

often simply could not be exercised," and South Carolina colonists relied upon widows as executrices even as they bequeathed valuable property, usually in the form of slaves, to wives and daughters.[120] Indeed, as Marylynn Salmon, John Crowley, and S. Max Edelson have shown, women in South Carolina enjoyed significantly more legal authority over property than women in other provinces, and this was a direct result of high mortality rates among white males. Because male heirs often were unavailable, provisions for South Carolina widows were "liberal." Nearly two-thirds of testators named their wives to share in the estate's residue (usually the most valuable portion of an estate), while childless testators also "made their wives their most important single heir."[121] In leaving property to widows, testators did not necessarily seek to ensure their maintenance. Rather, as Cara Anzilotti has argued, testators consciously arranged their affairs to ensure the "creation of a family estate, a rice plantation that would be passed from one generation to the next." Husbands hoped that their widows would serve as the "regents necessary to perpetuate" a dynasty, passing wealth in tact to the next generation.[122]

Generous provisions for wives in South Carolina were accompanied by a more equitable distribution of personal property among daughters.[123] As we have seen in Chapter 1, in 1712 South Carolina formally adopted English intestacy laws, which gave eldest sons the right to an intestate father's lands, but provided for partible inheritance of personal property regardless of sex. As slaves were the most valuable type of personal property in South Carolina, this could operate to the benefit of daughters. Likewise, as John Crowley discovered in his study of colonial South Carolina wills, testators frequently bequeathed slaves to their daughters, an inheritance that could be more valuable than a decedent's real estate, particularly if the land was unimproved. As was the case with wives, liberal provisions for daughters in South Carolina wills were not meant to set women up as female planters. Bequests to daughters, instead, primarily were meant "to attract suitors."[124]

[120] Crowley, "Family Relations and Inheritance in Early South Carolina," 43.

[121] *Ibid.*, 45; Salmon, *Women and the Law of Property in Early America*, 157; S. Max Edelson, "Reproducing Plantation Society: Women and Land in Colonial South Carolina," *History of the Family* 12 (2007): 130–131.

[122] Cara Anzilotti, *In the Affairs of the World: Women, Patriarchy and Power in Colonial South Carolina* (Westport: Greenwood Press, 2002), 143.

[123] Crowley, "Family Relations and Inheritance in Early South Carolina," 47.

[124] Edelson, "Reproducing Plantation Society," 133.

Testators' careful arrangements for daughters and widows, however, were contested in the Court of Chancery as litigants sparred over valuable patrimony in the form of slaves. Watching colonists argue over female inheritance in Chancery reveals that husbands were eager to use the court to collect the property they expected to receive in right of their wives. Rather than providing a venue for the expression of independent female agency, then, South Carolina's Chancery Court provided a mechanism by which husbands could claim a wife's marriage portion. In Chancery, enslaved people were transferred down the generations and across patri-archal lines through women. At the same time, however, Chancery litigation reveals that dynastic wealth building was a fraught process. Although women primarily were meant to hold and transfer property intact to heirs, in practice some women sought to retain during their lifetimes real familial power. Reluctant to cede control of slaves, widows in particular retained considerable authority over an estate's most valuable property when they maintained actual possession of enslaved people.

IN RIGHT OF MY WIFE

If Christian Arthur's suit was typical in some ways, in other respects the case deviated from the typical Chancery inheritance suit. Whereas Arthur sued alone on behalf of her minor son, most Chancery inheritance disputes were brought by husbands suing with and in right of their wives. Although married female complainants in South Carolina (and England) could sue without their husbands – which was not permitted at common law – most did not do so.[125] Rather, husbands and wives sued together in Chancery to recover female inheritance in the form of slaves. South Carolina's first equity case, in fact, assumed this procedural posture. In 1677, Margaret Yeamans and her spouse asked the Grand Council, sitting as an equity court, to enjoin her deceased husband's heir from transporting fourteen slaves out of the province. Yeamans and her new husband wanted "her thirds," her right to her first husband's property, and they sought relief in equity because a common law court could not grant her an injunction.[126]

---

[125] Erickson has observed, even though women might sue separately from their husbands in Chancery, in contrast to common law courts, "it was clearly prudent to do so in Chancery too, although it was not mandatory." Erickson, *Women and Property in Early Modern England*, 115.

[126] Alexander S. Salley, Jr., ed., *Journal of the Grand Council of South Carolina*, 2 vols. (Columbia: Historical Commission of South Carolina, 1907), 1: 81.

Yeamans's case was a harbinger of things to come, and throughout the colonial period, husbands and wives sued together to claim a wife's enslaved property.[127] George Bassett, for example, sued with his wife Mehatabel to demand slaves she had inherited from her deceased first husband. These slaves had been seized by the estate's executors, who gave "notice in Writing at all the public places" that they intended to sell the property, presumably to pay the estate's debts.[128] Male litigants like Bassett routinely claimed slaves "in right of" their wives, asserting that through intermarriage with an heiress widow, they acquired title to her property. Likewise, husbands also joined with their wives in Chancery to collect a wife's inheritance from her father. As John Crowley has noted, daughters in South Carolina typically inherited personal property, including slaves, equally with their brothers. If a father did not act to shield this property – either by inserting proper limiting language in a will or by creating a separate estate through a marriage settlement – when a daughter married her husband acquired a right to her slaves. In some instances, this was desirable from a father's perspective. Indeed, fathers in South Carolina specifically provided for their daughters in order to encourage eligible suitors, and single male colonists in South Carolina "unabashedly pursued women for their inheritances."[129] Through Chancery litigation, husbands sought to make good on a father's promise to provide for his daughter in his will, and they used the court to ensure that a wife's inheritance was managed properly. For example, Thomas and Ann Everleigh asked the Chancery Court to intervene to protect Ann's inheritance, which they complained was being grossly mismanaged by her uncle. Although the "[p]lantations and Negroes belonging to the Estate" were of "considerable" value, they argued, the uncle seldom could clear more than a two or three percent profit per year "owing to the Lands being unimproved or other Causes of Mismanagement." Thomas and Ann had "often applied" to her uncle "in a friendly Manner," asking him to sell the "[s]laves belonging to the Estate" and to put "the Monies to Interest," but to no avail.[130]

---

[127] Anzilotti, *In the Affairs of the World*, 143.

[128] *George Bassett on behalf of Mehatabel, his wife, late widow of James Gilbertson, and of Anne Gilberston, age 5 years*, January 1722, Chancery Case Papers, 1700–1791, Court of Chancery Bundle 1721–1735, Nos. 1–13, No. 2, Oversize; S142001, SCDAH.

[129] Edelson, "Reproducing Plantation Society," 133.

[130] *Thomas Eveleigh & Others v. Thomas Farr, Executor of James Simmons*, Decree filed 1777, Chancery Case Papers, 1700–1791, Court of Chancery Bundle 1770–1779, Nos. 1–16, No. 10, S142001, SCDAH.

That the Everleighs brought their case against an executor is not surprising. Indeed, husband-and-wife complainants in Chancery frequently alleged that executors and administrators mismanaged estates or refused to distribute assets. In South Carolina as in England, executors and estate administrators (who were appointed by the Court of Ordinary when a decedent died without a will) were endowed with significant power to manage estates, to pay creditors, and to make distributions to heirs. Appointing an executor was "the most important decision a testator made," and acting as an executor required a unique "combination of business and personal honor." Executing or administrating estates also could prove lucrative, and some colonists earned a livelihood from managing decedents' property.[131] This important role was not limited to male colonists, however. Indeed, in South Carolina widows were named as executrices "in a majority of estate cases," and many also served as administratrices.[132] Acting in this capacity gave them significant power over estates, including enslaved people. But it also brought them into conflict with their own children. Reading colonists' complaints about female estate managers reveals the extent to which widows could upset settled expectations about inheritance by refusing to deliver enslaved people to a decedent's heirs. Although women theoretically were meant to possess and transfer property intact to the next generation, in practice some women used their economic control over inherited property to continue to exert one household's influence over the next generation.

In Chancery, heirs and heiresses complained that widows refused to distribute assets and particularly enslaved people. Indeed, once in possession of valuable estate property, some widows proved reluctant to part with it, as Benjamin Schenckingh discovered. Although his father died possessed of a "very considerable personall Estate," including livestock and slaves, his mother convinced her children to "forbear giveing her any Trouble" about their inheritance because "she beleived she had butt a Little time to Live." She promised instead to provide for her children in her will, but much to Schenckingh's consternation, failed to make the expected bequests.[133] Abraham Saunders went so far as to accuse his sister-in-law, Mary Saunders, of forging a will "whereby she pretend[ed]"

[131] John E. Crowley, "The Importance of Kinship: Testamentary Evidence from South Carolina," *Journal of Interdisciplinary History* 16 (1986): 568.

[132] Edelson, "Reproducing Plantation Society," 132.

[133] *Benjamin Schenckingh et al v. Job Howes and Hugh Grange, Executors of Elizabeth Schenckingh*, December 28, 1704, Chancery Case Papers, 1700–1791, Court of Chancery Bundle 1700–1716, Nos. 1–17, No. 4, Oversize; S142001, SCDAH.

his deceased brother gave her "all his Estate both Real & Personal" and made her his executrix. Acting under "the Colour of the said Will" she had "taken & detained" twelve slaves, "their Issue & increase as Part of the Personal Estate."[134] Similarly, in 1719, George and Mary Flood sued Mary's stepmother, the administratrix of her father's estate, for threatening to "sell at Public Vendue" Mary's inheritance, including "Negroes Household Stuff Plantation Tool and Implements."[135] Whether widows technically had a right to enslaved property or not, mere possession put them in a position of significant strength vis-à-vis a decedent's heirs. Indeed, these women could put slaves to work on plantations or sell them knowing that, short of a time-consuming and expensive Chancery suit, heirs had few legal options for reclaiming slaves.

Chancery pleadings, which allowed colonists to complain at length about the behavior of widows, reveal the extent to which female control of property had the potential to disrupt settled expectations about the descent of land and slaves. Both male and female complainants reacted swiftly and severely when faced with recalcitrant widows, drawing upon timeworn stereotypes to depict these women as connivers, tempters, and conspirators. Complaints about one widow reached hyperbolic proportions in 1767 litigation over the estate of Royal Spry. Spry was a wealthy colonist who died "possessed of a very considerable personal Estate consisting of Negroes and other Slaves Horses Cattle Household Goods Plate and other Effects." He bequeathed his property to his son, Joseph, but if Joseph died without heirs, the property was to descend to Martha Ferguson. At the time of his father's death, Joseph was a "[m]inor very imprudent and easily imposed on" and a ripe target for one Catherine Tucker. Joseph was "drawn in and deluded without the Consent or approbation of his Mother ... to intermarry" with Catherine, who not only was a "[w]oman older than" Joseph but also was "without any Fortune whatsoever." What Catherine lacked in material wealth, however, she apparently made up for in "indigent and greedy Relations" who "surrounded" Joseph and drove him away from his family. Bereft of relatives to guide him, Joseph "was led to a Practice of Gameing Drinking Folly and Disperation" by Catherine, who sought to seize his

---

[134] *James Stewart & Mary, his wife* v. *Abraham Saunders*, Decree filed August 2, 1731, Chancery Case Papers, 1700–1791, Court of Chancery Bundle 1721–1735, Nos. 1–13, No. 10, Oversize, S142001, SCDAH.

[135] *George and Mary Flood* v. *Johanna Baker, Administratrix of Thomas Baker*, 23 July 1719, Chancery Case Papers, 1700–1791, Court of Chancery Bundle 1717–1720, No. 14, S142001, SCDAH.

sizeable "personal Estate." Indeed, while Joseph was "greatly impaired" he "was wrought upon to make a Will" that left all of his property to Catherine, and that also named her his executrix. Joseph finally succumbed to his debauchery, and Martha Ferguson, suing with her husband, tried to claim Joseph's personal estate. They complained that even though they were entitled to the property under Royal Spry's will, Catherine had "prevented and interrupted" them from "taking Possession of the said Slaves." Her actions, they argued, were "contrary to Equity and Good Conscience" and tended to "injure and defraud" the Fergusons.[136]

If complainants in Chancery found it difficult to dislodge slaves from widows like Catherine Tucker, they discovered that forcing a distribution was even more difficult when widows remarried. When heiresses were widows, the extent to which new husbands could make a colorable claim to slaves depended entirely upon whether the decedent died with or without a will. In South Carolina, when a husband died intestate, his widow received one third of his estate, with a life interest in the real property and outright ownership of the personal property, including slaves. This meant that if the widow of an intestate remarried, under the common law doctrine of coverture her new husband gained title to her personal property. Testates could alter these dispositions, and indeed, many male colonists chose to write wills in order to circumvent intestacy rules that allowed slaves to pass outside the family when a widow remarried. As Chancery suits against widows and their new husbands show, however, it was difficult in practice to prevent second husbands from asserting claims to a widow's slaves, particularly when she joined him in a suit.

Colonists frequently brought Chancery claims against widows and their new husbands, claiming that they refused to make a distribution of personal property, including slaves. For example, Abraham Saunders alleged that his brother's widow and her new husband had "detained in ther Possession" twelve "[s]laves their Issue & increase" and that her second husband now "use[d] and employ[ed]" the slaves "in Pretence of the Right of his s[ai]d Wife." Saunders asked the court to issue a Decree directing the couple to deliver "ye s[ai]d twelve Slaves with their Issue & Increase," and he moreover wanted his sister-in-law to "account with & pay" to him "all the Profits which have been made of

[136] *Thomas Ferguson and Martha His Wife v. Catherine Spry and Joseph Fabian, Administrator CTA of Royal Spry, Deceased,* filed October 12, 1767, Chancery Case Papers, 1700–1791, Court of Chancery Bundle 1763–1766, Nos. 1–12, No. 12, S142001, SCDAH.

the s[ai]d Slaves."[137] When a widow died, it could be particularly difficult to
regain control over assets if a second husband remained in possession of the
estate, as John Cantey learned. He sought relief in Chancery because his
stepfather had secreted away his mother's estate, including "all the
Household Goods plantation Tools and Implements and Even some of your
petitioners Wearing apparel." More significantly, he had "[c]arr[ied] away the
Slaves" that belonged to his deceased father's estate.[138] Although Cantey's
stepfather did not technically have a legal right to the slaves, the fact that he
actually possessed them made it difficult for Cantey to enforce his rights.

Chancery litigation could become particularly acrimonious when
widows remarried, and disputes over slave inheritances led to bitter family
quarrels. When Sarah Lewis's father died leaving a "considerable personal
Estate consisting of Negro Slaves Cattle Household Goods etca.," her
mother Mary remarried John Saseau, a planter who took it upon himself
to manage the estate. Family relations became strained, however, when
John and Mary refused to deliver Sarah's inheritance. As Sarah and her
husband complained, "Since his Intermarriage with the said Mary," John
"hath had the whole Management of the said real and personal Estate,"
and he had "made great profit and Gains as well by the work as the hireing
out of the said Negroes." In fact, he had benefitted from the "considerable
Increase of the said Negroes To the Number of four or five Children or
Thereabouts." Rather than relinquishing them to Sarah, however, John
and Mary maintained that Sarah's father had "dyed considerably in Debt"
and that his personal estate had been used to discharge these debts as well
as to clothe and educate his children. Taking full advantage of Chancery
bill procedure to hurl invectives at her mother and stepfather, Sarah and
her husband suggested that John and Mary in fact spent a paltry sum in
maintaining the children. Indeed, there "was very little difference or
distinction made" between Sarah and her siblings and "the Negroes."
They "were never Taught to Write Read ... or any other School Work or
Learning" and "wore nothing but Negroe Cloathing."[139] Not to be

---

[137] *James Stewart & Mary, his wife* v. *Abraham Saunders*, Decree filed August 2, 1731,
  Chancery Case Papers, 1700–1791, Court of Chancery Bundle 1721–1735, Nos. 1–13,
  No. 10, Oversize; S142001, SCDAH.
[138] *John Cantey, on behalf of the Children of Joseph Child, deceased*, filed March 8, 1722,
  Chancery Case Papers, 1700–1791, Court of Chancery Bundle 1721–1735, Nos. 1–13,
  No. 3, Oversize, S142001, SCDAH.
[139] *Evan and Sarah Lewis* v. *John and Mary Sauseau and Jonathan Milner*, filed
  October 1716, Chancery Case Papers, 1700–1791, Court of Chancery Bundle
  1700–1716, Nos. 1–17, No. 16, Oversize, S142001, SCDAH.

outdone, Mary and John replied that before Sarah was married, she "lived much better than plaintiff Evan now keeps her."[140]

CONCLUSION

In bitter and protracted Chancery suits, colonists like Sarah and Evan Lewis exposed the intimate power struggles over slaves that prompted them to seek relief in equity. Indeed, South Carolina colonists' "liberal" provisions for widows and daughters led directly to contentious disputes over enslaved people, disputes that were too complicated and too personal to be resolved at common law. Colonists called upon South Carolina's Chancery Court to resolve these disputes. There, pleadings that were highly individualized gave them space to describe in detail their specific complaints, to make it plain why they should inherit slaves. Drawing upon English legal traditions, they used the timeworn language of equity to frame their complaints. Like English litigants, they claimed to have lost records; they argued that "unknown" persons had colluded to defraud them; they insisted that the behavior of widows and stepfathers was "contrary" to equity and good conscience. But unlike English litigants, they deployed this discourse to claim human property.

Although few Chancery decrees survive, it seems clear that the court did not hesitate to resolve colonists' familial conflicts at the expense of enslaved people, to reach equitable solutions that involved selling slaves or separating enslaved families. The court ultimately satisfied litigants like Thomas and Ann Everleigh, for example, by ordering eighty-one slaves to be "publickly Sold" by the Chancery master.[141] In fact, South Carolina's Chancery Court provided legal consumers with precisely what they desired, which helped to make the jurisdiction consistently useful throughout the colonial period even as English Chancery business declined. In a colony where white colonists died frequently and slaves were increasingly valuable commodities, Chancery provided litigants with a meaningful alternative to common law, one that gave them the procedural flexibility to make claims to slaves that belonged to female heiresses.

Understanding the court in this way lays bare the invidious consequences of jurisdictional diversity. It allows us to see that variegated

---

[140] *Ibid.*

[141] *Thomas Eveleigh & Others* v. *Thomas Farr, Executor of James Simmons*, Decree filed 1777, Chancery Case Papers, 1700–1791; Court of Chancery Bundle 1770–1779, Nos. 1–16, No. 10, S142001, SCDAH.

legal landscapes did not always empower the disempowered; rather, jurisdictional complexity and competition created spaces for colonists to treat human beings as property in different venues. It multiplied colonists' options as they sought to manage enslaved people, constricting rather than expanding opportunities for slave agency. Indeed, in equity, colonists deployed but another language of English law, another discourse that allowed them to claim slaves in a highly individualized way. South Carolina colonists did not critically examine the morality of deploying an equitable discourse to claim people as property; in Chancery they merely saw useful procedures and remedies, albeit expensive ones. The use of equitable language gave them access to those procedures, justifying Chancery jurisdiction and delivering them from the constraints of common law. Drawing upon a language of conscience and equity in connection with their claims to slaves did not lead colonists to interrogate slaveholding as a practice or generate cognitive dissonance over the ethics of human enslavement. Rather, pleas of fraud, unfairness, collusion, and injustice were mere jurisdictional triggers, devoid of independent ideological content.[142]

Just as the availability of alternative courts like Chancery negatively affected slaves, like those sold on behalf of the Everleighs, jurisdictional diversity in South Carolina failed to provide tangible benefits for female colonists. In fact, attending to Chancery litigation complicates narratives that assume non-common law jurisdictions provided opportunities for women to assert control over their own lives. Amy Louise Erickson, for example, has argued that ecclesiastical and chancery courts treated early modern English women more fairly than common law venues. Marylynn Salmon also has depicted the availability of chancery jurisdictions as a net positive for women, while Laura Edwards has argued that local law in the early republic offered women opportunities to obtain justice that were unavailable at common law.[143] In South Carolina, however, female Chancery litigants were not empowered by equity procedures that allowed wives to sue without their husbands. In fact, few women did so.

---

[142] This view supports and extends the work of scholars who have suggested that legal pluralism had invidious consequences in colonial contexts, providing practical and theoretical justifications for a variety of unfreedoms in the Atlantic World. Tomlins, *Freedom Bound*, 143, 188.

[143] Erickson, *Women and Property in Early Modern England*, 19; Salmon, *Women and the Law of Property in Early America*, 12; Laura F. Edwards, *The People and Their Peace: Legal Culture and the Transformation of Inequality in the Post-Revolutionary South* (Chapel Hill: University of North Carolina Press, 2009), 8.

Although it is possible that some female Chancery litigants acted in concert with their husbands, women were impleaded in South Carolina Chancery proceedings primarily to establish a husband's claim to female inheritance, not to allow women to obtain control over property in their own right. Far from a proto-feminist institution, Chancery worked to ensure that testators' patriarchal dynastic ambitions were fulfilled, despite the fact that some women sought to retain power over the next generation by exercising control over slaves.

Most important, Chancery litigation in colonial South Carolina lays bare the complicated and interlaced customary arrangements that made plantation economies work, and the court's institutional role in facilitating those arrangements. Indeed, Chancery was a useful venue because its procedures allowed judges to adjudicate the space between the customary and the explicitly legal when it came to owning slaves. Despite the commonplace assumption that the master-slave relationship was of primary importance in slave societies, the reality was more complex. Legal ownership and mastery were not synonymous, particularly in a place where the mobility and liquidity of slaves was highly valued. Slaves were routinely hired, raising important questions about who should be held financially accountable for their well-being. Plantation leases, conducted with a handshake, might leave room for determining who was entitled to benefit from the labor of particular slaves and how much. Widows, though not technically the owners of enslaved people, could benefit from the actual possession of slaves even when they had no legal right to them. Chancery sanctioned this world of flexible mastery, in which legal ownership, customary use, and temporary command were all ways in which slaves could be put to work in the Lowcountry.

5

Res Publica

In November 1781, the Board of Police, an administrative entity responsible for governing Charlestown, South Carolina, during the British occupation of 1780–1782, heard the petition of Nathaniel Cary. Cary, who was one of the king's "Liege Subjects," complained to members of the Board that British troops had destroyed his property during the reconquest of the colony. Despite the fact that Cary had always been "well disposed for Government," he had "[s]uffered greatly" at the hands of the king's men, who demolished "twenty three Houses & three Gardens." More importantly, he also claimed that marauding American soldiers had taken his most valuable property, his "[s]laves." Thus "reduced to Indigent Circumstances," Cary and his family had been "obliged to fly to Town," where they endured conditions far worse than those to which elite planters were usually accustomed. Cary hoped that the Board would remedy his increasingly desperate situation. Couching his claim in suitably deferential language that would have been familiar to British subjects throughout the globe, he prayed that the Board's members would provide a "place of Shelter to accommodate his distressed family," and he asked them to grant "such further relief" as they in their "[w]isdom" saw fit.[1]

---

[1] Petition of Nathaniel Cary, November 27, 1781 [signed May 21, 1781], CO 5/520, 34v–35r, Records of the Board of Police (BOP), British Occupation of Charleston, May 1780–October 1782, B800127, South Carolina Department of Archives and History, Columbia, South Carolina (SCDAH). For an extensive discussion of how Britons made claims on the state that were framed using the language of subjecthood, see Hannah Weiss Muller, *Subjects and Sovereign: Bonds of Belonging in the Eighteenth-Century British Empire* (Oxford: Oxford University Press, 2017).

It is unclear whether the Board ever compensated Cary for his losses, but his circumstances were not unusual. Throughout the southeastern campaigns of the American Revolution, soldiers and civilians on both sides claimed, stole, and sold enslaved enslaved people, and slaves themselves took advantage of wartime disruptions to run away from their owners. As historians have recognized, the Revolutionary War in the southeast triggered an unprecedented movement of enslaved people over land and sea, as brutal partisan warfare devastated the plantation economies of British North America and displaced thousands of enslaved people. The mobility of slaves – both forced and voluntary – complicated an already difficult situation for British military commanders and civilian leaders, who debated how slaves should contribute to the war effort as people and as property. These leaders balanced a desire to tap the strategic advantage of threatening a slave uprising against concerns about the moral and practical consequences of destabilizing the institution upon which plantation America's wealth rested.[2] The stakes of this balancing act were high: British leaders hoped to maintain a functioning plantation economy in order to provide military forces in the southeast with labor and supplies. At the same time, loyalist slave owners, whose allegiance Crown officials sought to maintain, expected officials to uphold their property rights in people. Slaves who sought refuge with the British military, however, envisioned an entirely different result, one in which their military service would entitle them to freedom in a postwar Anglophone world.[3]

---

[2] Studies of the role of slaves in the American Revolution include Benjamin Quarles, *The Negro in the American Revolution* (Chapel Hill: University of North Carolina Press, 1996); Alan Taylor, *The Internal Enemy: Slavery and War in Virginia, 1772–1832* (New York: Norton, 2013); Jim Piecuch, *Three Peoples, One King: Loyalists, Indians, and Slaves in the American Revolutionary South, 1775–1782* (Columbia: University of South Carolina Press, 2013); Woody Holton, *Forced Founders: Indians, Debtors, Slaves, & the Making of the American Revolution in Virginia* (Chapel Hill: University of North Carolina Press, 1999); Silvia R. Frey, *Water from the Rock: Black Resistance in a Revolutionary Age* (Princeton: Princeton University Press, 1991); Robert Olwell, "'Domestick Enemies': Slavery and Political Independence in South Carolina, May 1775–March 1776," *The Journal of Southern History* 55 (1989): 21–48; Bobby G. Moss and Michael C. Scoggins, *African-American Loyalists in the Southern Campaign of the American Revolution* (Blacksburg, SC: Scotia Hibernia Press, 2005).

[3] For an examination of how Black military service figured prominently in early antislavery thought, see Christopher L. Brown, "From Slaves to Subjects: Envisioning and Empire without Slavery, 1772–1834," in *Black Experience and the Empire*, edited by Philip D. Morgan and Sean Hawkins (Oxford: Oxford University Press, 2004), 133–135.

Most historians agree that British civilian and military leaders ultimately never answered the strategic, logistical, and moral question of what to do with slaves in the Revolutionary-era southeast. This lack of a coherent policy meant that at the conflict's end, ad hoc decisions determined the fate of the estimated 20,000 enslaved people who sought refuge with the British army.[4] Some slaves found that their claims to freedom were honored, and they joined a global loyalist diaspora that Maya Jasanoff has so eloquently charted.[5] Others, however, discovered that promises of freedom were ephemeral; that the evacuating British prioritized the property claims of white loyalists over the liberty of slaves who flocked to the king's standard.[6]

This was true despite the fact that some Britons (and Americans) were openly critical of slavery by the second half of the eighteenth century. Although few in the Anglo-American world "were prepared to debate" emancipation in 1776, a burgeoning transatlantic "antislavery sentiment" led some to question the morality of slave owning.[7] In fact, the Revolutionary War marked a turning point in British attitudes toward slavery. During the war and in its immediate aftermath, Britons favorably juxtaposed "the horrors of American slavery" against "the virtues of metropolitan customs, manners, and laws" as they fashioned a new national identity in the midst of a civil war.[8] As slavery became a heated topic in the British public sphere, it in turn "deepened perennial questions about the morality of slavery."[9] These questions would eventually ripen in a full-fledged attack on Britain's role in the transatlantic slave trade in the 1780s and 1790s.

---

[4] Andrew O'Shaughnessy, *The Men Who Lost America: British Leadership, the American Revolution, and the Fall of the Empire* (New Haven: Yale University Press, 2013), 6–7; Brown, "From Slaves to Subjects," 135–136; Maya Jasanoff, *Liberty's Exiles: American Loyalists in the Revolutionary World* (New York: Knopf, 2011), 8.

[5] Jasanoff estimates that 15,000 slaves ultimately left the new United States with British evacuation fleets. *Ibid.*, 6.

[6] For Sylvia Frey, the British failed to balance their need to maintain a functioning plantation economy with the moral imperatives of honoring promises of freedom made to enslaved people. Their inability to formulate a coherent plan with regard to the treatment of slaves had serious consequences for British war efforts, they argue; indeed, it "fatally weakened" Britain's southern strategy. Frey, *Water from the Rock*, 141. Jim Piecuch, too, has characterized British slave policy in the southern campaigns as "ambiguous," and like Frey has argued that this ambiguity led to British defeat as officials failed to tap the military potential of enslaved people. Piecuch, *Three Peoples, One King*, 270.

[7] Christopher Leslie Brown, *Moral Capital: Foundations of British Abolitionism* (Chapel Hill, University of North Carolina Press, 2006), 26–27; Piecuch, *Three Peoples, One King*, 270.

[8] Brown, *Moral Capital*, 121.   [9] *Ibid.*, 134.

Despite their mounting criticism of American slaveholders, however, Britons did not actively seek to abolish slavery, curtail the slave trade, or liberate slaves as a matter of official policy during the American Revolution. In fact, when faced with the dilemma of what to do with enslaved people during the war and in its immediate aftermath, commanders and administrators in North America conformed their practice as much as possible to colonial precedents. Their legal solutions to the problem of mobile slave populations were inherently conservative ones that respected rather than challenged colonists' expectations about the administration of slave law. Although the military occupation of Charlestown dramatically altered the colony's legal landscape – the courts were closed and the Commons House of Assembly did not meet – customary slave law persisted. This persistence is not surprising given the fact that many administrators had previously served in South Carolina, often as judges or lawyers. Familiar with the colony's laws and its people, they replicated Lowcountry legal traditions, drawing upon the substance and procedure of a displaced legal system to govern the colony during wartime. Indeed, this is a story of continuity more than change, one that recognizes the disruptive power of a bloody and violent conflict, but also the compelling pull of legal custom. Britain's southern military campaigns may have set unprecedented numbers of people in motion, but British soldiers and administrators wielded old laws as they sought to return them to their proper places.

These wartime administrators betrayed little concern about the moral implications of recognizing property rights in people. Although some individual Britons expressed qualms about slaveholding as a practice (and particularly the cruel treatment of slaves by American slaveholders) these qualms did not prevent them from brutally repressing slave rebellions, personally profiting from the work of enslaved people, and using slaves to perform hard labor in support of Britain's war effort. In plantation America, slavery remained a thriving, economically viable institution that benefitted not only the oldest South Carolina planting families, but also recently arrived British soldiers and administrators who occupied Charlestown and its immediate hinterland. These newcomers to South Carolina quickly adopted an economic calculus that required the commodification of human beings in pursuit of profit. They learned to buy, sell, and argue over slaves as they sought to supplement their incomes in an economy organized around slave labor. In fact, when we look at daily practice, we can see that their treatment of slaves differed little from that of American colonists in rebellion.

Because American colonists and British administrators shared
a practical worldview that acknowledged slaves as property, the administration of law during the British occupation of South Carolina reinforced
rather than challenged slavery.[10] Individuals may have been willing to
grant some slaves freedom, but during wartime slavery's laws operated
according to a conservative logic, regardless of moral sensibility. This was
in part because the British were not interested or willing to disrupt the
principles and precedents that these laws established: they had been
proven effective in suppressing rebellion, policing mobile slave populations, and maximizing the value of enslaved people. As a practical matter,
displacing a workable colonial system made little sense. At the same time,
respecting local customs and laws helped the British to win and keep the
support of loyalist slaveholders. American colonists in the run-up to the
American Revolution had equated British tyranny with the displacement
of local government and local justice. By respecting and enforcing local
slave laws, British administrators appeased these fears and appealed to
slave-owning colonists whose military support they both expected and
desired. In practice, this meant perpetuating the chattel principle in all its
legal manifestations. British soldiers and administrators not only followed
colonial precedents when it came to policing the movement and activities
of enslaved people; they also protected loyal colonists' property rights in
people, even when it meant betraying promises to the enslaved men and
women who risked life and limb to serve the Crown. Laboring on behalf of
the British military, slaves forced soldiers and administrators to reckon
with their humanity on a daily basis, but British occupiers found themselves both unable and unwilling to jump the ruts of a legal system built
upon the proposition that Black people were property.

Watching these men as they sought to govern the Lowcountry at war is
a useful reminder that law's categories retained their power to shape
reality, even in an Age of Revolutions. As we have seen in other contexts,
the categorization of slaves as chattel property worked in Revolutionary-
era South Carolina to block alternative "trajectories of possibility" that
might have produced a more liberationist response to the problem of
slavery in an Age of Revolutions.[11] It made it "just a tiny bit more

---

[10] This position conforms to that of Davis, who argued that despite wartime disruptions, the
"war brought no major weakening of the slave system, except in the North." David
Brion Davis, *The Problem of Slavery in the Age of Revolution, 1770–1823* (Oxford:
Oxford University Press, 1999), 79.

[11] Robert W. Gordon, "Critical Legal Histories," *Stanford Law Review* 36 (1984): 112.

unthinkable" and "a tiny bit more difficult to imagine something altogether outside the scope of familiar possibilities," that slaves could be treated as human beings at law or as subjects of the king.[12] When Samuel Johnson wondered why he heard "the loudest yelps for liberty among the drivers of negroes," he identified an apparent core contradiction at the heart of the American Revolution: that some of the most ardent critics of British "tyranny" were in fact slave-owning planters in colonies like South Carolina and Virginia.[13] Slavery and liberty, he implied, were opposite binaries. How could the owners of human property not perceive their own hypocrisy when they used the language of English liberty to assert their independence from the Crown? Nonetheless, as the British evacuated places like Charlestown, South Carolina at the end of the War, they, too, had come to treat human beings as property at law and to view them as such. Certainly, a crude economic calculus helps to explain why Britons acted as a "shield" to slavery rather than a "sword" during the American Revolution, but so does the very language of law itself.[14]

In this chapter, I follow the Britons who struggled to maintain order in a Lowcountry ravaged by war and transected by enslaved people on the move. In "People in Motion" and "Policing Slaves," I provide an institutional overview of the Charlestown Board of Police as well as an analysis of its practices. Supplanting South Carolina's courts, grand juries, and legislature, the Board of Police functioned as an administrative entity and as a judicial tribunal, and was the only operating court during the occupation of South Carolina (with the exception of the Court of Ordinary, which probated wills, and courts martial, which tried cases involving military personnel). Although the Board represented a distinct break with institutions of colonial government, it nonetheless drew extensively upon colonial precedents as members sought to regulate slave life in Charlestown.

In "'Poor Distressed' Loyalists," I examine the plight of loyalists like Nathaniel Cary, who positioned themselves as the king's "Liege Subjects" in order to claim relief from British civilian and military officials. Drawing upon a long history of rights-talk, American loyalists invoked the reciprocal bonds of allegiance that bound them to the king, hoping that the return of their slaves would allow them to recover from

---

[12] *Ibid.*, 111.

[13] Samuel Johnson, *Taxation No Tyranny: An Answer to the Resolution and Address of the American Congress*, 4th ed. (London, 1775), 89.

[14] Frey, *Water from the Rock*, 141.

the devastation wrought by partisan conflict in the Lowcountry. The Board of Police and military authorities were generally receptive to these claims, as I show in "Adjudicating Ownership." Sympathizing with the plight of these "poor distressed loyalists," they upheld property rights in people in the context of debt litigation and disputes over slave stealing. They did so despite the fact that some Britons, including high-ranking military officers, felt obligated as a matter of strategy and a matter of honor to grant slaves freedom in exchange for their military service. Military and civilian officials alike balanced the need to return these slaves to their owners with promises of freedom made to slaves, and especially those who had served in the military. As I show in "A Matter of 'Serious Concern'" and "The Case of Negro Will," however, whether or not an enslaved person would be emancipated depended not upon the slave's military service, but rather upon a master's allegiance. Once again, the fate of the enslaved hinged far less on who they were or what they did as people, and far more on how white subjects of the king related to one another in the eyes of the law. Whereas slaves belonging to loyal colonists were "private" property and must be returned, those belonging to rebels were "public" slaves, who, after serving in the military or on public works projects, would be freed. Officials sought to balance the property demands of loyalists against the freedom claims of slaves with this public/private distinction. Nonetheless, as I show in "*Res Publica,*" it ultimately proved to be a distinction without a difference. The sequestration system that British officials established to manage so-called "public" slaves operated from its inception upon the assumption that public slaves were property that the military held in trust for the benefit of loyalists. For these officials, enslaved people remained valuable commodities that could be used to offset economic losses, rather than individuals who might be entitled to their freedom.

The commodification of public slaves extended to the management of individual sequestered plantations, and I conclude by following one administrator, Robert McCulloh, as he profited from slave ownership during the British occupation of the Lowcountry. McCulloh, like other British newcomers, quickly adopted the chattel principle; they learned to buy, sell, and argue over slaves like seasoned colonists as they sought to supplement their incomes in an economy organized around slave labor. In fact, when we look at daily practice, we can see that their treatment of slaves differed little from that of American colonists in rebellion. Rather than undermining chattel slavery, then, they perpetuated English law's unremarkable treatment of enslaved people as property.

PEOPLE IN MOTION

After enduring a grueling three-month siege, Continental General Benjamin Lincoln formally surrendered Charlestown, South Carolina to British General Sir Henry Clinton on May 12, 1780. The American defeat at Charlestown was the "largest loss sustained by the Continental Army during the Revolutionary War" and gave Britain possession of the most populous port town south of Philadelphia, along with a significant number of vessels, naval stores, gunpowder, and ordnance.[15] The terms of surrender foreshadowed the bitter and bloody conduct that would come to characterize the southern campaigns of the American Revolution. Still smarting from the Continental Congress's failure to honor the surrender terms granted to General John Burgoyne after the battle of Saratoga, Clinton denied Lincoln and his men the full honors of war, which would have enabled them to "surrender with their flags flying and drums beating as an acknowledgement of their honorable resistance."[16] Instead, the 2,571 captured Continental troops were "confined as prisoners of war" to hulks in the harbor, while officers were housed at Haddrell's Point, located on the mainland across from Sullivan's Island. Civilians in the town and militia members were deemed prisoners on parole and were permitted to return home.[17]

Surrender was a legal matter as much as it was a military one. Although the conquest of the mainland's largest southern port was a feather in Clinton's cap, it also posed significant questions of governance. Military officials drew upon their experiences administering other occupied cities during the war, including New York, Philadelphia, and Savannah, as they sought to restore order in the colony. They divided South Carolina into military districts, closed Charlestown's courts, and placed the town "under the jurisdiction of a military commandant," Nisbet Balfour.[18] Although Clinton had initially promised to return citizens to "the full possession of that Liberty in their Persons and Property, which they had before experienced," he ultimately never restored full civil government in the province.[19]

---

[15] O'Shaughnessy, *The Men Who Lost America*, 230.   [16] *Ibid.*, 230–231.

[17] George Smith McCowen, *The British Occupation of Charleston, 1780–1782* (Columbia: University of South Carolina Press, 1972), 9.

[18] *Ibid.*, 13. South Carolina patriot and historian David Ramsay characterized Balfour as a military autocrat who displayed "all the frivolous self-importance, and all the disgusting insolence, which are natural to little minds when puffed up by sudden elevation." David Ramsay, *History of South Carolina* (Newberry, SC: Duffie, 1858), 253.

[19] Proclamation (dated May 1780) in *The Royal South Carolina Gazette*, Thursday, June 8, 1780, SCDAH, Series P900046. The decision to retain military rule was a direct response to earlier experiences with the reinstitution of civil government in Georgia. There, Clinton

Instead, for most of the British occupation, a Board of Police governed the town. Modeled directly after Boards of Police that had been formed to manage other British-occupied cities, including New York, Savannah, and Philadelphia, the Board was headed by an Intendant of Police who was appointed by the Commandant, and also included local representatives from the merchant, planting, and military "interests."[20] Board intendants typically had "extensive legal and administrative experience," and most had served in South Carolina prior to the Revolutionary War. For example, James Simpson, the Board's first Intendant, was a former attorney general of South Carolina who made himself useful to American Secretary George Germain by providing intelligence about the strength of loyalism in the southern colonies. Sir Egerton Leigh, who later served as Intendant, also was familiar with the colony and its legal system, having acted as a colonial Vice Admiralty judge, attorney general, and royal council member. William Bull, who succeeded Simpson in February 1781, was a former lieutenant governor of the colony, and Thomas Knox Gordon had served as its chief justice.[21]

Throughout the British occupation, these men directed the Board as it acted in place of South Carolina's now-defunct courts, grand juries, and Commons House of Assembly. In fact, a review of the Board's records reveals an astonishingly broad purview for action that was sometimes specifically delegated, and other times merely assumed by members as they searched for solutions to tangled problems of governance.[22] In its administrative capacity, the Board was charged with a wide variety of tasks, including overseeing poor relief, maintaining proper weights and measures, and preventing price gouging, particularly by bread, flour, and fish sellers.

More importantly, the Board was also responsible for the day-to-day management of slaves in Charlestown and on surrounding plantations. Although colonial Charlestown had always had a large Black presence, the number of enslaved and free Black people in the town swelled with the arrival of the British army and navy. Slaves themselves were in large part responsible for this demographic transformation. Indeed, historians have

had reluctantly agreed to allow a governor and royal assembly to govern the colony, but these civilians repeatedly clashed with military officers over war goals and policy issues. Frederick Bernays Wiener, *Civilians under Military Justice: The British Practice since 1689 Especially in North America* (Chicago: University of Chicago Press, 1967), 151.
[20] McCowen, *The British Occupation of Charleston*, 14.   [21] *Ibid.*, 16–18.
[22] Inhabitants of Charlestown could be tried by courts martial for crimes. See Wiener, *Civilians under Military Justice*, 58.

charted the manifold ways in which enslaved people exerted agency in plantation America, but the American Revolution offered new opportunities for slaves to risk it all on a bid for freedom. It is difficult to imagine the agonizing process that must have preceded a decision to leave. Enslaved people sundered the connections they had worked so hard to forge, farewelling friends and family for unknown places. Their actions are filtered through the words of white interlocutors, but we know that in spite of the many obstacles strewn in their paths, they ran away in unprecedented numbers. They included Titus, a native "of Africa," who escaped to Charlestown "about a week before the town surrendered." Titus's master thought he might "pass for a fool," but he proved he was far from foolish when he slipped away during the siege and took refuge in Charlestown.[23] Jack, who was "by trade a caulker," likewise headed for the harbor, where his owner expected he would try to find work.[24] The same was true for Prince, "a great rogue" who was "fond of rum" and could "tell a very plausible story." Prince's owner suspected that he was working as a ship's cook because he had previously labored in this capacity on "several voyages on board a Guinea vessel."[25]

Enslaved people like Titus, Jack, and Prince may have abandoned plantations in direct response to General Clinton's 1779 "Philipsburgh" proclamation. Issued from his headquarters in Philipsburgh, New York, the proclamation threatened that all slaves found in the service of rebel masters would be sold for the benefit of their captors, but also gave slaves who deserted the rebels "full security to follow within [British] Lines." The proclamation "did not directly alter the legal status of slaves." It did, however, "raise the specter of emancipation," and upon Clinton's landing in South Carolina "thousands" of enslaved people interpreted the proclamation as an offer of freedom.[26] They absconded to the British much to the chagrin of colonists like John Harleston, who complained that "56 of the primest" of his "Negroes Followed the Army some to Charlestown," and wondered whether he should "ever gett them again."[27] Daniel McCormick provided an answer to this often-repeated question: slave owners "might as well enquire for last years snow, as the Runaway Negroes."[28]

---

[23] *RSCG*, vol. 1, no. 6, June 20, 1780 (advertisement dated June 19, 1780).
[24] *RSCG*, July 6, 1780.
[25] *Royal Gazette*, vol. 1, no. 4, March 10–14, 1781, P900047, SCDAH.
[26] Frey, *Water from the Rock*, 113–114, 118.
[27] John Harleston to Robert McCulloh, June 5,1780, TNA, C 106/89.
[28] Daniel McCormick to Robert McCulloh, December 11, 1780, TNA, C 106/89.

Many of the slaves who fled to Charlestown sought service with the British military, acting as "teamsters, wagon drives, guides, scouts, spies, and pioneers."[29] Although most worked as physical laborers, some enslaved people served in important posts. Others served in British military departments, including the 214 adult slaves and four children listed in the *Royal South Carolina Gazette* as "NEGROES in the ENGINEER DEPARTMENT that joined the Army since the landing under SIR HENRY CLINTON."[30] Slaves also worked in the Commissary General's Department, the Quarter-Master General's Department, the Barrack Master's Department, and the Commissary of Prisoner's Department. The Royal Artillery Department employed slaves as artificers and drivers, while enslaved men and women also worked in Charlestown's General Hospital as nurses.[31]

A smaller proportion of runaway slaves who sought refuge with the British military performed more highly specialized roles. Some were messengers and couriers, including an "Ethiopian Refugee" who had fled from his owner after "making Love Successfully to a White Girl."[32] These slaves used their knowledge of South Carolina's roadways and its people to collect and transmit vital information to British officials. Perhaps more important, South Carolina's slaves offered their services to the British as boatmen, pilots, and guides. In fact, British officers actively sought out these "[b]oat Negroes" because they were familiar with the complex waterways that connected plantation neighborhoods across the "country." As we have already seen, enslaved people throughout plantation America routinely worked as sailors, pilots, fishermen, divers, and in other maritime trades. Familiar with the Lowcountry's waterways and Charlestown's treacherous harbor, these slaves provided British invasion forces with crucial geographic knowledge that could be translated into a military advantage.[33]

Runaway slaves employed by military departments in Charlestown were joined by countless others who were sent to town by loyalist slave owners as they sought to shield their valuable human property from rebel capture. Between the capture of Charlestown in 1780 and 1781, the war in South Carolina was characterized by increasingly violent partisan conflict

---

[29] Moss and Scoggins, *African-American Loyalists*, vi.
[30] *Royal Gazette (RG)*, March 7–March 10, 1781, vol. 1, no. 3, P900047, SCDAH.
[31] *RG*, March 10–March 14, 1781, vol. 1, no. 4.
[32] A. Innes to Robert McCulloh, May 22, 1780, TNA, C 106/89 (emphasis in original).
[33] A. I. [Alexander Innes] to Robert McCulloh, May 19, 1780, TNA, C 106/89.

in the backcountry as the Continental Army and local militia units pushed British troops back into the vicinity of Charlestown.[34] These partisan bands, acting on their own authority or with the support of the revolutionary government-in-exile, took slaves from loyalists' plantations and put them to work as noncombatants with General Nathanael Greene's army, or distributed slaves to new recruits as an enlistment bounty. To prevent their slaves from being carried away, loyalist owners sent them to Charlestown. In 1780, for example, James Clitherall asked his overseer to send his slaves to town by the "first safe opportunity by water."[35] Robert McCulloh's plantation manager, fearing for "the worst," likewise ordered all of his "Negros and those of Doctor Clitherals to town" where they would "endeavour to find work for them."[36]

British soldiers, too, brought slaves into Charlestown, claiming them as spoils of war.[37] Indeed "[b]y custom and by law, slaves were regarded as property, subject, therefore, to the practices governing spoils," and military commanders had considerable discretion to distribute captured property, including slaves, to soldiers.[38] Although American forces in the southeast were notorious for stealing slaves and using them to "attract recruits and to pay officers and men," British soldiers also stole slaves and routinely received them as booty.[39] Plantations and slaves, in fact, were "plundered on both sides," as American and British troop alike took "Negroes and property."[40] This practice occasionally received official sanction from British high command. Prior to the Charlestown siege, General Clinton went so far as to make formal arrangements to distribute property taken from rebel plantations, appointing Lt. Col. James Moncrief and two other loyalist civilians to gather slaves and forage, and to disperse them among British troops as needed.[41] As a result, many British officers came to believe that they owned the slaves that they captured or received as booty, which created tensions between troops and colonists, who expected that their property rights in people would be

---

[34] By September 1781, only Charlestown and its immediate environs remained in British control. Robert M. Weir, *Colonial South Carolina: A History* (Columbia: University of South Carolina Press, 1997), 336.
[35] James Clitherall to Robert McCulloh, July 15, 1780, TNA, C 106/89.
[36] Crookshanks & Speirs to Robert McCulloh, May 15, 1782, TNA, C 106/89.
[37] Moss and Scoggins, *African-American Loyalists*, vi.
[38] Frey, *Water from the Rock*, 91.   [39] *Ibid.*, 134.
[40] Bernard Hale to Earl Cornwallis, November 6, 1780, TNA, PRO 30/11/3, Cornwallis Papers.
[41] Piecuch, *Three Peoples, One King*, 216.

honored under the British military government as they had been under the
British colonial government.[42]

The Board of Police was responsible for managing these slaves, who had
been funneled into Charlestown by a staggering variety of means and for a
wide variety of reasons. In regulating slave life in town, members theoretically were to exercise broad police powers to develop solutions to daily
problems of governance. Watching the Board at work, however, reveals
that members closely adhered to colonial precedents. This was particularly true when it came to identifying and remedying nuisances. For
example, the Board was preoccupied with preventing the congregation
of slaves, and especially nocturnal gatherings that involved alcohol.
Concerns about the dangers posed by "disorderly Persons and negroes"
gathering in punch houses closely tracked pre-Revolutionary complaints
about the social habits of Charlestown's enslaved and free Black people,
who were characterized in 1772 as "idle, loose, disorderly, vagrant and
run-away negroes" interested in little more than "loitering, gaming,
drinking," and "thieving."[43]

    The Board's desire to prevent such gatherings and to limit slaves' access
to alcohol was directly linked to a more pressing concern that they shared
with colonists of all political persuasions: preventing a slave insurrection.
This possibility seemed increasingly likely given Charlestown's expanding
slave population as well as the presence of large numbers of unsupervised
slaves on abandoned outlying plantations. In theory, plantations and
slaves belonging to rebellious colonists were assigned to the custody of
the commissioner of sequestered estates, John Cruden, who put the slaves
in his charge to work on abandoned plantations producing food for the
British military.[44] Nonetheless, the difficulties of administering the
sequestration system meant that many slaves remained largely

[42] General Alexander Leslie to Sir Guy Carleton, October 18, 1782, item 5924, Sir Guy
    Carleton Papers, B800120, SCDAH.
[43] September 29, 1780, CO 5/520 (1780–1781), 17r, BOP, SCDAH; Letters of "The
    Stranger," *South-Carolina Gazette*, September 17 and 24, 1772. The Board's concerns
    likewise differed little from those expressed by a grand jury in 1742, which complained
    about the "disorderly assembling and caballing of the Negroes in Charles-Town," espe-
    cially "on the Sabbath Days" when it was more difficult to monitor their behavior. *SCG*,
    November 8, 1742.
[44] Frey, *Water from the Rock*, 125.

unsupervised. Cruden himself feared that "numbers of Negroes" had been taken from sequestered estates into town and went "about uncontrolled, to the distress of the inhabitants, the detriment of the Government and in direction violation of orders that have been repeatedly issued to prevent such practices." Although he sought to institute a pass system and "empowered" a delegate to "hire out all such negroes as shall not be employed," Charlestown continued to teem with masterless enslaved men and women, much to the chagrin of military and civilian officials alike.[45]

Even slaves who remained subject to their masters' oversight seemed to pose a constant threat, as they took advantage of wartime disruptions of the plantation economy to run away or shirk work. Throughout the British occupation William White, a barely literate overseer at Silk Hope plantation on the Savannah River, supplied his employer, Robert McCulloh, with countless missives lamenting the fact that his "Negers" refused to follow orders. They were "a g[ai]en out in the Woods," he complained, and refused to "[c]um to town."[46] Indeed, he "[c]ould not git the hands to Work For the Space of 2 Mont[h]s," and even then, they refused to perform their "[c]ustemmerey Dayes Works." As White explained to McCulloh, if he failed to "[c]om to Rectefi the negers" he would be forced to "[l]uck out For Besnes [business]" at the end of the year; his meager salary was not adequate compensation for the headaches he endured managing McCulloh's increasingly unruly slaves.[47]

Fielding complaints about rebellious slaves on sequestered estates and abandoned plantations, the Board acted swiftly and brutally to prevent insurrection. After receiving a report that slaves owned by absentee patriot Ralph Izard had manifested an "ill behaving and insurrectious Conduct ... towards their Overseer," members asked the Commandant to send "a party of Soldiers" to the plantation "to inflict such Punishment upon the Principal offenders in the Insurrection as may be adequate to their Crimes." This show of force not only was meant to be retributive; the Board also believed that it was "most likely to prevent such Behavior in the future."[48] In repressing this potential slave uprising using military force, the Board mimicked the behavior of South Carolina colonists and pre-Revolutionary legal institutions, which quickly responded to the threat of slave rebellion with violence. This included South Carolina's

[45] *RG*, December 22–26, 1781.
[46] William White to Robert McCulloh, March 6, 1782, TNA, C 106/89.
[47] William White to Robert McCulloh, October 23, 1780, TNA, C 106/87.
[48] July 14 and 18, 1780, CO 5/519 (1780), 4r–5r, BOP, SCDAH.

revolutionary government, which the British invasion had displaced. After the effective collapse of British rule in 1775, the colony was run by a Provincial Congress, which in turn empowered a Council of Safety to act as executive.[49] The Council was preoccupied with anticipating and preventing a slave insurrection. Acting on rumors that the British sought to arm Indians and slaves in advance of an invasion, Council members stringently enforced slave laws that previously had been ignored.[50] They also reacted violently to rumors of a planned slave uprising that they suspected was led by Thomas Jeremiah, a free Black harbor pilot, by capturing, trying, and hanging Jeremiah on flimsy evidence.[51] Members of a committee tasked with defending the colony from invasion proposed removing slaves from coastal plantations to prevent them from uprising and collaborating with the British.[52] In fact, South Carolina colonists and British officials were united in their concerns about the dangers inherent in a massive slave revolt, dangers that seemed all the more pressing given the growing numbers of slaves in town and on sequestered estates.

In addition to exercising police powers, the Board also functioned as a clearinghouse for requests for enslaved labor. During the British occupation of Charlestown, the Board exercised authority to impress and distribute slaves to labor on public works, a power once wielded by the Commons House of Assembly. For example, in order to execute their responsibility for maintaining roads and bridges in and around Charlestown, Board members routinely requisitioned slaves from local planters. When they received a complaint that fallen trees were preventing "the free Intercourse between Town and Country," the Board recommended that an order be issued to "Some proper person" to remove the obstructions from roads and bridges. This person would be empowered to "go to the nearest adjoining Plantations," and to "require" local planters "to send so many negroes to work upon the Road or to repair the Bridges as may be necessary."[53] Similarly, the Board routinely requisitioned slaves

---

[49] In the spring of 1776, South Carolina adopted its first constitution, which was replaced by a state constitution in 1778. For an extensive discussion of these constitutions, see Scott Douglas Gerber, *A Distinct Judicial Power: The Origins of an Independent Judiciary, 1606–1787* (Oxford: Oxford University Press, 2011), 213 ff.

[50] Weir, *Colonial South Carolina*, 322.

[51] See J. William Harris, *The Hanging of Thomas Jeremiah: A Free Black Man's Encounter with Liberty* (New Haven: Yale University Press, 2009) and William R. Ryan, *The World of Thomas Jeremiah: Charles Town on the Eve of the American Revolution* (Oxford: Oxford University Press, 2012).

[52] Piecuch, *Three Peoples, One King*, 77.

[53] August 1, 1780, CO 5/520 (1780–1781), 5v–6r, BOP, SCDAH.

to keep the streets of Charlestown clean and free of refuse. In the spring of 1782, for example, the Board fielded a request from the Commissioners of Streets in Charlestown to provide the town scavenger (who was responsible for removing "[r]ubbish and dirt thrown into the Streets and vacant Lots") with "twenty Negroes for the Space of four or five days" to clean the town.[54] The Board also took on responsibility for "Cloathing the Negroes who are employ'd in cleaning & keeping the Streets &c in order" and "for paying an Overseer of the said Negroes his wages."[55]

The Board's power to impress slaves for road repair and rubbish removal extended to requisitioning slaves to construct and repair fortifications. Working in conjunction with different military departments, the Board supplied the army and navy with slaves that were employed to complete a wide variety of military jobs, and particularly tasks requiring hard physical labor. For example, on November 7, 1780, the Board issued warrants directing the recipients to "make a Requisition from the Owners of the Slaves in your District (always having a due regard to their respective abilities and their attachment to His Majesty's Government) of so many Slaves as you shall judge they can, conveniently, and, in fairness and Equity, they ought to furnish." These slaves would work on fortifications "for one Month and no longer," and would be housed and fed by the army. Neither the Board nor the army, however, would provide oversight, and therefore, the Board requested owners "to send down" "[o]verseers or other White Persons" with their slaves "to take the Charge and Care of them" and to "prevent any loss."[56] The Board also supplied slave labor to the navy, fielding requests for slaves to assist with emergency ship repairs. For example, when His Majesty's Ship *Sandwich* required emergency repairs, the Board ordered its agents to "immediately take possession" of the "[p]ublick Warf, Stores, &ca. at Hobcaw, and also of three fourths of the Negroes lately employed there."[57] These slaves, some of whom were likely skilled in maritime trades, would labor for the navy until necessary repairs were completed.

---

[54] April 18, 1782, CO 5/525 (1782), 4r-4v, BOP, SCDAH.

[55] October 22, 1781, CO 5/520 (1780–1781), 36r, BOP, SCDAH.

[56] November 7, 1780, CO 5/520 (1780–1781), 21r-21v, BOP, SCDAH. The Board also could authorize the impressment of slaves from specific plantations, as was the case in 1780, when "one hundred able bodied Negroes were wanted for about a Fortnight to repair some of the Works and Lines about the Town." These slaves were to be provided from plantations belonging to Thomas Ferguson, William Skirving, Thomas Osborne, William Clay Snipes, Thomas Bee, John Matthews, Philip Smith, and Joseph Glover. September 8, 1780, CO 5/520 (1780–1781), 11v, BOP, SCDAH.

[57] September 8, 1780, CO 5/520 (1780–1781), 11r-11v, BOP, SCDAH.

In impressing slaves at the Hobcaw wharf and plantations near Charlestown, the Board was not engaged in an innovative practice. Rather, they built upon a long-established colonial custom of requisitioning slaves from local planters to labor on public works projects. Indeed, throughout the colonial period, the Commons House of Assembly empowered commissioners to impress local slaves to clear roads, build fortifications, and even serve in militias. Slave owners were familiar with (although they frequently grumbled about) the requisitioning process.[58] For example, patriot Henry Laurens, like many other colonists, complained of this practice in 1765, seeking an "indulgence" from the Commissioners for High Roads in St. John Parish to "postpone the execution of it until" he had "got thro" his "first cutting of Indigo." Although Laurens's "inclination" was "at all times to be obedient to Laws," in this case "rigid compliance" would be "very distressing."[59]

The colonial government's requisitioning of slaves to labor on public works, which Laurens and other colonists complied with even if they occasionally found it onerous, extended to work on fortifications. South Carolina's revolutionary government, in fact, provided a recent precedent for conscripting slaves to work as military noncombatants on labor-intensive fortification projects. For example, rumors of a British invasion in 1777 prompted the Council of Safety send slaves belonging to loyalists to fortify Charlestown. These slaves ultimately were put to work digging a channel connecting the Cooper and Ashley rivers.[60] Familiar with customary practice when it came to impressing slaves, Board members simply extended this practice as they sought solutions to the day-to-day problems of labor management that occupied a great deal of their time. In fact, the everyday tasks of governing South Carolina were so bound up in the legal use of slave labor for various projects that even the disruption of invasion and occupation by a force that was willing to use manumission as a military tactic followed a path of least resistance. Because colonial slave law gave administrators the procedural mechanisms and precedents for mobilizing enslaved laborers, it continued to be of practical utility, and

---

[58] "An Act for Raising and Enlisting Such Slaves as Shall be Thought Serviceable to this Province in Time of Alarms," (1704), in *The Statutes at Large of South Carolina*, edited by Thomas Cooper and David J. McCord, 10 vols. (Columbia: A. S. Johnston, 1836–1841), 7: 347.

[59] Henry Laurens to James Cordes, Jr., August 30, 1765, Philip M. Hamer et al., ed., *The Papers of Henry Laurens*, 16 vols. (Columbia: University of South Carolina Press, 1968–2003), 4: 670.

[60] Piecuch, *Three Peoples, One King*, 122.

therefore, a means by which British administrators reinforced slavery as a working institution despite the political, military, and economic upheaval of the war.

"POOR DISTRESSED" LOYALISTS

The Board's decision to build upon rather than work against existing colonial precedents made the institution more responsive to the white community's needs when it acted as an administrative body. In the Board's judicial capacity, it also sought to conform its practice to colonial precedents, although its procedures initially marked it as innovative. As a court, the Board was a hybrid tribunal, hearing a variety of disputes that would otherwise have been adjudicated in the Court of Common Pleas and the Court of Chancery, and it followed a unique blend of equity and common law procedures.[61] Like South Carolina's Chancery Court, the Board proceeded by petition rather than writ in order to streamline the resolution of claims, even when claims were brought as common law causes of action. Those who thought "themselves aggrieved by the non-performance of any Bargain or Agreement," for example, were to petition the Intendant of Police "plainly and distinctly setting forth the Cause and Nature of their Complaint." The Clerk of the Board then would issue a summons in the Intendant's name bringing the defendant before for the tribunal. The Board likewise possessed enforcement mechanisms that made it similar to an equity court.[62] Nonetheless, the Board adhered to common law procedure by hearing testimony *viva voce* rather than through written depositions and interrogatories, as would have been the case in an equity jurisdiction.[63]

Although James Simpson, the Board's first Intendant, believed that South Carolinians "appeared to have a confidence" in the Board's "[j]ustice," the

---

[61] The court of ordinary eventually was opened for "the proving of Wills, granting Licenses and Letters of Administration, and other Matters incident to that Jurisdiction." James Simpson to Sir Henry Clinton, August 30, 1780, Clinton Papers.

[62] In cases where creditors were "apprehensive" that a debtor might "abscond and leave the province without making satisfaction," the Board could issue a warrant "to hold such Person to Bail in the amount of the sum Sworn to, and as much more as the Intendant may think will answer the Costs of prosecuting the Suit." CO 5/519, June 27, 1780, 2v, BOP, SCDAH.

[63] CO 5/519, June 27, 1780, 2r, BOP, SCDAH. They also adhered to a fee schedule set by the colonial legislature, requiring litigants to pay to the Gaoler and Clerk of the Board "such Fees as they would have been liable to pay if they had been litigated in Court of Justice, and as they are fixed by Acts of Assembly." June 1780, CO 5/519, 2v, BOP, SCDAH.

reality seems to be more complex.[64] Indeed, the Board's odd combination of common law and equity procedures and the fact that judges were account-able to military authorities may have been off-putting to potential litigants, who complained that the Board's "mode of proceeding" was "too sum-mary." Aware of this criticism, the Board eventually altered their procedures, providing more specific rules and a formal appeals process in order to make litigating before the Board "more consonant to the established Practice and Constitution of the Country."[65] The Board's use of arbitrators to find facts in most cases also proved unpopular and practically difficult. Although the Board persuaded the Commandant to allow them to exact penalties upon colonists who refused to serve as arbitrators, they eventually discarded arbitration in favor of a jury system that followed colonial precedents.[66] Ultimately, "the great number of Suits" litigated at the Board caused mem-bers to limit their caseload to litigation "of pressing and immediate necessity; such as where the Defendant" was "about to remove himself, or his property, out of the reach of process" or where there were allegations of fraud. They reserved the resolution of "all other Claims for a Season of Peace and Tranquillity" which would "admit of the full Establishment of a Civil Government."[67]

The Board's procedural volte-face represented an attempt to establish its legitimacy by adhering to the legal expectations of South Carolina colonists. Much of Britain's southern strategy depended upon mobilizing the support of slave-owning loyalists and in winning the support of rebellious or neutral slave owners. In South Carolina as in other colonies, pre-Revolutionary political conflicts had centered on the question of whether the colony's constitution was derived from the Crown, or whether local practice and precedents were a source of constitutional authority. Arguing that their rights sprang from their English subject-hood, colonists also insisted that local custom and precedents – "what has prevailed from the Beginning of the Colony" – were "[p]art of the Constitution."[68] Although British administrators in South Carolina dis-agreed with this sentiment as political theory, in practice they conformed

[64] James Simpson to General Sir Henry Clinton, July 16, 1780, Item 2915, Sir Guy Carleton Papers, B800120, SCDAH.
[65] September 11, 1780, CO 5/519, 29v-30v, BOP, SCDAH.
[66] January 30, 1782, CO5/523, 24r-24v, BOP, SCDAH; January 30, 1782, CO5/523, 34v-36v, BOP, SCDAH.
[67] January 30, 1782, CO5/523, 33v, BOP, SCDAH.
[68] Jack P. Greene, ed., *The Nature of Colony Constitutions, Two Pamphlets on the Wilkes Fund Controversy* (Columbia: University of South Carolina Press, 1970), 186.

to the colonial view, aligning their institutions to suit colonists' expectations about how justice should be administered in the colony. In doing so, they hoped to put to rest colonists' fears about the encroachment of British tyranny, and, by doing so, secure their allegiance to the Crown.

Key to assuaging loyalists' concerns in the immediate aftermath of the occupation was offering substantial legal protections for their rights as English subjects, and especially their property rights. Today, the term "subject" lacks a salient legal connotation. In the early modern British Atlantic World, however, subjecthood was a powerful legal concept that encapsulated how Britons were tied to the king. As we have already seen, the term was elastic, contested, and strategically invoked, but generally speaking it connoted the reciprocal bond – called *ligeantia* – between a monarch and those born within his or her dominions.[69] At the heart of subjecthood was an understanding that subjects owed allegiance to monarchs and monarchs offered protection to subjects.[70] Claiming subjecthood mattered precisely because of the benefits it conferred. When individuals like Nathaniel Cary invoked subjecthood and protested their allegiance to the Crown, they did so in order to access "certain rights, liberties, and privileges."[71] Although early modern Britons disagreed about the precise nature of the "rights, liberties, and privileges" that they claimed, most understood that property rights were among the most significant.[72] This was especially true in the American colonies, where property rights assumed an inflated importance given the outsized political and social importance of property ownership in settler societies. In places that lacked a hereditary aristocracy, property ownership remained the single most important signifier of status; individuals with the most property also possessed the most liberties. As a result, "property qualifications were also liberty qualifications," and protecting property "was equivalent to a defense of liberty."[73]

When the British occupied the Lowcountry, therefore, loyalists like Nathaniel Cary channeled a long history of rights talk by demanding that the Crown protect their property rights, which under local law included property rights in people. As Alured Clarke complained to General Cornwallis, he received daily requests "from the Masters of

---

[69] Muller, *Subjects and Sovereign*, 6–9.
[70] *Sir Matthew Hale's The Prerogatives of the King*, ed. D. E. C. Yale (London: Selden Society, 1976), 29.
[71] Muller, *Subjects and Sovereign*, 26.   [72] *Ibid.*, 71.
[73] Michal Jan Rozbicki, *Culture and Liberty in the Age of the American Revolution* (Charlottesville: University of Virginia Press, 2011), 70.

Negroes" who sought help locating their runaway slaves in the town.[74]
Clarke was not alone. Robert McCulloh, the Deputy Superintendent of
the Port at Charlestown, fielded similar inquiries. In 1780, for example,
Dr. James Clitherall asked for his help finding his runaway slaves, and he
authorized McCulloh "to take" his "Negroes where ever they" were "to
be found."[75] Thomas Boone, a resident of London, wrote to Cornwallis in
1780 and asked for aid in locating his slaves, who were likely "following
the British army."[76] Cornwallis also entertained a plea on behalf of "two
very amiable Ladies" whose "negroes" had run away. Would Cornwallis
"take these poor distressed Ladies under [his] favour and protection, by
obtaining Justice for them from those who have injured Them"?[77]

British officials were sensitive to pleas from the "poor distressed"
loyalists who pestered them with letters and petitions about stolen or
runaway slaves. After all, for the men and women who had refused to
abjure their oaths to King George III, the American rebellion had been an
unmitigated economic disaster. "Nothing but the Evidence of my Senses,"
James Simpson wrote, "would have convinced me, that one half of the
distress I am a Witness to could have been produced in so short a Time, in
so rich and flourishing a Country as Carolina was when I left it." Families
"who four Years ago abounded in every convenience and Luxury of Life,
are without Food to live on, Clothes to cover them, or the Means to
purchase either." This included Rawlins Lowndes, who wrote to
Simpson that before the Revolution he "annually made at least 1000
barrels of Rice," and his "[a]nnual Income was ... upwards of £3700
Sterling." Over the course of the War, however, his plantation failed to
clear "upwards of £250 Sterling a Year." His horses had been confiscated
"for public Uses," and he had "from various Causes lost upwards of 80"
of his "best Slaves."[78]

Although the exigencies of war reduced loyalists like the Lowndes
family to poverty, so too did the punitive legal measures that rebel

[74] Alured Clarke to General Cornwallis, July 10, 1780, TNA, PRO 30/11/2, Cornwallis Papers, 260r.
[75] James Clitherall to [Robert McCulloh], July 2, 1780, TNA, C 106/88. McCulloh's overseer eventually put Clitherall's slaves to work at Silk Hope. William White to Robert McCulloh, March 6, 1781, TNA, C 106/88.
[76] Thomas Boone to General Cornwallis, October 14, 1780, TNA, PRO 30/11/3, Cornwallis Papers, 228-228v.
[77] November 6, 1780, Bernard Hale to Earl Cornwallis, TNA, PRO 30/11/3, Cornwallis Papers, f45-45v.
[78] J. Simpson to Sir Henry Clinton, July 1, 1780, Item 2877, Sir Guy Carleton Papers, B800120, SCDAH.

colonists instituted in order to punish or terrorize their loyal neighbors. Historians once faulted loyalists for their failure to rally to the king's cause in South Carolina and Georgia, but scholars now appreciate that rebel colonists "relentlessly murdered, imprisoned, abused, and intimidated those who supported the king's government."[79] This "unremitting campaign of Whig cruelty" ultimately "drove many loyal Americans to abandon their allegiance."[80] The Whig "campaign" also had a legal arm. At the beginning of the War, South Carolina's rebel government required the state's citizens to take an oath renouncing their allegiance to the king and to transfer their "[f]aith and true Allegiance" to the State of South Carolina. Those who refused to do so were forced into exile.[81] In 1778, the legislature again required all male citizens over the age of seventeen to take an oath of allegiance, but this time those who abstained would forfeit their right to vote, to sue "either in law or equity," to hold office, or to hold any property in the state.[82] As a result of these measures, many South Carolina loyalists sold their property and abandoned the province, or forfeited their lands and slaves to confiscation.

Under these circumstances, it is not surprising that loyalists greeted British troops as liberators and looked to them for solutions to their financial hardships. They had lost everything by remaining loyal, and when the British retook Charlestown, loyalists invoked their subjecthood to convince the Crown to restore their slaves. As we have seen, colonists like Nathaniel Cary emphasized their unwavering loyalty and their status as "Liege Subjects" in order to make claims upon the king's justice.[83] The Crown had no obligation to protect rebel property, but loyal subjects were positioned differently in the eyes of the law. As General Clinton had promised, they eventually "would be restored to the full possession of that Liberty in their Persons and Property, which they had before experienced under the British Government."[84] In the meantime, administrators and military officials would work to protect loyalist property, including their slaves.

---

[79] Piecuch, *Three Peoples, One King*, 7.   [80] *Ibid.*

[81] Act Establishing an Oath of Abjuration and Allegiance, February 13, 1777, Cooper, *SAL*, 1: 135.

[82] Act Enforcing an Assurance of Allegiance and Fidelity to the State, March 28, 1778, Cooper, *SAL*, 1: 148.

[83] Petition of Nathaniel Cary, November 27, 1781 [signed May 21, 1781], CO 5/520, 34v–35r, BOP, SCDAH.

[84] Proclamation, May 1780, *RSCG*, vol. 1, June 8, 1780.

ADJUDICATING OWNERSHIP

Loyalists' claims resonated with members of the Board of Police, who felt honor-bound to administer justice to the king's loyal subjects in South Carolina. Just as the Board followed colonial precedents in regulating the lives of enslaved people, they also enforced the local laws that had allowed colonists to commodify slaves and maximize their value over the previous century. In practice, this meant that the Board perpetuated the legal fiction inherent in chattel slavery by adjudicating questions about slave ownership in the context of debt litigation.[85] As we have already have seen in Chapter 2, slaves were an important form of collateral in plantation America, and colonists routinely leveraged the value of enslaved people to underwrite the expansion of plantations and businesses through borrowing. For loyal South Carolinians, the Board provided a forum for attaching slaves that rebel debtors had risked as collateral at a time when many of these colonists were pressed to meet basic needs. By bringing a petition before the Board, these impoverished loyalist creditors could have the slaves of rebel debtors (many of whom had fled the

[85] At first, the Board only heard disputes over agreements entered into after the capitulation of Charlestown, but it eventually was empowered to hear suits for debts incurred "prior to the breaking out of the present Rebellion, and to do therein what appertains to Law and Equity." June 27, 1780, CO 5/519, 2r, BOP, SCDAH; Order from Nisbet Balfour, April 2, 1781, CO 5/521, 47v-48r, BOP, SCDAH. Sir Henry Clinton disliked the extension of the Board's jurisdiction to include debts incurred prior to the conflict, finding that "the Powers of the Police have been extended beyond what they themselves say the Courts at Westminster or any other civil Jurisdiction under the British Government have a Right to Exercise" and moreover were not exercised by the New York Board of Police. Sir Henry Clinton to Lieut. Gen. Leslie, March 17, 1782, Item 4248, Sir Guy Carleton Papers, B800120, SCDAH. As Clinton explained to Lord George Germain, he had been "uniformly of Opinion that Military Establishments taking Cognizance or enforcing the Payment of Debts contracted prior to the Rebellion, or an improper Interference with the Real Property of Rebels lying within the British Lines must ultimately embarrass Government, injure the British Merchant, and be always immediately fatal to the Loyalists in America." [Clinton] draft letter to Lord George Germain, March 18, 1782, Item 4249, Sir Guy Carleton Papers, B800120, SCDAH.

In addition to debt and contract litigation, the Board also heard cases involving the billeting of military officers in Charlestown and particularly disagreements over housing. Criminal cases, including frequent complaints about stolen watercraft, also occupied some of the Board's time. On any given day the Board heard (or referred to arbitration) a wide variety of cases, including litigation "for nonpayment of an Account for Furniture sold to the Defendant"; "for unlawfully obtaining possession of the Complainants House"; "for unlawfully taking & detailing the Complainant's Schooner"; "for unlawfully taking & detaining the Complainant's Boat"; "for nonperformance of an Agreement"; "for nonpayment of an accot. for hire as a Nurse"; and "for pulling down & destroying the Complainant's Wall." July 14, 1780, CO 5/519, 6v-7v, BOP, SCDAH.

province) seized by the Sheriff, appraised, and sold to pay outstanding debts. In 1781, for example, the Board awarded a creditor plaintiff possession of "three Negroes" who had been "adjudged the Property" of an "absent Debtor."[86] On the same day, the Board also awarded "thirty Negroes and a quantity of Rice in the Straw supposed to be about two hundred barrels on the Plantation of the Defendant" to a creditor plaintiff in payment of a debt.[87] Later that year, the Sheriff attached "a Negro Woman named Lucy," and after the Board determined that she belonged to the "absent Debtor," ordered her "appraised" and "delivered over" to the creditor.[88]

In debt cases, the Board adhered to colonial precedents as much as possible, even going so far as to selling attached slaves according to the procedures outlined in a colonial statute.[89] For example, when "a Negroe Wench named Binkey and a Negroe Woman named Lucretia and her five Children named Dye, Jeffrey, Binkey, Andrew and Well" were "adjudged to belong to the absent Debtor," the Board specifically ordered them to be appraised and sold by Sheriff "pursuant to the Act commonly called the attachment act," passed by the Commons House of Assembly in 1744, with money arising from the sale used to discharge the debt.[90] Indeed, South Carolina's colonial laws provided a legal framework that Board members did not seek to alter as they adjudicated disputes over slave property. Familiar with South Carolina's laws and aware that those laws were effective at balancing the needs of creditors and debtors in an economy where slaves commonly served as collateral, the Board assumed *arguendo* that slaves were property that could be claimed to satisfy debts.

This practice had real consequences for enslaved people. Although we cannot know what life was like for Lucretia and her children, we can make some assumptions. The Revolutionary War opened up unprecedented opportunities for resistance, but it also left slaves on outlying plantations vulnerable to starvation and the depredations of marauding armies. War posed dire threats to Lucretia and her family, and the looming threat of attachment and sale only compounded her burdens. In fact, Lucretia's fate throws into stark relief the process of commodification that British officials participated in when they acknowledged loyalists' property rights in

---

[86] January 3, 1781, CO 5/521, 20v, BOP, SCDAH.   [87] *Ibid.*, 21r.

[88] August 17, 1781, 5/522, 27r-27v, BOP, SCDAH.

[89] September 13, 1781, 5/522, 28v, BOP, SCDAH.

[90] *Ibid.* See "An Act for the Better Securing the Payment and More Easy Recovery of Debts due from Any Person or Persons Inhabiting, residing or Being Beyond the Seas," *SAL* 3:616.

people. Rather than evidencing a concern about the fate of individual slaves, officials instead sought to satisfy white loyalists, who expected institutions like the Board to protect their investments in enslaved people and to treat slaves as property under local law.

We can detect a similar pattern in the slave-stealing cases that loyalist colonists brought to the Board. Because the Board technically retained jurisdiction over "Contests between Individuals concerning Matters of Property," members also heard disputes over the ownership of enslaved people, and particularly trover cases (for the taking of personal property) involving slaves.[91] Throughout the British occupation of South Carolina, slave stealing or "inveighling" was a particular problem as some loyalists took the law into their own hands to recoup the slaves they had lost to rebel incursions. In particular, they targeted slaves on sequestered estates, who were technically "the property of the enemy" but now labored to produce agricultural commodities for the British military. According to British officials, aggrieved loyalists "clandestinely carried away" these slaves with an alarming frequency and brought them to Charlestown, where they were hidden and then sold.[92] The Board and its arbitrators picked through complicated ownership histories in order to determine the rightful owners of these valuable slaves, who could be sold multiple times by colonists seeking to exploit the chaos of war. Often, Board members discovered that a fraudulent slave sale was at the heart of theft allegations. For example, in July 1780 John Night complained to the Board that Smith Clarendon had unlawfully taken and carried away his "Negro Wench named Suey." As the Board discovered, however, Suey actually "was the property of Mr. Clarendon's Child," and Night had purchased her from a man who in turn acquired Suey "at an illegal Sale." The case was ultimately dismissed when the seller agreed to indemnify Night for damages he sustained "on account of the said Negroe."[93] In a similar fact pattern, John Pearson sued Jacob Valk "for the value of a Negroe warranted by the said Jacob Valk & proved to be the Property of another person."[94]

[91] August 11, 1780, CO 5/519, 7v, BOP, SCDAH. The Board also heard cases seeking damages for the beating of slaves, although these were less common. In August 1780, for example, Robert Brisbane sued Peter Delacourt for "wounding and beating" his slave, "whereby he was deprived of his Service." The Board ordered arbitrators to determine the amount of damages. August 25, 1780, CO 5/519, 23r, BOP, SCDAH.

[92] *RSCG*, 30 April 1782; *RG* December 22–26, 1781.

[93] July 11, 1780, CO 5/519, 4v-5r, BOP, SCDAH.

[94] August 22, 1780, CO 5/519, 22r-22v, BOP, SCDAH.

Determining whether a slave was fraudulently sold could be a complicated matter, particularly when colonists fled outside of the province with enslaved people. For example, in 1780 the executrix of loyalist Charles McKinnon asked the Board to restore his slaves "for the benefit of his Widow and Orphan Children." The slaves in question had traveled with McKinnon to St. Augustine at the outbreak of the war, but were captured, condemned by a Congressional Vice Admiralty Court, and sold to South Carolina colonist Edward Weyman. Weyman, however, "refused to deliver the Negroes," arguing that "he had bought them at public Sale" and that they were his legal property. The Board sided with McKinnon's estate, ordering that "the Negroes in dispute should be delivered up to the Plaintiff, and that the Defendant" should "pay the Costs of Suit."[95] As the McKinnon case and other slave sale cases reveal, the breakdown of legal exchanges in wartime South Carolina created confusion about slave ownership. To restore order and to establish its legitimacy as a legal body, the Board sought to root out cases of fraudulent sale, something they did emphatically by adjudicating the distance between possession and ownership.

None of these legal practices led the Board's members to question the enslaved status of the Black people in dispute. Rather, the Board assumed *arguendo* that slaves were property, and sought to trace a chain of title back to the proper owner, to whom the slave would be returned or who was entitled to compensation. Indeed, the fate of McKinnon's slaves is a helpful reminder that the unprecedented movement of enslaved people across provincial boundaries, over oceans, and on battlefields provided unique opportunities for escape from the subjugation of their masters, which many slaves seized. Nonetheless, geographic mobility enabled by war also made enslaved people particularly vulnerable to capture and resale. When these individuals appeared before the Board, members treated them as objects, not subjects. Board members never questioned the legal validity or the morality of treating people as things,

[95] November 10, 1780, CO 5/521, 7r-9r, BOP, SCDAH. At times, the Board's jurisdiction in determining questions about slave ownership was questioned, particularly when soldiers were parties. In October 1781, for example, the Sheriff seized "a certain Negroe Man Slave named Edmund" pursuant to a writ of fieri facias. He was hindered in his duty, however, when the slave "was rescued and taken out of his Possession by Capt. Alex. Campbell of the South Carolina Royalists." Campbell then "threatened to split down the Head any Person who should again take hold of the said Negroe, and alledged he was his Property." The Board referred the matter to the Commandant of Charlestown. October 23, 1781, 5/523, 2r-2v, BOP, SCDAH.

in part because neither law nor the exigencies of the moment required them to do so. But more important, these administrators treated slaves as property because there was no space in the law's procedures for them to do otherwise. As was true in all of slavery's varied laws, slave law as administered in occupied South Carolina ultimately reinforced slavery as a system because it offered procedures for managing slaves that required individuals to follow a set pattern – one that never questioned that slaves were things.

A MATTER OF "SERIOUS CONCERN"

Rather than challenging slavery as an institution, the Board of Police played an important role in a broader legal-administrative system that governed in keeping with colonists' expectations about the administration of law in the colony, and particularly slave law. Nonetheless, records from the British occupation reveal that at least some British officials expressed qualms about the treatment of South Carolina's enslaved people, and especially those who had willingly undertaken service on behalf of the British military. Although few Britons questioned the legality of slavery or made structural critiques of slavery as an institution, a number of officers believed that military service drew slaves into a relationship with the king that triggered the Crown's obligation to protect them. Crucially, these soldiers and administrators drew short of suggesting that slaves were British subjects. Nonetheless, they invoked the very same bonds of allegiance and protection that gave subjecthood its legal significance when they described military service by enslaved people. For example, Alexander Leslie admitted that slaves who had served with the British military in the southern campaigns had acquitted themselves well. They had "been very useful, both at the Siege of Savannah and here," and he reminded Sir Guy Carleton that they had "from their loyalty been promised their freedom."[96] Lieutenant Colonel James Moncrief likewise expressed concerns about betraying the expectations of slaves who had gallantly served. He considered the "number of slaves who have attached themselves to the Engineer Department ... and who look up to me for protection" a "matter of serious concern." Like Leslie, he believed that "His Majesty's service" had received "many advantages" "from their

---

[96] [Lt. Gen. Alex. Leslie] to [Gen. Sir Guy Carleton], June 27, 1782, Item 4916, Sir Guy Carleton Papers, B800120, SCDAH.

labour," and he urged Clinton to formulate a plan for treating these slaves fairly.

Moncrief's reasoning was based in practicality. Failing to deal with slaves honorably might "lay aside the confidence which they always placed in us," which would in turn make it difficult to call upon their labor going forward.[97] Aware of the value of slaves as laborers, officers like Moncrief saw no benefit in alienating them from the Crown. Indeed, Moncrief had such a good opinion of their service that he considered "embodying a brigade of the Negroes of this Country" a "great advantage."[98] But Alured Clarke expressed a more robust view of British obligations. He reminded Cornwallis that slaves had "served in the defence of Savannah, and on many other occasions," and that they feared "being treated with cruelty in consequence of it, if they go back." Although "policy may interfere in favor of the Masters," he insisted that "an attention to Justice, and good faith, must plead strongly in behalf of the Negroes."[99]

These officers' qualms about the treatment of slaves reflected a broader Atlantic context in which British writers and politicians were beginning to openly criticize slavery and American slaveholders. These attacks were less systemic critiques of slavery and more commentaries on the politics of rebellious American slaveholders. As Christopher Leslie Brown has shown, "[a]ntislavery statements and gestures emerged as frequently to meet tactical needs, to answer immediate ideological objectives, or to erase doubts about individual or collective self-worth. In the Revolutionary era, expressing opposition to chattel slavery was a means to other ends as often as an end in itself."[100] Nonetheless, as the war reached its conclusion, we can see the development of a line of thinking that might have led Britons to consider slaves to be subjects. This was legally possible. Case law and the practical experience of sorting diverse peoples into subjects and nonsubjects as the British Empire expanded had created a presumption that it was allegiance rather than geography or birthright that made one a subject.[101] Particularly in the period after the Seven Years' War, when the British Empire expanded dramatically, the "flexibility and fluidity" of subjecthood as a legal concept allowed diverse

---

[97] Lieutenant Colonel James Moncrief to Sir Henry Clinton, March 13, 1782, Item 9955, Sir Guy Carleton Papers B800120, SCDAH.

[98] *Ibid.*

[99] Alured Clarke to General Cornwallis, July 10, 1780, TNA, PRO 30/11/2, Cornwallis Papers, 260r.

[100] Brown, *Moral Capital*, 113.   [101] Muller, *Subjects and Sovereign*, 24.

peoples throughout the globe to position themselves as loyal subjects based upon their allegiance to the Crown.[102]

There were also legal precedents for viewing the service of enslaved people as a marker of subjecthood. In 1725, the Board of Trade deemed enslaved Bermudian mariners British subjects for the purposes of the Navigation Acts. In this decision, which was couched as an appeal from a Vice Admiralty Court case, the Board took notice of the fact that the slaves in question had served in the local militia.[103] The decision seems to have received little attention, and it failed to otherwise alter the legal status of Bermudian slaves. Nonetheless, it exposed a potential legal avenue – one ultimately not taken – that might have allowed Britons to treat slaves as subjects rather than as commodities.

This tantalizing possibility reappeared in the 1772 Somerset decision, albeit in a different procedural posture. Lord Mansfield heard arguments about whether the return of a writ of habeas corpus, which was used to protect the bodies of the king's subjects, was sufficient to detain the slave, James Somerset. Mansfield ultimately determined that it was not, and he ordered Somerset's release. This decision is intriguing in part because all of the lawyers and the judges in this case assumed that the writ of habeas corpus, which applied to subjects, might be used to free James Somerset. None of the lawyers, "[e]ven the lawyers who argued against James Somerset's release from his master," insisted "that his status as slave or his birth in Africa made him an alien or barred his use" of the writ. Slaves, it seems, could be subjects "for the purpose of investigating the legality of one person's detention by another."[104] The potential implications of this decision were staggering, as antislavery activists like Granville Sharp perceived. Sharpe, in fact, argued that subjecthood and its protections might be extended to enslaved people in the American colonies. Colonial slaves were "as much the king's natural born subjects as the free natives of England," he insisted. Therefore, local laws that authorized slavery were a violation of the king's prerogative rights.[105] The power to free slaves

---

[102] *Ibid.*, 9.

[103] For an excellent description of the Navigation Acts and the colonial trade system, see Nuala Zahedieh, *The Capital and the Colonies: London and the Atlantic Economy, 1660–1700* (Cambridge: Cambridge University Press, 2010), 35–55. Michael J. Jarvis, "Maritime Masters and Seafaring Slaves in Bermuda, 1680–1783," *WMQ* 59 (2002): 598.

[104] Paul Halliday, *Habeas Corpus: From England to Empire* (Cambridge, MA: Harvard University Press, 2010), 208.

[105] Granville Sharp, *A Representation of the Injustice and Dangerous Tendency of Tolerating Slavery* (London, 1769) (Cambridge: Cambridge University Press, 2014), 92.

would flow from the king, who was the font of all justice and could bring the bodies of his subjects (or those in the control of his subjects) under his protective mantle.

Given this broader context, we can imagine a situation in which military officials might have chosen a different path, one that acknowledged the humanity of slaves and honored their military service by protecting them. For the British in South Carolina, however, this was a road not taken, in part because they prioritized the demands of the king's white subjects over those of enslaved people. Because white subjects were entitled to the protection of their property – which under local law included human beings – British officials found themselves unable to jump the well-worn ruts of a colonial legal system built around the chattel principle. Indeed, when the British occupied the Lowcountry, they entered a world in which slaveholding had been legal for over a century. Colonial courts routinely heard disputes about slaves, and local statutes outlined a comprehensive code that governed the conduct of enslaved people and, to a lesser extent, slave owners. Chattel slavery – the classification of human beings as personal property – formed the core of South Carolina's written and customary constitution by the 1780s. As we shall see, British military and civilian officials ultimately perpetuated the legal fiction inherent in this slaveholders' constitution by honoring white subjects' claims to slaves. They did so despite the fact that thousands of enslaved people in the Lowcountry were busy putting the lie to the notion that people were things. At great risk to themselves, South Carolina's slaves resisted their commodification in ways small and large during the British occupation. They stopped work; they flouted the colony's myriad policing laws; and they ran away in unprecedented numbers. Crucially, many of these slaves took up the king's standard and served with dignity and bravery. They did what loyal subjects do, evidencing their faith and allegiance with their actions. Nonetheless, throughout the war and especially at its end, British officials would weigh their claims to freedom and find them wanting. As an Black man named Will discovered in 1781, even when slaves performed valuable military service, British officials continued to treat them as objects, not subjects, in the eyes of the law.

THE CASE OF "NEGRO WILL"

In 1781 "Negro Will" found himself in a magistrate's court in the Bahamas. Will had faithfully served the king during the War, and whether he was a free man or not as a result of that service was the subject of dispute in this case. According to Will, he was the former slave of Bermudian colonist Willis Morgan, "who sent him to Carolina" to be sold prior to the outbreak of hostilities. When the war began, "his Master" in South Carolina "became an Officer in the American Service," and therefore, "forfeited" all of his property. Will was ambitious, and at some point he decided to join "the King's Army." He testified that he served in the "Defence of Savanna against the French & Rebels," and that this had earned him "a free pass" from the Georgia Board of Police. It seems that Will believed this pass documented his emancipation; he testified that after receiving it he was "employed as a free Man in the Transport Service at the Reduction of Charlestown." After serving in Charlestown, Will traveled to the Bahamas, where he planned to catch a Bermuda-bound ship and reunite with "his old Master."[106]

At this point in Will's journey, questions about his legal status began to trigger official scrutiny. As he searched for a vessel that would take him to the Bahamas and, from there, to Bermuda, he discovered that captains were reluctant to take him aboard absent definitive proof that he was free. Their reluctance was informed by an accurate understanding of local laws that held ships' masters accountable for transporting slaves without a license. In South Carolina, for example, two statutes (passed in 1698 and 1739) required captains to enter into a £1,000 penal bond with two securities, in which they agreed not to "take on board and carry away or suffer to be taken on board and carried away, any person or persons whatsoever" without permission.[107] These statutes were originally meant to prevent slaves from stowing away on outbound vessels, but, during the Revolution, British officials also used them to prevent colonists from stealing sequestered slaves and transporting them out of the province. For example, Cornwallis specifically ordered captains landing in

---

[106] [unknown] to John Maxwell Esq. Captain General, Governor, and Commander in Chief of the Bahama Islands, September 20, 1781, TNA, C 106/88.

[107] Masters who failed to enter into a bond in a timely manner were subject to a £50 penalty. It is unclear whether the penalty amount was £50 South Carolina currency or Sterling. An Act for the Entry of Vessels (1698), *SAL* 2: 140; an additional and explanatory Act to an Act for the Entry of Vessels (1739), *SAL* 3: 526. The Board specifically recommended the forty-eight-hour provision to the Commandant, noting that it "would be attended with beneficial Consequences if such parts of the Acts of Assembly for the Entry of Vessels as direct the Masters to wait upon the Commandant in forty eight hours after their Arrival and to give Bond with Security not to carry away any Persons inhabiting or residing in this Province without the License of the Commandant" were to be adopted. June 27, 1780, CO 5/519, 2v-3r, BOP, SCDAH.

Charlestown to comply with the 1698 and 1739 statutes because he had heard complaints that "[s]everal Negroes" had been "carried off ... by Masters of trading vessels and others."[108]

In this context, Will found it difficult to secure a passage to the Bahamas, even though he reassured potential captains that "he had a Pass from Genl. Prevost." Will's persistence eventually paid off, however, and he convinced one Captain Lighbourn to bring him from Charlestown to Providence. Was Lighbourn justified in transporting Will? The answer hinged upon Will's precise legal status. Will had testified that he was a free man, but Lighbourn insisted that Will had deceived him; that he was not, in fact, from Bermuda "but that he was sold in Georgia." Another witness suggested that Will was a runaway, and that Lighbourn had purposefully concealed him after discovering him on board his ship. According to this witness, the captain had confided that "he did not know any such Negro as Will untill he had left Charlestown and was laying in five fathom Hole." Afraid that he might be held legally accountable under local statutes for carrying Will away, Lighbourn told the magistrate that he was willing to "deliver" Will to any "such Person" who would take him back to South Carolina.

Ultimately, the Court agreed with the facts as Will presented them. The magistrate held that Will "was a Bermuda Slave & Sold to a Person in Rebellion," and that he had subsequently "joined the King's Army & was in actual Service at the Sieges of Savannah & Charlestown." Moreover, he concurred that Will "had a Passport signed with Genl. Prevost's Name and was afterwards in the King's Service in the Transport Department." However, the magistrate did not consider Will's "passport" to be a "free pass," and did not at any point identify Will as a "free man," as Will himself did in his testimony. Having found these facts, the Court then admitted its own ignorance in this particular case: "In what Manner Negroes, circumstanced as Will is, are treated, and upon what Footing they are put by the King's Officers, we know not." Was Will free by virtue of his military service? The Court was unsure, largely because the judge could not answer one dispositive question: Had Will's rebellious owner returned his allegiance to the Crown? "[I]t is undoubtedly true," the magistrate observed, "that Pardons are granted to all who come in to the King's Standard & take the Oath of allegiance to him." In such cases, "their Property wherever found, is restored & secured to them." Therefore, the Court held that "should Will's Master return to his

[108] August 29, 1780, CO 5/519, 25v, BOP, SCDAH.

Allegiance, he would have an undoubted Right to Will, as his Property."[109] Unable to determine whether Will's owner had returned his allegiance, the Governor of the Bahamas transported Will back to Charlestown along with the Magistrate's report, and he left it to administrators in Charlestown to resolve the case.[110]

We do not know what happened next to Will. What is certain it that his fate rested upon the subject status of his alleged owner. Indeed, Bahamian officials refused to resolve the case because they did not know whether Will's alleged master had taken an oath of loyalty. They assumed that the distinction between subject and rebel was the distinction that made a difference when it came to honoring a slave's claim to freedom. Although in Will's case many of the individuals he encountered seemed sympathetic to his claims, they found themselves bound by the law to respect the chattel principle. They agreed that Will came in "to the King's Standard," but this did not result in his automatic emancipation. Instead, Will remained object, not subject, in the eyes of local administrators, who did not hesitate to respect property rights in people and to peg those rights to an owner's loyal status, not a slave's service.

RES PUBLICA

Will's fate in many respects reflected the implementation of broader British policy, which tended to respect rather than undermine the treatment of slaves as property under local law. Although British military officials gestured at the humanity of enslaved people, especially those who had served the Crown, the language of property law created a nearly inexorable logic of its own: classifying colonists as loyal subjects triggered an obligation to protect their property, including their slaves. Aware that slave ownership was the key to wealth in the Lowcountry, British officials used slaves to win and maintain the loyalty of whites during the occupation. For loyalists who had suffered in the king's cause, actions to safeguard their valuable human property worked to shore up support for a fight that had become bitter and protracted. The prospect of reclaiming confiscated slaves likewise must have operated powerfully upon lukewarm rebels who were wavering in their allegiance.

---

[109] [unknown] to John Maxwell Esq. Captain General, Governor, and Commander in Chief of the Bahama Islands, September 20, 1781, TNA, C 106/88.
[110] John Maxwell to Robert McCulloh, September 26, 1781, TNA, C 106/88.

We can see this balancing act in a memorandum that General Clinton issued in June 1780, which included advice about how officials should treat runaway slaves belonging to loyalists. The document comes closer than any other to representing an official British "policy" position on slavery, and it reveals the extent to which the commanding language of property law shaped outcomes for both white colonists and enslaved people in occupied South Carolina. Clinton began by suggesting that military and civilian officials should sort slaves in Charlestown and outlying plantations into "public" slaves and "private" slaves. Slaves of loyal colonists were to be deemed private slaves: they would be treated as private property and returned to their former masters. However, runaway or confiscated slaves owned by "[r]ebels and those persons who are not under Protection of Government" belonged "of course . . . to the Public." According to Clinton, "after serving faithfully during the War," these "public" slaves were "entitled to their freedom."[111]

We can imagine that Clinton hoped to tread a middle path with this public/private distinction. He honored the Crown's obligation to protect the property of loyal subjects, and he created a legal formula for balancing the freedom claims of slaves against the property demands of loyalists. Simultaneously, he sought to assuage his officers' concerns about protecting slaves who served with the British military by holding out the possibility that some might obtain their freedom at the end of the War. Read charitably, the memorandum manifests Clinton's real concern that British officials should treat enslaved people humanely. For example, Clinton was aware that owners would likely punish the runaway slaves who were returned to them. As a result, he ordered officers not to return slaves until their loyalist masters "promised in the presence of the Negro not to punish him for past Offences." He also insisted that public slaves should receive sufficient food, clothing, and even compensation for their work, and went so far as to muse whether these slaves might be settled on "Forfeited Lands" after the War. "Perhaps they would be a check upon the others," he suggested, or maybe "just the contrary Captures."[112] Despite his attempts to ameliorate the conditions of enslaved people, however, both public and private slaves remained vulnerable to theft and sale throughout the War. Although Clinton sought to make

[111] Memoranda for the Commandant of Charlestown and Lieutenant General Earl Cornwallis Head Quarters Charles Town, June 3, 1780, Item 2800, Sir Guy Carleton Papers, B800120, SCDAH.
[112] *Ibid.*

a distinction that would leave room for the emancipation of individual slaves, it was ultimately a distinction that failed to make a difference because it was hitched to the proposition that slaves were things at law.

We can see a similar principle at work as the Board of Police sought to implement Clinton's policy on a broader scale. As the Board created a bureaucracy for inventorying and returning "all Slaves" who came "into the British Lines," members gestured at the humanity of enslaved people by seeking to protect runaway slaves from punishment upon their return. According to the Board, loyalist owners could only receive slaves after making a "solemn promise not to resent the Behaviour of the Slave for having left his Service." Those who punished slaves in contravention of these regulations would receive no aid in recovering other runaways.[113] However, this meager attempt to protect enslaved people was counteracted by the fact that the Board construed the category of "loyalist" expansively, and therefore, increased the number of slaves that were returned. In practice, loyalists included not only "[p]ersons whose Sentiments have been ever loyal," but also those who had repented and taken an oath of allegiance; colonists whose paroles had been discharged by Sir Henry Clinton's proclamation but who later took an oath of loyalty; and former militia members who agreed to return to their allegiance.

There were practical reasons for such an expansive view of loyalty. One reflected the Board's desire to return slaves to their owners speedily in order to revive South Carolina's plantation economy. Although slaves were a "large and valuable pool of laborers for the army and simultaneously diminished the rebels' labor resources," the army also had attracted "more slaves ... than it could possibly employ."[114] British military and civilian officials understood that these slaves would be more useful to Britain's war effort if they could be returned to agricultural labor. In fact, the British army suffered from significant supply problems throughout the American Revolution, and maintaining a functioning plantation economy powered by slave labor was essential for ensuring that military forces were properly provisioned.[115] The Board in particular believed that it was crucial to begin the process of returning slaves to their loyalist owners as soon as possible because "the advanced Season of the year required the

[113] June 13, 1780, CO 5/520, 1r-3r, BOP, SCDAH.
[114] Piecuch, *Three Peoples, One King*, 216.
[115] O'Shaughnessy, *The Men Who Lost America*, 14.

immediate Labour of the Negroe to cultivate the Crop, which otherwise must be lost."[116]

More importantly for our purposes, military officials read the category of "loyalist" broadly because they were aware that wavering colonists might be induced to change sides if the British government offered to return their slaves. Enslaved people were always valuable commodities, but in the war-ravaged southeast, slave ownership was the key to rebuilding wealth. British officials understood this, and they offered to return slaves to rebellious colonists who were willing to take an oath of loyalty to the king. Following the capitulation of Charlestown, Clinton issued several proclamations that offered pardons to rebels who would return their allegiance to the Crown (with the exception of those who were "pol[l]uted with [spilling] the blood of their fellow-citizens"). He issued these with the understanding that former rebels could resume ownership of their confiscated property, including their slaves, upon renouncing their rebellion.[117] In fact, one of the Board's many tasks was sifting through lists of erstwhile rebels who wished to be "admitted to the Priviledges of British Subjects" in order to determine whether they had truly conformed and were, therefore, entitled to confiscated property.[118]

It is difficult to gauge how often rebels claimed that they had "conformed, and become good Subjects" in order to recover their slaves.[119] As Maya Jasanoff has shown, loyalism was not monolithic; individuals remained loyal or returned their allegiance to the Crown for different reasons.[120] For southeastern loyalists, the potential restoration of slave property may have been a compelling reason to take an oath. Certainly, unwavering loyalists and British officials assumed that erstwhile rebels routinely took advantage of the policy, and swore oaths of allegiance solely for pecuniary reasons. They found the practice extremely irritating. One Georgia plantation manager confided his suspicion that rebels who had plundered "this province & all the kings friends" had changed sides in order to "[c]laim & forcibly take" the "negroes" that had been "[c]aptured from them or that under the Sanction of Sir Henry Clinton's

[116] June 13, 1780, CO 5/520, 1r-3r, BOP, SCDAH.
[117] Proclamation (dated June 1, 1780), *RSCG*, June 8, 1780, vol. 1, P900046, SCDAH.
[118] The Board typically consulted colonists who were more familiar with the applicants' reputations before they made this determination. August 15, 1780, CO 5/520, 9v, BOP, SCDAH.
[119] Alured Clarke to Lord Cornwallis, July 10, 1780, TNA, PRO 30/11/2, Cornwallis Papers, 260r.
[120] Jasanoff, *Liberty's Exiles*, 8–9.

Proclamation came & join'd the British troops." He condemned this
policy as perverse. The "more a Rebel has Sinned & made himself
conspicuous in a daring Rebellion," he lamented, the "better terms he
is intitled to." A rebel may have been "a man who had some parts," but
a "[l]oyal Subject" was "a dull fool – unworthy of any notice."[121] This
view must have been common among those who were steadfast in their
allegiance. Those who had "positively refused" to "abjure" the king
from the onset of the conflict no doubt felt betrayed by policies that
seemed to reward those who were less scrupulous.[122] However, the real
victims of offers of pardon were the individual enslaved people who
found themselves commodified in the service of British policy aims.

While slaves belonging to loyalists were subject to the property claims
of their owners, in practice even those ostensibly entitled to freedom
because their owners were rebels trod a narrow path to freedom. Many
of these "public" slaves had been sequestered on plantations, where they
were forced to labor on behalf of the British war effort. According to
Clinton's memorandum, they were entitled to their freedom at the end of
the war. However, the very language that British officials used to establish
and administer the sequestration system reflected a belief that they were
property. Rather than describing slaves on sequestered plantations as
human beings, officials imitated the colonial practice of listing slaves
alongside other valuable chattels in the legal documents that undergirded
sequestration. For example, Cornwallis conflated slaves with other property when he authorized his agents to seize and sequester "Slaves, Houses,
Cattle, Horses, Household Furniture, Plate," and produce.[123] He also
included "[l]ands and negroes" in his definition of "the Capital Stock"
of sequestered plantations, replicating rather than challenging a view of
slaves as productive capital.[124] Cornwallis was not alone in adhering to
local legal norms when he considered enslaved people to be units of value.
John Cruden, the Commissioner for the Seizure, Care and Management of
all Sequestered Estates and Property in South Carolina, also understood
that the slaves he managed on confiscated estates were a "species" of
property, and that "Negroes and of Course their Labour" were the
"principal" part of the property on these estates.[125] For Cruden and for

[121] F. P. Fratia to [Robert McCulloh], July 28, 1780, TNA, C 106/87.
[122] Robert Baillie to Mother from Camp Necessity in East Florida, March 3, 1778, Scottish
National Archives, GD1/1155/72/11.
[123] Earl Cornwallis to John Cruden, TNA, PRO 30/11/7, Cornwallis Papers, 22v.
[124] *Ibid.*, 23r.   [125] To Alexander Leslie, TNA, PRO 30/11/7, Cornwallis Papers, 14r.

other British officials, treating sequestered slaves as property in official documents made sense in practical as well as legal terms. Like colonists, they recognized that slaves were valuable as laborers and as commodities, and that enslaved people would constitute a significant portion of confiscated property. Officials also understood that they occupied a world in which the language of chattel slavery shaped everyday practice, and in this context it made sense to conform their language to colonial precedents in order to make their desires legible.

British officials did not merely conform to linguistic precedents in discussing sequestered slaves, however. Intriguingly, they enlarged upon this discourse to characterize enslaved people on sequestered plantations as more than mere commodities; together with confiscated lands, sequestered slaves constituted a public trust that might appreciate in value over time. Collectively, they were a form of public property that should be managed on behalf of the public. Cornwallis himself expected sequestered estates to be run "for the publick advantage," and he gave John Cruden the authority to manage them in any way that was "conducive to the publick Interests," as long as it kept "the Capital Stock, consisting of Lands and negroes" in "the best State of Improvement and increase."[126] For Cornwallis and other officials, this "Improvement and increase" would directly benefit the military; sequestered estates could yield much-needed supplies, including foodstuffs, timber, indigo, tobacco, and hemp.[127] The "public" that they invoked was the British public, which would indirectly benefit from military victory. At the same time, however, they also expected that the sequestration system would benefit loyalists as a particular subset of the public. Many British officials were genuinely moved by the plight of the king's loyal subjects in South Carolina, and they took seriously their responsibility to make them financially whole. Cruden, for example, styled himself as the "responsible Guardian" of sequestered estates "for the Benefit of the suffering Loyalists," and he conceived of the estates and slaves in his charge as a "Fund" that must be preserved and improved for their benefit. These loyal subjects had a "fair" and "just Claim" to confiscated rebel property "for immediate support and future Indemnification," he insisted.[128] Where the Crown had

---

[126] Earl Cornwallis to John Cruden, TNA, PRO 30/11/7, Cornwallis Papers, 23r.

[127] Sundry Queries upon which Mr. Cruden tryes to have the Opinion of the Right Honorable Earl Cornwallis, TNA, PRO 30/11/7, Cornwallis Papers, "The Commissioners Narrative," 38r.

[128] To Alexander Leslie, TNA, PRO 30/11/7, Cornwallis Papers, 14v.

initially failed to protect the persons and property of its loyal subjects, it would indemnify them and make them financially whole.

Cruden, for one, took his obligation to manage sequestered estates seriously. He demanded that officers and administrators account to him for all seized rebel slaves, and he took them to task when they failed to do so.[129] He also expected officers to promptly pay him for hired out slaves. For example, when Colonel Moncrief of the Engineering Department failed to reimburse him for the "Labour of at least two hundred Negros," Cruden petitioned the Board of Police for redress.[130] Perhaps more importantly, he took steps to prevent colonists from stealing sequestered slaves from plantations by instituting a pass system that differentiated public slaves from private slaves.[131] Finally, he managed the plantations in his charge with an eye toward cutting costs, placing estates under the control of deputies of "approved Loyalty Integrity and Abilities" and keeping their "[c]harges ... as light as possible."[132] Taken together, these measures suggest that Cruden was guided by an understanding that the efficient management of slaves on sequestered estates could produce returns that would benefit not only the British military, but also "those faithful Subjects" who suffered "from the Vengeance and predatory Laws of the Rebels."[133]

ROBERT MCCULLOH'S WAR

The commodification of "public" slaves persisted at the level of individual sequestered plantations. If military officials and Board members believed that "public" slaves should be held in trust for the benefit of loyalists, individuals who managed sequestered plantations leavened this patriotic impulse with self-interest. This was true for Robert McCulloh, who used his influence and connections to become a manager of sequestered properties and, finally, a slave owner himself. McCulloh's experiences stand in for those of other sequestered estate administrators. Far from challenging

---

[129] March 7, 1782, TNA, PRO 30/11/7, Cornwallis Papers, 12v-13r.
[130] Sundry Queries upon which Mr. Cruden tryes to have the Opinion of the Right Honorable Earl Cornwallis, TNA, PRO 30/11/7, Cornwallis Papers, "The Commissioners Narrative," 39v.
[131] *RG*, December 22–26, 1781, vol. 1, no. 86.
[132] Sundry Queries upon which Mr. Cruden tryes to have the Opinion of the Right Honorable Earl Cornwallis, TNA, PRO 30/11/7, Cornwallis Papers, "The Commissioners Narrative," 38r-38v.
[133] To Alexander Leslie, TNA, PRO 30/11/7, Cornwallis Papers, 14r.

slavery as an institution, administrators like McCulloh supplemented their salaries through slave ownership and learned to treat people as property like born-and-bred South Carolinians. They replicated the day-to-day practices of managing slaves that colonists had long found effective, just as they reinforced and extended slavery's law in the context of war. And they had the same financial stakes in preserving the vernacular and official legal cultures that made slave property secure, productive, and easily exchanged. Even as the war disrupted the plantation economy and set thousands of slaves in motion, British administrators took advantage of this tumultuous situation to profit from owning people, just as thousands of colonists had done before them.

Robert McCulloh was an experienced administrator by the time he arrived in Charlestown to serve as Deputy Superintendent of the Port in 1780, and he was a logical choice for the post. McCulloh already had served as Deputy Collector of the Port of Charlestown, but lost his office in 1776 when it "was taken from him by the Rebels." In the early years of the war, he worked in various posts in North America, including the Quarter-Master General's department in New York and the provincial store in Philadelphia. When he embarked with the army for the siege of Savannah in 1779, he served as Collector of the Port there, until he finally was promoted to the Deputy Superintendent Post at Charlestown, when "that Nest of Pirates & Robbers," was "reduced to His Majesty's Arms."[134] An important figure in South Carolina's British establishment during the War, McCulloh went on to become a justice of the peace, Deputy Post Master General of the Southern District of North America, and Paymaster of the Provincial Troops.[135]

McCulloh quickly resettled into life in Charlestown after his appointment as Deputy Superintendent, working tirelessly to administer the busiest port in the mainland southeast. In 1779, in "consideration" of his "[s]ervices," Lieutenant Archibald Campbell granted him "the use of a Plantation lately occupied by John Habersham (a Rebel) Called Dean's Forrest."[136] McCulloh later acquired Silk Hope plantation, another

---

[134] The Memorial of Robert McCulloh of Charlton in the County of Kent late Deputy Collector of the Port of Charlestown in the Province of South Carolina, March 22, 1784, TNA, C 106/88; Step[hen] Prosser to Robert McCulloh, May 24, 1780, TNA, C 106/89.

[135] George Dirbage to Robert McCulloh, December 8, 1779, TNA, C 106/89; Commission to Robert McCulloh, July 3, 1780, TNA, C 106/87; F. P. Fratia to Robert McCulloh, July 12, 1780, TNA, C 106/87.

[136] January 6, 1779, TNA, C 106/87.

confiscated Habersham property. These estates were in disarray when he received them. Slaves from a nearby plantation had "[s]tole" all the hogs, while rootless white "[c]rackers and Others passing in the late Alarm" had "destroy'd the greatest part of the rice in the Straw."[137] Both were filled not only with slaves from the Habersham estates, but also from nearby plantations. A "[r]eturn" of slaves from Silk Hope, for example, reveals that in 1780 forty-four adult slaves and ten children, gathered from several other sequestered or abandoned plantations, lived on the premises.[138]

Like South Carolina planters before the Revolution, McCulloh sought to manage Habersham's estates and the slaves that worked them from afar. From his residence in Charlestown, he hired managers and installed overseers to improve the properties in his charge. These included William White, who acted as overseer at Silk Hope and corresponded frequently with McCulloh, advising him as to crop prospects, seeking supplies (and particularly clothing) for the slaves, and alerting McCulloh about the slaves' welfare. This correspondence reveals the extent to which the war altered plantation life, prompting supply problems, work stoppages, and, most significantly, the forced and coerced movement of large numbers of slaves. At the same time, these letters show that the McCulloh, White, and other estate managers took advantage of these disruptions to profit from slavery, buying choice slaves that had been sold for debts and installing them on the plantations in their care.

Both McCulloh and White were particularly concerned to safeguard the enslaved people on the plantations from theft. Indeed, Silk Hope and Dean Forest were routinely threatened by troops from both sides, as well as loyalists who recently had taken an oath of allegiance and sought to claim the slaves that they had lost. One of McCulloh's correspondents found these "[r]ebel Carolinians newly converted to the faith" particularly worthy of scorn. He warned McCulloh that they were "very thick in the Woods, Skulking to get back what they presume to Call their negroes runaway," and advised that they had already stolen a number of his slaves from Silk Hope.[139] American troops were equally predatory. When a party of "[r]ebels Came With in Five Miles of the plantation" they "put

---

[137] Robert McCulloh to Lewis Johnson & Martin Jollie, August 21, 1779, TNA, C 106/87.

[138] "Return of the Negro's at Silk Hope, &c.," January 10, 1780, TNA, C 106/87.

[139] F. P. Fratia to Robert McCulloh, July 12, 1780, TNA, C 106/87. In July 1780, the same correspondent advised that sixteen slaves had been taken off his plantations "without any formality whatsoever." P. Fratia to [Robert McCulloh], July 28, 1780, TNA, C 106/87.

the negers to the Rout." However, White managed to get "them togather a gain" and planned to remain "on Duty" in the near future to prevent further depredations.[140] Moving slaves out of the path of armed whites to more protected outlying plantations, into the woods, or into towns was the overseer's most promising option as he sought to protect the slaves in his charge from theft. For example, in response to information that rebel forces planned to indemnify officers and troops for back pay "by the Capture of the different Persons Negroes – in the Neighbourhood obnoxious to their Government," McCulloh's property managers ordered his slaves to Savannah for their protection.[141]

Disciplining slaves during this tumultuous time was difficult. Aware of the movement of troops nearby, slaves stopped work or stole provisions. In October 1780, White warned McCulloh that the crop would be poor because he "Could not git the hands to Work For the Space of 2 Monts."[142] He routinely begged McCulloh to travel to his plantations to "Mak[e] a proper Regulation among the negers," who continued to "[r]ob the Field of Corn and grabble the purtaters" to sell in town. These depredations were not limited to one or two slaves. Indeed, if "it Wos one two or three that Did it" he "would Floug them." However, the bewildered White lamented that "thare is a number of them So that" he could not "tell What to Dow."[143] Not only did the slaves on Dean Forest and Silk Hope steal and market the meagre crop; they also left the plantation, sometimes running away permanently, other times absenting themselves for short periods of time. As his property managers informed McCulloh in December 1781 the "whole" of his "Negroes (excepting four) ha[d] absented themselves, from the plantation."[144] In early 1782, White also informed McCulloh that nine of his slaves had run away, including the cooper, a skilled slave employed to make the barrels in which the crops were packed and shipped.[145] Some of these slaves eventually returned, but some did not. These included "8 or 9 of Lucenas negroes that" did "not come back," White complained, as well as two of McCulloh's own slaves.[146]

---

[140] William White to Robert McCulloh, May 18, 1781, TNA, C 106/88.
[141] Crookshanks & Speirs to Robert McCulloh, May 15, 1782, TNA, C 106/89.
[142] William White to Robert McCulloh, October 23, 1780, TNA, C 106/87.
[143] William White to Robert McCulloh, October 30, 1780, TNA, C 106/87.
[144] Crookshanks & Speirs to Robert McCulloh, December 11, 1781, TNA, C 106/89.
[145] William White to Robert McCulloh, January 4, 1782, TNA, C 106/89.
[146] Crookshanks & Speirs to McCulloh, January 18, 1782, TNA, C 106/89.

As the custodian of slaves that did not technically belong to him, McCulloh, his overseer, and his managers also were particularly concerned to ensure that these slaves were not arbitrarily removed from the plantations in payment of debts. As we have seen, litigation before the Board of Police often involved debt disputes over slaves, and White kept his employer informed when slaves on his plantations were attached for debt or when colonists engaged in self-help. For example, on September 7, 1780, he wrote that "5 negeres" had been "taken From the Plantation" that were "Formerley the properte of John:a Berthams," and that these slaves had been "[s]eased For Former Dets."[147] White's vigilance helped to ensure that McCulloh carried out his obligations as a caretaker of a sequestered estate by preventing the improper loss of human property.

However, McCulloh's desire to be kept informed of slave attachments was not merely an exercise in good stewardship. Rather, he also sought to profit from the attachment of slaves, authorizing his agents to make purchases of debt slaves that he would then put to work on the plantations in his charge. This was the case when Moses Nunis sought to attach slaves belonging to a Mr. Dupont for a debt of £91.[148] McCulloh's agent "prevailed" upon the parties to postpone the sale of the attached slaves, and particularly a slave named Ben and his family, so McCulloh would have an opportunity to purchase them.[149] Nunis, however, became "anxious for a Settlement," and threatened to move forward with the sale.[150] His concerns apparently were warranted, as soon after that the debtor, "with a white man & a Negro," visited Dean Forest at night "and forcibly carried off Twelve Negroes Working fellows & four Children."[151] Nunis was "very uneasy about it as he might have secured the amount of his Debt long since," but had "put off the Sale" at McCulloh's request.[152] However, this self-help not only caused problems for Nunis, who now lacked slaves to sell in payment for the debt. It also disrupted life for slaves

[147] William White to Robert McCulloh, September 7, 1780, TNA, C 106/87.
[148] J. Evans to Robert McCulloh, December 10, 1780, TNA, C 106/89.
[149] J. Evans to Robert McCulloh, December 28, 1780, TNA, C 106/89. The sale had been planned in order to "secure the debt and prevent the Negroes running off to Carolina." J. Evans to Robert McCulloh, December 29, 1780, TNA, C 106/89. The real value of the slaves Nunis sought to seize was far in excess of the value of the debt. In 1774 the average price of a slave in South Carolina was £58.63. David Eltis, Frank D. Lewis, and David Richardson, "Slave Prices, the African Slave Trade, and Productivity in Eighteenth-Century South Carolina: A Reassessment," *The Journal of Economic History* 66 (2006): 1056.
[150] J. Evans to Robert McCulloh, March 17, 1781, TNA, C 106/89.
[151] J. Evans to Robert McCulloh, April 7, 1781, TNA, C 106/89.   [152] *Ibid.*

who remained on the plantation. These slaves had been "put ... in a quondarey" by the theft because they believed that "thare Master" would come to "tak them next." Although White tried to "ke[e]p them in heart a[s] Mutch" as possible by telling them that "thare Master is Reables that they Cant tak them" and that McCulloh was "a Bout Byen them," such assurances were probably cold comfort for enslaved people concerned that their families might soon be forcibly separated.[153]

McCulloh profited from his management of Silk Hope and Dean Forest, learning to buy and sell slaves as deftly as a seasoned South Carolinian. For example, after the affair with Nunis, he purchased Ben and his family for £110.10, a price his agent hoped he did not think "too high."[154] He also bought other slaves from James Habersham's estate, including "a Negro man named Donold" who had been "employed as a Driver" on one of McCulloh's plantations; "Lupes, July, Boson his Wife Sally & Child & Phibo a Negro Woman," and "a Negro Man Named Ben his Wife Nanny & Child Billy late the property of Jonathan Bryan of Georgia."[155] Producing evidence of these purchases when he presented his claim for compensation as a loyalist, McCulloh described an exodus from South Carolina that suggests he had readily adapted to life in a slave society. He complained that he had been "cast away" and lost "the greatest part of his effects on the bar of Saint Augustine" as well as "Cattle plantation tools and Ten Negroes besides a Crop of Rice which he computes at £500." However, McCulloh still retained possession of a number of his slaves.[156]

In the postwar period, he would seek to rebuild his fortunes from the labor of enslaved people and from the value inherent in their capacity for labor. After spending a brief time in St. Augustine, he ultimately transported most of his slaves to Jamaica.[157] Like other slave-owning loyalists, McCulloh found in Jamaica an environment that was well suited for

---

[153] William White to Robert McCulloh, April 20, 1781, TNA, C 106/89.

[154] Crookshanks & Speirs to Robert McCulloh, June 13, 1781, TNA, C 106/89. This figure is presumably in pounds sterling.

[155] John Simpson to Robert McCulloh, May 22, 1781, TNA, C 106/88; May 16, 1783, C 106/87; May 17, 1783, TNA, C 106/89. Bryan was one of Georgia's richest colonists. See Allan Gallay, "Jonathan Bryan's Plantation Empire: Land, Politics, and the Formation of a Ruling Class in Colonial Georgia," *The William and Mary Quarterly*, 3rd ser. 45 (1988): 253–279.

[156] The Memorial of Robert McCulloh of Charlton in the County of Kent late Deputy Collector of the Port of Charlestown in the Province of South Carolina, March 22, 1784, TNA, C 106/88.

[157] Ann McCulloh to Robert McCulloh, February 2, 1783, TNA, C 106/87.

plantation agriculture and a culture in which the chattel principle was equally pervasive. He quickly hired a Jamaica-based agent, who helped him to devise a strategy to maximize the value of his human property in the British Empire's richest colony. Rather than "desposing" of his slaves, the agent counseled him to rent them out as long as possible. This would insulate him from a market that was glutted with the slaves of American loyalists, which were sold on the cheap compared with "New Negroes." However, if he could get an "adequate price" for several of the slaves that were "running Old," he advised McCulloh to "let them go." Quickly moving from an expression of concern for the slaves to an expression of even greater concern for the bottom line, his agent promised to "get them a good Master," but he also reassured McCulloh that he would "make them return ... as much as can be got by their Labour."[158]

Robert McCulloh's experiences as a manager of slaves and later as a slave owner encapsulate the larger process by which British soldiers and administrators adapted to life in a slave society. This process of adaptation featured little adaptation at all. Men like McCulloh saw great opportunities to profit from the labor of enslaved people, and they did not hesitate to take advantage of those opportunities. As a practical matter, this meant adhering to a legal framework and a worldview in which enslaved people were chattels at law, in which people had a price, and in which that price carried with it clear expectations and obligations. Although extended contact with enslaved people may have led some to question the morality of treating people as property, the vast majority of Britons experienced chattel slavery as McCulloh did: as a thriving economic system that could produce astonishing wealth if slaves were managed properly at law and in practice.

CONCLUSION

When the British evacuation fleet finally departed Charlestown on December 14, 1782, it carried on board 3,794 people of European descent and 5,333 people of African descent. These men and women joined a larger loyalist diaspora that fanned across the British Empire, as individuals and families sought to rebuild their lives and fortunes with varying degrees of success.[159] For many loyalists, slave ownership meant the difference between prosperity and poverty as they sought to rebuild

---

[158] Anthony Roxburgh to Robert McCulloh, January 30, 1784, TNA, C 106/88.
[159] Jasanoff, *Liberty's Exiles*, 15–16.

their fortunes elsewhere in the British Empire. Because slaves were moveable rather than fixed property in fact as well as law, they had become even more valuable to loyalists who faced the prospect of abandoning their South Carolina real estate. These included loyalists whose property had been confiscated and sold under legislation passed by the "Rebel Assembly," which authorized the seizure of the estates of "the most notorious Loyalists."[160] In order to recoup their losses, individuals named in confiscation acts carried off enslaved people "found on the sequestered Estates," often with military assistance. Alexander Leslie, for example, explicitly authorized British troops to "rescue" slaves in order to compensate these loyalists. On one mission, after receiving a "report that the enemy were driving away the negroes from the plantations of the loyalists," he detached cavalry "across the Cooper River" to catch them. The cavalry failed to arrive in time, but he "brought away about a hundred of the enemies' negroes" to redistribute to loyalists in place of their stolen slaves.[161] Slave catching on behalf of loyalists flowed naturally from a belief that sequestered slaves were valuable assets that could and should be used to indemnify the king's loyal subjects. But where once officials had carefully managed slaves as a public trust, they now haphazardly confiscated and redistributed human property on the eve of evacuation.

In fact, the scramble to evacuate South Carolina lays bare the extent to which the chattel principle had infused the worldview of British occupiers. British soldiers and officials – as well as loyalists – unabashedly claimed and removed slaves from the colony at the end of the war on the assumption that they, too, had property rights in people. They often did so in contravention of a 1782 treaty between British and American commissioners. The treaty stipulated that the British should restore possession of "all the Slaves of the Citizens of South Carolina" to their owners, with the exception of slaves that "rendered themselves particularly obnoxious on account of their attachment and Service to the British Troops, and such as have had Specific promise of Freedom."[162] However, some officers tried

---

[160] Piecuch, *Three Peoples, One King*, 281. Other loyalists were charged a twelve-percent fee on their estates. *Ibid.*

[161] Lieutenant General Alex. Leslie to Sir Henry Clinton, March 30, 1782, Item 9957, Sir Guy Carleton Papers, B800120, SCDAH.

[162] October 10, 1782, Item 5844, Sir Guy Carleton Papers, B800120, SCDAH. Owners would be compensated for the value of these slaves. The British secured a promise that slaves restored to their former owners "by virtue of this agreement" would not be punished "for having left their Masters and attached themselves to the British Troops,"

to include their slaves in "the number to be brought off," and were prepared to go to great lengths to ensure that their slaves could be evacuated in British transports. Because they were aware of the terms of the 1782 treaty, they "pretend[ed]" that their slaves were "spys, or guides, and of course obnoxious, or under promises of freedom" in order to lade them on ships.[163] Even John Cruden, commissioner of sequestered estates, hoped to be made financially whole by the sale of slaves he held in trust. Owed 10,000 pounds for administering sequestered estates, he asked to be repaid "from a proportional sale of the Negroes" in his charge. Cruden effectively revised his definition of the loyal "public" to include himself.[164]

For the vast majority of British military officers and administrators, the decision to treat slaves as commodities for the benefit of evacuating loyalists flowed almost inexorably from their inability to see enslaved people as human beings. If officials described the relationship between slaves and the king's army as possessing all the markers of subjecthood, they stopped short of declaring enslaved people subjects whose claims to freedom should be honored. As a result, they offered an extremely constricted path to freedom for some slaves in South Carolina, one that was built around the idea of special exceptions for individuals to general policies. When it came to enforcing order among slaves collectively, they were conceived of as a threatening internal enemy, not as human beings or subjects of the Crown who might be entitled to protection or rights.[165]

This is in part because Britons who served in slave societies during the American Revolution did not experience slavery as a crumbling economic system. Rather, they eagerly sought access to a plantation economy that was thriving on the eve of the Revolution, and that despite wartime

---

and that "no violence of Insult shall be offered to the persons or Slaves of the Families of such person as are obliged to leave the State for their adherence to the British Government when the American Army shall take possession of the Town." Any slaves confiscated from loyalists who subsequently ran away and were carried off by British subjects were not held to violate the agreement. *Ibid.*

[163] Alexander Leslie to Sir Guy Carleton, October 18, 1782, Item 5924, Sir Guy Carleton Papers, B800120, SCDAH.

[164] A. Leslie to Sir Guy Carleton, August 10, 1782, Item 5262, Sir Guy Carleton Papers, B800120, SCDAH. It is unclear whether Cruden calculated this debt in South Carolina currency or pounds sterling. In 1775 the average rate of exchange in South Carolina currency for £100 sterling was £758.67. John J. McCusker, *Money and Exchange in Europe and America, 1600–1775: A Handbook* (Chapel Hill: University of North Carolina Press, 1992), 224.

[165] Alan Taylor, *The Internal Enemy: Slavery and War in Virginia, 1772–1832* (New York: Norton, 2013).

devastation remained potentially viable. Slave ownership gave individuals like Robert McCulloh access to this system, as it had done for newcomers throughout the colonial era. At the same time, slave labor remained vital for a British military that was pressed to solve the problem of supplying a large army fanned out across a vast territory. As agricultural workers and as laborers in other military departments, slaves provided the manpower that was necessary to keep Britain's military operating in the American southeast – they were the sinews of war that made the British army work.

The usefulness of slaves to the British military and their profitability to individual Britons goes a long way toward explaining why these newcomers did not act decisively to undermine slavery during the American Revolution. But the enduring power of legal categories also helps us to understand why Britons during the Revolutionary War failed to do more to undermine chattel slavery in the southeast. We cannot forget that late eighteenth-century Britons inhabited a world in which slaveholding was normal, legal, and customary, despite growing antislavery sentiment in the British Isles and in some parts of the American mainland. Even in the wake of the *Somerset* decision, which historians now agree produced only a narrow holding as to the status of enslaved people in England, slavery was widely accepted and practiced in Britain's colonial possessions, where it was a source of great profit.[166] Moreover, colonial legislatures had classified slaves as chattel property in local statutes, which even the *Somerset* decision acknowledged as binding.

Britons also inhabited a world in which being a British subject meant something. In many ways, the American Revolution was fought over what that "something" was. For Britons who occupied South Carolina, subjecthood emphatically meant that the property of loyalists, including their slaves, should be protected. Failing that, the Crown would compensate loyalists for their losses. The Loyalist Claims Commission, which embodied this impulse, was not its only manifestation. The sequestration system, as we have seen, was another, as was the overarching desire among British officials to compensate departing loyalists with slaves. By honoring property rights in people, Crown officials made it emphatically clear that subjecthood marked the same rights for Britons in South Carolina as it

[166] George Van Cleve, "Somerset's Case and Its Antecedents in Imperial Perspective," *Law and History Review* 24 (2006): 602–603.

did for residents of Middlesex; they belied the claims of rebels that colonial subjecthood was unequal or lesser. The spiritual and visceral connection between King George III and his colonial subjects would be upheld as a matter of honor and as a matter of law, and it would be upheld through the bodies of Black people.

Conclusion

In 1783, South Carolinian John Sommers waxed optimistic about the future of his new state, writing to his father in England that the "happy effects of peace" already were beginning to be "felt." Not only did "all Kinds of European goods ... most Amazeingly sell," but Charlestown's wharfs were "Crowded with Ships of Different nations," including "prusians, Danes, Swedes, British, French, Duch, & Ships of the United States of A." True, money was scarce, but crops were "promising," and Sommers himself had recently invested in a new plantation on credit. This acquisition, when improved through the labor of enslaved people, would allow Sommers and his family to make their way in "this new world." For Sommers, who initially did not "expect to see any Satisfaction more in this country," the opportunity to profit from planting was too alluring to abandon.[1] Just as had been the case for countless colonists before him, purchasing land and slaves remained the key to wealth-building in post-Revolutionary South Carolina.

Despite Sommers's optimism, much about this "new world" was frightening for European Americans. The Revolutionary War not only physically devastated South Carolina; it also cut off merchants and planters from trade with Europe and the Caribbean, leading to economic stagnation in the last two decades of the eighteenth century. This stagnation was exacerbated by a manpower shortage in the immediate aftermath of the war, as South Carolina and Georgia plantations lost nearly "one-quarter of their pre-Revolutionary slave populations."[2] The "desertion & death of their Slaves" combined "with the destruction of their Crops & Cattle" brought

---

[1] John Sommers to Father, June 28, 1781, John Sommers Papers, Fl. 1777–1789, Misc. MSS Collection, AC17, 415, Library of Congress, Manuscripts Division, Washington, DC.

[2] Philip D. Morgan, *Slave Counterpoint: Black Culture in the Eighteenth-Century Chesapeake & Lowcountry* (Chapel Hill: University of North Carolina Press, 1998), 666.

"most of the Planters" to "a low ebb," explained Josiah Smith, Jr., to a London correspondent.[3] Slaves who had not successfully escaped with the British had to be retrieved and made to return to work, a process that proved difficult in practice. As Elias Ball complained, he was having a "grate deal of trouble" bringing his "new perchased Negroos" to "a proper method of work" because they had been in "such an ill habet of work last year."[4] Slaves in Charlestown (which was incorporated and formally renamed in 1783) were reluctant to give up the autonomy that had accompanied wartime disruptions. As Sarah DeFollenare, who had hired out her "Wench," Nanny, for "three years in Town," complained, Nanny now refused to remit her wages to her mistress, and she threatened her with sale "at Public Vendue" to compel her obedience.[5] Although the war did not result in significant legal changes for slaves, the continued mobility of enslaved people in the conflict's immediate aftermath posed significant challenges for owners like Ball and DeFollenare, who sought to reclaim their slaves and to put them back to productive work. As these owners understood, it was only through mobilizing slave labor that they could revive plantations and businesses and thereby attain prewar levels of prosperity. The unprecedented mobility of enslaved people during the war, then, ultimately had the effect of shoring up rather than undermining "slaveholder commitment to bondage" as South Carolinians sought to reassemble an enslaved labor force in the immediate postwar period.[6]

In addition to forcing slaves they already owned to return to work, planters and merchants also purchased new slaves. Between 1783 and 1784, the average price of a slave jumped from £59.79 to £67.82 as a result of increased demand and the expectation of planters like Sommers that crops were "promising." Although prices dropped again in 1785 due to crop failures in 1783 and 1784, by 1806 slaves were trading at an average price of £70.66.[7] Indeed, during the postwar period

---

[3] Josiah Smith, Jr. to James Poyas, December 5, 1780, Josiah Smith Letterbook, 411, 413, Southern Historical Collection, University of North Carolina, Chapel Hill, North Carolina.

[4] Elias Ball to [unknown], July 25, 1784, Ball Family Papers, 369.01 (c) 03–01, South Carolina Historical Society, Charleston, South Carolina.

[5] Sarah DeFollenare to [unknown], May 28, 1784, Grimke Papers, 11/172/11, SCHS.

[6] As Davis has observed, slavery "had done more than simply survive the disruptions of a half-century of war and revolution. The system had proved to be far more vigorous, adaptable, and expansive than critics had imagined." David Brion Davis, *The Problem of Slavery in the Age of Revolution, 1770–1823* (Oxford: Oxford University Press, 1999), 83.

[7] David Eltis, Frank D. Lewis, and David Richardson, "Slave Prices, the African Slave Trade, and Productivity in Eighteenth-Century South Carolina: A Reassessment," *The Journal of*

the "Lower South witnessed a huge expansion of slavery," in part to meet the growing demands of the state's backcountry region.[8] Fueled by extensive immigration from the middle colonies, the backcountry's white population had nearly doubled between 1750 and 1770.[9] By 1760, 50 percent of the colony's white population lived in the backcountry, and this figure reached nearly 75 percent in 1770.[10] These backcountry settlers provided a ready market for slaves as they turned to indigo planting or provisions farming in service of Lowcountry plantations.[11] Twenty years earlier Henry Laurens, who began his mercantile career as a slave trader, had identified this region as a "large field for trade," observing that the "vast number of people seting down" in the backcountry would pay "the highest prices" for slaves.[12] Peter Manigault agreed, noting that the "back parts" had "settled extremely fast" and that as a result more than "two thirds" of the slaves imported into South Carolina had "gone backwards."[13] Their appraisal of the region's potential as a market for slaves proved prescient. In the last decade of the eighteenth century and into the early 1800s, South Carolina imported 15,000 slaves from Africa. A majority of these new slaves "went inland," where they labored on backcountry farms and plantations.[14]

With this recommitment to slavery came a recommitment to slavery's laws. Disciplining unruly slave populations after the war became an issue of prime concern, particularly as South Carolinians, participating in what would soon become a booming internal slave trade, began to import more slaves from the Chesapeake. As Virginia transitioned from a labor-intensive tobacco export economy to cereal cultivation, Chesapeake planters found themselves "with a surplus of human property."[15] By the

---

Economic History 66 (2006): 1056. South Carolina outlawed the transatlantic slave trade in 1787, but trade was reopened between 1803 and 1808. Joyce E. Chaplin, *An Anxious Pursuit: Agricultural Innovation & Modernity in the Lower South, 1730–1815* (Chapel Hill: University of North Carolina Press, 1993), 320.

[8] Morgan, *Slave Counterpoint*, 666.

[9] Robert M. Weir, *Colonial South Carolina: A History* (Columbia: University of South Carolina Press, 1997), 205–206.

[10] *Ibid.*, 209.

[11] S. Max Edelson, *Plantation Enterprise in Colonial South Carolina* (Cambridge: Harvard University Press, 2006), 258.

[12] Henry Laurens to Richard Oswald & Co., February 15, 1763, *HLP*, vol. 3, 259–260.

[13] Peter Manigault to W[illiam] Blake [December 1772], Manigault Papers, 11/278/7, Peter Manigault Letterbook, 1763–1773, 192–193, SCHS.

[14] Chaplin, *An Anxious Pursuit*, 321.

[15] Steven Deyle, *Carry Me Back: The Domestic Slave Trade in American Life* (Oxford: Oxford University Press, 2005), 4.

1790s, Virginia, Maryland, and Delaware had become net exporters of slaves into South Carolina and the opening frontiers of the Deep South.[16] Between 1790 and 1860, traders transported more than 1 million slaves from the Upper South to the Lower South, while twice that number were traded within the South at the local level.[17] South Carolina alone received approximately four thousand slaves from the Chesapeake region between the 1790s and the early 1800s. While this internal slave trade began slowly between 1787 and 1807, it accelerated after the closure of the transatlantic African slave trade, feeding the labor demands of backcountry and Deep South cotton plantations.[18]

The influx of new slave populations into the backcountry raised fears of slave insurrection, particularly on the part of Lowcountry planters who believed that backcountry settlers, as less-experienced slave owners, neglected the law. Indeed, the backcountry's reputation for lawlessness, which arose in part due to the Regulation movement of the 1760s, aroused concerns that these poor white "crackers" were unwilling or unable to manage their slaves properly.[19] One Lowcountry judge, after touring the backcountry, expressed his concern that settlers had "neglected" the "patrole law" and that this was particularly disturbing given "great introduction of so many people of color into this State from Maryland, Virginia, & No Carolina." Just as colonists had once considered slaves from the West Indies to be prone to rebellion and, therefore, less desirable, so too did South Carolina slave owners fear that Chesapeake slaves would prove particularly unruly. As a result, enforcing South Carolina's slave laws was "more requisite" than it ever had been, according to the judge. He urged backcountry jurors to "carefully peruse that Law & the other Acts relative to the Government of Slaves" and to educate their neighbors about their findings. Paying "more attention" to "those useful Laws" would "be followed by the happiest consequences."[20]

These "useful Laws" were South Carolina's colonial slave laws. Despite the significant legal changes wrought by the Revolution, much remained the same.[21] South Carolinians became citizens of a state, not

---

[16] Michael Tadman, *Speculators and Slaves: Masters, Traders, and Slaves in the Old South* (Madison: University of Wisconsin Press, 1989), 11–12.

[17] Deyle, *Carry Me Back*, 4.   [18] Tadman, *Speculators and Slaves*, 17.

[19] For a discussion of the Regulator movement in South Carolina, see Rachel N. Klein, *Unification of a Slave State: The Rise of the Planter Class in the South Carolina Backcountry, 1760–1808* (Chapel Hill: University of North Carolina Press, 1990).

[20] [J. F. Grimke] Grand Jury Charge [undated], Grimke Papers, 11/172/33, SCHS.

[21] Jack P. Greene, "Colonial History and National History: Reflections on a Continuing Problem," *The William and Mary Quarterly*, 3rd ser. 64 (2007): 235–250.

subjects of a king. The state's judicial system was reorganized, and in 1785 the state legislature, now called the General Assembly, passed a statute establishing a county court system.[22] Nonetheless, citizens continued to view the 1740 Negro Act as a guide for managing their slaves in the new republic. Indeed, colonial slave statutes remained in force with little change through 1865. This meant not only that the policing of slaves in the state would be similar. It also meant that slaves would continue to be treated de jure and de facto as chattel property. South Carolinians did not choose to alter the English property law framework that had served them so well in the past. Rather than taking the Revolution as an opportunity to remake their entire system of slave laws, they doubled down on a colonial system, derived from English law, which had proven responsive to their commercial need to treat slaves as things.

As a practical matter, the continuation of chattel slavery into the new republic also meant that South Carolinians would continue to replicate English legal forms and procedures as they conducted routine transactions involving slaves and as they litigated over slaves in state courts. John Phillips's legal precedent book, written between 1788 and 1839, contained a multitude of English forms that he believed remained useful to a lawyer practicing in the new United States. These included form declarations to "recover for an unsound Negro sold for a sound price," for "covenant on Warranty for selling an unsound negro," and "for harboring a Negro." He also included a form of a "Writ retorno habendo in fi[eri] fa[cias]" for failure to prosecute a slave detention case, and a "Writ of Injunction in Equity" to restrain a defendant from removing a slave. Just as Phillips substituted "Negro woman slave" for "iron gray horse" in his precedent book, citizens and lawyers substituted the word "colony" for the word "state" in preprinted English forms that they used to buy, sell, and mortgage slaves. In a 1777 printed writ of attachment, for example, the word "colony" is stricken out and "state" written in.[23] A printed bill of sale for a slave from 1784 follows the form of colonial bills of sale with two exceptions: a caption that reads the "State of South Carolina" has been added, and references to the regnal year are replaced with a tally of years since independence.[24] Phillips himself copied out a slave mortgage form in his book of legal precedents. As South

---

[22] "An Act for Establishing County Courts, and for Regulating the Proceedings Therein" (1785), *SAL*, vol. 7, 211.
[23] January 7, 1777, Baker Family Papers, 1138.00, 11/535/29, SCHS.
[24] August 19, 1784, Broughton Papers, 11/93/9, SCHS.

Carolinians like Phillips discovered, English law and English legal procedure continued to be readily adaptable for citizens living in a slaveholders'
republic. Republican forms were not, in the end, different from forms used
under a monarchy: both could be used to manage slaves at law.

Perhaps most importantly, at the level of practice, the language of
English law and the authority that language conveyed continued to be
deployed by South Carolinians as they managed their slaves on a daily
basis. Citizens, like colonists, continued to use the language of "issue and
increase" to transfer slaves, adhering to an older worldview in which
property was bifurcated into chattels and real estate. For example, in
1795, Mary Allston, a "Spinster," gave to her brother "[t]o have and to
hold" in trust for his daughters her "Wench Catharine and her Two
Children Dinah and Jenny with all their Future Issue and Increase Also
to Charlote Atchinson Allston Wench Jenny and Two Children Besty and
Peter with all their future Issue and Increase."[25] As they wrote their wills,
South Carolina's slave-owning citizens also continued to group slaves
with livestock. When John Coming Ball drafted his will in 1792, for
example, he grouped his slaves with his cattle, giving his sister the pick
of "any Negro girl among my female Slaves she may prefer" and John Ball
the right of first refusal for his "Stock of Cattle at Jericho."[26] Also, South
Carolinians continued to finance their purchases with slave bonds and
mortgages. When a member of the Pringle family disposed of a plantation
"[f]or the sum of Thirty two thousand Doll[ars]," the land and slaves were
"secured by Bonds & Mortgage with the mortgage of additional property
as Security."[27] In fact, slaves were a source of collateral for more than
80 percent of the capital raised in recorded mortgages during the early
national period. This trend was in keeping with patterns established
during the colonial period, as citizens used the value that inhered in the
bodies of enslaved people to finance postwar recovery and expansion.[28]

Mobilizing enslaved labor also continued to result in complicated arrangements like those colonists once litigated in the colonial Chancery Court. These
included an 1819 "swap" of slaves, in which John H. Fisher and his wife,
Elizabeth, gave Charlotte A. Allston the use of an enslaved women and her
two youngest children "during her life time." The parties agreed that Allston

---

[25] July 17, 1795, Allston Family Papers, 1164.01, 12/6/14, SCHS.
[26] Will of John Coming Ball, December 3, 1792, Ball Papers, 11/5/5–27, SCHS.
[27] [undated], Mitchell-Pringle Collection: James R. Pringle Papers, 11/323/13, SCHS.
[28] Bonnie Martin, "Slavery's Invisible Engine: Mortgaging Human Property," *The Journal
of Southern History* 76 (2010): 840.

would be responsible for paying "their taxe's and finding them in cloathing & victuals" and that Allston also would "put out" the slave's older children. The female children would "be taught to sew, wach & c.," while her son would be "put to the carpenters trade." After their apprenticeship, these slaves would "return" to the Fishers's service. In order to compensate the Fishers for Suzy's labor, Allston also agreed to give them "during her life Boson," who would nonetheless be "considered as her property at her death."[29] Just as mastery and ownership were not necessarily synonymous during the colonial period, so too did legal flexibility, inherited from English law, open up space for citizens to craft individualized legal solutions to their labor needs.

English law also continued to be a cultural touchstone for South Carolinians as they sought to reorganize the state's institutions in the wake of independence. Drawing upon a shared English legal past, some South Carolinians defended the maintenance of jurisdictional diversity in the face of legislative attempts to consolidate the state's judiciary. For example, South Carolina's common law judges cited English law and legal precedents as they complained about the legislature's attempts to merge the state's common law, equity, and ecclesiastical jurisdictions. In part, their concerns stemmed from the fact that they were asked to do more work for less pay. Judicial independence, it seemed, came at a high price for judges who found themselves no longer entitled to fees, which had been "taken altogether" and replaced with salaries that were "not one third of their amount." These judges defended the autonomous jurisdiction of multiple courts based upon English practice, drawing a line of continuity between medieval legal precedents and their own constitutional roles. Although the judges admitted that the legislature had the authority under the 1790 constitution to erect "Superior & Inferior Courts both of Law & Equity," they denied that legislators were empowered "to blend either the Superior & Inferior Jurisdictions in one Court, or to authorize those who are appointed Judges of a Court of Common Law, to entertain appeals brought as from an inferior Court whose mode of decision is guided by the rules of the Canon or Civil Law." Citing Blackstone, they claimed that blending these jurisdictions violated the "forms & principles of our particular Constitution," and they warned of the "great confusion" that would follow from "overturning long established forms & new-modelling a course of proceedings that has now prevailed for 7 Centuries."[30] In South Carolina, colonial traditions and

---

[29] February 27, 1819, Allston Family Papers, 1164.01, 12/6/14, SCHS.
[30] Draft letter from Judges to Governor, February 19, 1791, Grimke Papers, 11/172/18, SCHS.

practices modeled on English law continued to be an important source of legal authority despite the upheavals of war and the proliferation of republican institutions in the immediate postwar period.

This legal continuity calls into question Laura Edwards's suggestion that the confusion created by the Revolutionary War created space for enslaved people to seek justice at the local level. Before the hegemony of state law, she argues, citizens sought to maintain "the peace." Doing so, as a practical matter, meant ceding authority to local actors despite their race and gender.[31] This narrative assumes that consistently administered state law – and particularly appellate practice that disciplined lower courts – was necessary for subjugating slaves. In early republican South Carolina, however, the legal status of enslaved people was clearly established both by statute and custom. Although the war disrupted life on plantations, it did not disrupt the legal classification of slaves as property or, more importantly, daily legal practices that taken together dehumanized slaves and denied them legal status before the law. Citizens brought with them into the nineteenth century not only an English legal heritage in which maintaining the king's peace was important. They also carried with them a host of other English legal precedents and practices that facilitated the buying, selling, and bequeathing of slaves. Formal institutions of state law were not necessary for deploying either.

Ultimately, South Carolina's doubling down on slavery's laws increasingly set South Carolinians' other citizens in the Deep South apart from the rest of the United States. Although the Revolutionary War did not alter South Carolina's slave laws, it did spark lasting legal changes in northern and Mid-Atlantic states that would come to heighten legal distinctions between places where slaves were property and places where they were not. Vermont's 1777 state constitution, for example, asserted that no individual "born in this country, or brought from over sea, ought to be holden by law to serve any purpose, or servant, slave or apprentice," without their consent.[32] Massachusetts's courts likewise construed the state's 1780 constitution to prohibit chattel slavery, articulating this principle for the first time in a series of decisions related to litigation over the legal status of the slave Quock Walker. Other states followed

---

[31] Laura F. Edwards, *The People and Their Peace: Legal Culture and the Transformation of Inequality in the Post-Revolutionary South* (Chapel Hill: University of North Carolina Press, 2009), 7–8.

[32] Gordon S. Wood, *Empire of Liberty: A History of the Early Republic, 1789–1815* (Oxford: Oxford University Press, 2009), 519.

suit – perhaps most famously Pennsylvania – instituting a series of gradual emancipation schemes.[33] Northern courts also increasingly grew unwilling to grant comity to the slave codes of southern states in the context of freedom suits. Whereas northern judges had traditionally denied freedom to slaves travelling with southern masters into their states, over the first three decades of the nineteenth century, they began to deny comity and free enslaved plaintiffs. This jurisprudential transformation was epitomized in *Commonwealth v. Aves* (1836) in which Chief Justice Shaw held that a slave carried to Boston could not, as a matter of public policy, be recognized as property in Massachusetts, over arguments that the state should grant comity to the laws of Louisiana.[34] The process by which this transition occurred was by no means uniform, nor was it predestined. In 1783, South Carolinians were not yet "crouched in a defensive posture against the North that they assumed in the decades before the Civil War."[35] Nonetheless, the post-Revolutionary abolition of slavery in northern and middle states via state constitutions, gradual emancipation

---

[33] *Ibid.*, 520.

[34] *Commonwealth* v. *Aves*, 35 Mass. 193 (1836). This is not to suggest that post-Revolutionary waves of emancipatory legislation in the North and Mid-Atlantic flowed from the elimination of racist sentiment. Indeed, as a number of scholars have noted, the status of northern free Blacks became increasingly tenuous as Revolutionary zeal faded. Richard Newman, for example, has shown that the free Black community in Philadelphia faced persecution over the course of the early nineteenth century as a post-Revolutionary window of opportunity for interracial harmony closed. Richard S. Newman, *Freedom's Prophet: Bishop Richard Allen, the AME Church, and the Black Founding Fathers* (New York: New York University Press, 2008), 191–194. Claire Lyons, too, in her study of the free Black community in Philadelphia concurs that possibilities for free Blacks were foreclosed as sexual deviance was reinscribed, via cultural processes, onto the bodies of lower class and free Black women. Claire Lyons, *Sex among the Rabble: An Intimate History of Gender & Power in the Age of Revolution, Philadelphia, 1730–1830* (Chapel Hill: University of North Carolina Press, 2006), 3–4. In his social history of free Black seamen in the north, W. Jeffrey Bolster, too, has argued that the lives of these men gradually worsened as revolutionary zeal faded. W. Jeffrey Bolster, "'To Feel Like a Man': Black Seamen in the Northern States, 1800–1860," *Journal of American History* 76 (1990): 1174, 1177. Likewise, scientific racism took hold in north and south and was even used to justify the activities of nascent antislavery movements and especially the American Colonization Society. See, e.g., Newman, *Freedom's Prophet* and Richard S. Newman, *The Transformation of American Abolitionism: Fighting Slavery in the Early Republic* (Chapel Hill: University of North Carolina Press, 2001). The "unrelenting mob terrorism against immediate abolitionists and African-American communities that swept the North between 1831 and 1838" represented the full flowering of this racial thinking. James Stewart, "The Emergence of Racial Modernity and the Rise of the White North," *Journal of the Early Republic* 18 (1998): 181.

[35] Edelson, *Plantation Enterprise*, 260.

schemes, or judicial decisions signaled sectional divergence in the period immediately following the American Revolution.

This process of entrenchment had far-reaching and negative consequences for slaves. As South Carolina's statutory law of slavery became the model for slave codes in the Deep South, so too did the language, practices, and precedents of chattel slavery. The economy of the nineteenth-century internal slave trade, which nineteenth-century historians have only begun to reconstruct, is the legacy of a legal culture that in prescription and practice treated slaves as things. Considered chattel property in nearly every Deep South state, slaves could be bought, sold, and mortgaged at will. Owners and slave traders devised increasingly ingenious ways to maximize their value as property, taking advantage of advances in communication, transportation, and finance to traffick in human beings.[36] In the long term, the removal of restraints on alienation and inheritability that South Carolinians pioneered does not map easily onto a post-Revolutionary triumphalist narrative that takes the removal of feudal restraints at its end point. As we have seen, this was the continuation of an older and far more tragic story in which English law was both prop and principal actor. We still live with its consequences today.

---

[36] Deyle, *Carry Me Back*, 119; Adam Rothman, *Slave Country: American Expansion and the Origins of the Deep South* (Cambridge: Harvard University Press, 2005), 4;223; Calvin Schermerhorn, *Money over Mastery, Family over Freedom: Slavery in the Antebellum Upper South* (Baltimore: Johns Hopkins University Press, 2011), 211–212.

Index